THE POLITICS OF NATURE AND SCIENCE
IN SOUTHERN AFRICA

The Politics of Nature and Science in Southern Africa

EDITORS
Maano Ramutsindela
Giorgio Miescher
Melanie Boehi

BASLER AFRIKA
BIBLIOGRAPHIEN

ACKNOWLEDGEMENTS

The idea for this edited volume came out of the graduate workshop on 'The Politics of Nature and Science in African History' that took place at the University of Basel on 15–16 April 2014. Most of the chapters in this volume emerged out of papers presented there. Patrick Harries, who sadly passed away as we were finalising this volume, inspired and supervised research on the history of science, some of which is presented in chapters by his graduate students in this volume. His guidance was highly appreciated and acknowledged. We thank the Basel Graduate School of History, Basler Afrika Bibliographien, Centre for African Studies Basel, Freiwillige Akademische Gesellschaft Basel and Swiss South African Joint Research Programme for generously funding the workshop, follow-up meetings of the editors and the publication of this book. The editors and authors are extremely thankful to the reviewers for their willingness to review chapters, and for their useful comments which helped to improve the quality of this volume. We wish to record our sincere gratitude to our commissioning editors, Petra Kerckhoff and Sarah Schwarz, and to Jo-Anne Friedlander and Nina Maister for the layout, proofreading and indexing of the volume.

© 2016 Authors and photographers
© 2016 Basler Afrika Bibliographien

Namibia Resource Centre & Southern Africa Library
Klosterberg 23
P O Box 2064
4001 Basel
Switzerland
www.baslerafrika.ch

The Basler Afrika Bibliographien is part of the Carl Schlettwein Foundation

All rights reserved

Design and typesetting by User Friendly Cape Town

COVER: Veterinary Cordon Fence, also known as Red Line, at the edge of the Namib desert. This fence traverses the whole country from west to east and – not only physically – continues to separate northern and central Namibia (Photographer: G. Miescher, 1993).

ISBN 978-3-905758-77-1

Contents

Part I – Reflections on the Politics of Nature and Science

1   Introductory notes on the politics of nature and science   9
    Maano Ramutsindela, Giorgio Miescher, Melanie Boehi
    and Tanja Hammel
2   Political dynamics of human-environment relations   20
    Maano Ramutsindela

Part II – Institutionalised Scientific Power

3   Racial difference in Mary Elizabeth Barber's knowledge on insects   39
    Tanja Hammel
4   Hamburg's Botanical Museum and German colonialism: nature
    in the hands of science, commerce and political power   59
    Gabriele Kranz
5   Circulating nature: from north-eastern Namibia to South Africa
    and back, 1960–1990   87
    Luregn Lenggenhager
6   Rehabilitating the 'Ovambo cattle': veterinary science and
    cattle breeding in early colonial Namibia   106
    Giorgio Miescher and Anna Voegeli

Part III – Plants and Power

7   Medicinal plants in South Africa   127
    Diana Gibson
8   "Flowers are South Africa's silent ambassadors": flower shows
    and botanical diplomacy in South Africa   149
    Melanie Boehi

Part IV – Impoverished Environmentalism

9   The comprehensive hunting ban: strengthening the state through participatory conservation in contemporary Botswana   179
    Annette LaRocco

10 Land relations and property rights in central-north Namibia's communal areas   208
    Romie Vonkie Nghitevelekwa

11 Local community disempowerment at the (trans)frontier   231
    Ndidzulafhi Innocent Sinthumule

12 On identities, ways of knowing and interactions across difference in collaborative urban nature conservation at Macassar dunes, Cape Town   252
    Marnie Graham

13 Fragile ground, contested soil: dynamics of tenure and policy in the Bamenda wetlands   281
    Sandro Simon

Part V – Interventions

14 Hidden struggles in conservation: people's resistance in Southern Africa   311
    Frank Matose

15 'Before we start': science and power in the constitution of Africa   323
    Elísio Macamo

List of Contributors   335

Index   337

PART I

Reflections on the Politics of Nature and Science

CHAPTER 1

Introductory notes on the politics of nature and science

Maano Ramutsindela, Giorgio Miescher,
Melanie Boehi and Tanja Hammel

Introduction
A number of phrases have developed around the term 'politics'. We hear of the 'politics of the belly', 'politics of knowledge', 'politics of gender', 'politics of love', and so on. A common ground for these phrases is not clear except that they all refer to the term 'politics'. This lack of common meaning is to be expected since the question of what politics is has been a subject of extensive debates among social scientists. Moreover, debates about the definition of politics are themselves political in that they are informed by particular conceptions of politics. Yet they provide an avenue through which we can deepen our understanding of politics in nature and in science. Notions of politics have long been used in analyses of environmental matters and scientific knowledge production. Journals such as *Environmental Politics* serve as a forum for scholarship that explores the interface between the goals of nature conservation and a radical reordering of political and social preferences.[1] Such an interface is more pertinent now in light of talks of environmental crises in the age of the Anthropocene.

This book brings together original work written mostly by young scholars at the beginning of their careers. Our goal is to explore from a variety of vantage points how politics is enacted in nature conservation and preservation in Southern Africa, as well as how such enactments are enabled by the scientific study of nature in historical and current contexts. This spatio-temporal juxtaposition is lacking in contemporary research on political ecology while the politics of science deserves

---

1 Environmental Politics 2015: http://www.tandfonline.com/action/journalInformation?show=aimsScope&journalCode=fenp20#.Vp8y_rX8KUk (accessed 20 January 2016)

more attention in critical scholarship on society and nature. In South Africa, critical scholarship became prominent in the 1990s when attention was drawn to the role of race and the relationship between power and knowledge across the disciplines. This scholarship has particularly focused on twentieth-century South Africa.[2] The histories of science in Southern Africa however remain sparse.[3]

The book tries to fill these gaps with the hope of attracting more research into forms of politics that guide or result from the study of nature. We aim to contribute to the field of critical history of science studies in and on Southern Africa by focusing on the science of nature that shapes ideas of nature as well as policies and practices of nature conservation, preservation and science. Our premise is that nature, science and politics are interrelated and also co-constitutive of one another. The science of nature is loaded with power that permeates scientific inquiry, research agendas, and practices on the ground. There is therefore a need to understand how such power is constituted and the kinds of relations it creates in time and space. We try to understand all these by first examining the politics of nature before we tease out its manifestation in science. This separation of nature and science is meant to clarify our conception of politics in this book rather than to assume that the two are completely distinct subject matters.

Politics and nature

Any discussion on the politics of nature and science has to appreciate that there is no universal agreement on what politics as an activity is. It is, however, imperative to clarify meanings of politics so as to arrive at an operational definition, and for clarity of thought and intelligible analysis. There are at least two broad approaches to politics that not only dominate the debate on what politics is but that also profoundly influence conceptions and the theorisation of politics. The first is the arena or site approach, which "holds that politics is an activity found only in certain kinds of societies (normally those with states) and in certain kinds of institutional sites or processes within those societies".[4] This approach predominantly focuses on the state and institutions, because it is premised on the view that "only governments define goals, policies and binding decisions".[5] Thus, it conceptualises politics as a formal activity. The second approach focuses on the process and "holds that politics is a much more generalised and universal process which has existed whenever the human species has been found … and hence is a characteristic and

---

2   Jansen 1991; Dubow 2000; Harries 2007
3   See, for example, the special issue of *Kronos* on the 'micro-politics of knowledge' edited by Jacobs/Bank 2015
4   Leftwich 2004: p. 2
5   Leftwich 2004: p. 13; see also Forsyth 2015

necessary feature, if not function, of all societies, past and present".[6] In the process approach, politics occurs in a wide range of settings and involves various groups of people. It occurs "whenever questions of power, control, decision-making and resource allocation between two or more people [are raised]".[7]

The two approaches sketched above raise the following questions: what constitutes the politics of nature? What is the methodological inquiry necessary for uncovering that politics? Scholars such as Neil Carter have approached these questions through the lens of environmental politics. As a sub-discipline of politics, environmental politics is primarily concerned with the "relationship between human society and the natural world".[8] For Carter the three components of environmental politics are "the study of political theories and ideas relating to the environment; the examination of political parties and environmental movements; [and] the analysis of public policymaking and implementation affecting the environment at international, national and local levels".[9] These components and the material Carter used in his book, *The Politics of the Environment: Ideas, Activism and Policy*, bring his analysis of environmental politics closer to the arena or site-based institutional approach.

Our view is that while the two approaches and the notion of environmental politics enable the analysis of politics in the domain of the environment, there is still a need to understand how these approaches are used simultaneously in the practice of nature conservation and preservation. Adrian Leftwich's view that politics "consists of all the activities of conflict (peaceful or not), negotiation and co-operation over the use and distribution of resources, wherever they may be found, within or beyond formal institutions" is a helpful starting point.[10] We expand this view of politics to encompass the politics of science that has profoundly shaped our ideas and meanings of nature and how humans should or ought to relate to it.

Nature conservation projects, often armed with scientific findings, should be understood as a platform on which particular human-environment relations are forged and also contested. It is in, and through, these projects that class, racial and gender differences are constructed into lived realities. This process has its roots in the historical separation between society and nature, which has not only fundamentally changed the relations people have with their biophysical environment, but has also resulted in the hierarchical ordering of humans in relation to their relationship with nature.[11] The separation between nature and society ignores the fact that the

---

6   Leftwich 2004: p. 2
7   Leftwich 2004: p. 14
8   Carter 2007: p. 3
9   Carter 2007: p. 3
10 Leftwich 2004: p. 15
11 Ramutsindela 2004

environment is a domain of entanglements, meaning the biophysical environment does not exist in isolation from humans.[12] Nature conservationists, who see nature as something external to the human experience, undermine these entanglements.

For us, this society-nature dualism—as scholars call it—is not only underpinned by science but it is, more importantly, the site of politics. We can see this clearly in the history of hunting in Southern Africa under colonialism which echoes medieval European traditions. One of the core privileges of the European nobility was (and partly still is) exclusive hunting rights for at least certain animals. These hunting privileges were paralleled by a century-old hierarchical classification system of animals based on observation as well as allegoric and moral ascriptions to each species. The European order of animals is based on the Aristotelian order, which was passed on and popularised through texts like the *Physiologos*.[13] This text from the second century AD combined the classic descriptions of animals based on observation with a Christian allegoric and moral order.[14] A strong reminder of such a classification reflecting the human social order is the term 'royal game', describing the most protected animals.[15] Basically, the creation of the first generation of national parks in many parts of the world primarily served to install exclusive hunting rights for the colonial elite. Mark Cioc captures the underlying politics well when writing that "the major animal-protection treaties of the early twentieth century are best understood as international hunting treaties rather than as conservation treaties".[16] He goes on to say that the force behind such treaties were prominent hunters and ex-hunters who were "far more concerned with the protection of specific hunting grounds and prized prey than with safeguarding of entire habitats, ecosystems, or bioregions".[17] It is estimated that 800,000 kilograms of ivory were shipped out of Natal (part of the present-day province of KwaZulu-Natal in South Africa) between 1844 and 1895.[18] The excessive off-take of ivory and commercial hunting caused a decline in wildlife and threatened the practice of hunting. Hence, hunting regulations were imposed on hunters.[19] Some commercial hunters such as Frederick Selous, after whom the Selous Game Reserve in Tanzania is named, became champions of the protection of wildlife after they had slaughtered hundreds of elephants.[20]

---

12 Ingold 2000
13 The text was translated into many languages.
14 Delort 1987; Miescher 2012, especially chapter one: pp. 19–42
15 The term 'royal game' was used in South African hunting regulations at least until the twentieth century.
16 Cioc 2009: p. 1
17 Cioc 2009: p. 1
18 Nustad 2015
19 MacKenzie 1997
20 MacKenzie 1988

Jane Carruthers has shown that, in apartheid South Africa, hunting transformed the relations between farmers and urban elites, and between whites and Africans.[21] White urban elites who hunted for pleasure saw themselves as superior to white farmers who hunted for the pot, i.e. subsistence hunting. For their part, Africans, who were part of networks of hunter-traders and who assisted whites in hunting expeditions, were relegated to the status of poachers when white hunters no longer required their hunting skills. Thus, hunting was instrumental to social stratification and also served as a tool by which property rights in wild animals could be imposed. One way of imposing these property rights was to categorise methods of hunting by Africans as destructive and illegal. This was also meant to prevent Africans from participating in the lucrative wildlife trade. One noticeable development regarding the protection of nature is the emergence of regulatory regimes that have broadened the social stratification.

Politics and science

At least since the publication of the seminal works of Michel Foucault and Edward Said, scholars in the humanities have been concerned with the politics of knowledge production.[22] Steven Shapin and Simon Schaffer, in their 1985 study of knowledge production, and the debates of Robert Boyle and Thomas Hobbes showed that the content of science could not merely be explained by its context but that content and context of science were inextricably linked and interdependent.[23] Feminist scholars of science have studied how politics of gender and race impacted on and were shaped by practices of scientific knowledge production.[24]

The role of scientific expertise and its complex relationship to (British) imperial politics has been meticulously discussed, for instance, by Helen Tilley. According to Tilley, Africa served as a living laboratory for European science, especially in the fields of environmental, medical and social sciences. Interpretations of science and empire or, in our case, science and (imperial) politics, focused on three central issues, namely: "the power colonialism conferred to science, the ways sciences were used as 'tools of empire', and the agency of non-European peoples and places to reshape sciences".[25] Although histories of science and politics focusing on Southern Africa in particular are still sparse and often have a strong biographical bias, there

---

21 Carruthers 1995
22 Said 1978; Foucault 1970
23 Shapin/Schaffer 1985
24 See, for example, Haraway 1989; Bauchspies/Puig de la Bellacasa 2009; Subramaniam 2014
25 Tilley 2011: p. 15. The term 'tools of empire' refers to the title of the seminal book by Daniel Headrick (1981) in which he explores the role of technology for the successful imperial expansion of the 19th century.

is some research which tries to understand the above-mentioned complexities in historical contexts.[26]

A number of scholars have been concerned with how settlers in South Africa in the late 19th and early 20th century constructed senses of belonging and national identity in botanical, archaeological and ornithological publications.[27] Historians analysed how early naturalists produced a Eurocentric and linguistic imperialist picture of the nature they encountered in Southern Africa or how understandings of nature emerged in cross-cultural collaboration.[28] The debate in *The Journal of African History* in 2004/2005 showed how deeply political the historical study of the politics of nature conservation and science is.[29]

Among the existing studies of the history of science in Southern Africa, the field of veterinary science, in particular, has thrived and grown, and a number of important publications have emerged. Theory and practice of veterinary science in a colonial framework was of particular interest for historians of Southern Africa, mainly due to the devastating rinderpest in the late 19th century, which had a dramatic impact on the socio-political landscape in many parts of the subcontinent. Whereas early studies primarily focused on African reactions, later ones elaborated how the discipline of veterinary science emerged in the colonial context of Southern Africa.[30] The field laboratories in the Southern African veld were the places where theoretical knowledge was developed as well as tested and applied.[31] Case studies show that the eventual success of the inoculation campaigns depended heavily on the almost absolute power the scientists were granted by the colonial authorities. The campaigns benefited from the knowledge and support of local stock-owners, and had a long lasting impact on the pattern of land ownership and land use. In Namibia, for instance, the presence or absence of veterinary surgeons and their assessment of local stock played a crucial role in classifying and dividing the country into healthy and unhealthy areas with long-lasting socio-economic and political consequences.[32]

The case of veterinary science in Southern Africa, not least due to the dramatic economic consequences of the outbreak of an epizootic animal disease, exemplifies very clearly how the politics of science can enable the politics of nature through the

---

26 For an approach on particular individuals and life histories see the latest issue of *Kronos* edited by Jacobs/Banks 2015; for a very recent example focusing on a particular science, its theoretical framework and practice, here colonial survey in South Africa, see Frederick Braun 2015.
27 Carruthers 2004; Dubow 2004; Van Sittert 2002
28 Pratt 1992; Beinart 1998, Green Musselman 2003; Jacobs 2006
29 Van Sittert 2004; Beinart 2005
30 For a very early study see Van Onselen 1972; see also Phoofolo 1992
31 Gilfoyle 2003
32 Miescher 2012

former's classificatory power with regard to the quality of dry-land farming. The complete failure of an inoculation campaign against lungsickness in north-western Namibia in the late 1930s precluded the presence of commercial stock-farming in the region.[33] Its absence soon after put the region in the spotlight of conservationists who worried much more about the resistance of settler than African farmers.

Setting the scene

The chapters in this book tackle the question of politics in nature-related practices from various angles. In an effort to facilitate the flow of the discussion, we have divided the book into five parts and also grouped chapters according to certain themes. In Part I of the book, we grapple with the question of what politics in nature and science entails and how it is manifested. This introduction is a contribution to that question. Maano Ramutsindela draws on literature from political ecology to examine the forms that politics take in nature conservation. He emphasises the inseparability of politics and ecology, the role of scale in political struggles over natural resources, and how nature conservation and preservation offer a platform on which we can investigate the politics of nature and science.

Chapters in Part II of the book variously highlight the politics of science through the lens of history. The common thread binding these chapters is their collective concern with the institutionalisation of scientific power. Tanja Hammel (Chapter 3) shows how Mary Elizabeth Barber negotiated racial difference in her descriptions of insects. Hammel calls for research to go beyond the 'entrapment in white mythologies' and for further critical investigations into the works of entomologists.[34] Gabriele Kranz (Chapter 4) analyses the collection, research and display of plants from Southern Africa in the Botanical Museum of Hamburg. The city's botanical institutions were deeply embedded in German colonialism. Kranz shows that the meaning of the botanical collections has changed considerably since their inception.

The history of nature conservation is replete with modes of resource control. In Southern Africa, colonial ideas of development and welfare were brought together in remote and marginal areas to enable control over natural resources through the creation of protected areas. Luregn Lenggenhager (Chapter 5) demonstrates that power relations that underpinned protected areas in colonial Namibia are enacted through the present transfrontier conservation areas. These emerged out of a close cooperation between ecological experts and armed security units, both

---

33 A detailed study of this failed inoculation campaign is presented in Rizzo 2012: pp. 208–252
34 Mbembe 2015, 'Decolonizing Knowledge and the Question of the Archive': http://wiser.wits.ac.za/content/achille-mbembe-decolonizing-knowledge-and-question-archive-12054 (accessed 10 November 2015)

financed by and originating from the centres of political, economic and academic power. Colonial Namibia also experienced the development of a scientific standard reference for cattle breeding. As Giorgio Miescher and Anna Voegeli (Chapter 6) show, this was not just veterinary science in practice but it was an exercise in the exoticisation and musealisation of a specific type of cattle that can be traced back through a longer process of experimentation, segregation and marginalisation that had been shaped by a close interplay between breeding practices, veterinary science, disease control and colonial politics of exclusion and inclusion.

Part III of the book addresses questions of power and politics in activities concerned with plants. As already introduced by Kranz and Lenggenhager, the chapters of this section expand on how plants function in complex ways as subjects of politics and how they are deployed by a variety of actors for various reasons. Diana Gibson (Chapter 7) discusses the institutionalisation of medicinal plants in South Africa since 1994. She argues that medicinal plants are not only material objects, but are also relational as they are embedded in assemblages with people, ecologies, knowledge systems, texts and legal networks. Melanie Boehi (Chapter 8) shows that plants were deployed in political propaganda and protest by a variety of actors in South Africa throughout the twentieth and twenty-first centuries. She discusses how the Kirstenbosch National Botanical Garden in Cape Town emerged as an institution where plants were charged with political meanings.

Part IV of the book brings together fieldwork data to reflect on how policy frameworks that place nature conservation above the needs of the poor, especially in rural areas, shape human relations and livelihoods. Such frameworks also favour the elite and have led to what scholars call elite capture, i.e. the manner in which powerful individuals in society use the apparatus of the state to control and benefit from access to public resources. Popular processes such as community participation mask this inequality in resource access. As Annette LaRocco (Chapter 9) shows, a small elite in Gaborone, the capital of Botswana, undermines socio-ecological institutions such as community-based natural resource management by imposing a hunting ban. The ban means that rural dwellers are denied access to natural resources while the politically connected photographic tourism industry stands to benefit.

Romie Vonkie Nghitevelekwa (Chapter 10) explores land relations and property rights in communal areas in central-north Namibia. She argues that communal land is a complex and contested terrain comprising of different social actors, who manoeuvre and struggle to control and use land while also ascribing different meanings to it. The politics of land is enabled by the Namibian constitution that individualises communal land while also allowing the same land to be used as commonage. The result is the class difference between those with individual property rights and those with communal rights.

Ndidzulafhi Innocent Sinthumule (Chapter 11) takes the theme of conservation policy and inequality further by tackling the question how and why processes that are routinely touted as empowering end up disempowering local communities. These chapters make it clear that nature conservation policies marginalise the interests of the poor. This raises the question of the nature of conversation that ordinary people could have to influence nature conservation. Specifically, the question is how do local people exert influence on the conservation enterprise? Marnie Graham (Chapter 12) suggests that a process that facilitates dialogue on nature through cross-social interaction might be a useful starting point to bring out local understandings of nature and to infuse them in nature conservation paradigms. She shows that such interactions contribute to post-apartheid social reconciliation while, at the same time, drawing closer ties between nature conservation areas and neighbouring communities. Sandro Simon's study of the Bamenda Wetlands (Chapter 13) brings together issues of land and conservation. He traces changes in land tenure from commons and customary tenure to nationalisation and privatisation. He thereby demonstrates that use of and authority over wetlands is determined by legal and normative pluralism.

Part V of the book includes two interventions in the form of shorter chapters. In Chapter 14, Frank Matose tackles the question why there are no open uprisings in Southern Africa's forests, given the history of dispossession in the region. He argues that local people who are dispossessed of their land and other natural resources are not quiet but engage in hidden struggles against the state. He develops a typology of resistance from which he concludes that the hidden struggles of local people take place in the form of what he calls 'articulatory' resistance and 'existential' resistance. The book concludes with a rejoinder by Elísio Macamo (Chapter 15), who challenges us to think about science and power in the construction of Africa, and also how we use methodological tools in the study of Africa. He calls for an engagement with the knowledge production of Africa because such a process takes place in theoretical frameworks, conceptual categories and methodological procedures. In his view, our study of 'real Africa' is dependent on uncovering epistemological assumptions and the scientific power underpinning constructions of Africa.

References

Bauchspies, W.K. and M. Puig de la Bellacasa (2009), Feminist Science and Technology Studies: A Patchwork of Moving Subjectivities. An interview with Geoffrey Bowker, Sandra Harding, Anne Marie Mol, Susan Leigh Star and Banu Subramaniam. *Subjectivity*, 28: 334–344.

Beinart, W. (1998), Men, Science, Travel and Nature in the Eighteenth and Nineteenth-Century Cape. *Journal of Southern African Studies*, 24(4): 775–799.

Beinart, W. (2005), Academic Amnesia and the Poverty of Polemics. *Journal of African History*, 46(1): 127–134.

Braun, L.F. (2015), *Colonial Survey and Native Landscapes in Rural South Africa, 1850–1913*. Leiden/Boston: Brill.

Carruthers, J. (1995), *The Kruger National Park: A Social and Political History*. Pietermaritzburg: University of Natal Press.

Carruthers, J. (2004), "Our Beautiful and Useful Allies": Aspects of Ornithology in Twentieth Century South Africa. *Historia*, 49(1): 89–109.

Carter, N. (2007), *The Politics of the Environment: Ideas, Activism and Policy* (2nd edn). Cambridge: Cambridge University Press.

Cioc, M. (2009), *The Game of Conservation: International Treaties to Protect the World's Migratory Animals*. Athens: Ohio University Press.

Delort, R. (1987), *Der Elephant, die Biene und der Heilige Wolf: Die wahre Geschichte der Tiere*. München/Wien: Hanser.

Dubow, S. (ed.) (2000), *Science and Society in Southern Africa*. Manchester: Manchester University Press.

Dubow, S. (2004), Earth History, Natural History, and Prehistory at the Cape, 1860–1875. *Comparative Studies in Society and History*, 46(1): 107–133.

Environmental Politics (2015). http://www.tandfonline.com/action/journalInformation?show=aimsScope&journalCode=fenp20#.Vp8y_rX8KUk. Accessed 20 January 2016.

Forsyth, T. (2015), Integrating Science and Politics in Political Ecology. In R.L. Bryant (ed.), *International Handbook of Political Ecology*. Cheltenham: Edward Edgar: 103–116.

Foucault, M. (1970), *The Order of Things: An Archaeology of the Human Sciences*. New York: Pantheon Books.

Gilfoyle, D. (2003), Veterinary Research and the African Rinderpest Epizootic: the Cape Colony, 1896–1898. *Journal of Southern African Studies*, 29(1): 133–154.

Green Musselman, E. (2003), Plant Knowledge at the Cape: A Study in African and European Collaboration. *International Journal of African Historical Studies*, 36(2): 367–392.

Haraway, D. (1989), *Primate Visions: Gender, Race, and Nature in the World of Modern Science*. New York: Routledge.

Harries, P. (2007), *Butterflies and Barbarians: Swiss Missionaries and Systems of Knowledge in South East Africa*. Oxford: James Currey.

Ingold, T. (2000), *The Perception of the Environment: Essays on Livelihood, Dwelling and Skill*. New York: Routledge.

Jacobs, N. (2006), The Intimate Politics of Ornithology in Colonial Africa. *Comparative Studies in Society and History*, 48(3): 564–603.

Jacobs, N. and A. Bank (eds.) (2015), *The Micropolitics of Knowledge: Special Issue of Kronos*, 41.

Jansen, J. (1991), *Knowledge and Power in South Africa: Critical Perspectives across the Disciplines*. Johannesburg: Skotaville.

Leftwich, A. (ed.) 2004, *What is Politics? The Activity and Its Study*. Cambridge: Polity.

MacKenzie, J.M. (1988), *The Empire of Nature: Hunting, Conservation and British Imperialism*. Manchester: Manchester University Press.

MacKenzie, J.M. (1997), Empire and the Ecological Apocalypse: The Historiography of the Imperial Environment. In T. Griffiths and L. Robin (eds.), *Ecology and Empire: Environmental History of Settler Societies*. Pietermaritzburg: University of Natal Press: 215–228.

Mbembe, A. (2015), Decolonizing Knowledge and the Question of the Archive. Wits Institute for Social and Economic Research (WISER). http://wiser.wits.ac.za/content/achille-mbembe-decolonizing-knowledge-and-question-archive-12054. Accessed 29/06/2015.

Miescher, G. (2012), *Namibia's Red Line: The History of a Veterinary and Settlement Border*. New York: Palgrave Macmillan.

Nustad, K.G. (2015), *Creating Africas: Struggles over Nature, Conservation and Land*. London: Hurst and Company.

Phoofolo, P. (1992), Epidemics and Revolutions: The Rinderpest Epidemic in Late Nineteenth Century Southern Africa. *Past and Present*, 138: 112–143.

Pratt, M.E. (1992), *Imperial Eyes: Travel Writing and Transculturation*. London: Routledge.

Ramutsindela, M. (2004), *Parks and People in Postcolonial Societies: Experiences in Southern Africa*. Dordrecht: Kluwer (Springer).

Rizzo, L. (2012), *Gender and Colonialism: A History of Kaoko in North-Western Namibia, 1870s–1950s*. Basel: Basler Afrika Bibliographien.

Said, E. (1978), *Orientalism*. New York: Vintage Books.

Shapin, S. and S. Schaffer (1985), *Leviathan and the Air-Pump: Hobbes, Boyle, and the Experimental Life*. Princeton: Princeton University Press.

Subramaniam, B. (2014), *Ghost Stories for Darwin: The Science of Variation and the Politics of Diversity*. Urbana/Chicago/Springfield: University of Illinois Press.

Tilley, H. (2011), *Africa a Living Laboratory: Empire, Development, and the Problem of Scientific Knowledge*. Chicago/London: University of Chicago Press.

Van Sittert, L. (2002), From 'Mere Weeds' and 'Bosjes' to a Cape Floral Kingdom: The Re-imagining of Indigenous Flora at the Cape, c. 1890–1939. *Kronos* 28: 102–126.

Van Sittert, L. (2004), The Nature of Power: Cape Environmental History, the History of Ideas and Neoliberal Historiography. *Journal of African History*, 45(2): 305–313.

Van Onselen, C. (1972), Reactions to Rinderpest in Southern Africa 1896–97. *Journal of African History*, 13(3): 473–488.

CHAPTER 2

Political dynamics of human-environment relations

Maano Ramutsindela

Introduction
The relationship between people and their biophysical environment is shaped by multiple forces, one of which is politics, which is understood here as the exercise of power in "production, distribution and use of resources in the course of social existence".[1] Politics mediates social relations as well as society's relations with its biophysical environment. I argue that politics in this sphere is aided by constructions of scale through which power is exercised. In other words, the level or combination of levels (i.e. local, national, regional, global) at which power is exercised determines the control and distribution of natural resources. This chapter contributes to the theme of the book by examining the forms that politics takes in nature conservation and the scales that enable these forms to emerge. The chapter adds to literature on political ecology by demonstrating the inseparability of politics and ecology through the lens of nature conservation.

Political ecology emerged as a field of study concerned with "the fusing of biogeophysical processes with broadly social ones".[2] At face value, the division between politics and ecology in human-environment relations appears logical but, in reality, politics and ecology are made together.[3] That is to say, politics and ecology are mutually constitutive and also intersect at various levels. In the first part of the chapter, I briefly recount the debate on politics and ecology to highlight the tension between the two. Next I show the significant role of scale in power

---

1 Heywood 2000: p. 34
2 Zimmerer 2000: p. 153
3 Forsyth 2015

relations as it manifests in human-environment interactions.[4] The objective here is to highlight the ways in which scale is used in the pursuit of environmental goals and the political possibilities that arise therefrom. Thereafter I suggest how nature conservation is a useful platform for examining these possibilities. As the literature shows, nature conservation embodies ideas of nature that are clearly articulated through the practices of nature conservation. These practices have huge implications for ordinary people living in and around nature conservation areas, whose livelihood, production and political organisation are often disrupted or marginalised by conservation non-governmental organisations.[5]

Inserting politics into ecological research

Scholarly interest in what constitutes the political in ecology traces to analyses that sought to understand what Swyngedouw calls the political conditioning of physical process.[6] Such conditioning implies that ecological problems are interwoven with socio-economic processes. The co-evolution of politics and ecology has nonetheless been marginal to ecological studies that seek to explain ecological conditions outside their political contexts. For example, ecologists ascribed environmental degradation of, say, soils, to poor management, poverty, population growth, and so on.[7] They held the view that farmers in developing countries were acting irrationally and irresponsibly toward their land and, as a result of this, there was much land degradation in those countries.[8] In other words, farmers were deemed to have little or no knowledge of their biophysical environment and therefore needed to be educated and disciplined so they could use the land properly. These solutions were suggested without asking the crucial questions of why farmers behaved in certain ways and what they were doing about the deteriorating conditions of their land. These studies ignored the fact that land-use options and their impact on the environment cannot be understood outside broader land and agrarian questions.[9]

The above-mentioned weaknesses in ecological explanations triggered questions on the social, political and economic conditions under which ecological systems operate. Attempts to answer these questions crystallised into what we call political ecology today. The concern with the political in ecology was articulated by proto-

---

4 Neumann 2009: p. 398
5 Anderson/Grove 1987; Ramutsindela 2004; Dowie 2009; Oldekop et al. 2016
6 Swyngedouw 2015
7 Tiffen/Mortimore/Gichuki 1994
8 Duraiappah 1998
9 For example, land degradation in South Africa is highest in areas of the former bantustans (Hoffman/Ashwell 2001). The apartheid government blamed black farmers and population growth for the demise of agriculture in the bantustans but ignored the fact that the majority of black people were pushed into marginal land on which they made a living.

political ecologists such as Gourou in the late 19th and early 20th centuries.[10] Proto-political ecologists with different professional backgrounds broadly shared "an ethos about how politics, political economy and ecology interweave under capitalism to degrade peoples and environments, and how this provokes a backlash among those who are oppressed".[11]

In the early 1970s the journalist Cockburn, the anthropologist Wolf and the environmentalist Beakhurst referred to political ecology to cover the "panoply of ways in which environmental concerns were politicised in the wake of the environmentalist wave that broke in the late 1960s and early 1970s".[12] Accordingly, early framers of political ecology in academia such as Blaikie, Watts and Hecht sought to bring the complexity of human systems to the fore, and to link human-environment experiences with the broader political and economic factors that shaped them. Deriving inspiration from peasant studies and Marxist theory, these early writings on political ecology observed "unequal power relations, conflict and cultural 'modernisation' under a global capitalist political economy as key forces in reshaping and destabilising human interactions with the biophysical environment".[13] Watts went further to inquire whether "a form of economic disequilibrium in the socio-economic system [was] being transmitted as a form of ecological disequilibrium".[14] In the mid-1980s, political ecologists drew clear links between environmental conditions and political interests, and worked from the assumption that environmental change and ecological conditions are products of political processes.[15] This assumption has been central to the work of political ecologists to this day.

The fusion of politics and ecological scientific research on human-environment relations has become fertile ground for debating the (im)balance between the science of ecology and the political interpretations of ecological knowledge and practice. The debate is captured in phrases such as 'political ecology without politics' and 'politics without ecology'.[16] This debate is well documented in the pages of journals such as *Progress in Human Geography* but has not been closed. I have no intention to close it here either as I think the debate should continue in light of the collision between pressing environmental and socio-political challenges, and the need for scholars to clarify their normative standpoints on socioecological questions. Emphasis on either ecology or politics as a central concern in studies of

---

10 Bryant 2015
11 Bryant 2015: p. 17
12 Gregory et al. 2009: p. 545
13 Walker 2005: p. 74
14 Watts 1985: p. 30
15 Robbins 2012
16 Peter Walker even described the place of ecology in political ecology as a recurrent and unresolved question. Walker 2005

human-environment relations should be seen as a political choice. Take the initial central goal of political ecology that was to explain accelerated degradation by using "combined analytical tools of both natural and social sciences".[17] As a result of more emphasis on the political, the goal of the field was redefined as a "broader social project of raising the emancipatory potential of environmental ideas and to engage directly with the larger landscape of debates over modernity, its institutions, and its knowledges".[18] Writing on urban political ecology, Holifield and Schuelke endorse the goal of political ecology as to "identify conditions of possibility for imagining and enacting more democratic and egalitarian socioecological futures".[19]

Ecology, scaling and political dynamics

The development of political ecology sketched above highlights the significance of scale in answering ecological questions. The question of scale is crucial for understanding the broader political processes that shape the relations between humans and their biophysical environment. While a cascade of hierarchical levels is often used to match research questions and the scale of analysis, the politics of production, distribution and use of resources discussed in this chapter can best be understood by paying attention to the recursive relationship between ecological scales and the scales of political process. Ecological scales here are understood as the appropriate scale at which ecological systems are protected while political scales emphasise political processes that mediate and define power relations, which in turn affect the governance and distribution of natural resources. Engel-Di Mauro commented that "if one wishes to define and explain the interaction of social and nonhuman systems, understanding the scale of interaction and the scale of different environmental and social processes is of paramount importance".[20] Analyses that take smaller-scale dynamics as their central focus are likely to fail to relate these dynamics to general patterns or to see how general patterns underscore local political dynamics.[21]

At the macro-level, ecological research has adopted world systems approaches to engage ecological questions related to local conditions. Such approaches mirror those of new ecology, where broader levels of ecological organisation (landscape or ecosystem) have impact on the dynamics of subsidiary levels such as communities and populations.[22] It is at this macro level where the production, distribution and use of resources are shaped through various international agreements such as

---

17 Walker 2005: p. 79
18 Peet/Watts 1996: p. 37
19 Holifield/Schuelke 2015: p. 295
20 Engel-Di Mauro 2009: p. 117
21 Ramutsindela/Noe 2015
22 Turner 2014: p. 618

conventions and treaties. This formalisation of politics in turn triggers day-to-day struggles over control of, and access to, natural resources, i.e. the environmentalism of the poor.

Environmental struggles by ordinary people are captured in the notion of the environmentalism of the poor that is considered part of the broader environmental movement.[23] As Martinez-Alier explains, the environmentalism of the poor does not imply that "poor people are always and everywhere environmentalists", but instead suggests that "in ecological distribution conflicts, the poor are often on the side of resource conservation and a clean environment, even when they themselves do not claim to be environmentalists".[24] The environmentalism of the poor arises from the "unavoidable clash between economy and environment" and implies that ordinary people, especially in developing countries, have "material interest in the environment as a source and a requirement for livelihood".[25] Shiva concurs that "communities are resolutely defending and evolving living economies that protect life on earth and promote creativity" but goes further to propose Earth Democracy as an alternative future built on living economies, living cultures and living democracies.[26] These broad conceptions of environmentalism are underpinned by a poststructuralist approach to human-environment relations. This approach goes beyond institutionalised and formalised politics and opens up possibilities for imagining the informality of politics.

Holifield and Schuelke think that institutionalised politics has two sides: one being moments of egalitarian demands that interrupt and disrupt established orders and the other relating to conventional, institutionalised politics. One example of institutionalised politics is participation in decision-making processes considered a sign of increasing democratisation. Participation is a buzzword in environmental and development projects yet it often stifles opposition and resistance. There is a

---

23   Broadly speaking, environmentalism is made up of three main intertwined clusters, namely the cult of wilderness (made up of groups and institutions preoccupied with saving nature as it has been), the gospel of eco-efficiency (with its emphasis on using technology and other means to both plunder and heal the planet), and the environmentalism of the poor rooted in notions of justice. Martinez-Alier 2002
24   Martinez-Alier 2002: p. viii
25   Martinez-Alier 2002: pp. ix, 11. It would be wrong to associate the environmentalism of the poor to local scale politics as locals are able to tap into resources located far and wide through their networks. For example, indigenous peoples in Suriname used multiple scales to harness specific types of information needed to aid them to reject a proposed protected area at Kaboeri Creek. Haalboom/Campbell 2012
26   Earth Democracy is a name Shiva gave to a project in which people around the world are engaged in reclaiming the commons and in building an inclusive, nonviolent future for all beings. Its underlying philosophy is the connectedness between people and the planet as a family and the rejection of global privatisation and its consequent "Ownership Society". Shiva 2005: p. 2

view that "participation, carefully managed and typically oriented toward building consensus is symptomatic of the absence of the political".[27] As I show below, the formal/informal dichotomy is insufficient for explaining the density of local and extraterritorial forces that shape the conservation enterprise.

Issues of scale cannot be separated from institutionalised politics in the human-environment interaction. Scale is integral to political ecologists' analyses of human-environment relations, mainly because understanding these relations demands an approach that encompasses "the contribution of different geographical scales and hierarchies of socio-economic organizations".[28] Scale is conceptually relational and socially produced through and by political struggles.[29] To comprehend the role of scale in power dynamics of human-environment relations we need to free scale of its limiting cartographic qualities—that is, avoid treating scale as a pre-given and fixed space arranged in hierarchical fashion.[30]

Critical scholarship has shown that scale is a result of political and economic processes but that also enables them.[31] For example, scale enables capital accumulation by aligning particular actors operating at quite different scales to work toward a clearly defined capitalist goal. This explains the reasons for upscaling or downscaling or even crossing scales such as in glocalisation, where actors at the local and global levels could be connected without the assistance of national governments.[32] Glocalisation not only redefines political and ecological scales but also significantly alters power geometries in society. Of importance here is how relations are forged or broken down or re-produced by connecting or disconnecting local and global scales.[33] The manner in which ecological and political scales intersect and rebound upon one another determines issues of access, control and ownership of natural resources. Political interests are pursued through the arrangement of scale. For example, once natural resources like the Amazon forests are determined to be of global concern, the decision of people living in the Amazon or by the Brazilian government over the same resources is weakened because the resources are deemed to belong to humanity as a whole. The Amazon is a good example of this scaling process because it is claimed by powerful nations as a storehouse of carbon for the

---

27 Holifield/Schuelke 2015: p. 295
28 Neumann 2009: p. 398
29 Marston 2000; Howitt 1998; McCarthy 2005
30 Marston 2000
31 This scholarship is espoused in the works of Harvey, Swyngedouw, Robbins, and Watts, among others.
32 Upscaling entails moving from a lower to a higher scale. For example, an activity or decision-making power could be moved from, say, a ward level to a national level in order to effect desired political changes. Downscaling means relocating power from a higher office such as national government to local communities as a democratisation process.
33 Smith 1996

world. Such claims, however, do not translate into equality and equity as the needs of poor nations are often sacrificed in the interests of global environmental goals. This way, ecology becomes a political subject because it entails policy-making that connects global and local actors.

Nature conservation as a site of politics

In this section I discuss nature conservation through the lens of political ecology to make two interventions. The first intervention relates to power relations in the domain of nature conservation. Nature conservation is characterised by ways of dominating nature and people. It is an act of ordering nature in line with human aspirations that are pursued by using guidelines that regulate human behaviour toward nature. In the second intervention I show how ecological and political scales produce unequal power relations in nature conservation. This process not only transcends the binaries between formal and informal politics but also enables us to imagine the political ecology of nature conservation across different scales.

Power relations

Nature conservation, and the environmental movement associated with it, have been a subject of study of political ecologists for many years.[34] The discussion in this chapter adds to this literature by drawing attention to the intersection between nature conservation and the politics of scale. It emphasises the point that scale is a vehicle through which political struggles are waged over natural resources and in the protection of nature. Such struggles are unavoidable because nature conservation areas involve land that is under various tenure regimes. West's book, *Conservation is our Government Now: The Politics of Ecology in Papua New Guinea,* emphasises the power of conservation.[35] Where does conservation get all this power? The answer to this question is a complex one since the idea of conservation is dynamic and has drawn its power from multiple sources over time and space. Nature conservation in the form of protected areas such as national parks was initially influenced by the interests of the hunter. For example, the excessive off-take of ivory and other wildlife products in Africa in the 19th century led to the decline in wildlife. As a result of this, European hunters and colonial administrators feared that nothing would be left to hunt, hence they imposed stricter hunting regulations.[36] While sport hunting became a norm for the elite, subsistence hunting was condemned as uncivilised and lacking any sportsmanship.

---

34 Bryant/Bailey 1997
35 West 2006
36 MacKenzie 1988; Gissibl/Höhler/Kupper 2012

Subsistence hunting was seen as a cause for declining wildlife populations.[37] Much of nature conservation is currently guided by scientific knowledge, often produced by specialists in natural sciences who pay less or no attention to social, political and economic systems. While these scientific specialists have developed intimate knowledge about species and the nonhuman world, they have also encultured and politicised nature.[38] The emergence of specialists however also brings with it hierarchies of people and their knowledge. The knowledge of non-specialists is seen as of lower value compared to that of academic specialists. The power dynamic at play in such hierarchies of knowledge is that some people's understanding of flora and fauna is undermined, mainly because it is seen as irrelevant to the hegemonic idea of nature conservation.[39]

In its globalised sense, nature conservation privileges one form of knowledge system about nature above the other; this often leads to the condemnation of the ways in which marginalised groups relate to, and interact with, their biophysical environment. Marginalisation takes different forms. For example, most nature conservation projects are imposed on local communities without consultation as happened during the creation of Limpopo National Park in Mozambique in 2001, and when Maramani (Zimbabwe) was made part of the Greater Mapungubwe Transfrontier Conservation Area in 2006.[40] Generally, possibilities for changing power relations in nature conservation have been thwarted by a conservation-for-development discourse that perpetuates unequal power relations. According to this discourse, local citizens appear as beneficiaries of nature-based economies rather than as owners of natural resources.[41] The loss of power over natural resources by local citizens under colonialism is yet to be successfully resolved in Southern Africa. In other words, most post-independence governments have not yet fundamentally transformed land and agrarian relations for the benefit of local citizens.[42] In the absence of resource rights, local residents lack the necessary power to challenge the encroachment of nature conservation onto their land, and are therefore vulnerable to green grabbing.[43]

To return to the question of the power of conservation, scholars have shown that a hegemonic bloc established at the global level and operating through multi-layered networks consisting of conservation non-governmental organisations, business,

---

37 Neumann 2009
38 Lynch 2016
39 The idea of preserving nature by separating it from humans. See Nash 2014
40 See Sinthumule in this volume.
41 In Southern Africa, nature-based economies were made popular through the Communal Area Management Programme for Indigenous Resources (CAMPFIRE) and communal conservancies in Namibia.
42 See Nghitevelekwa in this volume
43 Land acquisition for environmental ends. Fairhead/Leach/Scoones 2012

governments and philanthropists is firmly established as each of these actors seeks to maximise gains from nature.[44] The tourism sector in particular has found new markets in nature conservation, hence there has been an increasing penetration of capitalism into nature conservation.[45] How nature is valued by business and the predominantly western ecotourism clientele accounts in part for the concentration of nature conservation projects in areas that guarantee maximum financial returns.

Crossing scales

The protection and preservation of fauna and flora takes place at localities where valuable species are found, yet decisions informing nature conservation strategies and practices come from various sources that can be located on and across a range of scales. On the global stage, interest and influential groups and institutions such as the International Union for the Conservation of Nature (IUCN), the Global Environment Facility (GEF), and the World Wide Fund for Nature (WWF) play a critical role in matters of nature conservation.[46] Most of these organisations take a big share of philanthropic funds that in turn give them enormous political power.[47] More importantly, they are channels through which ideas of nature conservation are formulated and translated into action. Take the World Parks Congress held in Sydney, Australia, on 12–19 November 2014, at which individual countries and organisations made commitments toward nature conservation.[48] At that Congress the GEF undertook "to support country-driven actions to help conserve and sustainably use biodiversity through effectively-managed protected area systems that are integrated into sustainable landscape and seascape mosaics in 146 developing countries and countries with economies in transition".[49]

---

44 Heynen et al. 2007; Brockington/Duffy 2010
45 Büscher et al. 2012
46 The IUCN claims to be the world's authority on biodiversity conservation, nature-based solutions and environmental governance, and boosts of over 1,200 members and 11,000 scientific experts. IUCN Online 2015: http://www.iucn.org/about/union/members (accessed 29 June 2015). The GEF is the environmental arm of the World Bank dedicated to financing environment-related projects.
47 Chapin 2004
48 For example, China announced its commitment to increase its protected areas territory to at least 20% by 2020 in order to match Chinese categories of protected areas to global standards. It also committed to increasing its forest area to 40 million hectars by 2020 (World Parks Congress Online 2014). These commitments are made at international platforms as a way of telling the world about the country's good intentions but also as a political gesture. China is heavily criticised for its pollution problem. It however makes public commitments such as these in order to silence its critics on environmental matters while also sending a message that its environmental commitments meet global standards.
49 World Parks Congress Online 2014: http://worldparkscongress.org/about/promise_of_sydney_commitments.html (accessed 29 June 2015)

Arguably, the institutionalisation and formalisation of the politics of nature conservation that take place at the global level are linked to actions and practices at localities. On the global stage, environmental regimes emerge in the form of conventions and treaties that are themselves shaped by powerful nations that use such regimes to pursue their economic and political interests. It is also the level on which global distributional justice—"how the global resources as well as the benefits and responsibilities arising from interstate relations may be equitably shared between states"—is fiercely contested.[50] Against this backdrop, environmental regimes should be looked at as vehicles for either exacerbating or correcting existing social and economic inequalities between nations.[51]

It is at the global level that ecological problems and political processes co-determine global institutional arrangements that shape nature conservation. The IUCN for instance holds World Parks Congresses and World Conservation Congresses as platforms on which scientific findings are used to inform resolutions that are adopted for implementation by parties to the Convention of Biological Diversity (CBD).[52] For its part, the Congress of the Parties on the CBD set the 20 Aichi Biodiversity Targets in Nagoya (Japan) in 2010 to address the underlying causes of biodiversity loss, reduce the direct pressure on biodiversity and promote sustainable use, improve the status of biodiversity, enhance the benefits of biodiversity and ecosystems to all, and enhance implementation. The Congress passed the resolution that each country should place 17% of terrestrial and inland water and 10% of coastal and marine areas under protected status. As MacDonald has convincingly argued, the World Conservation Congress is a platform on which politics is enacted and also serves as a site at which nature conservation is institutionalised.[53] Meetings such as these privilege certain positions like market-based solutions to nature conservation-related problems.[54]

Biodiversity targets set at the global level have huge implications for national policies on, and strategies for, nature conservation. In other words, these targets require national governments to devise strategies to achieve global goals of nature conservation.[55] In the process, government strategies collide with livelihood options and the interests of ordinary people, who are marginal to global discussions on how nature should be protected. Thus, conservation policies and strategies of national governments bring together global and national ideals that often clash with local aspirations. This clash leads to three main forms of politics that I now turn to.

---

50   Okereke 2007: p. 17
51   Okereke 2007
52   It will hold its next World Conservation Congress in Hawai'i on 2–5 September 2016.
53   MacDonald 2010
54   Corson/MacDonald 2012
55   Ramutsindela 2015

First, the nation state becomes an insulator at the edge of the global and the local, i.e. it simultaneously faces the global and the local in order to meet the expectations of global players and its local constituency. Globally, the state has to meet its obligations as, say, a signatory of the CBD mentioned above. Since most, if not all, of these obligations are voluntary, there is no direct force applied to the state. There is however a recognition that failure to meet these obligations has material and political consequences for signatory states. Materially, the state could lose foreign aid and donor funding designed to finance nationally-driven nature conservation projects. On the political front, the state could lose access to global fora that form channels for political interaction, influence and networking. The state usually responds favourably to demands by global institutions and globally-networked conservation non-governmental organisations such as the IUCN in order to keep their presence on the international stage.

The second form of the political manifests in state-society dialectical relations. The democratic state derives its mandate from the will of the people and governments are elected to serve people. Governing parties however tend to pursue narrow political interests once elected into office.[56] Such interests are also visible in the environmental domain, where governments are biased toward the private sector at the expense of ordinary citizens. There is a history to this. In the colonial past, the state used its brutal force to bully disenfranchised citizens into complying with conservation ideals. Examples that come to mind are the forced removals of black people from national parks such as Gonarezhou (Zimbabwe), Kalahari Gemsbok (South Africa), Kruger (South Africa), Etosha (Namibia) and Sehlabathebe (Lesotho). Variants of this violence continue today under the watchful eye of democratic states in much of the Global South, although states use different approaches to engage with local people. States in the Global South are under pressure from global actors to carry out their conservation mandate but often fail to do so because of conditions prevailing on the ground.[57] These conditions relate to the need for locals to have access to land and other natural resources, for example.[58]

Third, nature conservation ideals that are driven by global and local forces could trigger conflict but such conflict could also reflect local political dynamics. These dynamics have been ignored by analyses that ascribe environmental-related

---

56 Bayart 1993; Way 2005; Schedler 2014
57 The technocratic explanation of the failure by nation states in developing countries to meet biodiversity targets is that they do not have the capacity to do so. A more nuanced explanation is that such failures are indicators of shifting biodiversity values and priorities, and the overambitious goal of trying to protect everything under the sun (see Bottrill et al. 2008; Raymond 2014).
58 Ramutsindela 2015

conflicts at national and sub-national levels to two causal relationships, namely resource scarcity and resource abundance. It is not my intention here to go into a full discussion on these causal relationships. Rather, I refer to perspectives on environment-related conflicts to highlight that concerns with environmental protection could ignite local political contest.[59] For example, violent conflict has been experienced in the creation of wildlife management areas (WMAs).

In brief, WMAs originate from the need to devolve conservation authority to the local level in line with democratic values, interests in promoting nature conservation outside state land, and the need to create wildlife corridors. Of relevance to our discussion here is how the creation of WMAs engenders local politics. The decision to set aside communal land for purposes of nature conservation such as WMAs should be understood as a political act. Conservation groups encourage local communities to put land aside and this process involves the creation of political structures and business-savvy institutions at the village level. These structures exist in parallel with local government—as the arm of government—and also with other state agencies, especially those responsible for wildlife.[60] A stage for local politics is set at the site where these WMAs are established as various groups of land users and environmental non-governmental organisations (ENGOs) seek to control the process in their favour. For example, ENGOs remain focused on creating a wildlife corridor through villages while villagers seek to protect areas for grazing and cultivation—they do this while participating in the process. Where villagers appear to constitute a stumbling block toward the creation of a wildlife corridor, the head of the state intervenes in favour of nature conservation as examples of WMAs in Tanzania have shown.[61]

Local political dynamics also come to the surface in the wars against wildlife crimes such as poaching. For example, the rhino poaching crisis in South Africa's Kruger National Park (KNP) has become a site of brutal violence as both the South African National Defence Force and poachers fight over rhinos in the park. In the KNP an arms race has ensued between poachers and anti-poaching forces "as each side becomes more sophisticated and potentially lethal via militarised methods and technologies, the other follows suit to keep up".[62] Thus, poaching blurs the boundary between formal and informal process of production, distribution and use of resources in the course of social existence. Poachers exercise informal

---

59 For a debate on this see Maxwell/Reuveny 2000; Le Billion 2001; Devlin/Hendrix 2014; Eck 2014; Hough 2015
60 Ramutsindela/Noe 2015
61 In places such as Tanzania, the head of the state has a final say on communally held land, which is basically state land, and could therefore declare land for WMAs even though the process appears devolved to local communities. Noe 2009
62 Lunstrum 2014

power over natural resources that are formally enclosed and protected by a legal regime.[63]

The war against poaching, as conservationists call it, affects communities living near or within protected areas where poaching takes place. It is assumed that poor rural communities are lured by poaching syndicates who exploit their poverty to carry out illicit activities.[64] Members of these communities are also seen as poachers because they have nothing to live on other than to harvest natural resources, some of which are enclosed into protected areas. To succeed in the war against poaching, conservation groups enlist communities as partners. Massive investments are made into communities in the form of development projects but also in creating networks of informants. These networks in turn divide local communities into 'good citizens' and 'bad citizens'.[65] Good citizens are informants who track the movement of members of the community suspected of poaching, act as watchdogs against strangers suspected of poaching, and as volunteers who guard protected areas alongside park rangers.[66]

Conclusion

The politics of ecology embedded in scale promises to advance political ecological research. This becomes clear when examined together with the politics of scale in the environmental domain, where ecology and politics intersect to determine the production, distribution and use of resources. Scale is more than a plane at which structural processes operate but entails the organisation of power relations.[67] Environmental struggles are waged through the shifting of scales that open up new social relations. Scale analyses therefore enhance our understanding of power dynamics in the environmental domain. In the absence of such analyses we are unable to comprehend large-scale systemic processes that shape human-environment relations and that also account for most of the environmental problems we worry about.

This chapter has highlighted that examining the ecological scale and politics of scale together helps us understand the institutionalisation of politics at various scales. It sheds light on the significance of scale in shaping power relations. It also reveals that the formalisation of politics involves non-state actors such as non-governmental organisations that participate at global fora, where environmental

---

63 In the South African context, national parks are proclaimed and governed in terms of the National Environmental Management: Protected Areas Act, 2003 (Act No 57 of 2003). South Africa 2003
64 Kings 2014; Hübschle 2016
65 Büscher/Ramutsindela 2016
66 Büscher/Ramutsindela 2016
67 Legg 2009

agendas are drawn. In nature conservation such agendas are often at variance with demands for access to natural resources by local citizens. Contest over natural resources by local citizens is typical of informal politics in that it takes place outside formal institutions although this does not apply to all cases involving such contest.[68] In conclusion, issues of power relations in nature conservation and in human-environment interactions cannot be fully understood by analyses that do not pay attention to ecological scales and the politics of scale. These two are inseparable but are also crucial for the unfolding of politics in the environmental domain.

References

Anderson, D. and R. Grove (eds.) (1987), *Conservation in Africa: People, Policies and Practice*. Cambridge: Cambridge University Press.

Bayart, J.-F. (1993), *The State in Africa: The Politics of the Belly*. London: Longman.

Bryant, R.L. (2015), Reflecting on Political Ecology. In R.L. Bryant (ed.), *International Handbook of Political Ecology*. Cheltenham: Edward Edgar: 14–24.

Bryant, R.L. and S. Bailey (1997), *Third World Political Ecology*. London: Routledge.

Bottrill, M.C., L.N. Joseph, J. Carwardine, M. Bode, C. Cook, E.T. Game, H. Grantham, S. Kark, S. Linke, E. McDonald-Madden and R.L. Pressey (2008), Is Conservation Triage Just Smart Decision Making? *Trends in Ecology and Conservation*, 23(12): 650-654.

Brockington, D. and R. Duffy. (2010), Capitalism and Conservation: The Production and Reproduction of Biodiversity Conservation. *Antipode*, 42(3): 469–484.

Büscher, B. and M. Ramutsindela. (2016), Green Violence: Rhino Poaching and the War to save Southern Africa's Peace Parks. *African Affairs*, 115(458): 1–22.

Büscher, B., S. Sullivan, K., Neves, J. Igoe and D. Brockington (2012), Towards a Synthesized Critique of Neoliberal Biodiversity Conservation. *Capitalism Nature Socialism*, 23(2): 4–30.

Chapin, M. (2004), A Challenge to Conservationists. *World Watch Magazine* (November/December): 17–31.

Corson, C. and K.I. MacDonald (2012), Enclosing the Global Commons: The Convention on Biological Diversity and Green Grabbing. *Journal of Peasant Studies*, 39(2): 263–283.

Devlin, C. and C.S. Hendrix (2014), Trends and Triggers Redux: Climate Change, Rainfall, and Interstate Conflict. *Political Geography*, 43: 27–39.

Dowie, M. (2009). *Conservation Refugees: The Hundred-year Conflict between Global Conservation and Native Peoples*. Cambridge MA: MIT Press.

---

68 See Matose in this volume

Duraiappah, A.K. (1998), Poverty and Environmental Degradation: A Review and Analysis of the Nexus. *World Development*, 26(12): 2169–2179.

Eck, K. (2014), The Law of the Land: Communal Conflict and Legal Authority. *Journal of Peace Research*, 51(4): 441–454.

Engel-Di Mauro, S. (2009), Seeing the Local in the Global: Political Ecologies, World-systems, and the Question of Scale. *Geoforum*, 40(1): 116–125.

Fairhead, J., M. Leach, and I. Scoones (2012), Green Grabbing: A New Appropriation of Nature? *Journal of Peasant Studies*, 39(2): 237–261.

Forsyth, T. (2015), Integrating Science and Politics in Political Ecology. In R.L. Bryant (ed.), *International Handbook of Political Ecology*. Cheltenham: Edward Edgar: 103–116.

Gissibl, B., S. Höhler, and P. Kupper (2012), Towards a Global History of National Parks. In B. Gissibl, S. Höhler, and P. Kupper (eds.) *Civilizing Nature: National Parks in Global Historical Perspective*. Oxford: Berghahn: 1–27.

Gregory, D., R. Johnston, G. Pratt, M. Watts, and S. Whatmore (eds.) (2009), *The Dictionary of Human Geography* (5th edn.). Malden MA.: John Wiley & Sons.

Haalboom, B.J. and L.M. Campbell (2012), Scale, Networks, and Information Strategies: Exploring Indigenous Peoples' Refusal of a Protected Area in Suriname. *Global Networks*, 12(3): 375–394.

Heynen, N., J. McCarthy, S. Prudham and P. Robbins (eds.) (2007), *Neoliberal Environments: False Promises and Unnatural Consequences*. London: Routledge.

Heywood, A. (2000), *Key Concepts in Politics*. Basingstoke: Palgrave Macmillan.

Hoffman, T. and A. Ashwell (2001), *Nature Divided: Land Degradation in South Africa*. Cape Town: University of Cape Town Press.

Holifield, R. and N. Schuelke (2015), The Place and Time of the Political in Urban Political Ecology: Contested Imaginations of a River's Future. *Annals of the Association of American Geographers*, 105(2): 294–303.

Hough, P. (2015), Fighting over the Last Drop? A Critique of the 'Water Wars' Thesis. *Commonwealth Human Ecology Council Annual Journal: Water and Water Security*.

Howitt, R. (1998), Scale as Relation: Musical Metaphors of Geographical Scale. *Area*, 30(1): 49–58.

Hübschle, A.M. (2016), *A Game of Horns: Transnational Flows in Rhino Horn*, (PhD Thesis, International Max Planck Research School on the Social and Political Constitution of the Economy).

International Union for the Conservation of Nature Online (2015). http://www.iucn.org/about/union/members. Accessed 29 June 2015.

Kings, S. (2014), Why SA Cannot Win Rhino War. *Mail & Guardian* (17–23 January), Johannesburg.

Legg, S. (2009), Of Scales, Networks and Assemblages: The League of Nations Apparatus and the Scalar Sovereignty of the Government of India. *Transactions of the Institute of British Geographers*, 34(2): 234–253.

Le Billon, P. (2001), The Political Ecology of War: Natural Resources and Armed Conflicts. *Political Geography*, 20(5): 561–584.

Lunstrum, E. (2014), Green Militarization: Anti-Poaching Efforts and the Spatial Contours of Kruger National Park. *Annals of the Association of American Geographers*, 104(4): 816–832.

Lynch, M. (2016), Social Constructivism in Science and Technology Studies. *Human Studies*, 39(1): 101–112.

MacDonald, K.I. (2010), Business, Biodiversity and New 'Fields' of Conservation: The World Conservation Congress and the Renegotiation of Organisational Order. *Conservation and Society*, 8(4): 256.

MacKenzie, J.M. (1988), *The Empire of Nature: Hunting, Conservation and British Imperialism*. Manchester: Manchester University Press.

Marston, S.A. (2000), The Social Construction of Scale. *Progress in Human Geography*, 24(2): 219–242.

Martinez-Alier, J. (2002), *The Environmentalism of the Poor: A Study of Ecological Conflicts and Evaluation*. Cheltenham: Edward Edgar.

Maxwell, J.W. and R. Reuveny (2000), Resource Scarcity and Conflict in Developing Countries. *Journal of Peace Research*, 37(3): 301–322.

McCarthy, J. (2005), Scale, Sovereignty, and Strategy in Environmental Governance. *Antipode*, 37(4): 731–753.

Nash, R.F. (2014). *Wilderness and the American Mind*. New Haven, CT: Yale University Press.

Neumann, R.P. (2009), Political Ecology: Theorizing Scale. *Progress in Human Geography*, 33(3): 398–406.

Noe, C. (2009), Bioregional Planning in Southeastern Tanzania: The Selous-Niassa Corridor as a Prism for Transfrontier Conservation Areas, (PhD Thesis, University of Cape Town).

Okereke, C. (2007), *Global Justice and Neoliberal Environmental Governance: Ethics, Sustainable Development and International Co-Operation*. Abingdon: Routledge.

Oldekop, J.A., G. Holmes, W.E. Harris, and K.L. Evans (2016), A Global Assessment of the Social and Conservation Outcomes of Protected Areas. *Conservation Biology*, 30(1): 133–141.

Peet, R. and M. Watts (1996), *Liberation Ecologies: Environment, Development and Social Movements*. London: Routledge.

Ramutsindela, M. (2015), Transfrontier Conservation and Land Reform Policy. In B. Cousins and C. Walker (eds.), *Land Divided Land Restored: Land Reform in South Africa for the 21st Century*. Cape Town: Jacana: 175–190.

Ramutsindela, M. (2004), Parks and People in Postcolonial Societies: *Experiences in Southern Africa*. Dordrecht: Kluwer (Springer).

Ramutsindela, M. and C. Noe. (2015), Bordering and Scalar Thickening in Nature Conservation. In R. Bryant (ed.), *International Handbook of Political Ecology*. Cheltenham: Edward Elgar: 501–514.

Raymond, C.M. (2014), Identifying and Assessing Conservation Opportunity. *Conservation Biology*, 28(6): 1447–1450.

Robbins, P. (2012), *Political Ecology: A Critical Introduction*. Chichester: Wiley.

Schedler, A. (2014), The Criminal Subversion of Mexican Democracy. *Journal of Democracy*, 25(1): 5–18.

Shiva, V. (2005), *Earth Democracy: Justice, Sustainability, and Peace*. London: Zed Books.

Smith, N. (1996), Spaces of Vulnerability: The Space of Flows and the Politics of Scale. *Critique of Anthropology*, 16(1): 63–77.

South Africa (2003), *National Environmental Management: Protected Areas Act No 57*. Pretoria: Government Printer.

Swyngedouw, E. (2015), Depoliticised Environments and the Promise of the Anthropocene. In R.L. Bryant, (ed.), *International Handbook of Political Ecology*. Cheltenham: Edward Edgar: 131–145.

Tiffen, M., M. Mortimore and F. Gichuki (1994), *More People, Less Erosion: Environmental Recovery in Kenya*. Malden MA: John Wiley & Sons Ltd.

Turner, M.D. (2014), Political Ecology I: An Alliance with Resilience? *Progress in Human Geography*, 38(4): 616–623.

Walker, P.A. (2005), Political Ecology: Where is the Ecology? *Progress in Human Geography*, 29(1): 73–82.

Watts, M.J. (1985), Social Theory and Environmental Degradation: The Case of Sudano-Sahelian West Africa. In Y. Gradus (ed.), *Desert Development: Man and Technology in Sparse Lands*. Dordrecht: Springer: 14–32.

Way, L.A. (2005), Authoritarian State Building and the Sources of Regime Competitiveness in the Fourth Wave: The Cases of Belarus, Moldova, Russia, and Ukraine. *World Politics*, 57(2): 231–261.

West, P. (2006). *Conservation is Our Government Now: The Politics of Ecology in Papua New Guinea*. Durham, N.C: Duke University Press.

World Parks Congress Online (2014), The Promise of Sydney: Our Commitment to Action for the Promise of Sydney. http://worldparkscongress.org/about/promise_of_sydney_commitments.html. Accessed 29 June 2015.

Zimmerer, K. (2000), Rescaling Irrigation in Latin America: The Cultural Images and Political Ecology of Water Resources. *Ecumene*, 7(2): 150–175.

PART II
Institutionalised Scientific Power

CHAPTER 3

Racial difference in Mary Elizabeth Barber's knowledge on insects

Tanja Hammel

In South Africa, it has long been debated about whether monuments, which reproduce a history and culture of white supremacy, should be removed or not. In early 2015, at the University of Cape Town, a student movement called 'Rhodes Must Fall' formed and protested against the presence of Cecil John Rhodes's statue at the university that was established on land he had bequeathed to the South African nation.[1] On 9 April 2015 the statue fell. Achille Mbembe interpreted this act as "one of the many legitimate ways in which we can, today in South Africa, *demythologize that history and put it to rest*—which is precisely the work memory properly understood is supposed to accomplish". He suggested building a new institution, "partly a park and partly a graveyard", to put statues of racist figures to rest and to "recreate new public spaces" required by South Africa's "new democratic project".[2] Rhodes has attracted much critical scholarly attention, but what about less well-known imperialists and aspects in South African history?[3] They, too, should be explored, as this chapter will show.

The 1820 Settlers haunt Makhanda (formerly called Grahamstown) in the Eastern Cape, the home of Rhodes University, the annual National Arts Festival and South Africa's National Science Festival (Scifest Africa); statues and museum displays

---

1 See *Vanguard* (2015), Tag Archive for #RHODESMUSTFALL: http://vanguardmagazine.co.za/tag/rhodesmustfall/ and *The Johannesburg Workshop in Theory and Criticism* (2015), Special Edition of The Johannesburg Salon: http://jwtc.org.za/the_salon/volume_9.htm (accessed 10 November 2015)
2 Mbembe 2015, "Decolonizing Knowledge and the Question of the Archive": http://wiser.wits.ac.za/content/achille-mbembe-decolonizing-knowledge-and-question-archive-12054 (10 November 2015)
3 See, for example, Maylam 2005; McFarlane 2007

relating to them have not been removed. A number of people have, for years, been engaged in building alternative heritage spaces such as the eGazini Outreach Project or the eGazini Memorial Garden to communicate aspects of the long-neglected history of the amaXhosa and to complement the histories produced.[4] There is, however, still a large imbalance between hagiographic publications on the 1820 Settlers and critical or postcolonial work on the history of the amaXhosa, let alone a shared history. "History frictions", meaning "debates, tensions, collaborations, [and] conflicts" between "disparate communities, interests, goals and perspectives" are visible.[5] Grasping this situation, artist Mikhael Subotzky opened the Standard Bank Young Artist Exhibition in Grahamstown showing his first film *Moses and Griffiths* (2012), a portrait of the local Observatory Museum and its guide, Moses Lamani, and the 1820 Settlers Monument and its guide, Griffiths Sokuyeka. The two Xhosa guides give their official tours that they have given for twenty years. Then they give a personal tour. These are shown on four screens "to narrate the contrasting and conflicting institutional and personal histories" and present "a complex interwoven narrative that explores the relationship between personal and institutional histories".[6] In works like these, Subotzky raises awareness for Grahamstown's haunted past(s).[7]

The History Museum of the Albany Museum complex—to which the 1820 Settlers Monument and Observatory Museum also belong—was built in 1965 to celebrate British settler history, and to further consolidate it at a time when the National Party was primarily stressing Afrikaner history. Two massive staircases and Doric columns at the museum entrance welcome visitors. On entering, we pass

---

4 See, for example, Wells 2003, 2007, 2012. The eGazini Memorial Garden Project, a two-hectare communal park and memorial garden with indigenous plants in remembrance of the Xhosa chief, Makhanda, and his warriors' attack on the British in 1819 seemed particularly promising during my last visit in April 2014. It transgressed the nature-culture boundary and, according to township tour guide Mbuleli Mpokela, was much more meaningful to people living in Fingo Village and the Vukani settlements than the eGazini Memorial built in 2001. eGazini Memorial constituted one of a few township-based monuments but due to a lack of communication was built on the wrong spot. Sadly, due to vandalism and free roaming livestock, the garden has been destroyed and abandoned. Interview with Mbuleli Mpokela, 6 April 2014

5 Kratz/Karp 2006: p. 2

6 Subotzky 2012: http://www.magnumphotos.com/C.aspx?VP3=CMS3&VF=MAGO31_4&IID=2K1HRGZ652J (accessed 26 March 2015); Subotzky 2012: http://www.subotzkystudio.com/works/moses-and-griffiths/ (accessed 26 March 2015)

7 Mikhael Subotzky, Sticky-tape Transfer 01, Haunted Memories, 2014, Pigment inks, dirt and J-Lar tape on cotton paper, 290 x 240 cm in Art Basel 2016: https://www.artbasel.com/catalog/artwork/12566?blLocaleCode=zh_CN (accessed 27 March 2015). National Arts Festival, 2012: His works generally critique discourses that "pretend to be liberal but actually aren't". https://www.youtube.com/watch?v=_OBMkr8Oplk (accessed 27 March 2015)

FIGURE 1: Barber, Mary Elizabeth Butterfly—Drawing No 29. Precis sesamus, Trim. Var. Two specimens showing upper and lower surfaces of wings. Exhibited in the Bowker Case in the 19th Century Lifestyles Gallery in the History Museum, Albany Museum Complex, Makhanda, then Grahamstown (Photographer: T. Hammel, April 2014).

engravings of the English St George's Cross, the Lion Rampant of Scotland, one of the ships that brought the British settlers to South Africa, the Welsh Red Dragon and the Irish Saint Patrick's Saltire emblazoned on the wall. The first gallery one enters is the 19th Century Lifestyles Gallery. Not much has changed in the displays from the time when the museum was called 1820 Settlers Memorial Museum.

A framed aquarelle of the butterfly Gaudy Commodore (*Precis sesamus*) by English-born, South Africa-based naturalist Mary Elizabeth Barber, née Bowker (1818–1899), represents her entomological work.

In the display, Barber is decontextualised and presented as an independent, apolitical artist, botanist, poet and helpmate to male British scientists. Barber grew up on the remote farm, Tharfield, about 13 kilometres of Port Alfred, which she described as "the 'uttermost parts of the earth' so far removed from the civilised and scientific world".[8] Here, she wrote, butterflies were "almost" her "companions".[9]

---

8   Kew Library, Art & Archives, Director's Correspondence, Vol. 189, Letter 114, Barber to Hooker, Highlands, 9 May 1867
9   Kew Library, Art & Archives, Director's Correspondence, Vol. 189, Letter 118, Barber to Hooker, Highlands, 29 October 1868

She is presented as a local despite the fact that she said that she had "scarcely ever been a week or fortnight in one place" and had "been a vagabond upon the face of the earth", similar to the fluttering butterflies that captivated her.[10]

The display withholds several aspects of Barber's life and work. First, it veils the fact that she played a leading role in research on South African *Lepidoptera* and the circulation of evolutionary theory by natural and sexual selection at the Cape. In her late forties, married and a mother of three, her observatory skills became widely known when South Africa's smallest butterfly, with a wingspan of ten to fifteen millimetres, commonly called the Dwarf Blue, was named after her as *Oraidium barberae*.[11] By then she was already corresponding with entomologist Roland Trimen (1840–1916) in Cape Town.[12] She had provided him with vital information for his study of butterfly mimicry that in turn presented evidence for natural selection, as well as with information and specimens for the publication *South-African Butterflies* (three volumes, 1887–1889).[13] She had also published her own articles on the mimicry of the stone grasshopper, African Blue-banded Swallowtail (*Papilio nireus*) and the pollination and fertilisation of two species of plants.[14] Second, the display silences her feminism. In that respect, the Gaudy Commodore was of particular importance to Barber, as it was one of a series of butterfly paintings in which she stressed that there was little sexual dimorphism. Focusing on the slight differences between male and female species and sexual selection, Barber hoped to contribute towards timely gender equality.[15] Third, it silences the insight we can gain into Barber's racism by analysing her texts on insects. This chapter concentrates on the last aspect.

A few hagiographic articles have been published on Barber that mention her entomological work. The curator (emeritus) of the History Museum, Fleur Way-Jones, has collected these over the years to legitimise the display. Some of these texts have provided wrong information that has become part of the display. Barber is said to have contributed to Darwin's *On the Origin of Species* (1859) and to have been a life-long correspondent of Darwin. In fact, only one letter from Barber

---

10 Barber to Mary Anne Bowker (her brother John Mitford's wife), in Cohen 2011: p. 34
11 The butterfly is part of the *Lycaenidae* family. Royal Entomological Society Library & Archives, St Albans, England: Trimen Correspondence, Box 17, Letter 56, Barber to Roland Trimen, Highlands, 26 December 1866; Trimen 1887b: p. 57
12 Royal Entomological Society Library & Archives, St Albans, Trimen Correspondence, Box 17 and 18.
13 Barber 1874, 1878; Cohen 2002
14 Barber 1869, 1871b, 1871c, 1874, 1878, 1880; The Linnean Society of London Library & Archives: MSS SP 58 'On the fertilization of a species of Salvia', read 7 March 1872, MSS SP 56 'On the Stone Grasshopper of Grahamstown, S. Africa', read 4 February 1869
15 This chapter does not focus on her feminism, but the dissertation of the author will. In the meantime, see Hammel 2015 for an exploration of Barber's feminist ornithology.

to Darwin exists in the archive, and this was a questionnaire for his research on human emotions that was cited in *The Expression of the Emotions in Man and Animals* (1872).[16] Some of these articles were published after the end of apartheid to stress the importance of British settlers and their impact on South Africa.[17]

I add to previous articles and the display by critically examining Barber's knowledge on insects. The analysis of her insect descriptions opens a window on Barber's relationships with Africans. Studies concerned with the history of certain disciplines in Southern Africa have either stressed Europeans' 'imperial eyes' and exploitation of Africans or their dependence on and collaboration with African interpreters.[18] Scholars working on cross-cultural collaboration have been reluctant "to acknowledge the role of Eurocentrism and hidden colonialism", which "implies that 21st century anthropologists and historians may be inadvertently justifying their continuity".[19] Entomological research in South Africa, I argue, has always entailed close relationships between entomologists and their African collaborators that were bounded by the politics of race in the colonial context. Thus collaboration, racism and colonialism all deserve equal attention. I start with an exploration of the complex relationships and hierarchical "culture of collaboration" with Africans on which Barber's texts and illustrations were based.[20]

---

16 History Museum, Case 15, Mitford-Barberton 1934: p. 82; Department of Arts, Culture, Science and Technology 2000: p. 225; M.E. Barber to C.R. Darwin, after February 1867, Darwin Correspondence Project, Letter 5745 http://www.darwinproject.ac.uk/entry-5745 (accessed 16 March 2015). See also Shanafelt 2003. Darwin 1872: pp. 22, 108, 269, 274, 289, 320

17 Alan Cohen, a retired medical doctor in London, learned about Barber while volunteering in the archaeology department of the British Museum and has written several articles on her and her network. He sees "a problem rearing its head again now with all this business of removing Rhodes' statue. Even Mugabe just said he didn't know what Rhodes had to do with Zimbabwe. Well, Mugabe is a retired medic like me but obviously doesn't know his history." Email Cohen to Hammel, 10 April 2015

18 Pratt 1992. Green Musselman 2003 argues that there was in fact much collaboration between Europeans and Africans in Cape botany. Jacobs 2006; 2016 focuses on collaboration in birding. Harries stresses the role that Elias ('Spoon') Limbombo, among others, played in Swiss missionary anthropologist Henri Alexandre Junod's butterfly collecting in South-East Africa. Limbombo's contribution was to become part of Junod's ethnographic work and transformed his attitudes towards the Tsonga religion (Harries 2007: 136–137, 219–232). Bank/Bank 2013 focused on anthropologist Monica Wilson's interpreters such as Leonard Mwaisumo, Godfrey Pitje, Livingstone Mqotsi and Archie Mafeje. Shepherd (2003, 2015) focused on the role Adam Windwaai and others played in archaeologist Goodwin's archaeological work. An interesting recently-published article by Meier 2015 focuses on Boukary Porgo who was of much importance to Swiss researchers working in the field of tropical medicine in West Africa. The prime focus of this existing research was on male scientists, an exception is Bank/Bank 2013.

19 See Cereso 2013/14

20 Jacobs 2006: p. 569

"One finger does not catch a louse"[21]:
African collaborators in Barber's research on insects

According to Nancy Jacobs, "a continuum of acknowledgement" exists that ranges from complete anonymity, brief mentions of important contributors about whom we know hardly anything to a handful of collaborators with individual personalities and contributions to science.[22] Barber was concerned with women's role in entomology. In her butterfly and moth illustrations she continued German artist-cum-naturalist Maria Sibylla Merian's (1647–1717) iconographic tradition of including all the stages of metamorphoses, both sexes and the food plant in a plate.[23] She acknowledged her female relatives and quoted English economic entomologist Eleanor Anne Ormerod's (1828–1901) work on insects' impact on agriculture.[24] As she was engaged in opening up science for women, she acknowledged her nieces Mary Ellen White (1840–1915), Fanny Bowker (1850–1940) and daughter Mary Ellen Barber (1853–1938), who were collecting, painting and providing Trimen with important information on local butterflies by name.[25] Their information was adapted and the dichotomy between local people's cultural and traditional understanding and her and her peers' scientific observations and knowledge reinvigorated.

The invisibility of the amaXhosa and Khoikhoi in her work resulted from her construction of herself as a naturalist. She presented herself as superior to European travellers as a local expert with life-long experience. Her emphasis on the fact that she—unlike her European colleagues—was not dependent on local guides, translators and collaborators, can be understood as a part of her construction of supremacy. In her feminist entomology, she hardly acknowledged her African collaborators by name. Barber might have acted similarly to anthropologist (of Scottish descent) Monica Wilson (1908–1982), who in the Pondo community in Ntibane kept a bag of tobacco "which helped the conversation along"—that was seen as sufficient compensation for valuable information.[26]

Barber strictly controlled boundaries, but there was an exchange of knowledge as fragments of passages in letters reveal. They give the impression that Barber gained information from interview-like situations that she then translated without

---

21 "Nine kake nui ngmo" Dangme proverb, quoted in Arlt 2005: p. I
22 Jacobs 2006 quoted in Bank/Bank 2013: p. 90
23 For more on Merian see Davis 1995; Schiebinger 1989, 2004
24 See, for example, Trimen 1887a: pp. xi–xii; Barber 1886: p. 13
25 Royal Entomological Society, St Albans, Roland Trimen Correspondence, Box 17, Letter 64, Highlands, 29 February 1869; Letter 66, Highlands, 14 June 1869; Letter 75/1, Highlands, 10 April 1870; Letter 76, Highlands, 18 April 1870; Box 18, Letter 83, Highlands, 14 March 1871; Letter 81, Highlands, 11 January 1871
26 Wilson 1936: pp. 10–11 quoted in Bank/Bank (eds.) 2013: p. 75

acknowledging her informants. Until 1870 she had only been in contact with "the Kafir and Fingoe tribes", "with the other numerous races [she had] had no intercourse and kn[e]w nothing of their manners and customs".[27] She "probably knew" some Xhosa men and women, but "only from a reserved distance", as anthropologist Robert Shanafelt argued.[28] But letter passages that Irish botanist William Henry Harvey (1811–1866) glued on herbarium sheets at Trinity College Dublin show that she gained considerable information on "valuable plants" collected from the Boers, amaXhosa and Khoisan with whom she came into contact.[29] From "Kafir women" she learned about plants that they used to produce soap and dye. She was also interested in plants that were used as "valuable medicine for fever", "a cure for dysentery", and to "heal sores" or "inflamed spots".[30] From these glimpses we see that she admired the amaXhosa and Khoisan for their knowledge and use of medicinal plants. We can assume she learned about butterflies similarly, but she does not acknowledge her collaborators in this field.

Barber's travelogue includes references to her African collectors and informants by name but, even in the most elaborate passages of her travel account, they remain shadowy figures or are racialised and criticised. Most prominently, she refers to two individuals whom she describes as "Matabele boy" Kamel and Klaas from Cape Town.[31] They acted as wagon drivers and collected butterflies, cooked for her and allowed her to devote all her time to research. Klaas was harshly criticised for being unreliable and dumb. Barber never interpreted his losing a kettle and breaking the whipping stick for the oxen as acts of resistance, but they could have been such acts of defiance. Klaas was as unhappy with the travel group as they with him and so he left. Barber later writes "a few simple rules to aid my friends in making up a good collection", referring to "a Kafir wagon driver, who was inclined to think well of entomology", who brought her "a fine *Papilio*" that was "*a little spoiled*".[32] Later, she wrote about the mantis damaging butterflies.[33] However, she never believed that this insect could also have damaged the butterfly collected for her by her "Kafir wagon driver" or interpreted the providing of a damaged butterfly as an act of resistance. In Victoria, she employed Cobus with whom she was very satisfied as he treated the cattle well, worked hard, was balanced and "a

---

27 Barber to Darwin, after February 1867, Darwin Correspondence Project, Letter 5745, http://www.darwinproject.ac.uk/entry-5745 (accessed 14 May 2015)
28 Shanafelt 2003: p. 827
29 See e.g. Trinity College Dublin Herbarium, Boerhaavia 761, Letter: Highlands, 16 March 1865
30 Trinity College Dublin Herbarium, *Leucosidea sericea* or 'Dwadwa' in Leucosidea 2060; Lippia 5680; *Monsonia biflora* in Monsonia 981 in Helichrysum 3632; Erythrina 1793
31 See e.g. Cory Library, Vol. I, MS 10560 (a), pp. 1, 3, 9, 15, 25, 31, 32, 34, 44
32 Cory Library, Vol. III, MS 10560 (c), p. 88
33 Cory Library, Vol. III, MS 10560 (c), pp. 91–92

true South African wagon driver, full of fun, and anecdotes of 'the road': he was every body's friend, and always willing to make himself generally useful".[34] She described him as an obedient friend and useful servant who was well adapted to settler society, "a reformed, recognizable 'Other'" with "a difference that is almost the same, but not quite"[35] to use Homi Bhabha's words. This "mimicry" could unintentionally become subversive and be "one of the most elusive and effective strategies of colonial power and knowledge".[36] Describing him as a 'true South African' she stressed the 'ambivalence' between herself and him.

Barber silenced local butterfly names in the course of linguistic imperialism—"a politics of naming that accompanied and promoted European global expansion and colonization".[37] The reluctance to include African names in classification is also apparent in ornithologist Edgar Leopold Layard's *Birds of South Africa* (1867), a contemporary and correspondent of Barber. Layard listed 702 species among which he used "thirteen names that probably originated in Africa among speakers of West African, Malagasy, Khoesan, Germanic, and Bantu languages".[38] In the 18th century, there was a battle on how to name species. Swedish zoologist Carl Linnaeus's (1707–1778) binominal system gained acceptance and Barber stuck to it. Linguistic imperialism resulted from the Linnean victory over the French naturalist Michel Adanson (1727–1806) who had propagated a classification based on vernacular names. Adanson criticised botanists' naming plants after themselves and argued that "the vanity of botanists" was one of the main causes impeding the progress of the discipline.[39] Linnaeus rejected "generic names that do not have a root derived from Greek or Latin".[40] He argued that these non-classical languages were "barbarous" and "primitive, since they are from languages not understood by the learned".[41] Barber echoed Linnaeus, as the following passage to Roland Trimen shows:

> I am much obliged to you for the names of the Butterflies that you sent me, as for *Djalala* it certainly is a great curiosity a wonderful name, a name that cannot be forgotten! I am quite in love with it, but nevertheless I agree with Dr. Harvey "that all barbarous names ought by all means to be avoided" too many have already crept into our sciences, and I see you have been adding another to the list (I mean Macomo)

---

34 Cory Library, Vol. I, MS 10560 (a), 34–35
35 Bhabha 1994: p. 122
36 Bhabha 1994: p. 122
37 Schiebinger 2004: p. 224
38 Jacobs 2016: p. 118 (manuscript)
39 Schiebinger 2004: p. 221
40 Linnaeus 1938: p. 37
41 Linnaeus 2003: p. 172

how could you call a butterfly insect "child of the sun" after that son of darkness? That thing so evil, that brandy loving murderous Kafir Macomo? I like nearly all the names in your first part,[42] they are pretty and fanciful but there are some *terrible names* in the second part ... the specific names that I like are those that tell at once the species and the food plants, such as *Cardui Hippomenus Bramca* &c., these names also divide peculiarities in the plants, and they are truly scientific.[43]

Barber echoed the contemporary settler discourse on chief Maqoma.[44] Following the mass cattle starvation, he was arrested in 1858 and sentenced to death, which was commuted to twenty years of imprisonment and hard labour on Robben Island. Maqoma, who was "a particular favourite of Colonel Henry Somerset and this may have prejudiced Somerset's many enemies against him", "was widely suspected" of having been "removed to make way for Khoi settlement".[45] Regarding Barber's accusation that he was "brandy loving", it has to be borne in consideration that he was "encouraged to drink by the Colonial authorities because it kept him quiet" and that he "received a daily ration of liquor", but was "usually able to carry out his duties as a chief"[46]: visual sources such as a photograph of Maqoma and his wife from 1869, where he posed in Victorian fashion and represented African modernity, paint a rather different picture.

Barber misunderstood Trimen's use of vernacular names. Trimen, who was a friend of philologists Wilhelm Bleek and Lucy Lloyd whose "Bushmen Work", as they called it, fascinated him, was interested in indigenous South African people and culture.[47] He named various butterflies after Africans as a close reading of *South African Butterflies* (three volumes, 1887–1889) shows. I only focus on the butterflies mentioned by Barber here. With regard to "Nisoniades Djaelaelae, N. Mokeezi and N. Kobela", Trimen explains that they are "rather dull in colouring", "very dark" or "dark brown", "dusted" and include "dark triangles" or "spots".[48] While Barber interpreted this as a hagiographic practice to make

---

42 Trimen 1887a
43 Royal Entomological Society, St Albans, Roland Trimen Correspondence, Box 17, Letter 39, Highlands, 6 September 1864, in original.
44 Dynamic Africa tumblr: http://dynamicafrica.tumblr.com/post/50087670519/notable-africans-william-moore-attr (accessed 30 June 2015)
45 Peires 1982: p. 225
46 Peires 1982: p. 244
47 See, for example, Bennun 2004: p. 8; Skotnes 2007: p. 272
48 Trimen 1862–1866: pp. 310–312, Nisoniades Djaelaelae is now known as The Small Marbled Elf (*Eretis umbra*), N. Mokeezi as The Large Sprite, Large Flat or Christmas Forester (*Celaenorrhinus mokeezi*) and N. Kobela as The Mrs Raven Flat or Mrs Raven Skipper (*Calleagris kobela*).

these individuals endure in species names, Trimen in fact only named dark and dull butterflies and moths after Africans, such as the brown *Pamphila Macomo* with blackish dots.[49]

Barber seems to have known that Trimen did not share her racism. When we compare her letters to him with her articles for the *Cape Monthly Magazine* (*CMM*), her self-censorship is striking. The Macomo example is one of only very few instances in which her racism, here her linguistic imperialism, gleamed through. Established in 1857, the *CMM* promoted "the cause of intellectual improvement, progress, and civilization throughout the Colony".[50] The journal combined the genre of the British scientific quarterly with popular magazines including travel reports, poems, and fiction and thus informed and entertained its readers, which made it an important space for the circulation of ideas. Colonial naturalists fostered colonial nationalism and scientific racism through the widely circulating articles.[51] Barber's *CMM* articles provide insight into how she constructed her own supremacy.

The use of insect metaphors to establish social hierarchy

In 1865, the debate between missionary John Aitken Chalmers and the first African minister to be ordained, journalist, translator, missionary and intellectual Tiyo Soga (1829–1871) on the role of the amaXhosa in Cape Colonial society culminated in *Indaba* and the *King William's Town Gazette*.[52] Barber contributed to this discussion. In a letter to her brother Thomas Holden Bowker, she claimed that "the black fellows" had to "'go to the wall' for they [were] the weakest—both in intelligence and common sense and [could not] stand against the white races".[53] Either they obeyed the settlers' laws or they had to "be driven out", as she did not believe it would ever be possible for them to "live together as one people".[54]

In 1867, Barber answered the questionnaire for Charles Darwin's research on emotions. Anthropologist Robert Shanafelt's analysis showed that "when it came to human beings, ... she was a fierce social Darwinist".[55] For her and her brothers "Africans were not really people", "what she took from Darwin about them was the most crass 'survival of the fittest' mentality" and even "if she admitted that natives shared similar emotional expressions with Europeans, emotion was a much lower

---

49 Trimen 1862–1866: pp. 297–298
50 Dubow 2004: p. 109
51 See Dubow 1995, 2006
52 See, for example, Williams 1978, 1983; Attwell 1997; Bickford-Smith 2011
53 History Museum (Albany Museum), S.M.D. No 932, Barber to Thomas Holden Bowker, Highlands, 14 June 1865
54 History Museum (Albany Museum), S.M.D. No 932, Barber to Thomas Holden Bowker, Highlands, 14 June 1865
55 Shanafelt 2003: p. 828

faculty than the cool intelligent reason of civilization".⁵⁶ Darwin then processed the questionnaires he received and published *The Expression of the Emotions in Man and Animals* (1872), in which he claimed the universal nature of expressions and concluded that "the young and the old of widely different races, ... man and animals, express the same state of mind by the same movements".⁵⁷ When Barber received a copy of the book in 1873, she wrote to Trimen that she found it "very interesting tho' not exactly in [her] line".⁵⁸ From Darwin's racist passages in previous works, Barber had presumably hoped he would prove Africans' inferiority, which became all the more important to her when she lived on the diamond fields in the Northern Cape where her family hoped to be successful at digging.

Women were a small minority among the 30,000 people on the diamond fields. A traveller to Du Toit's Pan, for instance, wrote in 1871 that he could not "recall seeing a single white woman".⁵⁹ Olive Schreiner's eponymous character in the novel *Undine* discovers in Kimberley that "she is the victim of a perilous exclusion. Like Africans, she is barred from the white male scramble over the diamonds and the economy of mining capitalism". Women had no "right to labour, land and profit" and Undine learns that "money, public autonomy and sexual power [were] reserved for white men, while her allotted fare [was] dependency and servitude".⁶⁰ Barber's experiences in Kimberley seem to have been similar; she became painfully aware of women's subordinate position in settler society and subsequently stressed their superiority to Africans.

In the 1873 article "The dark races of the diamond-fields", Barber used insect analogies to voice her concerns about African mineworkers. Anthropologist Kathryn Weedman argues that Barber, at that time, "was best known in her community as a writer of short stories and poems that contrasted images of civilized Europeans and uncivilized Africans".⁶¹ Her evaluation of Barber's *CMM* contributions is adequate, but she does not take this article into consideration, which goes beyond the mere dichotomy between civilisation and barbarism and thus sheds little light on Barber's racism.⁶² The article starts by focussing on African miners who "are more than ten to one in comparison to the fair-complexioned individuals" on the diamond fields. Barber described "Christy Minstrels" and criticised whites that acted like blacks and under their "guise ... carry out the darkest designs".

---

56   Shanafelt 2003: pp. 835–836
57   Darwin (ed.) 2009: p. 372
58   Royal Entomological Society, St Albans, Roland Trimen Correspondence, Barber to Trimen, Box 18, 88.1, Oatlands, 10 March 1873
59   Rall 2002: p. 15
60   McClintock 1995: p. 276
61   Weedman 2001: p. 5
62   She quotes Barber 1871a in Robinson 1978 and Barber 1872

After the two first paragraphs, she suddenly shifts to flies. She argues that "black flies ... are the order of the day, buzzing forth in all directions, making themselves perfectly at home ...".[63] It is not an entomological article and the reader realises that she used insect analogies to criticise African mineworkers and played with the ambiguity whether she meant Africans or insects in many instances. She, for instance, provided the reader with information on blue-bottles, house and gad flies as well as the "long-winged English fly". But the reader never gains the impression of reading an entomological article. S/he realises that flies function as means for criticising African mineworkers. Barber described them as "little busy-body", "suicidal", occurring "in great force, quietly appropriating the dwelling-places", constantly "in search of food", "sitting upon every part as if we liked to be 'sat upon', and as if it had paid for 'a licence' for doing so", "taking a bath in your liquor" and living "for the sole purpose of bothering you".[64] She used the "common black crickets ... of Griqualand West" as an analogy to the local Griqua people, in order to criticise their "lift[ing] up their voices" in singing day and night, destroying things and being "not only a trouble by day, but a terror by night", as "this shadowy tribe" makes "the night hideous".[65]

At the same time, using fly-analogies helped her construct British supremacy. She did so by comparing flies, arguing that the English fly "is certainly the best-behaved. Probably, coming as it does from highly-civilized Europe, the creature has acquired superior manners to its swarthy savage South African brethren".[66] She saw the white settlers as martyrs and explained their suffering in the poem in rhyming couplets entitled "The New Rush Flea".

Her verses were, according to literary critic Jeanette Eve, "written for the amusement of herself and her friends" and "reveal no great talent as a poet".[67] In this poem, Barber writes that there is "no peace, no ease", as the flies "never, never cease to tease". She describes the relations between whites and blacks in Kimberley as "one unmitigated fight", "a war against the foe" and ends with eugenic descriptions of better "digging them in" and by hoping "that they at length may go/ And give me respite".[68]

In the entire article and poem she treats African mineworkers as non-people, fosters colonial nationalism and fans her readers' racist sentiments and thoughts of extermination. This strategy can also be observed in other British settler colonies, such as in Australia where Aborigines were perceived as "noble" as long as they did

---

63 Barber 1873: p. 378
64 Barber 1873: p. 378
65 Barber 1873: pp. 379–380
66 Barber 1873: p. 379
67 Eve 2003: p. 185
68 Barber 1873: pp. 380–381

not resist white settlers' land grabs. By 1850 they were described as rural pests and treated as practically non-human "savages".[69]

In her ecological article "Locusts and Locust Birds" (1880) Barber again used insect analogies to legitimate the social hierarchy in Cape colonial society.[70] The article explores "the laws of nature which rule the migrations of vast bodies of living creatures".[71] While ostensibly a paper on birds' dependency on locusts, Barber negotiated British settlers' land rights and legitimacy for their actions by referring to them as birds, to Africans as locusts and Boers as *voetgangers* (young locusts in the wingless stage). She established a theory of locusts' and locust birds' interdependence. Locust birds followed locusts and kept "each other in check, ever regulating the balance of their power".[72] She no longer used the 'vanishing race myth' as in the mid-1860s, but stressed locust birds' (British settlers') dependence upon locusts (Africans). The former consumed the latter, diminished their numbers greatly, but they were "never entirely exterminated".[73] "Many survive the catastrophe by picking up a precarious existence here and there, and by eventually finding their way back into the interior, when haply they may meet with other locust swarms", reminding of the San people.[74] She described Boers and Africans as capitalists who ignored nature and destroyed it, while the British settlers were intellectually superior and saved nature. Locusts (Africans) wanted to have everything and killed each other.[75] While *voetgangers* (Boers) were

> a terrible scourge to the country wherever they occur, clearing off fields of corn and gardens of vegetables, and leaving devastation and ruin in their wake—in fact, destroying every green thing, not only in the cultivated fields, but throughout the length and breadth of the land, to the utter destruction of all pasturage, leaving no food for cattle. They are considered worse even than the Imago locusts themselves.[76]

---

69 Peters-Little 2003: 26
70 She had apparently been working on this article since 1865. Royal Entomological Society Library & Archives, St Albans, Trimen Correspondence, Barber to Trimen, Letter 40, Highlands, 5 January 1865. She called it "a history of that gigantic struggle for life—the locusts and the locust birds!" According to Alan Cohen, the article "influenced the United States Government approach to locust control in America". Email Cohen to Hammel, 12 April 2015
71 Barber 1880: p. 193
72 Barber 1880: p. 195
73 Barber 1880: p. 193
74 Barber 1880: p. 193
75 Barber 1880: pp. 204, 217. Barber wrote an article on her brother's reports about "cave cannibals" amongst the mountains beyond Thaba Bosigo in the Trans-Gariep Country. See, for example: Layland 1869–1870
76 Barber 1880: p. 210

Barber similarly described Boers' and *voetgangers*' destruction of the land, as comparison of the above passage with the following quotation from her travelogue (1879) shows:

> The homesteads of the rude uneducated Boers are all alike throughout this country. They are pictures of squalid wretchedness and discomfort, entirely without the improvements which Civilization should carry in her wake; not that I have much faith in civilization, it may be a mistake altogether, however, we expect from it, and, I fear, reap but little. Let us bear in mind that these Boers are included in the list of civilized men. Is the country, I wonder, benefitted by their possessing it? They have certainly acted as pioneers, they have cleared the way, driven out the original inhabitants! Before their long rifles the magnificent herds of antelopes have almost entirely disappeared, together with the elephant, the buffalo, the giraffe, rhinoceros, hippopotamus, lion and the wild Bushman with his poisoned arrows: all are gone, even the reed beds which gave them shelter, which in former times fringed the margins of our rivers; rivers which were once running streams, but are no longer so; the scrubby, bitter, Karroo bush has taken the place of the once charming fields of grass, and other valuable pasturage plants. Such is the result of civilization, and the love of greed, of over-stocking and ruining a fine country: and after all this, what have we left? ... the ... Boers have undoubtedly been a drag on this colony.[77]

She argued that "voetgangers are a terrible scourge to the country" while Boers had been "a drag on this colony" and lamented that *voetgangers* leave "devastation and ruin" and Boers were "ruining a fine country". In her article, she described *voetgangers* as white but becoming black, assimilating while living in their adopted homeland and as "swifter than the locusts" (Africans).[78] The *voetgangers* (Boers) were said to lie dormant, be passive, "waiting for better times" and to clear the land leaving devastation and ruin, worse than Imago locusts (young Africans).[79] The *voetgangers* (Boers) lived on the Fish River heights, but were leaving the neighbourhood when the birds (British settlers) came, taking a "northern course, travelling always towards the interior" that reminds of the Great Trek i.e. Boers' north-eastward emigration away from British control in the Cape Colony during the

---

77 Cory Library, MS 10560 (a), Volume 1, pp. 11–12
78 Barber 1880: p. 200
79 Barber 1880: pp. 208–210

1830s and 1840s.[80] Barber stressed that British settlers saved nature by destroying its human foes—the Boers and Africans.[81] Her characterisation of Boers reminds us of Charles Reade's novel *A Simpleton: A Story of the Day* (1873), in which he described Boers as "degenerated into white savages", the British protagonist finds that amaXhosa "savages" are "socially superior" to Boers, which was a widespread argument before the Anglo-Boer War.[82]

Her article is at times more differentiated, when she constructs a hierarchy among the African ethnicities she encounters. These descriptions did not include references to biological aspects—what W.E.B. Du Bois synthesised as "colour, hair and bone"[83]—but referred solely to behavioural aspects that she criticises and places in the already established racial hierarchy that she strengthens and propagates. She used "the floating signifier"[84] race to justify the unequal distribution of power along racial lines. The "wandering Bushman" was the lowest in her constructed hierarchy.[85] She argued that the San people did not think about the future, lived from hand to mouth, were naive that there would always be food and consequently did not save any. She described the "Kafirs, Basutos, Batlapins, Griquas, Hottentots" and "Korannas" as superior to the San people. The "Bakalahari, or Masaras, a tribe of natives inhabiting the regions of the Kalahari, Lake 'Ngame, the Zambesi &c." were "a much finer race" than the San people.[86] Describing how the "Bakalahari" collected food, she idealised their cross-gender communality and shared labour.[87] In general, she imagined a social hierarchy: the amaXhosa at the highest, then the "Basutos, Batlapins, Griquas, Hottentots and Bakalahari" followed by the "Korannas" and then the San people at the lowest stage.

Conclusion

Mary Elizabeth Barber helped classify butterflies and moths, established a feminist entomology, contributed to mimicry research and advocated for sexual selection by providing corroborative evidence. In the misogynistic history of science her work on insects attracted hardly any attention. In the post-apartheid era, cross-cultural collaboration, gender and ethnic equality are important which is why historians have become eager to detect these aspects in the past. I showed that what Barber interpreted as her African collaborators' 'failures' can be seen as acts

---

80   Barber 1880: p. 211
81   Barber 1880: p. 196
82   Reade 1873: pp. 250–251, quoted in Brantlinger 1985: p. 194
83   See, for example, Du Bois 1897: p. 5
84   See, for example, Mehlman 1972: pp. 10–37
85   Barber 1880: p. 202
86   Barber 1880: p. 203
87   Barber 1880: pp. 203–204

of resistance and subversion. Barber interpreted them as 'failures' due to her wish for segregation and strict racial hierarchy that she aimed to strengthen through her more popular articles that provide insight into her racism, her attempt to legitimate land expropriation in Kimberley and her genocidal thoughts. Barber worked with and against indigenous South Africans. The display in the History Museum in Makhanda would profit from addressing these aspects of her research. Doing so would help the inhabitants of Albany not to be haunted by Barber any longer. As biologist and women studies scholar Banu Subramaniam has recently argued, ghosts, want "to be listened to, understood, acknowledged, recognized, and resolved".[88] Only after listening to them can we "demythologize history", the "versions of whiteness that produced men like Rhodes" and women like Barber, put them to rest and "free ourselves from our own entrapment in white mythologies and open a future for all here and now", as Mbembe suggests.[89]

References

Arlt, V. (2005), Christianity, Imperialism and Culture: The Expansion of the Two Krobo States in Ghana, c. 1830 to 1930, (PhD thesis, University of Basel).

Art Basel (2016), Sticky-tape Transfer 01, Haunted Memories. Basel 2016 Catalog. https://www.artbasel.com/catalog/artwork/12566. Accessed 7 August 2016.

Attwell, D. (1997), Intimate Enmity in the Journal of Tiyo Soga. *Critical Inquiry* 23(3): 557–577.

Bank, A. and L.J. Bank (eds.) (2013), *Inside African Anthropology: Monica Wilson and her Interpreters*. Cambridge: Cambridge University Press.

Barber, M.E. (1869), On Fascination. *Scientific Opinion* 2: 165–166.

Barber, M. E. (1871a), Night at du Toit's Pan: Notes from a Journal. *Cape Monthly Magazine*, 3: 331–333.

Barber, M.E. (1871b), On the Structure and Fertilization of *Liparis Bowkeri*. *Journal of the Linnean Society, Botany*, 10(48): 455–458.

Barber, M.E. (1871c), On the Fertilization and Dissemination of *Duvernoia Adhatodoides*, *Journal of Linnean Society, Botany*, 11(56): 469–472.

Barber, M.E. (1872). In the Claims. *Cape Monthly Magazine*, 4(19): 39–45.

---

88 Subramaniam 2014: p. 227
89 Mbembe 2015, "Decolonizing Knowledge and the Question of the Archive": http://wiser.wits.ac.za/content/achille-mbembe-decolonizing-knowledge-and-question-archive-12054 (10 November 2015).

Barber, M.E. (1873), The Dark Races of the Diamond-Fields: Notes from a Journal. *Cape Monthly Magazine*, 7: 378–381.

Barber, M.E. (1874), Notes on the Peculiar Habits and Changes which Take Place in the Larva and Pupa of *Papilio Nireus*. *Transactions of the Entomological Society of London*, 4: 519–521.

Barber, M.E. (1878), On the Peculiar Colours of Animals in Relation to Habits of Life. *Transactions of the South African Philosophical Society*, 4: 27–45.

Barber, M.E. (1880), Locusts and Locust Birds (Read 27th August and 30th September 1879). *The Transactions of the South African Philosophical Society*, 3: 193–218.

Barber, M.E. (1886), *A Plea for Insectivorous Birds*. Grahamstown: Richards, Slater, and Co.

Bennun, N. (2004), *The Broken String: The Last Words of an Extinct People*. London etc.: Viking, an imprint of Penguin Books.

Bhabha, H. (1994), *The Location of Culture*. Oxon/New York: Routledge.

Bickford-Smith, V. (2011), African Nationalist or British Loyalist? The Complicated Case of Tiyo Soga. *History Workshop Journal*, 71(1): 74–97.

Brantlinger, P. (1985), Victorians and Africans: The Genealogy of the Myth of the Dark Continent. *Critical Inquiry*, 12(1): 166–203.

Cereso, K. (2013/2014), review of A. Bank and L. Bank, Inside African Anthropology: Monica Wilson and Her Interpreters. *Leeds African Studies Bulletin*, 75: 129–132.

Cohen, A. (2002), Roland Trimen and the *Merope* Harem. *Notes and Records of the Royal Society of London*, 56(2): 205–218.

Cohen, A. (2011), *In a Quiet Way, the Life of Mary Elizabeth Barber, South Africa's First Lady Natural Historian 1818–1899*. Unpublished manuscript.

Darwin, C. (1872), *The Expression of the Emotions in Man and Animals*. London: John Murray.

Darwin, F. (2009), Concluding Remarks and Summary. In: F. Darwin (ed.), *The Expression of the Emotions in Man and Animals*. Cambridge: Cambridge University Press.

Davis, N. (1995), *Women on the Margins: Three Seventeenth-Century Lives*. Cambridge, Massachusetts: Harvard University Press.

Department of Arts, Culture, Science and Technology (2000), *Women Marching into the 21st Century: Wathint' Abafazi, Wathint' Imbokodo*. Human Sciences Research Council. Boksburg: Shereno Printers.

Du Bois, W.E.B. (1897), The Conservation of Races. *The American Negro Academy Occasional Papers*, 2.

Dubow, S. (1995), *Scientific Racism in Modern South Africa*. Cambridge: Cambridge University Press.

Dubow, S. (2004), Earth History, Natural History, and Prehistory at the Cape, 1860–1875. *Comparative Studies in Society and History*, 46(1): 107–133.

Dubow, S. (2006), *A Commonwealth of Knowledge: Science, Sensibility, and White South Africa 1820–2000*. Oxford: Oxford University Press.

Dynamicafrica (2013), Notable Africans. http://dynamicafrica.tumblr.com/post/50087670519/notable-africans-william-moore-attr. Accessed 30 June 2015.

Eve, J. (2003), *A Literary Guide to the Eastern Cape.* Cape Town: Double Storey Books.

Green Mussellman, E. (2003), Plant Knowledge at the Cape: A Study in African and European Collaboration. *International Journal of African Historical Studies,* 36(2): 367–392.

Hammel, T. (2015), Thinking with Birds: Mary Elizabeth Barber's Advocacy for Gender Equality in Ornithology. *Kronos: Southern African Histories,* 41(1): 69–95.

Harries, P. (2007), *Butterflies and Barbarians: Swiss Missionaries and Systems of Knowledge in South-East Africa.* Oxford/Athens, OH: James Currey/Ohio University Press.

Jacobs, N. (2006), The Intimate Politics of Ornithology in Colonial Africa. *Comparative Studies in Society and History,* 48(3): 564–603.

Jacobs, N. (April 2016), *Birders of Africa: History of a Network.* New Haven/London: Yale University Press

Kratz, C.A. and I. Karp (2006), Introduction: Museum Frictions: Public Cultures/Global Transformations. In I. Karp, C.A. Kratz, L. Szwaja and T. Ybarra-Frausto (eds.), *Museum Frictions: Public Cultures/Global Transformations.* Durham/London: Duke University Press: 1–34.

Layland, M. (1869–1870), The Cave Cannibals of South Africa. *The Journal of the Ethnological Society of London,* 2: 76–80.

Linnaeus, C. (1938), *The 'Critica Botanica' of Linnaeus* (tr. A.F. Hort). London: The Ray Society.

Linnaeus, C. (2003), *Philosophia botanica* (tr. S. Freer). Oxford: Oxford University Press.

Maylam, P. (2005), *The Cult of Rhodes: Remembering an Imperialist in Africa.* Cape Town: David Philip.

Mbembe, A. (2015), Decolonizing Knowledge and the Question of the Archive. Wits Institute for Social and Economic Research (WISER). http://wiser.wits.ac.za/content/achille-mbembe-decolonizing-knowledge-and-question-archive-12054. Accessed 29.06.2015.

McClintock, A. (1995), *Imperial Leather: Race, Gender and Sexuality in the Colonial Contest.* New York and London: Routledge.

McFarlane, R.A. (2007), Historiography of Selected Works on Cecil Rhodes (1853–1902). *History in Africa,* 34: 437–446.

Mehlman, J. (1972), The 'Floating Signifier': From Lévi-Strauss to Lacan. *Yale French Studies,* 48: 10–37.

Meier, L. (2015), Auf der Suche nach Boukary Porgo: Fragmente einer Schweizer Wissensgeschichte in Westafrika. In P. Kupper and B.C. Schär (eds.), *Die Naturforschenden: Auf der Suche nach Wissen über die Schweiz und die Welt, 1800–2015.* Baden: Hier und Jetzt: 245–256.

Mitford-Barberton, Ivan (1934), *The Barbers of the Peak. A History of the Barber, Atherstone, and Bowker Families.* Oxford: Oxford University Press.

National Arts Festival (2011), Standard Bank Young Artist Award for Visual Art 2012—Mikhael Subotzky. Youtube. https://www. youtube.com/watch?v=_OBMkr8Oplk. Accessed 27 March 2015.

Peires, J. (1982), *The House of Phalo: A History of the Xhosa People in the Days of Their Independence.* Berkeley/Los Angeles/London: University of California Press.

Peters-Little, F. (2003), 'Nobles and Savages' on the Television. *Aboriginal History,* 27: 16–38.

Pratt, M.L. (1992), *Imperial Eyes: Travel Writing and Transculturation.* London: Routledge.

Rall, M. (2002), *Petticoat Pioneers: The History of the Pioneer Women who Lived on the Diamond Fields in the Early Years.* Kimberley: Kimberley Africana Library.

Reade, C. (1873), *A Simpleton: A Story of the Day.* London: Chapman and Hall.

Robinson, A.M.L. (ed.) (1978), *Selected Articles from the Cape Monthly Magazine,* New Series, 1870–1876. Cape Town: Van Riebeeck Series Second Series No. 9.

Schiebinger, L. (1989), *The Mind Has No Sex? Women in the Origins of Modern Science.* Cambridge, MA: Harvard University Press.

Schiebinger L. (2004), *Plants and Empire: Colonial Bioprospecting in the Atlantic World.* Cambridge/London: Harvard University Press.

Shanafelt, R. (2003), How Charles Darwin Got Emotional Expression out of South Africa (and the People who helped him). *Comparative Studies in Society and History,* 45(4): 815–842.

Shepherd, N. (2003), 'When the Hand that Holds the Trowel is Black …': Disciplinary Practices of Self-Representation and the Issue of 'Native' Labour in Archaeology. *Journal of Social Archaeology,* 3(3): 334–352.

Shepherd, N. (2015), When the Hand that Holds the Trowel is Black. In: *The Mirror in the Ground: Archaeology, Photography and the Making of a Disciplinary Archive*, online version: http://mirrorintheground.com/when-the-hand-that-holds-the-trowel-is-black/. Accessed 30 June 2015.

Skotnes, P. (ed.) (2007), *Claim to the Country: The Archive of Lucy Lloyd and Wilhelm Bleek.* Johannesburg and Cape Town/Athens: Jacana/Ohio University Press.

Subotzky, M. (2012), *Retinal Shift,* Göttingen: Steidl.

Subramaniam, B. (2014), *Ghost Stories for Darwin, The Science of Variation and the Politics of Diversity.* Chicago: University of Illinois Press.

The Johannesburg Workshop in Theory and Criticism (publisher) 2015, Special Edition. *Johannesburg Salon,* 9. http://jwtc.org.za/the_salon/volume_9.htm. Accessed 10 November 2015.

Trimen, R. (1862–1866), *Rhopalocera Africae Australis: A Catalogue of South African Butterflies: Comprising Descriptions of All the Known Species with Notices of their Larvae, Pupae, Localities, Habits, Seasons of Appearance, and Geographical Distribution.* London/Cape Town: Trübner & Co./W.F. Mathew.

Trimen, R. (1868), On some undescribed Species of South-African Butterflies, including a New Genus of Lycaenidae. *Transactions of the Entomological Society of London,* 69–96.

Trimen, R. (1873), Genus Cylopides Hübn. *Cyclopides barberae*, n. sp., On some new species of butterflies discovered in extra-tropical Southern Africa. *Transactions of the Entomological Society of London*, 101–124.

Trimen, R. (1887a), *South-African Butterflies: A Monograph of the Extra-Tropical Species assisted by James Henry Bowker, Vol. I, Nymphildae*. London: Trübner & Co.

Trimen, R. (1887b), *South-African Butterflies: A Monograph of the Extra-Tropical Species assisted by James Henry Bowker, Vol II, Erycinidae* and *lycaenidae*. London: Trübner & Co.

Weedman, K. (2001), Who's 'That Girl': British, South African, and American Women as Africanist Archaeologists in Colonial Africa (1860s–1960s). *African Archaeological Review*, 18(1): 1–47.

Wells, J.C. (2003), From Grahamstown to Egazini: Using Art and History to Construct Post Colonial Identity and Healing in the New South Africa. *African Studies*, 62(1): 79–98.

Wells, J.C. (2007), *Rebellion and Uproar: Makhanda and the Great Escape from Robben Island, 1820*. Pretoria: UNISA Press.

Wells, J.C. (2012), *The Return of Makhanda: Exploring the Legend*. Scottsville: University of KwaZulu-Natal Press.

Williams, D. (1978), *Umfundisi: A Biography of Tiyo Soga 1829–1871*. Lovedale: Lovedale Press.

Williams, D. (1983), *The Journal and Selected Writings of the Reverend Tiyo Soga*. Cape Town: A.A. Balkema.

Wilson, M. (1936), *Reaction to Conquest: Effects of Contact with Europeans on the Pondo of South Africa*. London: Oxford University Press.

CHAPTER 4

Hamburg's Botanical Museum and German colonialism: nature in the hands of science, commerce and political power

Gabriele Kranz

Introduction
In his book *The Birth of the Museum*, Tony Bennett wrote that museums and their collections "fulfilled a variety of functions", among them "demonstrations of royal power, symbols of aristocratic or mercantile status [and] instruments of learning".[1] The creation of museums, particularly natural history or botanical museums, in the 19th century should be viewed in this context.[2] Prestigious buildings for these institutions were constructed, mainly around the year 1900. The buildings demonstrated the power of science and the prestige of the aristocracy or of the ruling elite who founded the museums. Susanne Köstering described natural history museums of the 19th century as "cathedrals of science".[3] She thereby referred to the monumental architecture of the museum buildings and to their collections' function for illustrating human knowledge, domination over nature, and the benefits offered by nature to science and commerce. Natural history museums were also used for recreation and aesthetic enjoyment. Furthermore, Bennett showed that public museums of the 19th century were technologies for instructing people in how to be obedient citizens.[4]

The Botanical Museum of the Hanseatic City of Hamburg (Figure 1) is an example of an institution with an impressive building and a history closely connected to

---

1 Bennett 1995: pp. 92–93
2 Köstering 2003: pp. 18–21
3 Köstering 2003: p. 67. The term was introduced first by Susan Sheets-Pyenson in her book *Cathedrals of Science* in 1988.
4 Bennett 1995: p. 94

FIGURE 1: The Botanical Museum of Hamburg in 1908 (Photographer: J. Rompel, published in E. Zacharias (1908), *Jahresbericht der Botanischen Staatsinstitute für 1907*. Hamburg: Gräfe & Sillem).

the politics and economy of Hamburg. Here, knowledge production was from the beginning shaped by deep entanglements of trade, science and politics. To mention only one example, the influential Hamburg merchant Adolph Woermann had asked for governmental protection for his African trading stations, which was instrumental in the foundation of German colonies on the African continent.[5]

Hamburg emerged as a major sea port of Germany and the city has been shaped by its harbour and trading networks, which included places in Europe, North and South America, Asia, Africa and Australia.[6] By the 1880s, Hamburg had become the port of call for ships importing products from the colonies for their further distribution, and for trading them on the Hamburg stock exchange. Industries also developed in and around the city. For example, for the processing of natural rubber the Harburger Gummi-Kamm-Compagnie was founded, for margarine and oil products the Altonaer Margarinewerke Mohr & Co, the Palmin-Werke H. Schlinck & Cie, for jute the Norddeutsche Jute-Spinnerei und Weberei, for cacao the Kakao- und Schokoladenfabrik Theodor Reichardt and for spices E.H. Worlée &

---

5   Speitkamp 2005: p. 18
6   Hücking/Launer 1986: p. 19

Co.[7] The Botanical Museum of Hamburg with its staff members had emerged as an important adviser for trading companies. The scientists performed research, including seed testing, on the African palm oil, caoutchouc, cacao, coconut, coffee, sisal and sanseveria for the companies.

The existing Botanical Garden of Hamburg was founded in 1821.[8] Until 1856, it was financed through plant sales to schools and by donations.[9] Since then it has been financed by the City of Hamburg. The first two directors of the Botanical Garden, Christian Lehmann and Gustav Reichenbach, had previously tried to establish a museum, first in 1856 and then in 1863, but both attempts failed.[10] In 1869 and 1879 respectively, the city received two large botanical collections of private wealthy citizens. Richard Sadebeck, a professor at the Gelehrtenschule des Johanneum (Academic School of the Johanneum), was eventually successful in establishing a botanical museum in 1883.[11] This motivated merchants and ship captains to donate more botanical objects to the collections of the Botanical Museum. In addition, the trading companies in Hamburg were in need of an independent reference collection and a testing laboratory to ensure the classification and quality of plants, and their products and, thus, encouraged donations to the museum.[12]

The Botanical Museum of Hamburg with its botanical collection—not to be confused with the Herbarium Hamburgense of the Biozentrum Klein Flottbek (Biocentre Klein Flottbek)—has since 2006 been called Loki Schmidt Haus.[13] The museum's collection focuses on useful plants and their products, especially those originating from tropical and subtropical countries. The German colonial era between 1884 and 1918 constituted a crucial collection period for the museum. During those years the import of colonial goods to Hamburg increased and the collections of the museum grew accordingly. Plants, plant products and animal products were shipped to Hamburg and then distributed by road and rail to other German and European cities and industrial centres.

---

7   Universität Hamburg (2016): http://www.biologie.uni-hamburg.de/museen/loki-schmidt-haus/museum/chronik/hbhafenhandel.html (accessed 10 January 2016)
8   There was a predecessor to the Botanical Garden in Hamburg founded in 1810 but it was completely destroyed after the French occupation of Hamburg in 1813. This garden was privately financed by shares.
9   Voigt 1901: p. 36
10 Voigt 1901: pp. 174–175
11 Lierau 1888: p. 4
12 Brand/Kotthoff/Kranz 2010: p. 38
13 The Loki Schmidt Haus was established as the successor of the Botanical Museum in Hamburg in 2006. It was renamed after the new building had been finished in honour of Hannelore 'Loki' Schmidt (1919–2010) for her commitment to nature conservation.

TABLE 1: Imports during the German colonial era (adapted from Voigt 1914: p. 318)

	Import to Germany (in billion marks)				
Year	1885	1895	1905	1909	1912
Raw materials of industry, products, foodstuffs and luxury foods	2,92	4,13	7,13	8,53	10,2

Throughout the 19th century, wealthy citizens, among them the merchant Cesar VI Godeffroy (1813–1885), accumulated scientific collections.[14] Godeffroy even owned a museum building for exhibiting and selling specimens from his collections. His economic and scientific concerns led to the creation of a collection which was of great interest to the scientific community. The impressive Godeffroy Museum was a demonstration of economic power, and its natural and ethnological collections reflected the worldwide trade relations of its owner.[15] The Godeffroy Museum existed in Hamburg from 1861 to 1885. Upon Godeffroy's death, the City of Hamburg bought most of the zoological and botanical objects for the Museum of Natural History and the Botanical Museum of Hamburg.

This chapter is concerned with the insights that can be gained about cultural and political history from studying the composition of Hamburg's botanical collections and supporting material, especially with regard to Africa. The chapter asks how power structures, e.g. of colonialism or the Third Reich can be studied in the current composition of the collections. How can histories of Africa, Germany and Hamburg be studied in the botanical collections? For the past 15 years the collection of the Loki Schmidt Haus has not been accessible to researchers because it was packed away. An actual archive connected to the collection never existed. However, an existing database as well as several publications concerning the museum, among them annual reports, and several exhibitions generated insights into the history of the museum and the botanical collection. The history of botany

---

14 The merchant Johann Cesar VI Godeffroy (1813–1885) employed several scientists and 'plant-hunters' to collect animals, plants and ethnographic objects in Australia and the South Seas for his museum. He wanted to accumulate special collections for resale to the scientific community. To call attention to his collection, he published the *Journal des Museums Godeffroy* which informed scientists about his collections and the newly-discovered plants and animals. Many important contemporary scientists published the first descriptions of the new species in this journal. The zoological and botanical objects were allocated to the Museum of Natural History and the Botanical Museum, and the ethnographic collection was acquired by the ethnological museum in Leipzig. Many duplicates were sold to other European museums like the Rijksmuseum in Leiden. Thousands of the objects are still present in the botanical and zoological collections in Hamburg. On Godeffroy's museum, see Scheps 2005

15 Glaubrecht 2013: p. 17; Kirschner 2007: p. 293

in Hamburg is further complicated by the multiple fusions and separations of the Botanical Garden of Hamburg and the Botanical Museum, both of which are regarded as essential to the discipline of botany in Hamburg. The museum and garden fused in 1901 and were separated again in 1912. They remerged in 2003, only to be separated once more in 2014.[16] This caused several rearrangements of the collections in new compositions. The goal of this chapter is to analyse African collections in the Botanical Museum of Hamburg. The analysis is based on existing digitised data sets.

The place of Africa in botany in Hamburg

Africa had and still has a very high impact on botany in Hamburg. The geologist, Kurt Walter, reported in an essay on "African plants in Hamburg" that long before Hamburg's botanists travelled to the African continent, the plants of Africa had come to Hamburg.[17] Many African plants were cultivated in private gardens in Hamburg as early as in the 18th century. At the end of the 18th and in the 19th century, several citizens of Hamburg and surroundings travelled to Africa to collect plants. The physician and naturalist, Carl Lichtenstein, the first citizen of Hamburg to travel to South Africa, collected plants, animals and ethnographic objects at the Cape between 1803 and 1806. According to Hugh Francis Glen and Gerrit Germishuizen, "his first journey [1803 through South Africa] was with quite a considerable cavalcade under the command of the Commissary General Jacob de Mist, which gave him ample opportunity to observe the country at leisure and to make natural history collections".[18] An expedition to Bechuanaland followed in 1805 in which Lichtenstein also took part and kept scientific records concerning natural history and indigenous people. On his third journey, this time to the Roggeveld in the Karoo region of the Northern Cape, Lichtenstein vaccinated more than 300 persons against smallpox, "as well as searching for new insects and plants during his spare time".[19] After Lichtenstein's return to Germany, "his insect collection went to the authority Illiger and his plants to Willdenow and von Hoffmannsegg in Berlin".[20] One of his successors was Jean François Drège from Altona, today part of Hamburg.[21] He travelled and collected with his brother Carl Drège in South Africa in the 1820s. Several plants came to the Herbarium Hamburgense via Drège's friend, Johann Jakob Meyer.[22] Christian Friedrich

---

16 Voigt 1902, 1913; Hahn 2008
17 Walther 1965: p. 87
18 Glen/Germishuizen 2010: p. 267
19 Glen/Germishuizen 2010: p. 269
20 Glen/Germishuizen 2010: p. 269
21 Glen/Germishuizen 2010: p. 154
22 Poppendieck 2001b: p. 81

Ecklon and Karl Ludwig Philipp Zeyher, two other important collectors at the Cape, had connections to the first director of the Botanical Garden in Hamburg. Their collections were investigated by the pharmacist and medical officer, Otto Wilhelm Sonder. Together with William Henry Harvey, he edited the *Flora Capensis* between 1859 and 1865.[23] When the museum was about to be founded, Sonder was an important curator for the museum's collections, especially for the big carpological collection of Heinrich Wilhelm Buek.

Museum and Herbarium and the changing patterns of collecting
In his publication about "Hamburg, Africa and Botany", Hans-Helmut Poppendieck distinguished three periods of plant collection in Hamburg. In the first period at the beginning of the 19th century, taxonomists like Drège, Ecklon, Lehmann and Sonder made Hamburg a centre for South African botany.[24] So-called "gentlemen scientists" carried out substantial research.[25] Several of their collections remained at the Botanical Museum, in the collection of the Loki Schmidt Haus as well as at the Herbarium Hamburgense, among them those of Drège, Ecklon, Ludwig Preiss, Buek, and Lehmann and part of Sonder's *Algae*.[26] Before 1914, the scientists of this herbarium were able to purchase collections from all over the world.[27] Collections were further acquired through donation, for example, the ones of J.A. Schmidt and Dietrich Brandis, and a large set of duplicates was received from the Botanical Museum in Berlin.[28]

The second period was at the time of the German colonial era, in particular from 1884 to 1914. Most of the African collections at the Herbarium Hamburgense were acquired during this time. Among them are the collections of Kurt Dinter whose journeys through Namibia were sponsored by the Scientific Society of Hamburg and the Botanical Garden.[29] The figure of Dinter stands for the direct influence of political power on the collection, since he was originally employed as official state botanist of the German colony, South West Africa, today Namibia.[30]

Despite the loss of the colonies, collecting continued after World War I and was further boosted by raising interest in regaining the former colonies, which eventually became official policy of the fascist Third Reich. This was an outstanding

---

23　Harvey/Sonder 1859–1860, 1861–1862, 1864–1865
24　Poppendieck 1987: p. 11
25　Poppendieck used the term 'gentlemen scientists' to refer to private scientific collectors, mostly wealthy merchants, pharmacists or teachers interested in science in Hamburg during the 19th century, when Hamburg had no university.
26　Poppendieck 2001a: p. 43
27　Poppendieck 2001a: p. 44
28　Poppendieck 2001a: p. 44
29　Walther 1965: p. 91
30　"Botaniker des Kaiserlichen Gouvernements"

period for the Botanical Museum's collection because many economic plants and their products were added to the collection to support German trade, especially in Hamburg. During World War II and the post-war period there was no botanical collecting to speak of in Hamburg.[31] The same applies to the collections of birds in the Bavarian State Collection of Zoology.[32] There was no access to the collection between 1941 and 1950 either.[33]

Poppendieck defines the beginning of the next period, which he described as the third period, in the early 1960s with its focus on *Aizoaceae* (ice plant family) and on the flora of Southern Africa, this time for general scientific reasons without economic implication, or at least no evident one.[34] In this collection are almost no useful plants, like coffee or cacao, which were of commercial interest. The ice plant family was mostly interesting for questions regarding systematic botany and ecological adaption mechanisms. The botanists Hans-Dieter Ihlenfeldt and Heidrun Hartmann travelled through South Africa and South West Africa and collected many *Aizoaceae*.[35] Hartmann published a book about the whole plant family in 2001.[36] The *Aizoaceae* collection is not only a collection of dried plants but includes living plants cultivated in greenhouses in the Biozentrum Klein Flottbek.

These three periods are nearly comparable with the inventories described by Hildegard Vieregg in her study on museums. She defines the following three inventories for museum collections. The first inventory between 1650 and 1820 was based mainly on journeys of exploration, a second one between 1860 and 1910 was based on global trade, and a third one starting in 1950 was triggered by the constellation of three factors affecting the "whole of mankind: environment protection, demographic explosion and development aid".[37] Krysztof Pomian described similar periods for the origin of museums. On the basis of journeys of exploration in the 16th and 17th century, exotic objects came to Europe[38]—these collections were mostly in private ownership.[39] In the 19th and 20th century, the foundation of public museums with public collections increased.[40] Herbert Abel described in his book about the Übersee-Museum-Bremen (Overseas Museum

---

31 Nieser 1954: pp. 7–18
32 Reichholf 2003: p. 57
33 Reichholf 2003: p. 55
34 Archive of the Loki Schmidt Haus, Hamburg, Ihlenfeld, H.-D. (1961), Travelogue, *Expedition nach Südafrika Oktober 1961*: pp. 1–11. A new archive is in progress since 2014.
35 Glen/Germishuizen 2010: pp. 226, 205
36 Hartmann 2001
37 Vieregg 2006: pp. 30–31 (author's translation)
38 Pomian 1998: p. 58
39 Pomian 1998: p. 66
40 Pomian 1998: p. 70

Bremen) collection journeys for this third period.[41] Two scientists of the museum, Helmut Knipper (1951–1953) and Abel (1952) travelled to East Africa and South West Africa. They wanted to complete the museum's collection of ethnological and commercial objects because the museum had been damaged and many collection objects were lost during World War II.[42] Knipper collected molluscs, insects, birds and small mammals. Abel's collection included the skin and skeletons of 45 large animals, an ornithological collection and a small ethnological collection. These journeys can also be understood as an attempt to re-inscribe a German presence in Namibia, as a part of what Lawrence G. Green described as an international competition to explore "the last frontier".[43]

Politics, especially colonial politics, triggered the development and increase of collections, but sometimes politics would be the cause of the complete loss of collections. For example, during World War II, the political leadership decided to keep the collections in the besieged Berlin instead of evacuating, as was done in Hamburg, in order to keep the city's inhabitants in a false sense of security. Poppendieck concluded that "since Diels as director of the Botanical Museum Berlin-Dahlem apparently made no preparation for evacuation, it is suspected that museums in the capital were under much more political pressure than 'provincial' ones like those at Hamburg".[44] By the end of the war most of the collection was lost.

Botanical Collection of the Loki Schmidt Haus

The botanical collection of the Loki Schmidt Haus has been in storage since the Institute for Applied Botany moved out of its old building in 2000. Therefore, it was nearly impossible to access this collection for research purposes. The collection was first stored in an office building on an industrial estate, where it remained partly accessible, so that the digitisation of the objects could be started. In 2008, it had to be moved again into old barracks, which made work on the collection impossible. However, nearly 73 percent of the collection had already been recorded digitally.[45] In 2014, the collection was moved to the warehouse of a removal company and has since been completely inaccessible. Unfortunately, under these conditions, it is nearly impossible to guarantee proper preservation of the collection. These unfavourable conditions are expected to change in the near future. The director of the museum, Petra Schwarz, said that only proper curatorial conditions will enable the preservation of the collection for the future.[46]

---

41 Abel 1970: p. 213
42 Abel 1970: pp. 184–188
43 Green 1952: p. 200
44 Poppendieck 2001a: p. 45
45 Petra Schwarz, Hamburg, 20 January 2015, interview by Gabriele Kranz
46 Petra Schwarz, Hamburg, 20 January 2015, interview by Gabriele Kranz

Hamburg's Botanical Museum and German colonialism

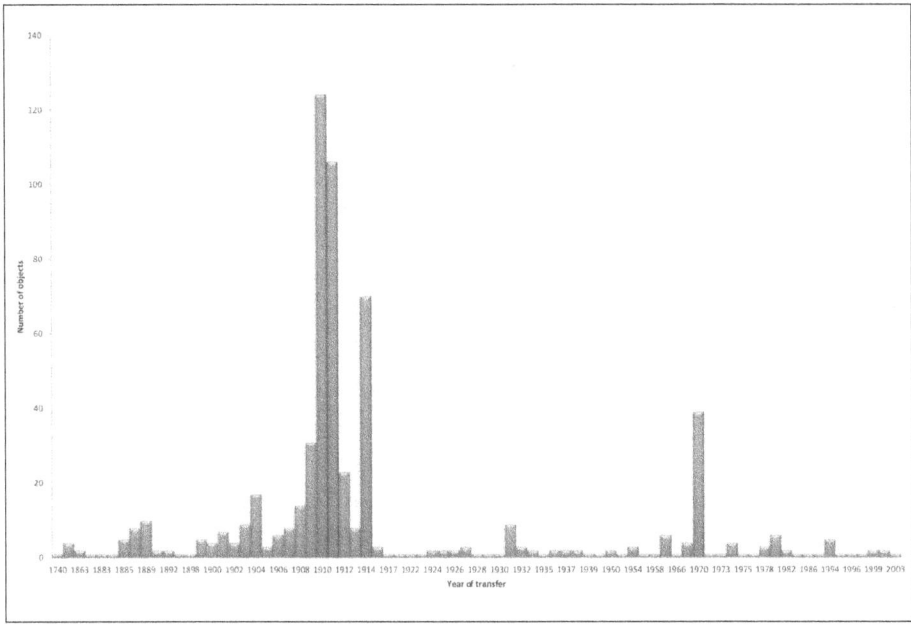

FIGURE 2: Dates of transfer of African objects to the collection of the Botanical Museum of Hamburg (Source: G. Kranz).

Descriptions of the collection had been previously published by Max Lierau in 1888, Richard Sadebeck in 1897 and Gerhard Brünner in 1983.[47] However, these publications focused exclusively on the description of the tropical economic plants exhibited, without even trying to analyse the complete collection. This chapter is the first time the African part of the collection has been analysed. Roughly five percent of the existing digitised data refer to African species. This amounts to nearly 2000 objects analysed with regard to countries, collectors, plant genera and collection time. Unfortunately, not all records are complete: 31,3 percent of the data are available for the timeline shown in Figure 2; 96 percent for the parts of the continent of Africa (Figure 3); 67,7 percent for the individual countries (Figure 5); 100 percent for the plant genera (Figure 6); and 61,4 percent for the collectors (Figure 8).

The analysis of the timeline shows a significant increase of the collection during the colonial period, especially in the years 1909, 1910 and 1914 (Figure 2). This surge in the number of specimens was a result of the activities of the Colonial Institute in Hamburg. Numbers varied but the collecting activities were ongoing until 2003. A small increase at the beginning of the 1930s was due to the activities

---

47 Lierau 1888; Sadebeck 1897; Brünner 1983

of Ilse Esdorn,[48] one of the first German professors of pharmacy. She taught pharmaceutical biology at the Institute for Applied Botany in Hamburg between 1927 and 1962.[49] She undertook several expeditions to Africa in search of new medicinal plants. In 1963, in an essay about her travel impressions, she wrote about her disappointment that she could not find any traditional indigenous herbal remedies in the pharmacies of Namibia.[50] Esdorn had previously found traditional remedies in the pharmacies during an expedition in the 1930s.[51]

The world wars are also clearly visible in the timeline of Figure 2 as periods when the collection stagnated. German politics in the 1930s is reflected by a small increase, as the former German colonies were now of interest again. In the 1970s a large increase can be found due to the activities of the botanical scientist, Dietrich Düvel. He collected mainly in Ethiopia, Malawi and Tanzania. He added plants and plant products such as rice, peanuts, teff grass, cotton and different beans to the collection. With his collection focusing on third world ecology, he is a representative of the abovementioned third inventory. Over the last few years the collection has only increased passively. Small collections have continued to be donated from time to time by schools, pharmacists or other private collectors.

Manifestations of power and science in the Botanical Museum

In the first 40 years of its existence, the Botanical Museum co-operated with many other botanical institutes in over 120 locations on nearly all the continents.[52] The botanists of the Botanical Museum of Hamburg were part of a worldwide network of scientists, dominated by the European view of nature and its inhabitants and, of course, by Europe's economic, political, and military interests. The colonies

---

48   Ilse Esdorn (1897–1987) was a German agronomist and pharmacist. She studied pharmacy in Rostock, finished her studies in Braunschweig in 1922 with Gustav Gassner and received her doctoral degree with a dissertation on the influence of X-rays on plants in 1924.
     The State Institute for Applied Botany in Hamburg employed her in 1927. Here Esdorn researched the hard shells of lupines in 1930. She was the first qualified female pharmacist in Germany and became a lecturer of pharmacognosy in the Institute in 1932. Medicinal plants, especially African ones, were her main interest until her retirement. With her colleague Pirson, she wrote a book about "useful plants of the tropics and subtropics in the world economy", published in 1961. During her journeys to Africa she often met scientists or her former students, who had established their own pharmacies in the interim, for example, in Namibia.
49   Universität Hamburg (2013): http://www.chemie.uni-hamburg.de/pha/publikationen/Esdorn.html (accessed 10 January 2016)
50   Esdorn 1963: pp. 78–79
51   Esdorn 1933
52   See the following annual reports: Jahresberichte des Botanischen Museums zu Hamburg for 1883–1902, Jahresberichte der Botanischen Staatsinstitute for 1902–1911, Jahresberichte Institut für Angewandte Botanik for 1912/13–1938.

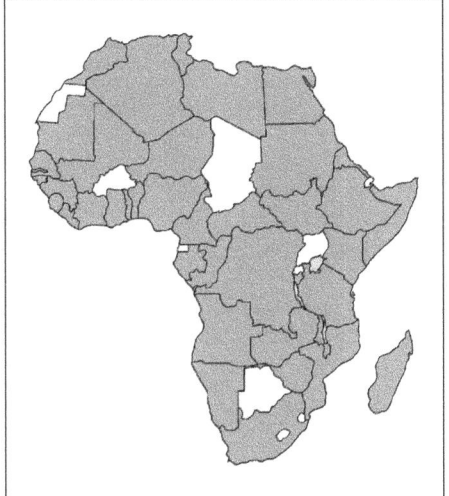 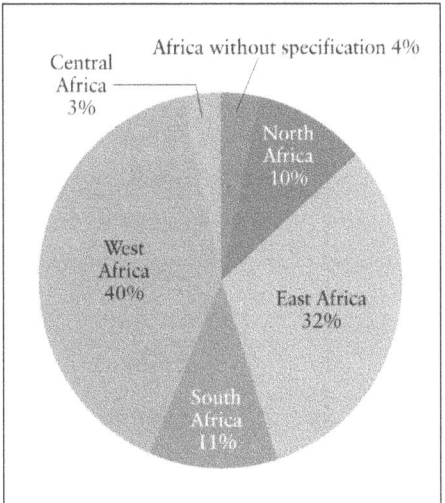

FIGURE 3: Objects in the botanical collection of the Loki Schmidt Haus come from African countries marked in grey (modern borders) (Source: G. Kranz).

FIGURE 4: Continental distribution of objects from Africa in the Botanical Collection of the Loki Schmidt Haus (Source: G. Kranz).

were represented exclusively by European colonialists. Only the countries and the landscapes with a climate suitable for the cultivation of tropical plants demanded by the European market were of interest to them. Indigenous people were of marginal interest to the Museum, unless they could provide information on exploitable plant specimens.

Raymond L. Bryant and Sinéad Bailey wrote that "the role of the colonies in Asia, Africa and Latin America in this economic order was to provide precious metals, spices, tea, coffee, timber, minerals, cotton, groundnut, copra and other products for consumption or manufacturing in Europe and North America".[53] Most of these plants can be found in the botanical collection, for example, coffee, groundnuts and cotton. African botanical objects from nearly all countries on the continent are found in the collection (Figure 3), sometimes just one specimen, with the majority originating from the former German colonies (Figure 4).

The top 20 specimens on the list show the origins of the items by country (Figure 5). Tanzania and Cameroon were the main sources, with 197 and 153 specimens, respectively. These two countries were important German colonies with many trading stations. Global traders were active in Cameroon (e.g. C. Woermann) and in Tanzania, formerly German East Africa (e.g. Hansing & Co.). The botanical collection in Hamburg was and still is a mirror of the society and the politics of the

---

53 Bryant/Bailey 1997: p. 7

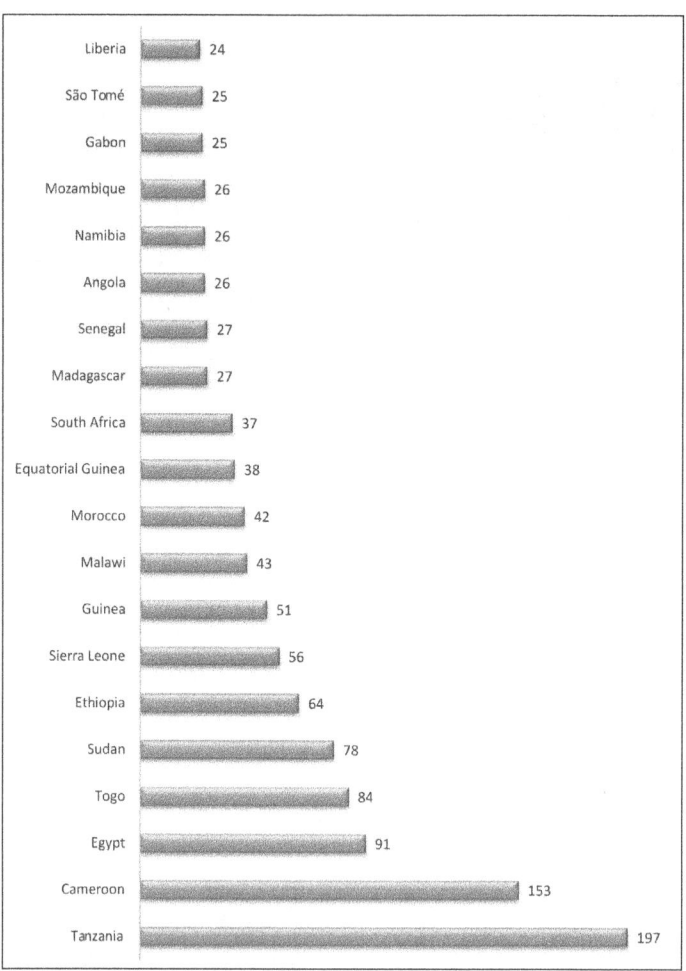

FIGURE 5: African countries with the most objects in the Botanical Collection of the Loki Schmidt Haus (top 20) arranged by number of objects (Source: G. Kranz).

past. As Gerhard Pfeisinger and Stefan Schennach wrote in 1989, the history of colonial products was also the history of economic growth of industrial societies.[54] Michael Flitner wrote that "the richness of Hamburg merchants is based to a substantial degree on the appropriation and use of natural resources in the tropics".[55] The industrialisation of Hamburg increased in the 1870s and 1880s, mainly due to the harbour that facilitated the import of raw materials such as leather, jute, wool, fats, rice, tobacco, coffee and cocoa. Raw materials imported from West Africa like

---

54   Pfeisinger/Schennach 1989: p. 7
55   Flitner 2000: p. 17

ivory, wood, rubber, palm kernels and oil became increasingly important.[56] The economic interests of the past can be inferred from a study of the composition of the existing collections of plants and products. It was possible to identify 476 different plant genera with 858 plant species in the collection. The most important genera are *Acacia* (mostly Acacia gum) and *Vigna* (different species of beans), followed by *Gossypium* (mostly cotton), *Phaseolus* (different species of beans) and *Theobroma* (mostly cacao), which reflect the interest in colonial plants (Figure 6).

Most of the colonial plants from the past are of interest to global trade to this day. The world economy depends on the exploitation of plants found and cultivated in the former colonies. Not only the most familiar economic plants like cotton, cocoa, coffee, cola or African oil palm can be found in the

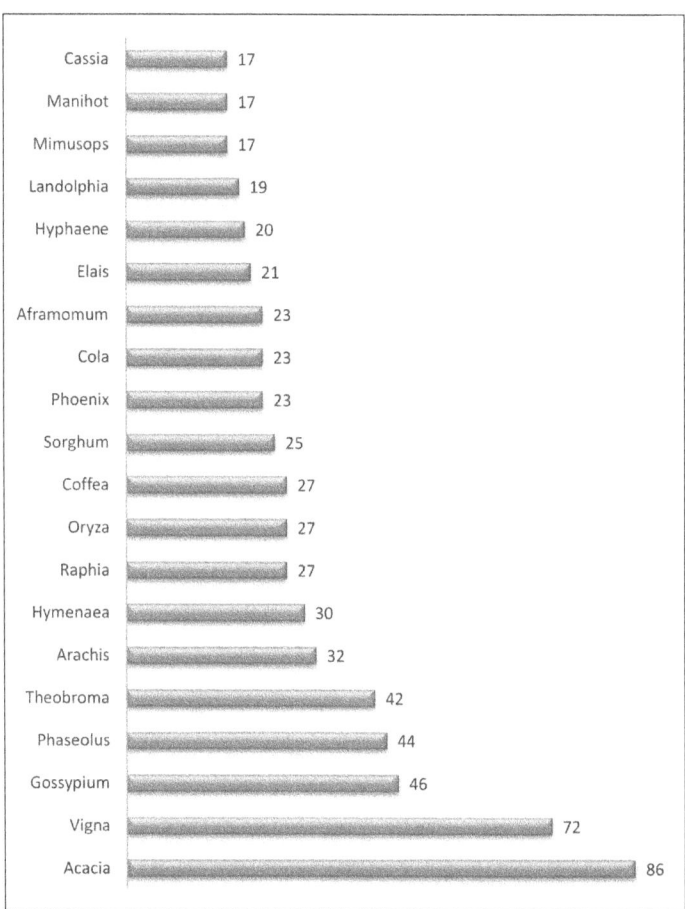

FIGURE 6: The 20 most frequently represented plant genera in the African part of the Botanical Collection of the Loki Schmidt Haus with their respective number of objects

---

56 Hücking/Launer 1986: p. 27

collection, but also other plant species relevant to indigenous peoples, edible plants like nara (*Acanthosicyos horridus* Welw. Ex Benth. & Hook f.) or medicinal plants like ricinus or aloe. However, these plant species, too, were only collected for economic reasons and without any anthropological curiosity with regard to indigenous people's knowledge of nature or how they used nature's products. One of the main purposes of the Botanical Museum in Hamburg was to carry out research for trade. This was, for example, described in a newspaper article in 1933 on the occasion of the 50th anniversary of Applied Botany in Hamburg:

> the scope of the effectiveness of this Institute [is] to a significant degree depending on the economic situation, especially on the import and export trade. Our birthday wishes for the next half century of the Institute are directed at a strong resurgence of the commercial enterprise, whose mirror the birthday child is.[57]

The museum was equipped with a laboratory for tests and investigations of plants and plant products, as requested by the merchants, just three years after its founding. A division for seed testing was added in 1891 and one of plant protection in 1898. The museum was so important for trade that in 1912 the Hamburg stock exchange opened two offices where museum experts could be consulted. In a special article in the anniversary report for the year 1933, Gustav Bredemann, the director of the State Institute of Applied Botany, reviewed the first 50 years of the museum. The information and examination results provided by the museum for trade, agriculture and industry increased from 77 cases in 1887 to 47,455 cases in 1930. Bredemann pointed out that these amounts "clearly reflect the development of the economic life from the beginning until today [1933], if one considers the nature of the studied questions and objects, the rising and falling of the single investigations".[58]

As a result, mainly those plant species that promised financial reward were collected. For example, the fruits and seeds of nara were staple food for people living in the Namibian desert, among them the so-called Topnaar in the Walvis Bay area.[59] During the colonial era, German traders sent specimens of nara to the Botanical Museum of Hamburg. Clemens Grimme, a chemist of the museum, analysed its ingredients and published his results in the journal *Der Tropenpflanzer* in 1910. He merely stated that the nara plant was very important for the indigenous people

---

57 Fünfzig Jahre Angewandte Botanik in Hamburg, *Hamburger Nachrichten*, 27 June 1933 (author's translation)
58 Bredemann 1934: pp. 1, 3
59 Moritz 1992: p. 9

without elaborating.[60] He neither mentioned which specific African community he was referring to; nor did he appreciate the elaborate way of preparing it by cooking it into a mush that was sieved and finally poured on to the sand for drying out and conservation in the form of flat cakes. Quite the opposite: he denigrated this way of preparing food supplies by pointing out that these nara flat cakes "had the consistency of leather ... so that it took a Negro's set of teeth to consume it in a raw state".[61] In sharp contrast to these racist descriptions, he extensively dwelt on the various possibilities of profiting from nara by large-scale industrial processing.[62] It took more than 80 years until Walter Moritz, a German missionary in Namibia, put forward a more adequate description of the various traditional indigenous uses of nara including its utilisation as an important medicinal plant[63]—notably, a form of usage Grimme only considered worth mentioning in a few words.[64]

Exhibitions

The industrial revolution of the 19th century was followed by what Stefanie Wolter called the "consumption revolution".[65] Some evidence suggests that the reverse might have been true as well.[66] The effort to show beautiful, exotic and attractive pictures of the world to the public in illustrated journals and world and colonial exhibitions created a particular view of nature.[67] According to Gregory, nature and its geographies were framed in botanical publications, botanical gardens' and zoos' specimens and museums displays "for a variety of audiences [...]. In their turn these orderings made possible a second dis-placement and re-placement that confirmed the power of colonial productions of nature."[68] The European view of nature was never neutral. As Vandana Shiva wrote,

---

60   Grimme 1910: p. 297
61   Grimme 1910: p. 298 (author's translation)
62   Grimme 1911: p. 226
63   Walter Moritz was born in Bielefeld-Sieker in 1933. He began his education in the seminary of the Rhenish Mission in Wuppertal in 1952 and passed his first theological examination in 1959. He went to South West Africa with his fiancée in 1960, first to Swakopmund to learn Afrikaans, Herero and Nama. He worked as a clergyman in Wuppertal, South Africa, from 1962 until 1965. Following that he worked in South West Africa in Walvis Bay until 1972, when he went back to Germany. He published several ethnological, historical and linguistic essays. He edited the series "Aus Alten Tagen in Südwest". (For more information, see Namibiana Buchdepot (2011): http:/www.namibiana.de/namibia-information/who-is-who/autoren/infos-zur-person/walter-moritz.html (accessed 10 January 2016))
64   Moritz 1992: p. 33
65   Wolter, 2004: pp. 22–30
66   Wolter 2004: p. 22
67   Wolter 2004: p. 28
68   Gregory 2001: p. 95

Europe colonized even nature, when it first colonized countries and cultures of the world. The metamorphosis of the perception of nature during the industrial and scientific revolution is illustrated by the fact, that the European way of thinking saw "nature" not as an inherently organized living system but as mere raw materials to be exploited by man and which needed to be administered and organized.[69]

What was visible in the exhibitions was the colonial nature of the tropics, which Wolter analysed, especially in the case of world exhibitions.[70] The information displayed and objects concentrated on trade and industrial countries and represented the present era, whereas ethnographic objects visualised the past.[71] The composition of the exhibitions served to educate the public.[72] The Botanical Museum in Hamburg had various exhibitions with colonial themes, presented from the perspective of an industrialised country in colonial times. For example, in 1897 a colonial section was established in the museum taking up more than 70 percent of the available space (Figure 7).

FIGURE 7: Exhibition room of palms in the Botanical Museum of Hamburg in 1897 (Archive of the Library of the Biocentre Klein Flottbek, Hamburg).

---

69 Shiva 2002: p. 115 (author's translation)
70 Wolter, 2004: pp. 32, 34
71 Wolter 2004: p. 34
72 Wolter 2004: p. 31

At the height of the colonial era in 1908 it was possible to build a representative building in the centre of Hamburg (Figure 1). More than half of the new building was allocated to the Botanical Museum's exhibition collection. As described by Köstering, the expansion of knowledge demonstrated in representative buildings corresponded to the self-image of the bourgeois society.[73] In the years 1913 and 1914 the museum also supported exhibitions of colonial plants and products in Windhoek, Namibia. Prior to that, the scientists Clemens Grimme and Wilhelm Heering from Hamburg, had researched fodder plants of Namibia, identifying and chemically analysing them in order to provide scientifically-based information on the nutritional value of the fodder plants. According to archival records, the exhibition in Windhoek was organised by the German Agricultural Society.[74]

Collections and collectors
Poppendieck remarked that "between 1883 and 1919, the Botanical Museum was developed into a local reference collection for colonial botany, a timely discipline".[75] This was one of the most significant and decisive periods for the museum in that "collectors were actors in the colonial context".[76] The extent to which the collectors were free to decide what to collect differed and could even vary in one and the same person depending on their status as an employee or a private collector at any given time. More than 200 different collectors donated objects to the African Section in the botanical collection between the 1860s and 2003. With regard to the numbers of objects, the most important collector was Franz Stuhlmann (1863–1928), a German zoologist and traveller in Africa.[77] He was also the director of the Colonial Institute in Hamburg. He is an example of a collector whose employment situation and collection focus varied during his lifetime. He collected first in his capacity as scientist on his journey of exploration with Eduard Schnitzer, also known as Mehmed Emin Pascha, to German East Africa from 1890 to 1892. Between 1903 and 1908 he was the director of the biological-agricultural Amani Institute in German East Africa. From there he sent many plants to Hamburg and Berlin, but also to other agriculture testing stations. As director of the Colonial Institute in Hamburg between 1908 and 1910 he no longer collected himself but organised the collecting through the Colonial Institute. The extent to which Stuhlmann's different professional positions influenced the composition of the plant collections brought together by him or under his coordination is a subject for future research.

---

73 Köstering 2003: p. 71
74 Voigt 1913: p. 8
75 Poppendieck 2001a: p. 49
76 Stoecker/Schnalke/Winkelmann 2013: p. 15
77 Bindseil 2008: p. 3

A further influential collector was Max Dinklage (1864–1935) whose number of contributions takes second place in this part of the botanical collection (see Figure 8). Dinklage was a German botanist and assistant of Sadebeck in the Botanical Museum of Hamburg. He was later employed by the company C. Woermann and collected mainly in Cameroon and Liberia. He is an example of a collector employed by trading companies.[78] His plant collection likely reflects the economic and commercial interests of his employer, a hypothesis still to be tested by a detailed analysis of surviving plant material. Other important collectors were Wölfert, Buek, Vosseler and Meinhof. Among them, Buek, a municipal physician in

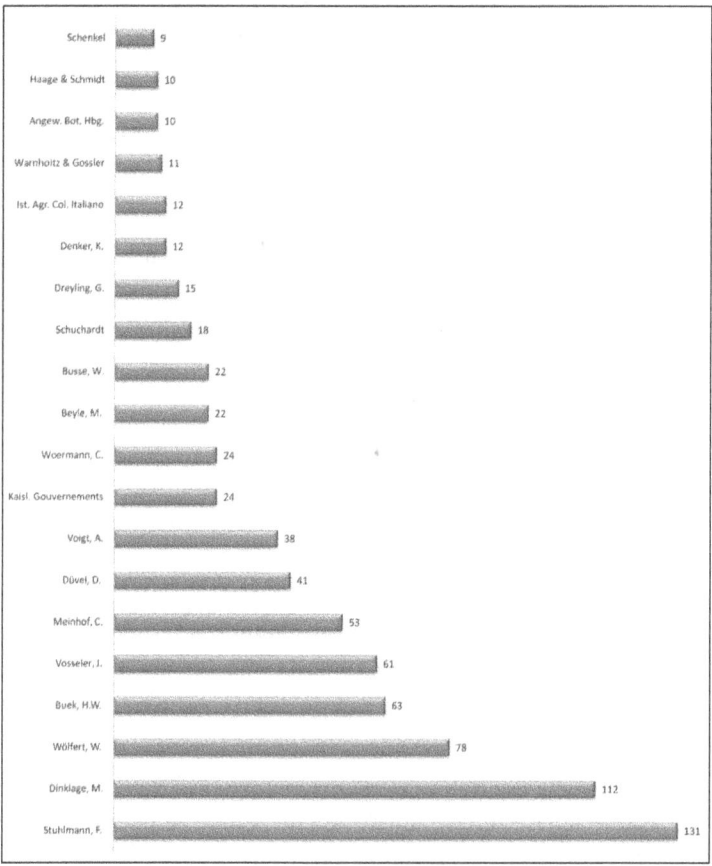

FIGURE 8: The names of the 20 collectors—individuals and companies—who contributed most to the African part of the botanical collection of the Loki Schmidt Haus by number of objects (Angew. Bot. Hbg. = Angewandte Botanik Hamburg (Institute of Applied Botany, Hamburg); Ist. Agr. Col. Italiano = Istituto Agricolo Coloniale Italiano (Italian Institute of Colonial Agriculture) (Source: G Kranz).

---

78 Mildbraed 1935: p. 413

Hamburg, is of special interest. He was a gentleman scientist and, in the 19th century, collected mainly out of personal interest. His big carpological collection with more than 10,000 objects is still one of the most important basic collections of the botanical collection of the Loki Schmidt Haus. The museum staff and later the staff of the Botanical State Institutes, among them Voigt, Düvel and Dreyling, also collected. These were collectors of the second and third period. Companies like Woermann, Schuchardt, Warnholtz & Gossler, and Haage & Schmidt contributed a quarter of the collection. Further objects came from official institutions like the Kaiserliches Gouvernement and the Istituto Agricolo Coloniale Italiano (Italian Institute for Colonial Agriculture).

Archives and publications

The Botanical Museum in Hamburg has never had its own archive. This chapter is based on published material relating to this museum, including data published in the annual reports. Information was also included in publications of the Colonial Institute, which were distributed in Germany and the German colonies. Other sources like Kurt Dinter's books were published in self-published editions. Richard Sadebeck, the first director of the Botanical Museum, published a book about colonial plants and their products,[79] to accompany to the 1897 colonial exhibition, in which 130 plant species or plant groups were described. Visitors were given an impression of the colonies, consisting mainly of colonial plants of economic interest, though the representation was highly selective and limited. The local names of the plant species were rarely mentioned, appearing in about 17 percent of the descriptions. Most likely they were only mentioned when the name was important for trade, perhaps when the name had become a trade name. The language of the book shows an imbalance, too. The perspective was the one of a European trader. For example, Sadebeck described sesame as one of the most important oilseeds, because of its importance for the European trade.[80]

In Dinter's book about *Die vegetabilische Veldkost Deutsch-Südwest-Afrikas* (The vegetable bush-food of German South-West Africa), published in 1912, the local names for the plants were mostly listed (85 percent).[81] He expressed an interest in linguistic research of the plant names used by the Herero.[82] This was in contrast to the volume he had published in 1909. His book *Deutsch-Südwest-Afrika: Flora-, Forst- und Landwirtschaftliche Fragmente* (German South-West Africa: Fragments of flora, forestry and agriculture) listed significantly fewer local plant names

---

79 Sadebeck 1897
80 Sadebeck 1897: p. 23
81 Dinter 1912: pp. 6–10
82 Dinter 1912: p. 4

(31 percent) and was directed to the broader colonial public such as officials, and settlers in Namibia such as veterinarians, doctors, soldiers and farmers.[83]

Alfred Voigt, the third director of the Botanical Museum, had close contacts with trading companies.[84] During the time of the Colonial Institute he twice went on collecting expeditions, to German East Africa, Togo and Cameroon in 1909 and 1911.[85] In 1914 he wrote an essay about the most important colonial products and their significance for Germany and the global market.[86] Between 1910 and 1914, two scientists of the Botanical State Institutes, Grimme and Heering, carried out research on forage plants from German South-West Africa and published their results in 1911 and expanded on them in 1914.[87] For this research they asked German farmers in the colony to provide them with forage plants and soil samples. The farmers further had to send them completed questionnaires about the samples. The results were published with the indigenous plant names. Indigenous people, however, were never involved except perhaps indirectly if consulted by the farmers. Heering determined the plants for this publication in collaboration with Hans Schinz, the director of the Botanical Museum of Zurich.[88] Schinz made a journey through German South-West Africa from 1884–1887 and he was deemed a specialist on the Namibian flora.[89] The forage plants with the questionnaires of this investigation are still in the Herbarium Hamburgense today.

Educational programmes

Hugo Schauinsland said in his opening speech at the Bremen Museum of Nature, Ethnology and Commerce in 1896 that the knowledge of nature ruled "the whole view of the world of this era".[90] Carsten Kretschmann wrote that Schauinsland declared knowledge of nature not only as the epitome of the modern world but much more as a natural part of education.[91] According to Gregory, "in consequence, the production of colonial knowledges of other cultures—through the spiral of representation, practices, and performances—also depends on the active

---

83   Dinter 1909: p. V
84   "On the stock exchange of Hamburg, where the Institute characteristically has its permanent status, is Professor Voigt, one of the best known personalities. Here he is purely merchant, flexible, witty and well informed." (author's translation) Hamburgisches Weltwirtschafts-Archiv, 38051–0002–000: Das Museum für Warenkunde.—Ein Ehrentag für Prof. Voigt, *Hamburger Correspondent*, 474, 9 October 1924
85   Zacharias 1910; Fitting 1912
86   Voigt 1914: pp. 318–329
87   Heering/Grimme 1914
88   Heering/Grimme 1914: p. VIII
89   Henrichsen 2012: pp. V–VI
90   Kretschmann 2006: p. 7
91   Kretschmann 2006: p. 7

involvement of those other cultures".⁹² A specific form of colonial knowledge production and representation took place in the lecture halls of the Botanical Museum and other institutions in Hamburg.⁹³ Since the founding of the Botanical Museum, its professors have given lectures on plants, specialising in economic plants. Between 1908 and 1919, the lectures were held as part of a General Lectures Series in collaboration with the Colonial Institute. Since 1919 they have been held under the auspices of the University of Hamburg. A chair for 'biodiversity of useful plants' exists at the Biozentrum Klein Flottbek to this day.

During the colonial era, especially between 1908 and 1919, the professors of Hamburg's botanical institutions taught students, merchants and customs officers about "colonial plants, their cultivation and their products" or "practical exercises in investigating and determining vegetable raw materials".⁹⁴ After World War I, the lectures focused on "vegetable raw materials of the world economy with special emphasis on agriculture in warm countries".⁹⁵ Under the fascist government of the Third Reich (1933–1945), lectures looked at "vegetable raw materials of the world economy with special emphasis on agriculture in colonial countries".⁹⁶ After World War II the lectures changed again to "tropical and subtropical useful plants and their products".⁹⁷ These changes in the naming of the lecture series already indicate how contemporary politics had an influence on the education programme.

Part of the permanent exhibition which the Loki Schmidt Haus has housed since 2009 is a so-called glass magazine with objects from the botanical collection, some of them originating from Africa, among them a big oysternut, manioc products, tropical and other pieces of African wood, breadfruit, a branch of coffee and a big strangler fig from Cameroon in the stairwell of the building. Special guided tours are offered in connection with the museum's education programme covering topics like "Colonial Plants – Old Hat?" or "Of Plant Hunters, Merchants and Quartermasters". Here the museum staff provides an insight into the history of the museum and establishes an understanding of useful plants and biopiracy.

Research

In the past, the Botanical Museum of Hamburg had emerged as an important adviser for trading companies. The research into questions of verification, application, cultivation and treatment of plant matter increased during the colonial time. The scientists of the museum studied diseases of colonial plants, plant fibres, the

---

92 Gregory 2001: p. 86
93 Ruppenthal, J. 2007: pp. 139–144, 200–217
94 Voigt 1913: pp. 12–14
95 Bredemann 1927: pp. 8–10
96 Bredemann 1934: p. 3
97 Nieser 1954: pp. 9–10

use and cultivation of the African palm oil, the taxonomy and determination of trade wood and so on. Further research subjects were caoutchouc, cacao, coconut, coffee, sisal or sanseveria, all of which were plants of economic value and thus of particular interest to Hamburg's trading companies. Between 1883 and 2000 more than 300 publications in this genre were produced.[98] During this time the Botanical Institute for Applied Botany offered services to trading companies, institutions and private persons. It seems that Hamburg's Botanical Museum with its orientation towards trade-relevant research from the very beginning of its existence established a powerful tradition that was followed and continued by the Institute for Applied Botany over decades. The question as to whether these circumstances form an example of path dependence is subject to further research and is part of an ongoing dissertation project by the author of this chapter.[99]

While the collection of the Botanical Museum is inaccessible nowadays, the situation of the Herbarium Hamburgense is certainly much better and its collections are an essential and important basis for research in Africa. Scientists of systemic botany of the Biozentrum Klein Flottbek in Hamburg are at present involved in projects like BIOdiversity Monitoring Transect Analysis in Africa (BIOTA), Southern African Science Service Centre for Climate Change and Adaptive Land Management (SASSCAL) and The Future Okavango (TFO).[100]

Concluding thoughts

The results of my analysis of the collection, the collectors, the exhibitions, publications, education, knowledge transfer and research illustrate the power of trade and politics and their considerable influence on the Botanical Museum of Hamburg in the past. In the present and future, ways to use such historical collections that differ from the ones of the past can be explored. For example, current ecophysical studies compare plant communities in nature with historical botanical collections. This is of great significance for biodiversity and climate research. The governments of several African countries, among them Namibia and South Africa, today permit cooperation on joint multinational projects like BIOTA in Africa.

The botanical collections of the 18th and 19th century that still exist are more or less well preserved and scattered all over the world, including in scientific collections

---

98 See the following annual reports: Jahresbericht des Botanischen Museums zu Hamburg for 1883–1886, Bericht Botanisches Museums zu Hamburg und Laboratorium für Waarenkunde for 1888–1901, Jahresbericht der Botanischen Staatsinstitute for 1902–1911, Jahresbericht Institut für Angewandte Botanik for 1912/13–1996
99 Beyer 2006: p. 12
100 BIOTA-AFRICA (2016): http://www.biota-africa.org (accessed 10 January 2016); SASSCAL (2016): http://www.sasscal.org (accessed 10 January 2016); The Future Okavango (2016): http://www.future-okavango.org (accessed 10 January 2016)

of universities and public museums. There is an opportunity to examine these collections and to compare historical and contemporary plants, so that changes in biodiversity can be detected. For example, the Herbarium Hamburgense, which was mainly collected for taxonomic reasons, allows for comparison of the historical collection with recent biodiversity. Such research enables one, for instance, to detect changes in plant distribution. This is one possibility for the use of herbaria today as environmental archives.[101]

Frein and Meyer give an example of how indigenous people can benefit from botanical collections and historical literature.[102] According to them, the neem tree (*Azadirachta indica* A. Juss), a large, evergreen tree, which occurs in India, constitutes such a case. For 2000 years, neem has been used as a medicinal plant and for pest control. It is mentioned in the Ayurveda medicines.[103] Farmers have always mixed neem leaves with grain for storage. Neem oil sprayed on rice plants was reported to inhibit brown plant hoppers and leaf folder.[104] But in 1985 the American company, Vowood Botanicals, patented an industrially-produced neem preparation. When science and industry patent their investment and intellectual efforts exclusively for product development, they also patent the traditional knowledge of the Third World. Between 1994 and 1998, 135 patents of neem were granted.[105] An Indian neem campaign fought against this. The well-documented historical local knowledge about neem allowed the patents to be declared invalid.[106] Nowadays, biopiracy and bioprospecting are major challenges for the former colonies. Shiva writes that

> The violence to farmers is threefold. First, their contribution to breeding is erased and what farmers have coevolved with nature is patented as an innovation. We call this 'biopiracy'. Patents on life are the hijacking of biodiversity and indigenous knowledge; they are instruments of monopoly control over life itself.[107]

Bioprospecting is described in a publication of the Buko-Kampagne[108] as the targeted investigation and collection of biological material within the frame of systematic biopiracy. Another definition for bioprospecting is "the commercial development of

---

101 Schwarz, 2015: p. 30
102 Frein/Meyer 2008: p. 113
103 Biswas et. al. 2002: pp. 1336–1339
104 Shiva 2014: p. 67
105 Frein/Meyer 2008: p. 114
106 Frein/Meyer 2008: p. 117
107 Shiva 2014: p. 225
108 The BUKO campaign against biopiracy is a free association of persons connected to the BUKO (Bundeskoordination Internationalismus), a network of grass-roots internationalist groups in Germany. Buko-Kampagne gegen Biopiraterie 2005: p. 16

biological compounds or genetic sequences by a technologically advanced country or organization without obtaining consent from or providing fair compensation to the peoples or nations in whose territory the materials were discovered".[109] Therefore special care must be taken to ensure that these scientific collections of the world are not misused for this purpose. As D.V. Field describes in his book, *Economic Botany Collection at Kew*, economic plant collections can be a source of vital information which can assist in future research on the uses of plants.[110]

Although the conditions for the botanical collection in Hamburg have been challenging, it was possible to analyse data and find African traces and historical power structures that permeated the composition of the collection. More than 20 percent of the objects of traders or trading companies document the influence of trade on the collection. These are the results of limited data sets only. Much data in the collection is waiting to be analysed and a real discussion of the museum with its own past is still to be launched.[111]

References

Abel, H. (1970), *Vom Raritätenkabinett zum Bremer Überseemuseum*. Bremen: Friedrich Röver.

Bennett, T. (1995), *The Birth of The Museum: History, Theory, Politics*. London/New York.: Routledge.

Beyer, J. (2006), *Pfadabhängigkeit: Über Institutionelle Kontinuität, Anfällige Stabilität und Fundamentalen Wandel*. Frankfurt am Main: Campus Verlag.

Bindseil, R. (2008), Franz Stuhlmann (1863–1928). In: Traditionsverband ehemaliger Schutz- und Überseetruppen (ed.), *Beiträge zur Kolonialgeschichte (Band 12)*. Halle/Saale: Projekte Verlag Cornelius.

BIOdiversity Monitoring Transect in Africa (BIOTA-AFRICA) (2016). http://www.biota-africa.org. Accessed 10 January 2016.

Biswas, K., I. Chattopadhyay, R.K. Banerjee and U. Bandyopadhyay (2002), Biological Activities and Medicinal Properties of Neem (*Azadirachta india*). *Current Science*, 82(11): 1336–1345.

---

109 http://www.thefreedictionary.com/biopiracy (accessed 16 January 2016)
110 Field 2001: p. 7
111 Many thanks to Melanie Boehi, Sylvia Hewuszt, Stefan Kirschner, Janine Peikert and Uta Ruett for detailed discussions and help with translation.

Brand, A., U. Kotthoff and G. Kranz (eds.) (2010), *Naturwissenschaftliche Museen und Sammlungen Hamburg VNSH*. Hamburg: Verbund der Naturwissenschaftlichen Sammlungen Hamburg.

Bredemann, G. (1927), *Jahresbericht Institut für Angewandte Botanik für 1917–1924*. Hamburg: Lütcke und Wulff.

Bredemann, G. (1934), Aus der Geschichte des Instituts 1883–1932. In *Jahresbericht des Staatsinstituts für Angewandte Botanik 1933*: 1–4.

Brünner, G. (1983), *Führer durch die Schausammlungen Institut für Angewandte*. Hamburg: Christians Verlag.

Bryant, L.R. and S. Bailey (1997), *Third World Political Ecology*. London: Routledge.

Buko-Kampagne gegen Biopiraterie (ed.) (2005), *Grüne Beute, Biopiraterie und Widerstand*. Frankfurt a.M. Trotzdem Verlag.

Dinter, K. (1909), *Deutsch-Südwest-Afrika: Flora-, Forst- und Landwirtschaftliche Fragmente*. Leipzig: Weigel.

Dinter, K. (1912), *Die vegetabilische Veldkost Deutsch-Südwest-Afrikas*. Okahandja: Self-published.

Esdorn, I. (1933), Deutschlands Einfuhr von Drogen und einheimischer Heil- und Gewürzpflanzenbau. In Heeger (ed.), *Der Heil- und Gewürzpflanzen-Anbau der deutschen Siedler (Veröffentlichung der Organisation "Deutscher Siedler Heil- und Gewürzpflanenanbau, 2)*. Stollberg: Keller: 11–16.

Esdorn, I. (1963), Afrikanische Reiseeindrücke in pharmazeutischer und kultureller Hinsicht. *Deutsche Apotheker-Zeitung*, 103(25): 765–789.

Field, D.V. (2001), The Economic Botany Collections, Royal Botanical Garden, Kew: A Treasury of the Past and Present and a Vision for the Future. In B.S. Rushton, P. Hackney and C. R. Tyrie (eds.), *Biological Collections and Biodiversity*. London: Westbury.

Fitting, E. (1912), *Jahresbericht der Botanischen Staatsinstitute für 1911*. Hamburg: Gräfe & Sillem.

Flitner, M. (2000), *Der deutsche Tropenwald: Bilder, Mythen, Politik*. Frankfurt am Main: Campus-Verlag.

Frein, M. and H. Meyer (2008), *Die Biopiraten: Milliardengeschäfte der Pharmaindustrie mit dem Bauplan der Natur*. Berlin: Econ.

Fünfzig Jahre Angewandte Botanik in Hamburg. *Hamburger Nachrichten*, 27 June 1933.

Glaubrecht, M. (2013), Der Schatz des Herrn Godeffroy. *DIE ZEIT*, 14 August 2013: 17.

Glen, H.F. and G. Germishuizen (eds.) (2010), *Botanical Explorations of Southern Africa*. Pretoria: South African National Biodiversity Institute.

Green, L.G. (1952), *Lords of the Last Frontier*. Cape Town: Timmins.

Gregory, D. (2001), (Post)colonialism and the Production of Nature. In N. Castree and B. Braun, *Social Nature: Theory, Practice and Politics*. Oxford/Malden, MA: Blackwell Publishers: 84–111.

Grimme, C. (1910), Narras, ein wichtiges Eingeborenen-Nahrungsmittel in Deutsch-Südwestafrika. *Der Tropenpflanzer*, 14(6): 297–302.

Grimme, C. (1911), Narras, ein wichtiges Eingeborenen-Nahrungsmittel in Deutsch Südwestafrika. *Die Umschau*, 11, 11. März: 224–226.

Hahn, H. (2008), *Geschichte der Abteilung Warenkunde*. Hamburg: Self-published.

Hartmann, H.E.K. (2001), *Illustrated Handbook of Succulent Plants: Aizoaceae A–E and F–Z*. Berlin/Heidelberg/New York: Springer Verlag.

Harvey, W.H. and O.W. Sonder (1859–1860), *Flora Capensis: Being a Systematic Description of the Plants of the Cape Colony, Caffraria, and Port Natal (Volume I: Ranunculaceae to Connaraceae)*. Dublin/Cape Town: Hodges, Smith and Co/A.S. Robertson.

Harvey, W.H. and O.W. Sonder (1861–1862), *Flora Capensis: Being a Systematic Description of the Plants of the Cape Colony, Caffraria, and Port Natal (Volume II: Leguminosae to Loranthaceae)*. Dublin/Cape Town: Hodges, Smith and Co/A.S. Robertson.

Harvey, W.H. and O.W. Sonder (1864–1865), *Flora Capensis: Being a Systematic Description of the Plants of the Cape Colony, Caffraria, and Port Natal (Volume III: Rubiaceae to Campanulaceae)*. Dublin/Cape Town: Hodges, Smith and Co/A.S. Robertson.

Heering, W. and C. Grimme (1914), *Die Futterpflanzen Deutsch-Südwestafrikas und Analysen von Bodenproben, Botanische und chemische Untersuchungen im Auftrage des Hamburgischen Kolonialinstitutes ausgeführt von W. Heering und C. Grimme*. Berlin: Deutsche Landwirtschafts-Gesellschaft.

Henrichsen, D. (2012), *Hans Schinz: Bruchstücke: Forschungsreisen in Deutsch-Südwestafrika: Briefe und Fotografien*. Basel: Basler Afrika Bibliographien.

Hücking, R. and E. Launer (1986), *Aus Menschen Neger machen: Wie sich das Handelshaus Woermann an Afrika entwickelt hat*. Hamburg: Galgenberg.

Kirschner, S. (2007), Die Geschichte des Naturhistorischen Museums. In G. Wolfschmidt (ed.), *Hamburgs Geschichte einmal anders: Entwicklung von Naturwissenschaft, Medizin und Technik*. Norderstedt: Books on Demand: 287–298.

Köstering, S. (2003), *Natur zum Anschauen: Das Naturkundemuseum des deutschen Kaiserreichs 1871–1914*. Köln: Böhlau.

Kretschmann, C. (2006), *Räume öffnen sich: Naturhistorische Museen im Deutschland des 19. Jahrhunderts*. Berlin: Akademie-Verlag.

Lierau, M. (1888), *Das Botanische Museum und bot. Laboratorium für Waarenkunde zu Hamburg: Eine Uebersicht seiner Sammlung und Einrichtungen*. Kassel: special edition of Botanisches Zentralblatt.

Mildbraed, J. (1935), Max Dinklage: Nachruf. *Notizblatt des Königlichen Botanischen Gartens und Museum zu Berlin*, 12(113): 413–315.

Moritz, W. (1992), *Die Nara, das Brot in der Wüste*. Windhoek: Meinert.

Namibiana Buchdepot (2011), Walter Moritz. http://www.namibiana.de/namibia-information/who-is-who/autoren/infos-zur-person/walter-moritz.html. Accessed 10 January 2016.

Nieser, O. (1954), *Jahresbericht Institut für Angewandte Botanik für 1939–1950*. Hamburg: Carstens & Homovc.

Pfeisinger, G. and S. Schennach (eds.) (1989), *Kolonialwaren: Die Schaffung der ungleichen Welt*. Göttingen: Lamuv.

Pomian, K. (1998), *Der Ursprung des Museums: Vom Sammeln*. Berlin: Wagenbach.

Poppendieck, H.-H. (1987), Hamburg, Africa and Botany. *Mitteilungen aus dem Institut für Allgemeine Botanik Hamburg*: 11–22.

Poppendieck, H.-H. (2001a), A Botanical Odyssey: The Evacuation of the Hamburg Herbarium 1943–1990. In B.S. Rushton, P. Hackney and C.R. Tyrie (eds.), *Biological Collections and Biodiversity*. London: Westbury: 43–50.

Poppendieck, H.-H. (2001b), Botanik und Botanisches Sammlung am Altonaer Museum 1901–1979. In T. Hinrichsen (ed.), *In Ottos Kopf: Das Altonaer Museum 1901 bis 2001 und das Ausstellungskonzept seines ersten Direktors Otto Lehmann*. Hamburg: Dölling und Galitz: 79–85.

Reichholf, J.H. (2003), Kriterien, Möglichkeiten und Grenzen wissenschaftlichen Sammelns. In J.H. Reichholf and C. Deigele (eds.), *Biologische Vielfalt: Sammeln, Sammlungen und Systematik*, München: Verlag F. Pfeil: 55–68.

Ruppenthal, J. (2007), *Kolonialismus als "Wissenschaft und Technik": Das Hamburgische Kolonialinstitut 1908 bis 1919*. Stuttgart: Steiner.

Sadebeck, R. (1897), *Die wichtigsten Nutzpflanzen und deren Erzeugnisse*. Hamburg: Gräfe & Sillem.

Scheps, B. (2005), *Das verkaufte Museum: Die Südsee-Unternehmungen des Handelshauses Joh. Ces. Godeffroy & Sohn, Hamburg, und die Sammlung "Museum Godeffroy"*. Hamburg: Goecke und Evers.

Schwarz, P. (2015), *Sammeln: Von Leidenschaft, die Wissen schafft*. Hamburg: Universität Hamburg/Biozentrum Klein Flottbek/Loki Schmidt Haus.

Sheets-Pyenson, S. (1988), *Cathedrals of Science: The Development of Colonial Natural History Museums during the Late Nineteenth Century*. Kingston/Montreal: McGill-Queen's University Press.

Shiva, V. (2002), *Biopiraterie: Kolonialismus des 21. Jahrhundert: Eine Einführung*. Münster: Unrast.

Shiva, V. (2014), *The Vandana Shiva Reader*. Lexington: The University Press of Kentucky.

Speitkamp, W. (2005), *Deutsche Kolonialgeschichte*. Stuttgart: Philipp Reclam.

Southern African Science Service Centre for Climate Change and Adaptive Land Management (SASSCAL) (2016). http://www.sasscal.org. Accessed 10 January 2016.

Stoecker, H., T. Schnalke and A. Winkelmann (eds.) (2013), *Sammeln, Erforschen, Zurückgeben? Menschliche Gebeine aus der Kolonialzeit in akademischen und musealen Sammlungen*. Berlin: Links Verlag.

The Future Okavango (2016), Welcome: www.future-okavango.org. Accessed 10 January 2016.

Universität Hamburg (2016), Hamburg, Hafen, Handel. www.biologie.uni-hamburg.de/museen/loki-schmidt-haus/museum/chronik/hbhafenhandel.html. Accessed 10 January 2016.

Universität Hamburg (2013), Ilse Esdorn. www.chemie.uni-hamburg.de/pha/publikationen/Esdorn.html. Accessed 10 January 2016.

Vieregg, H. (2006), *Museumswissenschaften: Eine Einführung*. Paderborn: Fink.

Voigt, A. (1901), *Die botanischen Institute der Freien und Hansestadt Hamburg*. Hamburg: L. Voss.

Voigt, A. (1902), Bericht Botanisches Museum und Laboratorium für Waarenkunde für 1901. In E. Zacharis, *Jahresberichte der Botanischen Staatsinstitute für 1901*. Hamburg: Lütcke & Wulff: 3–7.

Voigt, A. (1913), *Jahresberichte Institut für Angewandte Botanik für 1912/13*. Hamburg: Lütcke & Wulff.

Voigt, A. (1914), Die wichtigsten Kolonialprodukte und ihre Bedeutung für Mutterland und Weltmarkt. In Kaiser-Wilhelm-Dank Verein der Soldatenfreunde, *Deutschland als Kolonialmacht, Dreißig Jahre deutsche Kolonialgeschichte*. Berlin: Kameradschaft, Wohlfahrtsgesellschaft m.d.H.: 318–329.

Walther, K. (1965), Afrikanische Pflanzen in Hamburg, Hamburger Botaniker in Afrika. *Mitteilungen der Geographischen Gesellschaft in Hamburg*, 56: 87–103.

Wolter, S. (2004), *Die Vermarktung des Fremden: Exotismus und die Anfänge des Massenkonsums*. Frankfurt am Main: Campus.

Zacharias, E. (1908), *Jahresberichte der Botanischen Staatsinstitute für 1907*. Hamburg: Lütcke & Wulff.

Zacharias, E. (1911), *Jahresberichte der Botanischen Staatsinstitute für 1910*. Hamburg: Lütcke & Wulff.

CHAPTER 5

Circulating nature: from north-eastern Namibia to South Africa and back, 1960–1990

Luregn Lenggenhager

South Africa's unfinished empire

The control of Namibia's nature was central to South Africa's imperial practices in Namibia, particularly in the Caprivi Strip in north-eastern Namibia.[1] It has been prominently discussed how colonialism and imperialism were tied to the politics of and control over nature—in the form of deliberate or non-deliberate introduction of plants, animals and particularly germs into the colonised ecosystems.[2] Both forms clearly impacted not only the ecosystems in the colonies, but also ecological science in general and the networks and practices established around it.[3] In this chapter I elaborate on the circulation of nature between the centres of power in South Africa and the Caprivi Strip between the late 1960s and 1990, the period in which South Africa's presence in and power over Caprivi was the strongest.[4]

---

1 See generally: Kreike 2013. In regard to water and irrigation also: McKittrick 2015. By using the term 'Namibia' for the area of the modern nation-state, even when referring to a time when it was not yet commonly named as such, I follow a common practice among historians of describing ex-colonies by their current names (see e.g. Wallace 2014: p. 8, or Silvester et al. 1998.) Unless otherwise noted, I use the term 'the Caprivi' to refer to the entire geographical region of the Caprivi Strip, consisting of the present-day Namibian Zambezi Region (formerly Caprivi Region, under South African rule known as Eastern Caprivi) and the area that is commonly known as Western Caprivi, nowadays split between the Zambezi Region and the Kavango East Region.
2 On the importance of the exchange of nature in global history see the highly influential book by Alfred W. Crosby: Crosby 1972. See also Crosby 1986, Steinberg 2002, Carney/Rosomoff 2009, or for an overview: Nunn/Qian 2010 and with focus on settler colonies MacKenzie 1997: pp. 215–228
3 As, for example, Joseph M. Hodge convincingly shows for agricultural science in the British Empire of the 20th century. Hodge 2011: pp. 209–231
4 An overview of Caprivi's history: Kangumu 2011

South Africa's direct political and military rule over Namibia began with the conquest of the former German colony during World War I and, after decades of armed resistance against it, ended in 1990 with the founding of the independent Republic of Namibia. This period is commonly referred to as the South African period in Namibia's history, even though the details of South Africa's politics and Namibia's legal and administrative situation within South Africa shifted during this time. After Namibia's independence in 1990, scholars of Namibian history increasingly began to reflect on South Africa's rule over the country, and to write against the often grid-locked assumptions that Namibian history was simply an extension of South African social history.[5] Categories and patterns of understanding the histories of a settler colony proved not to be accurate, particularly when applied to discussion of the northern regions of Namibia, such as Caprivi, that were mostly seen as unsuitable for the settlement of white farmers.[6]

South African historiography has long failed to understand the importance of Namibia for South Africa's own past as a colonial state, and even more so as an "unfinished" empire.[7] Only recently, a group of scholars of Namibia and Southern Africa proposed to use the concept of a South African empire to analyse Southern African history not only from its centres of power in Cape Town and Johannesburg, but also from its "backwaters" in Namibia and other regions under less direct South African control.[8] They recalled that empire "has expressed itself through networks of people, things and ideas that have moved between and circulated within metropoles and peripheries of imperial systems, as colonial cultures were created, and in which empire was constituted in the colonies".[9]

I focus on the circulation of natural objects between the Caprivi and the centres of power in South Africa, and how this circulation had contradicting impacts on the local situation in the region. Further, I discuss how it contributed towards the construction of what I call a South African nature space: a South African space that incorporated its peripheries also through the circulation of nature.[10] I agree

---

5 Silvester et al. 1998: p. 13
6 While there is no evidence of plans for white settlement in the Caprivi or other parts of Namibia, up to the 1920s the boundary of white settlement was shifting and never strictly drawn. Only in the late 1920s were the few white settlers from outside the police zone resettled. Later all whites were banned from entering the northern territories without a permit. Miescher 2012b: pp. 772, 778–781
7 Henrichsen et al 2015: p. 431
8 See the Special Issue on South African Empire (2015): *Journal of Southern African Studies*, 41(3). In its introduction, Henrichsen et al. (2015: p. 433) stressed that particularly Namibia, which was considered as being the periphery of South Africa, was entangled with other metropoles through the liberation movements.
9 Henrichsen et al. 2015: p. 432
10 See also: Lester 2003: p. 609

with Alan Lester who stated that the "studies of material, symbolic, personal and discursive flows connecting South to Southern Africa are one way into more complete historical geographies of Southern, rather than just South Africa".[11] With regard to the Caprivi's particular geographical and historical position as a military stronghold of Southern Africa, it is worth looking at South Africa's political and economic attitude towards the region, and its policies of incorporating peripheral regions into its own vision of a diverse but united space.[12] In order to do so, it is crucial to depart from a rigid model of colonial centres and peripheries, but rather to see such divisions as constituted also through the practices of exchange depicted here.[13] In proposing to look at Namibia through the lens of a South African empire, Henrichsen et al. pointed out that this offers a

> vantage point on South Africa from the margins, particularly out of the ambiguities of the South West African territory, entangled as it was with multiple metropoles (Berlin, Cape Town, Pretoria, London, Geneva, New York, Lusaka), and whose status and history was constantly renegotiated.[14]

In other words, what was often understood as peripheries were also dynamic sites "where power relations and constellations came to the force and remained contested".[15]

Ecology, I argue, was a field where the relations between and the construction of such centres and peripheries took place. It is not only that "ecology and empire went hand in hand" as it was said for the American West, even more it was the particular place in which the ecology was produced that impacted the construction of an imperial nature space.[16] Referring to such "geographies of scientific knowledge", as proposed by David Livingstone, allows one to understand South Africa's ecological research not only as a "provincial practice", but as an undertaking

---

11 Lester 2003: p. 609
12 I use the term 'natural objects' to refer to all objects and living organisms closely linked to nature, here particularly animals (living and dead), plants and seeds. For a deeper debate on the terminology of nature as opposite to culture, see for example: Atran 1987: pp. 27–32. The term 'nature-space', referring to the German word *Naturraum*, includes the meanings of ecologically defined spaces, such as bioregion or ecozone, as well as much broader defined concepts of landscape. I use the term 'circulation' for the total of the different transfers.
13 See also Rizzo 2012: p. 2
14 Henrichsen et al. 2015: p. 433
15 Rizzo 2012: p. 2
16 Cronon et al. 1992: p. 12

within a broader Southern African space.[17] The geographies of science constituted new spatial and power relations, in this case particularly through the circulation of ecology and what belongs to it, namely people, plants, or practices. Along with this circulation, "a whole range of mechanisms" were created to keep up credibility for the "knowledge of the faraway": "observers have been drilled; bodies have been disciplined; pictures have been painted; photographs have been taken; maps have been charted; measurement have been standardized."[18]

My argument will be structured along four different transfers of nature between the Caprivi and South Africa. The first two transfers that I discuss were directly linked to South Africa's military presence in the area.[19] These are the so-called translocations of big game from the Caprivi into South African national parks in the 1970s and 1980s, and the mostly illegal purchasing and hunting of living and dead animals by South African servicemen as souvenirs to take back to South Africa during the same time. The other two transfers were related more to South Africa's strategy to mask its occupation as development, and to promote it locally and internationally as supportive to local people. These transfers began in the 1960s and included the gathering of specimens of Caprivi's fauna and flora for South African museums and research institutions while doing ecological research in the region, and the shipment of seeds and seedlings from or through South Africa for the purpose of forestry and agricultural field trials in Caprivi.

As I will show, the four transfers happened in a close interconnection of war, development, and ecological research. There were many joint interests and requirements, but also conflicts, between these three fields of South African interventions in the Caprivi. The circulation of nature impacted South Africa's understanding of the Caprivi and became a powerful practice of domination in the Caprivi itself. As such, the circulation of nature underlines an understanding of apartheid South Africa as an unfinished empire that is also constituted through complex relations of knowledge based on the collection and systematic research of its nature.[20]

South Africa's Caprivi

The Caprivi borders Angola and Zambia in the north and Botswana in the south, and is connected to Namibia only through a narrow stretch of land. Because of its particular geographical situation, the first German colonisers described the region as remote and useless. This narrative did not change when the Union of

---

17 Livingstone 2003: pp. 1–13
18 Livingstone 2003: p. 178
19 On South Africa's military strategy in Namibia see e.g.: Dale 2014: pp. 73–111
20 Rassool 2015: p. 653

South Africa took control of the region after the First World War.[21] Up to the late 1930s, the Union's administration of the Caprivi still had plans to surrender it to the United Kingdom.[22] Nevertheless, South African officials started to survey the region to find potential ways to make use of it shortly after they came into power.[23]

In the late 1950s and early 1960s, the Caprivi became of high strategic importance for the South African security forces because of two main developments. Firstly, the suppression of the Namibian independence movements became a major issue for South Africa after 1964. In that year the Caprivi African National Union (CANU) began its struggle for independence, and merged with the South West Africa People's Organization (SWAPO) in the armed struggle against the South African occupation.[24] Secondly, in the same year, Zambia gained independence, and became an important base for SWAPO.[25] During this period, independence movements also began to emerge in Angola. Academic literature on the Caprivi described South Africa's response to these changes as having led to a strong militarisation of the region.[26] During this time, the South African colonisers merged what they called development for the people in Caprivi—the incorporation of Caprivi into the South African mainland—and warfare into their efforts for the management of nature.[27] Therefore, nature became a battleground not only for military conflicts, but also for the struggle over interpretive power.[28]

Consequently, South Africa's strategy to win these battles had to take place on three levels: firstly, the militarisation of the region; secondly, the so-called development of its people; and, thirdly, a closer incorporation of the periphery into South Africa's political, economic and academic centres. As we will see later on, these three levels were closely entangled and based on the region's natural potential, i.e. agriculture, forestry, fishery and, later, nature conservation and tourism. To gain the support of local people and to present South Africa internationally as being supportive to Namibia, rather than an oppressive colonial power, it was important not only to find potential fields for local profit, but also to make South

---

21 I neither discuss the (few) impacts that the German colonial administration had on the region nor the reasons for imperial Germany's interest in the region. For a general overview, see, for example: Zeller 2009: pp. 142ff and Flint 2003: pp. 413ff. In more detail, see Kangumu 2011: pp 55–71
22 See, for example: National Archives of Namibia (NAN), South West Africa Administration (SWAA) A503/4. L.F.C. Trollope, Inspection Report, 1937
23 See also on South Africa's policy in the Caprivi before 1960: Lenggenhager 2015: pp. 469–472; Gewald 2013: pp. 81–93
24 Wallace 2014: pp. 259–271; Kangumu 2011
25 Dobell 1998; Katjavivi 1989
26 Kangumu 2011; Taylor 2012: pp. 73–78; Fisch 1999: pp. 14–15
27 See also for the former Ovamboland: McKittrick 2015
28 See also: Kreike 2004: pp. 90–110

Africa's effort visible.[29] This need prompted the intensive ecological survey and research activity in the Caprivi.

"The time when they stole our animals"

During South Africa's militarisation of the region, most big game animals nearly became extinct in the Caprivi.[30] Most of the people I interviewed in the Caprivi between 2012 and 2015 related this loss of game directly to the presence of the South African Defence Force (SADF) in the area, particularly in regard to the translocation of animals by the SADF.[31] A former community leader in the Western Caprivi said that this period is still remembered as "the time when they [South Africans] stole our animals".[32] A former game guard working in nature conservation in the Caprivi in the late 1970s affirmed that one of his main tasks was to help track down big game for "military and security guys".[33] According to him, they caught big game to take home to South Africa.

It was a common practice for the South African government to catch wild animals from all over Southern Africa in order to build up wildlife numbers in South Africa's national parks, mainly in the Kruger National Park. In 1980 the SADF stated in its own official publication that the "re-location of game" was "one of the most important projects the SADF" was undertaking "to protect our vital natural resources".[34] Not surprisingly, the SADF officials did not see their practice of translocation as the cause for the diminishing numbers of game in the Caprivi. Rather, they presented the SADF as "saving Caprivi's nature", arguing that it was the hunting by local people that caused the loss of wildlife.[35]

---

29 McCullers 2012: p. 128; Ashforth 1990: pp. 1–2. Generally on post-WWII colonial investments into Namibia's nature, see: Kreike 2013: pp. 197–220
30 For example, on elephants: Chase/Griffin 2009: p. 224
31 For example, former high-ranking nature conservation officer in Namibia, Windhoek, 10 June 2014, interview by Luregn Lenggenhager. The author conducted around 35 interviews in 2012 and 2014. About ten of them were with Caprivians who worked in nature conservation, forestry or agriculture during the South African period, another ten with former South African officials in the Caprivi, five with (former) military personnel, five with (former) community leaders in the Caprivi and five with other experts. Most of the interviews are recorded. All interviewees prefer to stay anonymous. Finding local interpretations of and resistance against South Africa's power in defining and controlling Caprivi's nature still bears many methodological and archive-related challenges that can only partly be addressed in this paper.
32 Former community leader in Western Caprivi, Kongola, 20 May 2014, interview by Luregn Lenggenhager
33 Former game guard in Eastern Caprivi, Windhoek, 2 November 2012, interview by Luregn Lenggenhager
34 Preserving our natural riches, *Paratus*, July 1980: p. 14
35 See, for example, Nature Conservation in Caprivi: SADF Battles to Save our Heritage, *Paratus*, November 1982. pp. 10–11; 58

The huge impact of the loss of big game that many interviewees attributed to South Africa's military presence points to another level of the SADF's involvement in the Caprivi's wildlife. In the mid-1990s, Stephen Ellis and others uncovered the SADF's deep enmeshment in the international trafficking of ivory and rhino horn that was also a reason for the military's hunting activities in the Caprivi.[36] In 1996 the Commission of Inquiry into the Alleged Smugglings and Illegal Trade of Ivory and Rhinoceros Horn in South Africa (Kumleben Report) concluded that the SADF was directly involved in the smuggling of ivory and rhino horn from Angola, and also from within Namibia at least between 1978 and 1980.[37]

I do not discuss these topics further here, because the animals transferred to South African national parks, as well as the tusks and rhino horns traded on the international black market, did not necessarily come from the periphery, nor were they brought to alleged centres of power. In other words, there were few spatial or developmental aspects to these transfers. Rather, the extraction of wildlife on this level should be seen in the context of destabilising neighbouring countries, and financially supporting South Africa's war-machinery.[38] I now discuss the small-scale transfers of nature in the context of incorporating the assumed peripheral regions such as Caprivi into a South African space.

Souvenirs from the front

By the mid 1970s, the SADF had built up at least seven large camps and two major airfields in the Caprivi. It was there that South Africa trained some of its infamous special units, such as the Reconnaissance Commandos ('Recons'), the Battalion 32 (Buffalo Battalion) or later, Koevoet.[39] A former South African colonel estimated that in the late 1970s more than 10,000 servicemen were based in the Caprivi.[40] He described three particularities of doing service in the Caprivi as compared to other regions of South Africa. Firstly, Caprivi was very far away from the South African mainland and therefore the soldiers had to stay in the area for extended periods. Secondly, there were only a few direct combat operations in between long stretches of inactivity and waiting. Thirdly, higher ranked military personnel were allowed to take along their wives and children. As there were no urban centres

---

36   Ellis 1994: pp. 53–69. See also for the Caprivi the edited interview with the former SADF colonel Jan Breytenbach: Reeve/Ellis 1995
37   Kumleben 1996: p. 129
38   Ellis 1994: pp. 53–69
39   Kangumu 2011: p. 154
40   Former colonel of the SADF, Cape Town, 12 March 2014, interview by Luregn Lenggenhager. The exact figures were difficult to trace. On several memorial webpages of former members of the SADF they speak of 18,000 in total in northern Namibia, including the Caprivi, e.g.: A Site about the South African Border War: https://sites.google.com/site/sabushwarsite/overview (accessed 20 November 2015)

within reach, the military personnel (and their families) spent their free time out in nature. Many photographs and written accounts of former servicemen illustrate that it was common to have a braai (barbecue) at the rivers, go fishing and even go on photo-safaris in those areas that were considered relatively safe.[41]

According to many interviewees, numerous SADF staff members were involved in hunting and capturing wild animals in Caprivi.[42] As mentioned above, the shooting and stealing of wild animals by soldiers was for many Caprivians at the time a very dominant aspect of South Africa's occupation. Inhabitants of the small river-island of Impalila said that during the time that a South African military base existed on the island, most of the wild animals disappeared. This is particularly interesting, as there have never been large numbers of big game like elephants or rhinos on the island, but rather large numbers of small antelopes and monkeys. This suggests the possibility that hunting on the island was not primarily done for the international ivory and horn trade. Rather, low-ranking soldiers hunted small game like antelope or caught monkeys in order to take them home to South Africa as pet souvenirs. In 1977 J.K. Thompson, director of the Department of Nature and Environmental Conservation in Cape Town sent an exasperated letter to the Director of Veterinary Services in Pretoria, complaining about "the importation of wild animals from border military areas".[43] He stated that it was not allowed to import animals to the Cape Province even if the soldiers obtained an export permit from the region of origin. Thomson argued that animals brought from the border areas "might easily introduce human or animal disease".[44] He mentioned one case in particular of an export permit issued by an official in Katima Mulilo allowing a monkey to be taken to Cape Town. In a letter forwarded to the Department of Agriculture and Forestry in Katima Mulilo, the government in Pretoria reiterated that officially none of the veterinarians doing military service in Caprivi were "entitled to issue any movement permits for animals or animal products from Caprivi".[45] This disunity of different South African administrative units displays that what was often described as a single centre of power can not be understood as

---

41 See also: Hayes 2010: p. 15
42 For example, former Community leader in Western Caprivi, Kongola, 20 May 2014, interview by Luregn Lenggenhager.
43 National Archives of Namibia (NAN), Caprivi Agriculture and Forestry (CAF) 19_2. Thompson to the Director of Veterinary Services Pretoria, Importation of Wild Animals, 2 May 1977
44 National Archives of Namibia (NAN), Caprivi Agriculture and Forestry (CAF) 19_2. Thompson to the Director of Veterinary Services Pretoria, Importation of Wild Animals, 2 May 1977. This has to be understood within broader veterinarian policies and laws for the northern territories, see: Miescher 2012a
45 National Archives of Namibia (NAN), CAF, 19_2. Director of Veterinary Services Pretoria to Bezuidenhout, Importation of Wild Animals, 11 May 1977

such, but must rather be viewed as multilevelled sets and networks of relations that crisscrossed South Africa and Southern Africa, and that were also produced and contested through interactions with more marginal regions, such as the Caprivi.[46]

Although the law clearly did not allow the hunting and the export of animals from the Caprivi by South African soldiers, the transfer of Caprivi's fauna into the South African mainland took place nevertheless. Through this process, Caprivi's nature became not only "domesticated" but at the same time became part of an imagined South African space.[47] The inclusion of the Caprivi's nature in South Africa's public awareness is strongly reflected in various South African soldiers' accounts, TV shows, and news reports.[48] This public attention in combination with the transfer of fauna fed into the perception of Caprivi as an exotic wilderness that had to be successfully pacified by South African soldiers, not only during combat but also in the time between fighting, through what they called the bush experience of the soldiers. In the next paragraph I discuss how Caprivi's nature became part of South Africa's academic outreach and hence became incorporated in South Africa's natural history collections.

Collecting specimens

Aside from the transfer of animals from the Caprivi to South Africa by the SADF itself, major transfers were made by the civil administration in close cooperation with the military. These transfers show that South Africa's occupation did not end at its military aspects, but also included a systematic survey and collection of Caprivi's nature. In order to promote its occupation as 'doing good', this was framed by South Africa as helping to 'develop' local people. It also supported the military intelligence with more information on the region's natural features.[49]

The collection and hunting for museums was not new to the Caprivi and northern Namibia. Leslie Witz described several expeditions into the region for the purpose of 'collecting' game for natural history museums in London, New York and King William's Town in South Africa in the first half of the 20th century.[50] Using the example of the Kaffrarian Museum in King's William Town (now Amathole Museum), he described such expeditions as taking place in an "imperial museum

---

46 See also: Lester 2003: p. 609
47 Hayes 2010, p. 15
48 Most prominently in the books of a former colonel of the SADF in Caprivi, for example: Breytenbach 1986. See generally on nature in soldier's account on the Border War: Bains 2004: pp. 15–16
49 For the involvement of the SADF in economic projects in Namibia see: Dale 2014: pp. 53–73 and for water and development: Kreike 2013. For plans for water development, see also McKittrick 2015 and McCullers 2012
50 Witz 2015: p. 678

network that linked London, South Africa and India".[51] The collections were considered to be "representatives of the natural environment".[52] The transfers of animals and plants I discuss here must be seen in what Witz described as a second imperial network that was established through South Africa's colonisation of Namibia. According to this, it was South African colonial officials (and in my case the security forces particularly) that "opened up Namibia as [a] field for collectors from South African museums".[53]

Other than many earlier expeditions in the area that were concerned with big game, I describe here the collections of small animals, insects and plants that were mostly conducted in cooperation with larger ecological research projects. This could perhaps explain why in most of my interviews, such practices of 'extracting' nature were not as frequently recalled as the loss of the wildlife caused by the SADF. However, by looking at these transfers through the perspective of colonial knowledge production, they show that both South Africa's entrenched power in space and its colonial oppression materialised through the combination of ecological surveys and the military control of the area.[54]

On a practical level, the military and the researchers shared common interest in knowing the area profoundly. Natural features such as dense bush or swamps figure prominently on military maps of the area.[55] As one former member of the South African Air Force (SAAF) put it: "Knowing nature was and still is essential to win a war. Particularly in the Bush War, the bush was the only thing we shared with our enemies, for both of us, nature was enemy and ally."[56]

A particularly systematic survey of this 'bush' was conducted in the mid-1970s by the South African forestry department. It concerned a large part of Eastern Caprivi, along the border with Angola and Zambia. According to the forester in charge, the area was no longer inhabited: "All settlements were cleared from there, because that was the army operational area. When I came there, there was nobody living there."[57] His main task was to find usable timber and in the meantime "collect as much ecological information" as he could.[58] To achieve this he spent months in

---

51 Witz 2015: p. 678
52 Witz 2015: p. 674
53 Witz 2015: p. 679
54 Beinart/Hughes 2007; Kreike 2004: pp. 90–110
55 Maps held by the Archives of the South African Air Force Museum, Cape Town (no archival numbers)
56 Member of the South African Air Force, Pretoria, 1 June 2014, interview by the Luregn Lenggenhager.
57 South African forester working in Caprivi in the 1970s, George, 10 March 2014, interview by Luregn Lenggenhager
58 South African forester working in Caprivi in the 1970s, George, 10 March 2014, interview by Luregn Lenggenhager

the forest, systematically counting different types of trees and collecting leaves to send to the forestry's headquarters in Sedgefield (South Africa). While the leaf samples became part of the herbarium of the botanical garden in Sedgefield, other information was used to produce exact maps of the forest area and its vegetation types.

A closer look at the practice of collecting such data and samples highlights that research of the natural space was extremely labour-intensive. The above-mentioned forester explained that it was a very monotonous work, for which he had to spend a lot of time walking through the bush:

> My job was to go up there, and survey on foot with a chain. What I did was walking. I walked ten kilometres with a compass, then five hundred metres angular [to the direction of walking], and then at night ten kilometres back to my camp again. Every 150 metres I made a fifty metre circular survey of all the usable timber. I had a gun bearer with me all the time, and everybody had to work with a gang of six people. So we stood in a circle and I went into the centre [...], and then the others walked around the circle, and they were shouting to me the names of the trees. And I looked if there is any usable timber and I measured it and I dotted it down. So we walked around like this.[59]

The effort put into such surveys indicate that the ecological research was not merely a by-product of South Africa's occupation of Caprivi, but a central aspect of it. It illustrates that such intense work could only be done in close cooperation with the military. The military had to give security clearance to the researchers before they entered the forest and was responsible for their security while they were conducting surveys in the forest. The data and plant samples were then flown out to South Africa by the SAAF.[60]

Another example of sending specimens to South Africa for scientific reasons was the export of plants and even animals that did not exist in other parts of South Africa. It shows that the Caprivi was of particular interest to South African ecologists because it was seen as offering a distinct fauna and flora to the rest of South Africa's territories. This notion of Caprivi's nature being totally different from the rest of South Africa—or even tropical—can be traced back to the early years of South African occupation in the 1940s.[61] Leslie Trollope, the first South

---

59 South African forester working in Caprivi in the 1970s, George, 10 March 2014, interview by Luregn Lenggenhager
60 Most probably the SAAF was also in charge of flying out ivory and rhino horn, as mentioned above. See: Reeve/Ellis 1995
61 The SADF used Caprivi for example as a base for 'tropical training': Kangumu 2011: p. 148

African governor of the Caprivi described the Caprivi's fauna as "not resembling very much" the one of the Union.[62] This runs like a thread through descriptions of the Caprivi until the 21st century.[63] Arguably, the growing ban of apartheid South Africa's researchers in most (tropical) African countries made the nature of the Caprivi even more attractive for those scientists.

A prominent case of such transfers of specimens to South Africa is the collection of fish species in the Caprivi. South African officials understood fisheries as an extremely important means through which to 'develop' the Caprivi.[64] The fresh water reserve and the rich fish fauna of the Caprivi were seen as being of high strategic value for the occupied territory because other parts of it lacked these resources.[65] Furthermore, there were specific fish in the Caprivi that could not be found anywhere else in South Africa's territory. Starting from as early as the 1930s, academic institutions of South Africa regularly organised trips to the Caprivi to collect fish samples.[66] The most systematic surveys were done in 1973 and 1977, in which several hundred fish species were collected and sent to the Albany Museum in Grahamstown.[67]

The collection of fish specimens shows how important the Caprivi became as a 'tropical' outpost, and even more as a region where the South African government could implement its vision of development. An even more telling example of South Africa's policy of developing the Caprivi is the fourth transfer of nature, discussed in the following paragraph.

Sending trees to the Caprivi

Nature was also transferred from South Africa and further away towards the Caprivi. There were many transfers in this direction, including seeds and seedlings for agriculture and, in some cases, also cattle and other domestic animals.[68] I focus on the sending of tree seedlings with an assumed economical potential for the purpose of field trials in the Caprivi. Before coming to the particular case of sending eucalyptus trees to the Caprivi, it is worthwhile to recall the contested

---

62   Quoted in Gewald 2013: p. 87
63   For example, in 2000 German journalist and writer Rainer Bruchmann published a book on Caprivi's history with the title: *Caprivi, An African Flashpoint: An Illustrated History of Namibia's Tropical Region Where Four Countries Meet*. Bruchmann 2000.
64   Tvedten 2002: pp. 421–439
65   Van der Waal/Skelton 1984: p. 303. Some specimens were also taken to the JLB Smith Institute for Ichthyology (now called the South African Institute for Aquatic Biodiversity) in Grahamstown for further research.
66   Van der Waal/Skelton 1984: p. 304
67   Van der Waal/Skelton 1984: p. 313
68   See, for example, former officer in the Caprivi Government's Ministry for Agriculture and Forestry, Malengalenga, 18 May 2014, interview by Luregn Lenggenhager.

histories of eucalyptus in South Africa and position them within the different networks of empire.⁶⁹ Eucalyptus originates from Australia and was introduced by colonial forestry departments in most parts of the British Empire (and beyond) in the 19th century.⁷⁰ Planting trees was closely related to imperial visions of bringing water to seeming wastelands, enabling agriculture and, consequently, civilisation.⁷¹ In the 1890s, state foresters working for the Cape Colony's Forestry Department began pursuing a particular programme. They attempted to find areas within the British Empire with climates that were most similar to those of South Africa in order to find most suitable species for plantations in South Africa. They found the most favourable climate in Australia.⁷² Eucalyptus was particularly attractive, and they soon began to plant it all over South Africa. Because of the small amount of indigenous wood and the growing demand for timber, the planting of eucalyptus became popular amongst private farmers in the early 20th century as well.⁷³

While some South African foresters and scientists were still travelling the world in search for 'perfect' trees, others began to expand their trials and planting experiments towards their own imperial peripheries. In 1958, the first trials were conducted to evaluate the introduction of eucalyptus trees into northern Namibia. Ironically, this was at a time in South Africa when long-lasting concerns grew so dramatically about the 'impurity' of the seemingly untouched white settlers' landscape caused by exotic trees, that concerned people in South Africa began to eradicate them.⁷⁴

Such concerns were not apparent within the colonised territories in the north, where the planting and promotion of exotic species was done to prevent the local population from using their own trees. This enabled the colonial regime to intensify their control over local economies and access to forests.⁷⁵ Still, the transfer of eucalyptus trees to northern Namibia was never fully uncontested, even within the South African administration. The following case focuses on the destruction of eucalyptus field trials by the SADF at the border between Western Caprivi and Okavango. Although the military and the civil administration had similar practices of ruling the people and controlling space, there were also disagreements.

---

69 As mentioned above, Leslie Witz used the two networks of empire in his interpretation of the imperial hunting for museums. Witz 2015: pp. 674–79
70 Bennett 2010: pp. 125–145
71 Bennett 2011a: pp. 32; Barton 2002: pp. 99–104. See also the use of trees in the Israel/Palestine war and how such practices passed over to different colonial regimes: Braverman 2008: pp. 449–482
72 Bennett 2011b: pp. 265–280
73 Bennett 2011b: pp. 276–277
74 Bennett 2011b: p. 244 and Comaroff/Comaroff 2001: pp. 627–651
75 See, for example, on the Transkei: Tropp 2006

The state forester in Windhoek in the 1950s and 1960s was convinced that if the local people continued cutting wood, it would take only a few dozen years until all of the indigenous trees were gone. In response to this, he engaged in finding suitable, fast-growing trees to import, namely different varieties of eucalyptus. He was later approved to establish designated forestry reserves with a size of several thousand hectares where no one was allowed to live. These areas were reserved for the potential introduction of trees. In his own words, "although we don't need it now, we might need it in twenty or fifty years, to introduce exotic trees for wood production".[76]

One of the largest of these reserves was around Bagani at the border between Western Caprivi and Okavango. In 1974, the South West African Forestry Department tested eucalyptus and other fast-growing, dense trees on this land. However, one year later, the SADF removed all of these trees without explanation. The reason for this was discovered only afterwards by the state forester in Windhoek: "The terrorist hid behind the eucalyptus trees, because those were the densest bushes in the whole area, so the military just destroyed the trees so that the terrorists can't hide anymore."[77]

This contradicts two of South Africa's own fantasies about their control over the area. Firstly, it reconfirms that what was portrayed as one single power was rather different layers of powers, conflicting interests, and competing administrative bodies.[78] Secondly, it speaks against South Africa's vision of being able to hide its military goals under the cloak of 'development' and economic support. 'Doing good' was only possible as long as it did not pose a security threat. As soon as the economically valuable dense trees offered the hostile combatants a place to hide, the SADF destroyed them, although their 'economic' potential was yet to be identified.

Conclusion

I have discussed four transfers of natural goods from and into the Caprivi by South African officials in the 1970s. All of them can be positioned on the axis of military control, academic exploitation and economical integration of the Caprivi into what can be framed as a South African empire. I argue that these three practices of enforcing power over the large and often difficult-to-reach region were centred on the area's nature. Having physical and interpretive control over Caprivi's nature was a central means of power for the South African administration. In addition to

---

[76] Former head of the South West African Forestry Department in Grootfontein, Cape Town 21 April 2014, interview by Luregn Lenggenhager

[77] Former head of the South West African Forestry Department in Grootfontein, Cape Town 21 April 2014, interview by Luregn Lenggenhager

[78] Similar conflicts were also shown between different security organisations in Namibia, namely between the police and the military, see: Eloff de Visser 2011: pp. 91–94

the overlapping security and academic interests in knowing the region's ecology, I suggest that South Africa's intense examination of Caprivi's nature and the associated transfer of natural objects be understood within two further contexts: development and incorporation.

It was important for South Africa to promote its occupation of Namibia internationally as a development project, and to convince the Namibian population that the presence of South Africa would help them. In the Caprivi, the pretended uplifting of the local population evolved around its ecological potential. South Africa saw forestry and fishery in particular as important sectors for local development, and therefore forced the exploitation of timber and fish. This was meant to help the local people make some profit from the natural resources and therewith increase their economic dependency on South Africa.[79] To do so, South African officials intensively researched the ecological potential and introduced economically promising plants from South Africa to the Caprivi.

The incorporation of Caprivi into a South African nature space did not only take place on a discursive level through the production of ecological knowledge, but also materially through the inclusion of specimens into the collections of South African academic institutions, as well as through souvenirs that South African soldiers took back to their homes. This shows that more than just doing research on nature (on the ground) by mapping out the region's natural features, 'nature' also needed to be brought back to the alleged central areas of power.[80] This was often carried out on a practical level, by physically collecting Caprivi's nature and sending it back to South Africa or sometimes also sending plants from South Africa to the Caprivi.

The idea of an imperial nature that constituted a greater South Africa was a strong means for integrating peripheral regions such as the Caprivi. This needed clearly defined boundaries between 'own' nature and 'exotic' nature, as it was the case for post-colonial nation states and as I mentioned before.[81] Interestingly, when analysing South Africa through the lens of empire, collecting nature from the peripheries was also crucial for displaying diversity within the empire, and therefore including the 'exotic' nature in the 'own'.[82] Arguably, the incorporation of Caprivi's nature—perceived as a 'tropical' outpost of South Africa and lying at the immediate border of it—was particularly helpful in the constitution of such a united but diverse South African nature.

Thinking of Southern Africa as one natural space without any borders and boundaries, but internally diverse and manifold is still very present in postcolonial

---

79 Kreike 2013: pp. 197–220
80 Witz 2015
81 Comaroff/Comaroff 2001; Olwig 2003: pp. 61–74
82 MacKenzie 1997

visions for the area.[83] The colonial idea of bringing 'development' and welfare to marginalised areas through researching, protecting and capitalising on their natural potential survives in the 21st century: the highly celebrated plans for Transfrontier Conservation Areas show that this is widely seen as a solution for a multitude of problems. The enforcement of such projects builds on a close cooperation between ecological experts and armed security units, both financed by and originating from the centres of political, economical and academic power.[84]

References

Africa Focus Tours (2009), http://africafocustours.co.za/map.html. Accessed 20 November 2015.

Ashforth, A. (1990), *Politics of Official Discourse in Twentieth-Century South Africa*. Oxford: Clarendon Press.

A Site about the South African Border War, A Short Overview of the South African Bushwar/Border War. https://sites.google.com/site/sabushwarsite/overview. Accessed 20 November 2015.

Atran, S. (1987), Ordinary Constraints on the Semantics of Living Kinds: A Commonsense Alternative to Recent Treatments of Natural-Object Terms. *Mind & Language*, 2(1): 27–32.

Bains, G. (2004), South Africa's Vietnam? *Safundi*, 5(3): 1–21.

Barton, G. (2002), *Empire Forestry and the Origins of Environmentalism*. Cambridge: Cambridge University Press.

Beinart, W. and L. Hughes (eds.) (2007), *Environment and Empire*. Oxford: Oxford University Press.

Bennett, B.M. (2010), The El Dorado of Forestry: The Eucalyptus in India, South Africa, and Thailand, 1850–2000. *International Review of Social History*, 55(18): 27–50.

Bennett, B.M. (2011a), A Global History of Australian Trees. *Journal of the History of Biology*, 44(1): 125–145.

Bennett, B.M. (2011b), Naturalising Australian Trees in South Africa: Climate, Exotics and Experimentation. *Journal of Southern African Studies*, 37(2): 265–280.

Braverman, I. (2008), "The Tree Is the Enemy Soldier": A Sociolegal Making of War Landscapes in the Occupied West Bank. *Law & Society Review*, 42(3): 449–482.

---

83 In tourism business the slogan "A whole world in one country" is often used for South Africa, sometimes also to advertise tours including Namibia and Botswana. See also the interactive tourist map on Africa Focus Tours 2009: http://africafocustours.co.za/map.html (accessed 20 November 2015)

84 Ramutsindela 2007; Büscher/Ramutsindela 2016

Breytenbach, J. (1986), *Forged in Battle*. Cape Town: Saayman & Weber.

Bruchmann, R. (2000), *Caprivi, An African Flashpoint: An Illustrated History of Namibia's Tropical Region Where Four Countries Meet*. Northcliff: Self-published.

Büscher, B. and M. Ramutsindela (2016), Green Violence: Rhino Poaching and the War to Save Southern Africa's Peace Parks. *African Affairs*, 115(458): 1–22.

Carney, J.A. and R.N. Rosomoff (2009), *In the Shadow of Slavery: Africa's Botanical Legacy in the Atlantic World*. Berkeley: University of California Press.

Chase, M.J. and C.R. Griffin (2009), Elephants Caught in the Middle: Impacts of War, Fences and People on Elephant Distribution and Abundance in the Caprivi Strip, Namibia. *African Journal of Ecology*, 47(2): 223–233.

Comaroff J. and J.L. Comaroff (2001), Naturing the Nation; Aliens, Apocalypse and the Postcolonial State. *Journal of Southern African Studies*, 27(3): 627–651.

Cronon, W., G. Miles and J. Gitlin (1992), Becoming West: Toward a New Meaning for Western History. In: Cronon,W., G. Miles and J. Gitlin (eds.), *Under an Open Sky: Rethinking America's Western Past*. New York: WW Norton & Company.

Crosby, A.W. (1972), *The Columbian Exchange: Biological and Cultural Consequences of 1492*. Westport: Greenwood Press.

Crosby, A.W. (1986), *Ecological Imperialism: The Biological Expansion of Europe, 900–1900*. Cambridge: Cambridge University Press.

Dale, R. (2014), *The Namibian War of Independence, 1966–1989, Diplomatic, Economic and Military Campaigns*. Jefferson: McFarland.

Dobell, L. (1998), *Swapo's Struggle for Namibia, 1960–1991: War by Other Means*. Basel: P. Schlettwein Publishing.

Ellis, S. (1994), Of Elephants and Men: Politics and Nature Conservation in South Africa. *Journal of Southern African Studies*, 20(1): 53–69.

Eloff de Visser, L. (2011), Winning Hearts and Minds in the Namibian Border War. *Scientia Militaria. South African Journal of Military Studies*, 39(1): 85–100.

Fisch, M. (1999), *The Secessionist Movement in the Caprivi*. Windhoek: Namibia Scientific Society.

Flint, L. (2003), State-Building in Central Southern Africa: Citizenship and Subjectivity in Barotseland and Caprivi. *International Journal of African Historical Studies*, 36(2): 393–428.

Gewald, J.B. (2013), Beyond the Last Frontier: Major Trollope and the Eastern Caprivi Zipfel. In M. de Bruijn, and R. van Dijk (eds.), *The Social Life of Connectivity in Africa*. Basingstoke: Palgrave.

Hayes, P. (2010), Bush of Ghosts. In J. Liebenberg and P. Hayes (eds.), *Bush of Ghosts: Life and War in Namibia 1986–1990*. Cape Town: Umuzi.

Henrichsen, D., G. Miescher, C. Rassool, and L. Rizzo (2015), Rethinking Empire in Southern Africa. *Journal of Southern African Studies*, 41(3): 431–435.

Hodge, J.M. (2011), The Hybridity of Colonial Knowledge: British Tropical Agricultural Science and African Farming Practices at the End of Empire. In B.M. Bennett and J.M. Hodge (eds.), *Science and Empire: Knowledge and Networks of Science Across British Empire, 1800–1970*. New York: Palgrave McMillan: 209–231.

Kangumu, B. (2011), *Contesting Caprivi: A History of Colonial Isolation and Regional Nationalism in Namibia*. Basel: Basler Afrika Bibliographien.

Katjavivi, P.H. (1989), *A History of Resistance in Namibia*. Paris: Unesco.

Kreike, E. (2004), War and the Environmental Effects of Displacement in Southern Africa, 1970s–1990s. In W. Moseley and B.I. Logan (eds.), *African Environment and Development: Rhetoric, Programme and Reality*. Aldershot: Ashgate: 89–110.

Kreike, E. (2013), *Environmental Infrastructure in African History, Examining the Myth of Natural Resource Management in Namibia*. New York: Cambridge University Press.

Kumleben, M.E. (1996), *Report of the Commission of Inquiry into the Alleged Smugglings and Illegal Trade of Ivory and Rhinoceros Horn in South Africa*. Pretoria: Government Printer.

Lenggenhager, L. (2015), Nature, War and Development: South Africa's Caprivi Strip, 1960–1980. *Journal of Southern Africa Studies*, 41(4): 467–483.

Lester, A. (2003), Introduction: Historical Geographies of Southern Africa. *Journal of Southern African Studies*, 29(3): 595–613.

Livingstone, D.N. (2003), *Putting Science in its Place: Geographies of Scientific Knowledge*. Chicago: Chicago University Press.

MacKenzie, J. (1997), Empire and the Ecological Apocalypse: the Historiography of the Imperial Environment. In T. Griffiths and L. Robin (eds.), *Ecology and Empire: Environmental History of Settler Societies*. Edinburgh: Keele University Press: 215–228.

McCullers, M. (2012), Lines in the Sand: The Global Politics of Local Development in Apartheid Era Namibia, 1950–1980, (PhD Thesis, Emory University).

McKittrick, M. (2015), An Empire of Rivers: The Scheme to Flood the Kalahari, 1919–1945. *Journal of Southern African Studies*, 41(3): 471–490.

Miescher, G. (2012a), *Namibia's Red Line. The History of a Veterinary and Settlement Border*. New York: Palgrave Macmillan.

Miescher, G. (2012b), Facing Barbarians: A Narrative of Spatial Segregation in Colonial Namibia. *Journal of Southern African Studies*, 38(2): 769–786.

Nature Conservation in Caprivi: SADF Battles to Save our Heritage, *Paratus*, November 1982. pp. 10–11.

Nunn, N. and N. Qian (2010), The Columbian Exchange: A History of Disease, Food, and Ideas. *Journal of Economic Perspectives*, 24(2): 163–188.

Olwig, K.R. (2003), Natives and Aliens in the National Landscape. *Landscape Research*, 28(1): 61–74.

Preserving Our Natural Riches, *Paratus*, July 1980. pp. 13–14.

Ramutsindela, M. (2007), *Transfrontier Conservation in Africa: At the Confluence of Capital, Politics and Nature*. Wallingford: CABI.

Rassool, C. (2015), Re-storing the Skeletons of Empire: Return, Reburial and Rehumanisation in Southern Africa. *Journal of Southern African Studies*, 41(4): 653–670.

Reeve, R. and S. Ellis (1995), An Insider's Account of the South African Security Forces' Role in the Ivory Trade. *Journal of Contemporary African Studies*, 13(2): 653–670.

Rizzo, L. (2012), *Gender and Colonialism: A History of Kaoko in North-Western Namibia, 1870–1950s*. Basel: Basler Afrika Bibliographien.

Silvester, J., M. Wallace and P. Hayes (1998), Trees Never Meet: Mobility and Containment: An Overview. In P. Hayes, J. Silvester, M. Wallace and W. Hartmann (eds.), *Namibia Under South African Rule, Mobility and Containment, 1915–1946*. Oxford: James Currey.

Steinberg, T. (2002), Down to Earth: Nature, Agency and Power in History. *American Historical Review*, 107(3): 798–820.

Taylor, J.J. (2012), *Naming the Land: San Identity and Community Conservation in Namibia's West Caprivi*. Basel: Basler Afrika Bibliographien.

Tropp, J. (2006), *Natures of Colonial Change: Environmental Relations in the Making of the Transkei*. Athens (OH): Ohio University Press.

Tvedten I. (2002), If You Don't Fish, You Are Not a Caprivian: Freshwater Fisheries in Caprivi, Namibia. *Journal of Southern African Studies*, 28(2): 421–39.

Van der Waal, B.C.W. and P.H. Skelton (1984), Check List of the Fishes of Caprivi. *Madoqua*, 13(4): 303–320.

Wallace, M. (2014), *A History of Namibia*. Oxford: Oxford University Press.

Witz, L. (2015), Hunting for Museums. *Journal of Southern African Studies*, 41(4): 671–685.

Zeller, W. (2009), Danger and Opportunity in Katima Mulilo: A Namibian Border Boomtown at Transnational Crossroads. *Journal of Southern African Studies*, 35(1): 133–154.

CHAPTER 6

Rehabilitating the 'Ovambo cattle': veterinary science and cattle breeding in early colonial Namibia

Giorgio Miescher and Anna Voegeli

Introduction

On 20 June 1929, a long-awaited cattle transport arrived at Onderstepoort (South Africa), then the leading veterinary scientific institute in Africa. The small herd consisted of six cows of a breed, common in the far north of Namibia, known as 'Ovambo cattle'.[1] The vets were excited as this breed had allegedly never been scientifically examined and classified; more importantly, they expected these animals to be of "the pure Ovambo type" since they originated from "probably the least accessible territory south of the Zambezi river". With joy they observed how the animals, exhausted from the long journey, at first refused food from the manger and water from the trough, and only after a while adapted to "these receptacles of civilisation".[2]

Throughout the following three years, the cattle were subjected to an intensive procedure of measuring, classifying and documenting their physical characteristics and productivity. Their general appearance was found to be small and narrow, with substantial horns; their meat and milk productivity small but of high quality; also, they were noted to have an impressively good health constitution. At the end of the process, some of the animals were killed and given to South African museums for conservation and display, be it stuffed or as a skeleton, where they henceforth were to serve as the scientific standard reference for the breed.[3]

---

1 As regretfully noted by the researchers, "it [had not been] possible to obtain an Ovambo bull from South West Africa". Groenewald/Curson: p. 606
2 Groenewald/Curson: p. 601
3 Groenewald/Curson: p. 612

GENERAL CHARACTERISTICS OF THE OVAMBO COW.

HEAD.

Forehead: Broad and flat, i.e. not much dished.

Horns: Curved forward, sideward and upward.

Face: Fairly long with veins showing slightly.

Fig. 3. Ovambo cow No. 3588.

Muzzle: Broad, strong and black.

Jaws: Strong and lips firm.

Eyes: Languid, with heavy fold of skin above.

Ears: Oval, pointed, stylish and alert.

NECK.

FIGURE 1: Detail of scientific description of 'Ovambo cattle' (Groenewald/Curson, 1933, p. 606).

What was seen to be the groundbreaking aspect of this veterinary study was that, for the first time, this 'pure' African cattle breed with all its specific strengths and weaknesses had been examined and documented.[4] All in all, the vets presented their findings as the scientific discovery of a native African breed untouched by the march of civilisation.[5] As we outline below, this exoticisation and musealisation of a specific type of cattle was the result of a longer process of experimentation, segregation and marginalisation; a process shaped by a close interplay between breeding practices, veterinary science, disease control and colonial politics.[6]

This chapter is divided into four sections. It begins with situating the conceptualisation of Ovambo cattle as a distinct breed in the context of the emergence of veterinary science and the professionalisation of settler farming in Namibia at the turn of the twentieth century. A second section examines the establishment of the police zone border and its effects on cattle in Owambo and the role cattle from this area occupied in the colonial farming industry and veterinary science up to World War I. The third section subsequently looks at the temporary revival of cattle mobility between northern and central Namibia as a consequence of the war, but centrally argues that the restitution of the police zone border in 1924 cemented previous segregationist tendencies of colonial policy and resulted in the general exclusion of Ovambo cattle from commercial breeding and veterinary services. A fourth and final section will then return to the Onderstepoort study presented at the beginning and concludes how a long history of colonial isolation of the Owambo region and its cattle formed the precondition for the scientific '(re-)discovery' as well as the musealisation of Ovambo cattle as an exotic breed.

The invention of the 'Ovambo cattle': rinderpest, settler farming and the emergence of veterinary services, before 1904

In retracing the historical process which, as we argue, prepared the ground for the exoticisation and musealisation of a particular breed of cattle, we need to start out with a critical examination of the origins of the term 'Ovambo cattle'. Ovambo cattle by no means refers to a naturally given, clearly demarcated group of animals of the same type. Quite the contrary is the case: as we will seek to show in this first section of the paper, the invention of Ovambo cattle as a cattle breed with distinct features must in itself be understood as the product of historical processes.

---

4 Groenewald/Curson: p. 603
5 Groenewald/Curson: p. 603
6 There is a growing and multifaceted literature on such politics of breeding and the (re)invention of specific breeds as well as the social role of animals in Southern Africa focusing in particular on dogs (Gordon 2003; Van Sittert/Swart 2008) and horses (Bankoff/Swart 2007; Swart 2010).

Considering Namibia's long history of multidirectional cattle mobility within and across regional boundaries, which also involved exchange of cattle between central and central north Namibia, it is first of all unclear to what degree cattle in the various regions actually manifested clear-cut phenotypical differences.[7]

As far as written sources from the first decade of German colonial presence in Namibia are concerned, these do not give evidence that the colonisers thought of the local cattle herds in terms of different breeds. When the first German military troops, settlers and traders began to establish themselves in Namibia, they joined an ongoing, intensive struggle over land and livestock resources within African societies.[8] Early reports on the development of the colony thus again and again eagerly point to the region's vast and economically promising cattle resources and champion how, often with the help of the German military, increasing numbers of cattle changed hands from African breeders to European traders and settlers.[9]

Despite this strong emphasis on the economic potential of the region's cattle resources, prior to the outbreak of the rinderpest panzootic, the monopoly for cattle breeding and meat production remained firmly in the hands of African breeders, while the majority of European settlers continued to rely on trading, the transport business or work as craftsmen for their subsistence, with cattle farming forming at best a sideline.[10]

Primarily concerned with giving a tentative overview of the actual numbers of cattle available in the colony on the one hand, and describing and measuring the effects of cattle diseases like lung sickness on the emerging settler herds and the steps taken to contain them on the other, colonial sources from the early 1890s usually

---

7   On cattle mobility in Namibia in the 18th and 19th century, see Voegeli 2008: pp. 16–27. For northern Namibia, see Siiskonen 1990, and for central Namibia, see Henrichsen 2011.
8   On struggles over cattle resources in the early years of German colonial presence, see Voegeli 2008: pp. 24–27; Gewald 1999: pp. 29–60; Drechsler 1966: pp. 84–85; Kaulich 2001: p. 362
9   See, for example National Archives of Namibia (NAN), ZBU 146 A.VI.a.3, vol. 2, annual report, *Gouvernement*, Windhoek, to *Reichskanzler*, Berlin, 20 October 1896, p. 235; *Jahresbericht über die Entwickelung der Deutschen Schutzgebiete im Jahre 1896/97*, Berlin, 1898, pp. 121–123; NAN, ZBU 146 A.VI.a3, vol.2, *Ortspolizeibehörde*, Windhoek, to *Gouvernement*, Windhoek, 5 August 1896, pp. 66–67
10 In the general annual report for the year 1894/95, 300,000 to 400,000 head of cattle alone were estimated to be in possession of Herero groups, while Theodor Leutwein later estimated the number of cattle in central Namibia in the mid-1890s to around 500,000. (Kaulich 2001: p. 363) For the other regions, estimates are only available for the year 1891, when von François roughly gauged a total of 200,000 head of cattle for central Namibia, 100,000 in Owambo, 3,000 in the Okavango region and 50,000 in southern Namibia. NAN, ZBU 146 AVI.a.3, vol. 1, von François to *Reichskanzler* von Caprivi, 31 December 1891, pp. 1k–1q. On early farming activities by European settlers, see Schlettwein 1914: p. 92

refer to local cattle simply as *Einheimischenvieh* or identify them by reference to a specific region or the ethnic group their owners were associated with.[11]

> Der Viehbestand des hiesigen Distrikts beläuft sich z.z. auf ca. 4000 Rinder, etwa 1000 Stück Kleinvieh (einschliesslich Beute-beester) und 25 Pferde. Das vor der Zeit des Oorlogs hier im Distrikt vorhandene *Vieh der Hereros* ist schwer abzuschätzen, nach meiner Schätzung belief sich dasselbe auf etwa 80'000 bis 100'000 Stück Grossvieh und etwa das Doppelte Kleinvieh.... Die Ausfuhr bestand zum grössten Theil in *Herero Vieh*, ferner in Hörnern, Fellen und Straussenfedern.[12]

It is in the mid 1890s, the period during which the first initiatives to promote animal husbandry breeding amongst settlers are documented, that we can find the first differentiation between local cattle breeds based on their physical characteristics in a number of reports. In his report for the southern district, for example, *Bezirkshauptmann* Duft explains that "Nama oxen" (*Namaochsen*) were the best-liked cattle type in his district when it came to draught oxen and slaughter cattle.[13] In a similar vein, the general annual report to Berlin for the year 1895/96 refers to the small constitution of "Herero cattle" (*Hererovieh*) and explains that "Afrikaner bulls" (*Afrikanerbullen*) would be taken from the southern parts of the protectorate to central Namibia as a first step towards 'upgrading' the cattle locally available.[14]

The phase where breed-classifications begin to appear more densely across colonial sources, however, falls into the years following the rinderpest panzootic of 1897, a time of intensified European settlement, professionalisation of settler cattle

---

11 See, for example, NAN, ZBU 146 AVI.a.3, vol. 1, *Landeshauptmann* von François to *Reichskanzler* von Caprivi, 31 December 1891, pp. 1k–1q; NAN, ZBU 146 A.VI.a.3., vol. 1, annual report 1891/92, *Landeshauptmann* von François, Windhoek, to *Reichskanzler*, Berlin, 14 August 1892, pp. 1r–1u. The German term 'Einheimischenvieh' can be translated both as 'cattle held by indigenous people' and 'indigenous cattle'.

12 NAN, ZBU 146 A.VI.a.3, vol. 2, annual report, *Distriktshauptmann*, Gobabis, to *Bezirkshauptmann*, Windhoek, 29 July 1896, pp. 82–84, authors' emphasis. Authors' translation of the quote: "The amount of stock in this district actually amounts to c. 4000 head of cattle, to 1000 head of small stock (including prey-cattle) and to 25 horses. The amount of *stock owned by Hereros* before the war is difficult to estimate, according to my estimation the numbers were 80,000 to 100,000 head of large stock and the double of small stock. (...) The export consisted of mainly of *Herero cattle*, complemented by horns, skins, and ostrich feathers."

13 NAN, ZBU 146 A.VI.a.3., vol. 1, annual report 1894/1895 for the southern district, *Bezirkshauptmann* Duft, Keetmanshoop, to *Landeshauptmann* Leutwein, Windhoek, 12 July 1895, pp. 274–276

14 NAN, ZBU 146 A.VI.a.3, vol. 2, annual report, *Gouvernement*, Windhoek, to *Reichskanzler*, Berlin, 20 October 1896, pp. 235–236

farming, and the establishment of veterinary science and services in the protectorate. As stated in previous studies, the rinderpest panzootic was a crucial event for the establishment and consolidation of veterinary science across Southern Africa: the devastating effects of the panzootic left no doubt that veterinary knowledge and well-functioning veterinary structures were vital for colonial rule; moreover, they offered a pioneering field for practical experimentation for leading scientists from all parts of the world.[15] Not surprisingly, then, the colonial administration of German South West Africa created a special department for veterinary medicine and animal husbandry, the Referat für Veterinärmedizin und Tierzucht in the aftermath of the panzootic in 1897/1898. As illustrated in the department's name (literally the 'Department of Veterinary Science and Animal Husbandry'), apart from disease control and prevention, the second major function of the governmental veterinary services was to assist and educate farmers in the management and development of their livestock according to the principles of 'rational' animal husbandry.[16]

With the unequal distribution of cattle losses, which was centrally determined by access to veterinary medical services (which in turn seems to have depended on the breeders' political and spatial proximity to the colonial state), the rinderpest panzootic also marked a radical turning point in socio-economic relations. While a large number of African cattle owners suffered severe cattle losses, the rocketing cattle prices following the panzootic opened up unprecedented opportunities for settlers to engage in commercially viable cattle farming.[17] In the years after the panzootic, the number of farmers and settlers almost tripled, and according to the first cattle census in 1902/1903, by then over fifty percent of the cattle in the area under colonial control were owned by settler farmers.[18]

It is in this early phase of the institutionalisation of veterinary science and the expansion of settler farming between the rinderpest panzootic and the outbreak of the Namibian colonial war of 1904 that the categorisation of local cattle into a discrete set of breeds became more broadly established in colonial debates and breeding practice. As a case in point, a newspaper report on the first Namibian agricultural exhibition held in Windhoek in June 1899 lists farmer Herpolsheimer

---

15 On the significance of the rinderpest panzootic for the institutionalisation of veterinary science, see further: Gilfoyle 2003; Miescher 2012: pp. 28–30
16 On the establishment of a veterinary department in the German colonial administration, see also Kaulich 2001: p. 90; Schneider 1994: pp. 150–151, 238
17 On the socio-economic effects of the rinderpest panzootic, see Miescher 2012: pp. 30–31; Voegeli 2008: pp. 29–30
18 Voegeli 2008: p. 30. The cattle census of 1902/1903 listed a total of 45,898 head of cattle in the hands of settlers and 44,487 head in the hands of Africans. However, the census only applied to the areas under effective colonial rule, and thus did not include cattle ownership in Kaoko and Owambo region. NAN, ZBU 184 A.VI.g.4, 'Viehzählungen Hauptstatistik', *Gouvernement*, Windhoek, ca. April 1903, pp. 1–4

with his "pure Nama cows" as the winner of the second prize in the category "collective exhibition with a minimum of 5 cows", followed by farmer Boysen from Windhoek with "Nama cows" and "Shorthorn cows", and farmer Hälblich with "crossbreeds of Damara- and Nama cattle".[19]

A more general glance at the different levels of breed specification in this prize list reveals two major tendencies in colonial debates on and practices in cattle breeding at the turn of the 20th century. First, debates on how to develop the local cattle industry centrally built on the presumption that cross-breeding local cattle with breeds imported from Europe was the primary strategy for improving the colony's stock resources. Debates on cattle breeding between government veterinarians and farmers thus centrally focused on the subject of imported stud cattle, their acclimatisation and their suitability for cross-breeding with local cattle.[20] Accordingly, from a total of eleven prizes awarded for stud cattle, the list gives detailed breed specifications for each prized animal within the five categories exclusively reserved for cattle of European origin; by way of contrast, the listings for the five categories awarding prizes to *Einheimischenvieh* (native stock) do not give any further information as to what breed the prized animals pertained to. As pointed out above, such breed specifications for local cattle were only made in the eleventh, mixed category.

The second major tendency in contemporary debates on cattle breeding is reflected in the fact that the local breed specifications in this eleventh category only include Nama and Damara cattle, while Ovambo cattle do not appear amongst the prized animals.[21] For it was mainly those local breeds identified in the colonial settlement area, that is, Damara or Herero cattle and the Nama or Afrikaner cattle, that became the subject of farmers' and veterinary debates, whereas the Ovambo cattle generally went unmentioned.[22]

Nevertheless, there is clear evidence that at least farmers in the northern districts from early on included cattle from the Owambo region in their breeding experiments and perceived them as a distinct breed. In a retrospective on his experience as a breeder, Carl Schlettwein stated that he had started to systematically breed with Ovambo, Herero and Bastard cows in 1901 and kept detailed records

---

19 'Die Ausstellung', *Deutsch-Südwestafrikanische Zeitung*, vol. 1, no. 18, 8 June 1899, p. 1
20 For a more extensive discussion of these debates, see Voegeli 2008: pp. 84–89
21 'Die Ausstellung', *Deutsch-Südwestafrikanische Zeitung*, vol. 1, no. 18, 8 June 1899, p. 1
22 This is most strikingly illustrated in a memorandum on cattle breeding by the director of the government stud farm in Nauchas, von Clavé. Although he was one of the few voices within the veterinary department strongly opposing the common practice of importing cattle from overseas for upgrading and instead highlighting the advantages of breeding with locally available breeds, i.e. Damara and Afrikaner cattle, he did not at all refer to Ovambo cattle. NAN, ZBU N.I.a.1, vol. 1, *Gestütsdirektor* von Clavé, Nauchas, to *Gouvernement*, Windhoek, ca. 1903, pp. 43–46

of the development of the different breeds and experiments in cross-breeding from that time onwards.²³

To sum up this section's observations, the conceptualisation of Ovambo cattle as a category and distinct breed, contrasted against other local breeds like Herero or Damara cattle, Nama cattle and Afrikaner cattle, must in itself be situated in the context of an increasing institutionalisation of veterinary science, veterinary services and the professionalisation of settler farming in Namibia at the turn of the 20th century. Yet, in spite of becoming conceptualised as a breed of its own around this time, the Ovambo cattle played only a marginal role in the first years of commercial farming in Namibia, as other local breeds were more readily available in the areas of colonial settlement.

The discovery of 'Ovambo cattle' as potential breeding stock and their strategic exclusion from government breeding policies, 1905–1914

With the eruption of the colonial war in 1904, the distribution of cattle resources in the region once again drastically changed. In the first months of the war, Africans succeeded in taking possession of large numbers of cattle from European farmers. As the war went on and took on genocidal dimensions, however, most cattle in the hands of Africans involved in the conflict were killed or died.²⁴

Ultimately, the war resulted in the large-scale dispossession of Africans from their large stock (Africans in central and southern Namibia were no longer allowed to own cattle)²⁵ and a near depletion of cattle resources in central and partly also southern Namibia.²⁶ European farmers, by way of contrast, received intensive governmental support for (re-)building farms and herds from 1905 onwards, so that the number of farms in the colony grew rapidly in the years following the war.²⁷ Along with major investments in the colony's infrastructure and administration, expanding the agricultural sector as part of a proactive settlement policy was regarded as a key to stabilising colonial rule and preventing further insurgencies.²⁸

---

23 Schlettwein 1911: p. 36
24 In July 1905, chief veterinary officer Rickmann estimated the number of cattle remaining in the hands of the colonial forces as low as 5000 head. NAN, ZBU 152 A.VI.a.3, vol. 11, annual report, *Gouvernement*, Windhoek, to *Kolonialabteilung des Auswärtigen Amts*, Berlin, ca. July 1905, p. 360. For a more detailed discussion of the effect of the war on the colony's cattle resources, see Voegeli 2008: pp. 48–52
25 Except with a special permission.
26 'Verordnung betr. Massregeln zur Kontrolle der Eingeborenen', *Deutsch-Südwestafrikanische Zeitung*, 9(72), 7 September 1907, p. 1
27 Kaulich 2001: p. 345
28 Schmokel discusses in detail the impressive dimension of state investment into the farming sector in the years following the war and particularly highlights the political and ideological rather than economic motifs for such lavish state subsidies. Schmokel 1985

In the aftermath of the 1904 war, the previously neglected Ovambo cattle suddenly came into focus of attention. As early as 1905, the government vets—who occupied key roles in planning and coordinating governmental measures to rekindle and promote cattle breeding amongst farmers—began to debate the question of how to best restock farms in central Namibia. With the herds of so-called Damara and Nama cattle critically decimated in central and southern Namibia, the Owambo region, which had largely remained unaffected by the war, was discovered as a possible source for the large numbers of breeding stock needed to rekindle the colony's farming industry.

As Wilhelm Rickmann, head of the veterinary department, stated in October 1905 in a letter to the *Gouvernement*, he found the Ovambo cattle, in spite of their comparatively small constitution, very well suited for the purposes of settler farming. He particularly emphasised that, unlike livestock imported from overseas, this breed was fully adapted to the local climate. Rickmann thus suggested that at least the colony's northern districts of Outjo, Karibib and Grootfontein, where he had observed a strong demand for this breed amongst farmers, should be restocked with cattle from Owambo.[29]

In this letter, Rickmann also addressed possible impediments to cattle imports from Owambo. First, he pointed out that, in terms of disease control, the cattle would need to be checked for lung sickness, as this disease was still endemic in the northern areas. He argued that this problem could be easily confronted by means of control posts and vaccinations. The only impediment that remained, then, was of political nature. Rickmann stressed that the prohibition of horse trade into Owambo had also brought cattle trade with that region to a standstill.[30]

While the chief veterinary officer thus evaluated the Ovambo cattle as very suitable for the purposes of commercial farming in terms of constitution, breeding characteristics and health conditions, political concerns impeded large scale acquisition of cattle in Owambo for farmers in the northern districts of the colony.[31] In spite of this entirely positive veterinary evaluation of the Ovambo cattle, the breed was not included in the governmental restocking schemes subsequently developed; instead, the colonial government focused on the import of female

---

29 NAN, ZBU 1230 N.IV.a2, vol. 1, Rickmann, Gammams, to *Gouvernement*, Windhoek, 12 October 1905, p. 1b. In a later publication, Rickmann again provided a very positive and even more detailed evaluation of the breeding qualities of Ovambo cattle. Rickmann 1908: pp. 28–29

30 Horses were much sought after by the Owambo elites, especially so-called "salted horses" which were resistant to *Pferdesterbe*, a deadly horse disease endemic in northern Namibia. Therefore the trading of horses (and other commodities) against cattle played an important role in the Namibian north-south trade. See Miescher 2012: pp. 39–40

31 NAN, ZBU 1230 N.IV.a2, vol. 1, Rickmann, Gammams, to *Gouvernement*, Windhoek, 12 October 1905, p. 1b

cattle from the Cape after experiments with imported cattle from Argentina had failed.³² The governmental decision to exclude Ovambo cattle from its restocking scheme was thus not based on veterinary scientific analysis of this breed's 'natural' breeding qualities; rather, it must be understood as linked to a broader process of increasing political and economic isolation of the Owambo region.

Indeed, in January 1906, *Gouverneur* von Lindequist issued a proclamation which cartographically defined the borders of the Owambo region as "*Land der Ovambo*" and prohibited the introduction of weapons, ammunition, horses and spirits into the area. Moreover, in general it prohibited that persons other than those permanently living in the area from entering Owambo until further notice.³³ Historiographic explanations for this radical closure of a part of the colony for trade and traffic have highlighted economic and political motifs. On the one hand, it has been argued that the colonial administration hoped to push the region's residents onto the colony's labour market as migrant labourers, as the prohibition of free trade would create a scarcity of goods in the region.³⁴ On the other hand, Eirola has highlighted political concerns informing the proclamation: fearing that insurgents in central Namibia might team up with resistance movements in northern Namibia, the administration sought to prevent the importation of military materials as well as limiting unwanted provocation of African resistance by, for example, European traders.³⁵

The increasing isolation of Owambo has to be seen as part of a broader colonial policy of spatial order. In the following year, the definition of the so-called police zone border—a measure primarily taken to restrict administrative and infrastructural investments to areas identified as economically viable and to steer settlement along these lines—further contributed to the separation of Owambo from the area under effective colonial control.³⁶ In addition, huge areas, especially in the northern parts of the colony, were proclaimed as game reserves with heavily restricted access.³⁷

The establishment of the police zone border in combination with the economic isolation of Owambo did, however, have effective repercussions upon the further

---

32 NAN, ZBU 153 A.VI.a.3, vol. 12, annual report, *Referat für Veterinärmedizin und Tierzucht*, Windhoek, to *Gouvernement*, Windhoek, 5 October 1906, pp. 162–163
33 *Die deutsche Kolonial-Gesetzgebung*, vol. 10, 1906, p. 25
34 Strassegger 1988: pp. 50–54
35 Eirola 1992: 281. For a more detailed summary of the debate, see Miescher 2012: pp. 49–51
36 NAN, ZBU L.II.a.5, vol. 1, *Kolonialabteilung des Auswärtigen Amtes*, Berlin, to *Gouvernement*, Windhoek, 15 March 1907. On the establishment of the police zone border, see Miescher 2012: pp. 43–68.
37 In 1908 the Caprivi strip, too, was closed for settlers so that the Kavango region remained the only region in the far north of colony remaining open for settlers. Miescher 2012: pp. 54–56. For a detailed map printed in colour, see Miescher 2013: p. 372

development of Ovambo cattle as a breed. First, the establishment of the police zone led to an increasing gap in veterinary knowledge on cattle and breeding practices beyond that border. For the border also demarcated the limits of colonial veterinary services, leading to an increasing division of the colony into areas with fairly sophisticated veterinary services comprising disease control and state-support for breeders, and areas 'beyond'. With veterinary work focusing on animals and breeding practices within the police zone, the Ovambo cattle as a breed mainly found beyond this zone fell out of the grid of analysis.[38]

Second, the increasing manifestation of the police zone border as a veterinary border had direct impact on the condition of cattle and breeding in Owambo. Most obviously, the systematic exclusion of cattle owners in Owambo from access to veterinary services led to a growing gap between the condition of cattle herds north and south of the border. Moreover, with the movement of cattle across this border becoming restricted and periodically even completely prohibited (e.g. between 1911 and 1914), breeders in Owambo could barely export their cattle to the police zone anymore and lost an important source of income.[39] In other words, the systematic isolation and segregation of Owambo from the area under colonial control led to an increasing isolation and segregation of the region's cattle resources. This, in turn, fundamentally affected the possibilities for working with and developing the breeding qualities of these animals.

It is interesting to note that, while the Ovambo cattle almost entirely disappears from the agenda of the colony's vets, the qualities of this breed and its integration into breeding schemes still remained an issue of debate amongst farmers in the northern districts. In revising his widely-read practical guide to farming in German South West Africa from 1907 for a new edition published in 1914, Carl Schlettwein complemented his section on Ovambo cattle with the note that Ovambo cattle continued to be very popular on farms with acid grass.[40] There is evidence that, until the closure of the police zone border to cattle in 1911, small-scale importation of cattle from Owambo beyond the control of the state veterinary apparatus continued to be common practice amongst farmers in the northern districts.[41]

---

38 Miescher 2012: pp. 65–68. Parts of the settler society, including a leading staff member of the veterinary service, challenged the isolation of Owambo and would have preferred to bring this part of territory under direct colonial control, too. NAN, ZBU 1310 O III b1, handwritten notes by chief veterinary officer Henning on the draft version of an article titled 'Ausdehung des Einfuhrverbotes auf das Amboland und die östlich gelegenen Gebiete in D.S.W.A.', 18 May 1911

39 On the complete closure of the border for cattle between 1911 and 1914, see Miescher 2012: p. 67

40 Schlettwein 1914: 96. See also Schlettwein 1907

41 NAN, ZBU 1295 O.I.i.2, vol. 1, Farmer Diesel, Farm Chamkubis, district Outjio, to *Gouvernement*, Windhoek, 10 June 1911, pp. 1–2; NAN, ZBU 1295 O.I.i.2, vol. 1,

All in all, the last decade of German colonial rule saw the implementation of a series of measures and policies which contributed to an increasing isolation of cattle in Owambo from breeding practices, veterinary services and research within the police zone. This process of segregation began with the isolation of the Owambo region for strategic political and economic purposes, followed by the institution of the police zone border, and culminated in the complete, if temporary, closure of the police zone border for cattle. However, despite these segregationist tendencies in colonial policy-making and their negative effects on cattle breeding in Owambo, Ovambo cattle continued to appear in debates and among the breeding stock of farmers in the northern districts of the police zone up to World War I.

Cementing segregation following a temporary reopening of the police zone border, 1915–ca. 1930

The collapse of German colonial rule and South Africa's takeover changed the conditions for African cattle breeders in the colony in many ways. Prior to the military clash, the northern police zone border was reopened for cattle imports to guarantee the alimentation of the German troops. The German defeat, then, was paralleled by a significant African repastorialisation in central and southern Namibia resulting in the emergence of new African settlements all over the police zone.[42] As a result, the colonial heartland changed from an almost homogenous European settler area into a zone of much more mixed African and European settlement.

In addition, movements of Africans between the former German police zone and territories in the far north of the colony like Owambo were hardly controlled any more,[43] although South Africa took over the general idea of limiting European settlement to central and southern Namibia and closed the northern boundary of the German police zone for Europeans.[44] After the South African forces had occupied the whole country including the far north (i.e. Owambo), the new government lost interest in the police zone boundary and the former police posts along this inner-Namibian border were mostly abandoned. Instead, another spatial

---

Bezirksamt, Outjo, to *Gouvernement*, Windhoek, 11 July 1911, p. 3; NAN, ZBU 1295 O.I.i.2, vol. 1, Ludwig Hölzer, Okaukwejo, to *Gouvernement*, Windhoek, 14 July 1911, p. 5

42 Silvester 1998; Werner 1998: pp. 56–57; Gewald 2000: p. 213

43 For example, in 1915/16 thousands of people from Owambo fled to central Namibia due to famine and Portuguese military attacks. As there was no border control at the police zone boundary these migrations never appeared in colonial statistics stored in the archives and were overlooked by historiography until recently. Miescher 2012: pp. 74–75, referring to Gewald 2003

44 The police zone boundary (i.e. the former northern German police zone boundary) was for the first time defined by the South African military government in 1916 (Martial Law Regulation No. 57); this was repeated in 1919 (Prohibited Areas Proclamation of 2 September 1919; Martial Law Proclamation 15).

segregation, most relevant for cattle breeders, was drawn further south, in the mid of the former German police zone.

The collapse of German rule meant a collapse of the colonial veterinary system based on the control over movements of people and stock, too. After outbreaks of lung sickness, a contagious cattle disease, in central Namibia in 1915, South Africa closed the international border and no imports from Namibia were allowed. Two years later, the international border was opened again for imports south of a deliberately drawn line along the 22nd latitude, lying just north of Windhoek. The territories north of this line were perceived as buffer zones comprising not only the far north like Owambo but also settler farming areas between the 22nd latitude and the northern police zone boundary.

After South Africa was granted the mandate for the territory by the League of Nations, the new colonial power started to install a civil government and began to transform the colony according to the South African settler society's needs. This included rebuilding a functioning state veterinary service, albeit not comparable to the previous German one in quality and quantity.[45] In order to regain control over the spread of contagious animal diseases and mitigate the lack of professional veterinarians in the colony, the police were integrated into the veterinary services.[46]

Another part of the transformation was the concentration of African settlement into reserves at the edges of the European settler area or beyond. The limits of such a European-dominated settler area were still disputed in the early 1920s, especially with regard to the northern boundary. Finally it was decided to draw the line at the police zone boundary by merging the concepts of a European settlement border and of a veterinary border against the threats coming from inner Africa. In 1924 the police zone boundary was closed for all cattle movement whereas the areas south of it were re-opened for unrestricted export to the South African market. To control the newly-defined police zone boundary, henceforth marked with red on the maps and therefore soon referred to as the Red Line, police posts along the border were re-opened or newly established.

The closing of the police zone boundary or Red Line brought an end to a vigorous cattle trade between Owambo and central Namibia which had gained some momentum in the previous years.[47] Classified as potentially 'sick', cattle from

---

45 For example, the number of South African veterinary services totalled seven veterinarians throughout the 1920s which was a considerably smaller number compared to the seventeen veterinarians employed at the end of German rule. Miescher 2012: pp. 84–86

46 In the early 1920s every policeman in the colony was also trained as "sheep inspector" and officially became part of the veterinary services. A process that is described as "veterinarisation of the police". Miescher 2012: p. 90

47 Veterinary permits were needed for taking cattle from and into Ovamboland from 1916. In the early 1920s the border traffic was quite significant, not least in northern direction, and

Owambo were no longer a breeding option for farmers inside the police zone; breeders in the north, on the other hand, no longer had any opportunity to upgrade their breeds through imports from the south. In the face of the difficulties inherent in controlling the movement of stock, the border control was conceptualised to rely not on the police post alone, but on an adjoining stock-free zone of up to 100 kilometres width. However, the stock-free zone was rather imagined than real at the time when the Red Line was established and it took decades to enforce such a zone on the ground.[48]

The re-establishment of the police zone boundary as a combined settlement and veterinary border eventually cemented the segregation and economic isolation of the far northern parts of the colony initiated under German rule.[49] *De iure*, the gates between central and northern Namibia were now definitely closed for Ovambo cattle and smuggling cattle over the border happened—if at all—only on a very small scale. Despite its precarious existence on the ground, the concept of a stock-free zone contributed to an increased symbolic isolation, adding to the physical isolation of Ovambo cattle in settler Namibia.

As a number of veterinary assessments from the late 1920s and early 1930s suggest, these multiple forms of isolation clearly affected the further development of cattle in Owambo.

The 1927 report of the Farm Industry Commission assessed the region's dominant cattle type as considerably degenerated due to inbreeding:

> The Ovambo type of cattle …, which has more or less disappeared from South West Africa owing to the closure of Ovamboland, has become very diminutive and small-boned in consequence of continuous inbreeding, but it possesses a redundancy of beef all the same.[50]

While the Farm Industry Commission at least still commented positively on the breed's good meat productivity, the senior veterinary surgeon in Windhoek more radically stated that cattle from Owambo were "of such an inferior type that there is no inducement for illicit movements".[51]

---

    between January and March 1924 alone 1624 head of cattle were officially transported from central Namibia into Owambo. Miescher 2012: pp. 92–93

48 It was only after World War II that the concept of a supervised stock-free zone got fully implemented. Miescher 2012: especially pp. 151ff

49 The establishment of this border was confirmed in the Prohibited Areas Proclamation in 1928 (Proclamation No. 26 of 1928).

50 Unpublished report: South West Africa, 'Report of the Farm Industry Commission', Windhoek, 1927, p. 26

51 NAN, AGV, 108.V2/70, vol. 2, Senior Veterinary Surgeon, Windhoek, to Director Veterinary Services, Pretoria, 14 September 1931

Whether or not these negative evaluations of breeding stock in Owambo accurately captured the state of breeding in the region must be left open here. We do contend, however, that it was a history of colonial policies working towards the isolation of the Owambo region which prepared the ground for such negative evaluations of Ovambo cattle and possibly affected the actual development of this breed.

Conclusion: Exoticising and rehabilitating the 'Ovambo cattle'

The increasing isolation of the Owambo region formed the foundation for an exoticisation of the Ovambo cattle as discussed in the introductory paragraphs of this chapter. For, at the time when the senior veterinary surgeon in Windhoek seemed to dismiss Ovambo cattle from both the scope of scientific analysis and commercial farming for years to come with his obliterative assessment, the veterinary scientists at Onderstepoort were already working intensively on their 'groundbreaking' study of cattle from Owambo.

The processes of segregation and isolation that had led to their eventual exclusion from colonial breeding practices were now reinterpreted as a stroke of luck: for the Onderstepoort team, the location of the African reserve Ovamboland outside the police zone implied that "Ovambo cattle ha[d] been less disturbed by the march of civilisation than elsewhere in the sub-continent"[52]—and thus still made it possible to obtain cattle "of the pure Ovambo type"[53]. Thus, the Onderstepoort scientists did not only define a standard reference for Ovambo cattle as a breed, but also established the foundation for further research on and experimentation with this breed. They were clearly concerned with documenting and preserving what they regarded as exceptionally "pure native cattle" as an exotic curiosity for generations to come: they provided the Onderstepoort and the Transvaal museum with skeletons and prepared exemplars from their herd.

In spite of this strong tendency towards exoticisation and musealisation, the researchers also highlighted the great breeding potential of these "native" animals due to their excellent adaption to the region's "vicissitudes associated with climatic, physiographic, edaphic and biotic factors" and envisioned the reintegration of such "native cattle" into commercial farmers' breeding schemes.[54] However, instead of acknowledging shortcomings of the breed with regard to the desired standard of excellence as the reverse side of the coin of isolation, the scientists lamented mismanagement on the part of African breeders and called on the administrative authorities for supportive interventions:

---

52 Groenewald/Curson 1933: p. 601
53 Groenewald/Curson 1933: p. 603
54 Groenewald/Curson 1933: pp. 612–613

It is clear that many decades will pass before native cattle under present management can attain the standard of excellence so desired by Europeans. The native idea of selection, e.g. pugnancy in a bull or mere coloration in a cow, etc., being so unscientific, it behoves the administrative authorities in the various tropical and sub-tropical areas to give scientific advice wherever possible.[55]

This paradoxical approach of championing one effect of isolation while failing to confront the other persists in economic and veterinary policies to the present. The 'survival' of indigenous cattle in sub-Saharan Africa—now more generally and neutrally referred to as "Sanga cattle"—continues to be appreciated; in this sense, the Ovambo cattle have been 'rehabilitated' with regard to their qualities and potential for commercial farming in Southern Africa.[56] By way of contrast, disadvantages of the above outlined history of segregation for breeders in northern Namibia, however, continue to exist: the colonial legacy of a continuing prohibition of cattle movements from northern Namibia south into the commercial farming area continues to bar northern breeders from the export market and access to high-standard veterinary services.[57]

References

Bankoff, G. and S. Swart (2007), *Breeds of Empire: The Invention of the Horse in Southeast Asia and Southern Africa 1500–1900*. Copenhagen: NISA Press.

Die Deutsche Kolonial-Gesetzgebung, Vol 1–13. Berlin: Ernst Siegfried Mittler.

Drechsler, H. (1966), *Südwestafrika unter deutscher Kolonialherrschaft: Der Kampf der Herero und Nama gegen den deutschen Imperialismus (1884–1915)*. Berlin: Akademie-Verlag.

Eirola, M. (1992), *The Ovambogefahr: The Ovamboland Reservation in the Making. Political Responses of the Kingdom of Ondonga to the German Colonial Power 1884–1910*. Rovaniemi: Societas Historicae Finlandiae Septentrionalis.

---

[55] Groenewald/Curson 1933: p. 613

[56] In his monograph on the meat industry in Namibia, for example, Rawlinson states: "The Ovambo Sanga is the only indigenous cattle breed to survive the upgrading practices followed by the various Colonial Authorities. [...] Since the 1970s it [the modern Sanga] has attracted great interest among scientists and breeders alike and with improvement through selection and feeding practices, has proved to be formidable opposition for beef breeds indigenous or exotic in South Africa." Rawlinson 1994: p. 75

[57] We thank Dag Henrichsen and Lorena Rizzo for commenting on this chapter at various stages.

Gewald, J.-B. (1999), *Herero Heroes: A Socio-Political History of the Herero of Namibia 1890–1923*. Oxford/Cape Town/Athens (OH): James Currey/David Philip/Ohio University Press.

Gewald, J.-B. (2000), Colonization, Genocide and Resurgence: The Herero of Namibia 1890–1933. In M. Bollig and J.-B. Gewald (eds.), *People, Cattle and Land: Transformations of a Pastoral Society in Southwestern Africa*. Köln: Rüdiger Köppe: 187–226.

Gewald, J.-B. (2003), Near Death in the Streets of Karibib: Famine, Migrant Labour and the Coming of Ovambo to Central Namibia. *Journal of African History*, 44(2): 211–239.

Gilfoyle, D. (2003), Veterinary Research and the African Rinderpest Epizootic: The Cape Colony, 1896–1898. *Journal of Southern African Studies*, 29(1): 133–154.

Gordon, R. (2003), Fido: Dog Tales of Colonialism in Namibia. In W. Beinart and J. McGregor (eds.), *Social History & African Environment*. Oxford/Athens (OH)/Cape Town: James Currey/Ohio University Press/David Philip: 240–254.

Groenewald, J.W. and H.H. Curson (1933), Studies in Native Animal Husbandry(6): A Note on Ovambo Cattle. *Onderstepoort Journal of Veterinary Science and Animal Industry*, 1(2): 601–627.

Henrichsen, D. (2011), *Herrschaft und Identifikation im vorkolonialen Namibia: Das Herero- und Damaraland im 19. Jahrhundert*. Basel/Windhoek: Basler Afrika Bibliographien/ Scientific Society Windhoek.

Kaulich, U. (2001), *Die Geschichte der ehemaligen Kolonie Deutsch-Südwestafrika (1884–1914): Eine Gesamtdarstellung*. Frankfurt a.M.: Peter Lang.

Miescher, G. (2012), *Namibia's Red Line: The History of a Veterinary and Settlement Border*. New York: Palgrave Macmillan.

Miescher, G. (2013), *Die Rote Linie: Die Geschichte der Veterinär- und Siedlungsgrenze in Namibia (1890er–1960er Jahre)*. Basel: Basler Afrika Bibliographien.

Rawlinson, J. (1994), *The Meat Industry of Namibia. 1835–1994*. Windhoek: Gamsberg Macmillan.

Rickmann, W. (1908), *Tierzucht und Tierkrankheiten in Deutsch-Südwestafrika*. Berlin: Schoetz.

Schlettwein, C. (1907), *Der Farmer in Deutsch-Südwestafrika: Eine Darstellung sämtlicher für den afrikanischen Farmer in Betracht kommenden Erbwerbszweige und ein Leitfaden für Anfänger*. Wismar: Hinstorff.

Schlettwein, C. (1911), Zehnjährige züchterische Beobachtungen der Rinderzucht (nach genauen Stammregister & Herdbuchaufzeichnungen). *Landwirtschaftliche Beilage des Amtsblatts für das Schutzgebiet Deutsch-Südwestafrikas*, 1(5): 36–37.

Schlettwein, C. (1914), *Der Farmer in Deutsch-Südwest-Afrika*. Wismar: Hinstorff.

Schmokel, W.W. (1985), The Myth of the White Farmer: Commercial Agriculture in Namibia 1900–1983. *International Journal of African Historical Studies*, 18(1): 93–108.

Schneider, H.P. (1994), *Animal Health and Veterinary Medicine in Namibia*. Windhoek: Agrivet.

Siiskonen, H. (1990), *Trade and Socioeconomic Change in Ovamboland, 1850–1906*. Helsinki: Suomen Historiallinen Jeura/Societas Historica Fennica.

Silvester, J. (1998), Beasts, Boundaries and Buildings: The Survival and Creation of Pastoral Economies in Southern Namibia. In P. Hayes, J. Silvester, M. Wallace and W. Hartmann (eds.) *Namibia under South African Rule: Mobility and Containment 1915–1946*. Oxford: James Currey: 95–116.

Strassegger, R. (1988), Die Wanderarbeit der Ovambo während der deutschen Kolonialbesetzung Namibias: Unter besonderen Berücksichtigung der Wanderarbeiter auf den Diamantenfeldern in den Jahren 1908 bis 1914, (PhD thesis, University of Graz).

Swart, S. (2010), *Riding High: Horses, Humans and History in South Africa*. Johannesburg: Wits University Press.

Van Sittert, L. and S. Swart (2008), *Canis Africanis: A Dog History of Southern Africa*. Leiden/Boston: Brill.

Voegeli, A. (2008), Improving the Cattle, Developing the Colony: Exploring the History of Cattle Imports into Namibia during the German Colonial Period, 1893–1914, (MA Thesis, University of Basel).

Werner, W. (1998), *"No one will become rich": Economy and Society in the Herero Reserves in Namibia, 1915–1946*. Basel: Basler Afrika Bibliographien.

PART III

Plants and Power

CHAPTER 7

Medicinal plants in South Africa

Diana Gibson

Introduction

In South Africa medicinal plants are often approached from different perspectives.[1] These frequently include science and Indigenous Knowledge Systems (IKS), or in a Latourian sense, nature and culture.[2] This was highlighted in 2014 at a South African symposium on medicinal plants. An anthropologist, who made a presentation on the selling, buying and use of such plants in the Eastern Cape, emphasised that plants and nature have long impacted on local people, shaping and being shaped by their beliefs and practices of healing in a vibrant interchange with their biophysical environment.[3] She alluded to the sizeable informal market in medicinal plants in South Africa and calls from the government and conservationists to protect the country's biodiverse natural resources. A biochemist in the sciences of biology and chemistry, said medicinal plants had been "held captive" by culture and should be studied scientifically. A medical biologist emphasised the science of plant-based medicines and presented the results of clinical trials with *Lessertia frutescens*, a medicinal plant powder, which was tested for safety in people.[4] He stressed that knowledge of the medicinal use of plants originated with local community members, such as his grandmother, who had taught him much about it. She did not

---

1   Medicinal plants are those that are turned into medicines in a variety of ways, and the products derived from this process are referred to as plant medicines.
2   IKS is broadly defined as a complex set of knowledge that exists and has been developed around specific conditions of populations and communities indigenous to a particular geographic area (Department of Science and Technology 2004). See also Latour 1993
3   See Alexander 2010; Cocks 2006
4   Phase 1a for safety in healthy people done in Cape Town (Johnson et al. 2007). Phase 2a for safety in people who are HIV positive but do not yet qualify for anti-retrovirals was done in Pietermaritzburg (Wilson et al. 2012); the first trial of its kind in South Africa

know what was in the plant, but she knew that it worked for certain conditions. The biologist's standpoint was that all the scientists are doing is explaining how the plant and the molecules work, and how they function in synergy; i.e, they are intersecting with local knowledge by systematically analysing how it works.

The above presentations indicate the current focus on indigenous medicinal plants in South Africa where a variety of interests converge: debates and concerns in relation to, for example, science and technology, health care, research projects, government legislation and policies, plant markets and commercial interests, as well as conservation.[5] In literature, media representations, policies and discussions on medicinal plants and their products (medicines), are positioned within the domain of traditional healing.[6] Plants and medicinal products have become deeply political, especially concerning the authority of "traditional" healing knowledge and the unregulated economy of plants with therapeutic properties. Respect and fairness in the utilisation and conservation of the environment and plant resources mark the debates on the social and intellectual dimensions and protection of plant-related knowledge and its use.

This chapter argues that medicinal plants are material as well as relational, in that they have histories and are caught in assemblages with people, ecologies, ways of knowing, texts and regulatory networks aimed at protecting indigenous medicinal plants.[7] Medicinal plants are part of nature-cultures, or even multiple natures.[8] I situate it in South Africa and argue that plants are increasingly immersed in modern techno-social arrangements such as laboratories, plant medicine markets, farms, development schemes, and the aims and policies of nature conservation. These assemblages have to be recognised and made visible.[9] To do so, I draw on my own research on medicinal plants, and work done with students in the Western Cape. For this chapter, I refer to a policy document on Traditional Medicine (TM) as a backdrop to my own multilevel argument on the above, and relate it to a wider South African setting.[10]

First there is a brief overview of the institutionalisation of TM in South Africa. I show how such initiatives are part of broader developments in Africa and in the strategies of international agencies like the World Health Organization (WHO).

---

5 The bulk of medicinal plants are sold at plant markets. There is also a strong market in alternative medicine in South Africa that includes the sale of herbal medicines in health shops, pharmacies and some chain stores. Medicinal plants used are cultivated on farms.
6 See Laplante 2009, 2014, 2015; Gibson/Kilian 2013
7 Law 2007: p. 1 stresses that material-semiotics analyse and understand "everything in the social and natural worlds as a continuously generated effect of the webs of relations within which they are located". See also Low 2007; Van Wyk 2008
8 See Haraway 1991; Viveiros de Castro 1996
9 Latour 1993; Michael 2000
10 See Republic of South Africa 2008a/b

I return to IKS in South Africa to show some of the ways in which this process has unfolded. The focus is on traditional plant-based medicines and the politics surrounding the institutionalisation and promotion thereof. The commercialisation and conservation of medicinal plants are scrutinised using South African examples, but with a particular focus on empirical work in the Western Cape. A material semiotic approach enables me to place human activities, material things, ideas and texts at the same level and helps to describe and disentangle "the enactment of materially and discursively heterogeneous relations that produce and reshuffle all kinds of actors".[11] These encompass objects, subjects, ideas, organisation, regulations, commercial and conservation efforts. The social and the natural are understood as effects constantly generated by the material and discursively heterogeneous relational webs within which they are located.

Finally, all of the above are shown to be intertwined with an array of documents and texts, such as the national Department of Health's Draft Policy on Traditional Medicine which supports my argument, principally in relation to the Western Cape.[12]

Institutionalisation of IKS and TM
Background
After 1994 the government took steps to institutionalise TM as part of the new national health care system.[13] This was in line with former President Thabo Mbeki's promotion of African medicine as part of an African renaissance and the Minister of Health Dr Manto Tshabalala-Msimang's support for the traditional use of plant medicines. The government aimed to put TM on the agenda as part of a wider nation-building project, not only to situate South Africa as a leader in and of Africa, but also to advance the field of TM and promote it for the development of a bio-economy. As a result "traditional healers, plant gatherers, petty traders, researchers and private investors were assembling around knowledge about plants".[14]

---

11 Law 2007: p. 1
12 Republic of South Africa 2008b
13 The South African Traditional Medicines Research Group (SATMeRG) was established in 1997. It aimed to advance the study of indigenous TM, as promoted by the WHO. Specific foci were the quality of plant medicines, development of "standards which define their identity, purity and potency" and formulation of related policies and guidelines. Later, an IKS policy was implemented for South Africa, an Institute for African Traditional Medicines was established, a National Indigenous Knowledge Systems Office was created within the Department of Science and Technology, and a draft National Policy on African Traditional Medicine was published in 2009 (Gibson 2011; Republic of South Africa 2009). An annual African Traditional Medicine Day was declared on 31 August.
14 Reihling 2008: p. 1

Unlike traditional Chinese medicine and traditional Indian medicine (Ayurveda), South Africa does not have a written pharmacopeia of TM.[15] Thus IKS and TM must often first be documented and investigated. Policies that aim to standardise and regulate this field are reflected in the development of the National Drug Policy of 1996, the Traditional Health Practitioners Act (22 of 2007), the Medicines and Related Substances Amendment Act (72 of 2008) and the draft Policy on African Traditional Medicine.[16]

The African context and its relation to South Africa

As a signatory to the African Union's Decade of African Traditional Medicine (2001–2010),[17] the South African government is committed to TM, its institutionalisation and the design, creation and implementation of policies and regulatory frameworks, that support the local production of traditional herbal medicines. Signatories were required to endorse the protection, cultivation and conservation of medicinal plants. Efforts were made to promote and protect intellectual property rights.

In 2007 a further declaration was signed, which prioritised research into African traditional herbal medicine and the strengthening of health systems through mechanisms such as scientific clinical trials on traditional plant medicines and the inclusion of traditional herbal medicines, in the lists of essential drugs.[18]

South Africa's research programme on herbal medicines has seen little progress on clinical trials. *Lessertia frutescens* was tested in Phase 1a for safety in healthy adults and Phase 2a for safety in HIV-infected adults who did not yet qualify for anti-retroviral medication.[19] A trial on the possible immunogenic properties of *Lessertia frutescens* in early management of HIV-positive patients has been cleared

---

15 Knowledge about traditionally used plant-based medicines was historically transmitted orally. One exception is a publication based on the notebooks of a Norwegian medical doctor Henrik Greve Blessing. He wrote them when visiting Natal between 1901 and 1904. Blessing described 98 plants, their Zulu names and local uses. The Norwegian government handed the original manuscripts over to the South African government in 2013. See Smestad Paulsen et al. 2012

16 Department of Health 1996; Republic of South Africa 2008a and b, 2009

17 World Health Organization 2011

18 For example, some African signatories such as Burkina Faso, Cameroon, Democratic Republic of Congo and Madagascar had included TM on their National Essential Medicines List (all for malaria) by 2011. In Mali *Argemone mexicana* decoctions have undergone a trial for the treatment of uncomplicated malaria. In Nigeria a plant medicine, based on traditional local treatment recipes, underwent a trial under the name Niprisan, for the treatment of sickle cell anaemia. See Siegfried/Hughes 2012

19 The numbers used, such as 1a, 2a and 2b above relate to the different phases of trials according to the regulatory framework set out by the Medicines Control Council (MCC). At each phase only specific kinds of trials can be done. See Johnson et al. 2007

by the South African Medicines Control Council (SAMCC).[20] There is also an unpublished trial on *Hoodia gordonii* for weight loss in South Africa.[21] The local herbal medicine, *Pelargonium sidoides—umckalaobo*—has undergone clinical trials in Russia and the Ukraine.[22] Unlike a number of other signatories to the African Union (AU) agreement, the South African government's anticipated support for the development of clinical trials on local plant medicines is proving to be complicated, with an array of regulatory documents and fraught with politics.[23] As a result, traditional herbal medicines have not been included on the essential drugs list.

Science and TM contestations
Making plant medicines scientific

While research on indigenous knowledge systems has in principle been promoted by various portfolio committees of the South African government, it has also been politicised, scrutinised and contested by different interest groups.[24] The initial impetus to promote the use of herbal medicine products in primary health care became deeply political and subsequently stalled in the wake of the controversy and contestation around HIV/AIDS, anti-retrovirals and the Treatment Action Campaign's strong opposition to the use of medicinal plants. Much of the objection to plant-based medicine was related to its being positioned as 'cultural', based in 'belief' and thus as inherently unscientific.[25] Instead of her rolling out a programme of anti-retroviral treatment, Dr Tshabalala-Msimang's promotion of TMs and nutritional resources was seen as flying in the face of science. Other issues included a lack of standardisation and concerns about the safety of plant-based medicines.[26] A perceived reluctance to address AIDS head-on hardened the scrutiny of plants

---

20 Participant 1, Cape Town, 6 November 2014, interview by Diana Gibson
21 In 2003, after legal action and negotiations about the filing of an international patent by the CSIR on Hoodia and its sale to Phytopharm (UK) to develop a drug, the San acquired a share of royalties from its sale. The Director of Phytopharm reportedly had been told that the San people were extinct.
22 Siegfried/Hughes 2012
23 The AU meeting in Zambia declared 2001–2010 the Decade of African Traditional Medicine. The agreement also addresses the contribution of Traditional Medicine to sustainable well-being, health development and poverty alleviation.
24 Flint 2012; Green 2008a, 2008b, 2012; Gibson/Kilian 2013; Lukani 2011; Xaba 2007
25 Van Niekerk 2012
26 The issue of safety has been raised by medical doctors and/or pharmacists in every forum where I have presented a paper on medicinal plants and their uses. Yet an extensive study on acute poisoning cases seen in a selection of South African hospitals showed the following causes: household chemicals (45.7%), modern medicines (17.5%), animal/insect bites (15.8%), agrochemical chemicals (9.7%), food poisoning (5.4%), drug abuse (3.3%), Traditional Medicines (2.4%), and plants (0.2%). See Malangu/Ogunbanjo 2009

through the lens of science.[27] For example, the draft National Policy on African Traditional Medicine, which is discussed in more depth below, had an ambiguous reception in health care circles.[28] While defining TM in an encompassing way, the policy emphasised that herbal medicines should be carefully scrutinised for safety and quality.[29] Many traditional health practitioners were adamant that such medicines were holistic and should by definition not be scientifically tested and the South African Medical Association (SAMA) issued a position paper stating that TM was not quantifiable through empirical scientific methods. The KwaZulu-Natal (KZN) Midlands Branch Council of SAMA responded that many medicinal plants were poisonous, suggesting that herbals be subjected to rigorous scientific study.[30] In 2013 Minister of Health Dr Aaron Motsoaledi unequivocally stated that "… all our policies in the Department of Health must be evidence-based".[31] Medicinal plants are thus increasingly scrutinised through the lens of science.[32]

While the promotion of indigenous plant-based medicines in the national health care system has faltered in South Africa, their potential as a field of scientific research and contributor to the economy has been more strongly emphasised. Herbal medicines and the knowledge related to them have been moving into the ambit of the Department of Science and Technology. The department's 2014 Bio-economy Strategy unambiguously declares that "the country's rich biodiversity and indigenous knowledge systems provide significant resources for bioprospecting herbal medicines/African TMs", as a flagship initiative.[33] Traditional plant medicine is thus shifting to the shared domain of science, technology and the bio-economy, rather than being solely situated in that of health.

Harvesting and marketing

While much of the debate and the texts generated concerning TMs and their related knowledge have set these up in a dichotomy with science, a material semiotic approach tries to address all knowledge on the same terms and for the

---

27 See Nattrass 2008. The author refers to the biomedical sciences, pharmacology and biochemistry.
28 Republic of South Africa 2008b
29 According to the document, TM draws on indigenous cultural wisdom and a concern for the well-being of the individual, the community and environment. Being unwell is perceived as a disruption of balance—between community members, the community and the ancestors etc. and healing is focused on restoring balance. Traditional medicines are thus enacted as holistic, spiritual and aimed at creating and maintaining equilibrium and as part of IKS.
30 KZN Midlands Branch Council, SAMA 2009: p. 206
31 Motsoaledi 2013: http://www.gov.za/keynote-address-health-minister-dr-aaron-motsoaledi-joint-nih-mrc-south-africa-research-summit-hiv (accessed 17 June 2013)
32 Particularly the biomedical sciences, pharmacy and biochemistry
33 Department of Science and Technology 2014

same reasons.³⁴ For Latour it is necessary to apply the same language, for instance, to knowledge and belief, human beings and material objects; or (to overcome the nature/society divide) as actors and actants, as he calls them. This applies equally to Western and African societal settings, or scientific and local knowledge practices.³⁵ Plants-as-medicines can thus not be detached from politics or current forms of social organisation and commercial activity, involving their cultivation, production and distribution.

In South Africa most medicinal plants are harvested in the wild by women and sold to and by local users, traditional healers, herbalists, *amayeza* or *intelezi* shops and *muthi* markets.³⁶ The sale of medicinal plants is big business. According to Street and Prinsloo, in 2013, up to 700,000 tonnes of plant material at a value of about US$150 million (about R2,400 million) was consumed annually by locals.³⁷ The trade in medicinal plants in South Africa is expanding so rapidly that wild stocks are being depleted and some species are extinct outside protected areas. These include the pepper bark tree (*Warburgia salutaris*) and wild ginger (*Siphonochilus aethiopicus*). A survey done in Cape Town found that around 1,300 tonnes of plant material is traded as TM locally, of which approximately 260 tonnes is harvested within the boundaries of the city, and 320 tonnes per year elsewhere in the province. The value of this informal market trading was approximately R170 million per year by 2014.³⁸

The knowledge about, access to and utilisation of medicinal plants run concurrently in the private, communal and public domains.³⁹ While traditional health practitioners know about and use medicinal plants, many people visit plant traders for information about ways in which to utilise the plants, and their uses.⁴⁰ The issue of intellectual property or, as Hayden writes in relation to South America, the "proper" parties of interest and knowledge that "come with" the plants, is much debated,⁴¹ as is the case in South Africa.⁴² Like the landscapes or environments that they inhabit, the plants are represented as somehow passive.⁴³ In material semiotics such plants would be understood as actants, i.e. material things that not only interact with humans and human factors in networks, but also affect them.

---

34 Latour 2004; Anderson et al. 2013: p. 281
35 Rottenburg 1998: pp. 62–54
36 Dold/Cocks 2002; Gibson/Kilian 2013
37 Street/Prinsloo 2013
38 Petersen 2014
39 See Rutert 2010; Rutert et al. 2011
40 See Cocks/Moller 2002; Olivier 2011; Philander et al. 2014
41 Hayden 2003: p. 128
42 See Rutert 2010; Rutert et al. 2011
43 See Whatmore 2002

Conservation

Access to plant biodiversity has progressively become a terrain of disagreement between traditional healers, herbalists and *kruiedokters* or *bossiesdokters*—who stress land-use and the plant-harvesting rights of local people, compared with conservation scientists and environmentalists who are concerned about the protection of the environment and biodiversity, including medicinal plants.[44] At the same time, environmentalism in South Africa is closely intertwined with the "scientific validation of nature" and the latter, in turn, is perceived as incontrovertible and "ideologically neutral".[45] In relation to conservation there is contention surrounding the harvesting and preservation of medicinal plant material, including access to and control of the environment in which it grows, because the bulk of the medicinal plants bought and sold in South Africa is still harvested in the wild. Since 1990, concerns for the conservation of the environment and plant biodiversity have increasingly intersected with development discourses and the politics of land restitution.[46] According to Weiner "every environmental story" is linked to power.[47] The environmental history of South Africa in relation to its medicinal plants was initially one of control but it has increasingly become one of activism,[48] involving contestations about "who best understands African environments, and who should have the right to control them—scientists, national governments, or local people".[49]

Plant medicines and their histories in the Western Cape

The documentation and research of medicinal plants has gained new impetus through policy developments and scientific and social science research, with some anthropological studies tending to understand medicinal plants as mostly acting at the level of meaning and symbolism.[50] Others focus on medicinal plants and "ecologies of well-being" to highlight numerous ways in "which plants, people and world bring one another into being".[51] Dold and Cocks illustrate how in the Eastern Cape people see the forest as providing food, medicines, animals, water or fuel, but also as an ancestral dwelling-place where children can learn about *isithethe* (the manner of doing things) of the amaXhosa.[52]

---

44 Carruthers 2014; Alexander 2010
45 Olivier 2011: p. 12
46 Walker, 2010; Olivier 2011
47 Weiner 2005: p. 409
48 Carruthers 2014; Alexander 2010
49 Beinart/McGregor 2003: p. 2
50 See Thornton 2009
51 Cohen 2013: p. 90
52 Dold/Cocks 2002: p. 17

In the Western Cape, knowledge of medicinal plants is often associated with the wisdom of the elders and intermixed with an array of knowledge heritages.[53] The first is Khoisan medicine, or what Van Wyk refers to as Cape herbal medicine, which reflects the intermixing of Khoisan ancestral healing knowledge and medicinal plants with historical Cape Dutch influences.[54] Such knowledge is increasingly the concern of herbal science and medicine research.[55] Current anthropological studies in the Western Cape show that local healing knowledge is dispersed and fragmented.[56] It includes historical as well as current ethnobotanical and medicinal plant knowledge, and related healing practices of the Khoisan—past and present— and other local users. Such knowledge is not yet well documented in South Africa.[57]

The Western, Northern and Eastern Cape contain the largest groups of descendants of people formerly referred to as the Khoisan, even though they were officially made to "disappear" through implementation of the Population Registration Act of 1950. Khoisan descendants were classified as "coloured", effectively effacing their identity, and assigning their healing knowledges and practices to the past.[58] Such knowledge and practices were also suppressed through cultural assimilation and the missionisation of South Africa.[59]

Where medicinal plants used by Khoisan have been recorded, they appear in large collections on medicinal plants in South Africa and Namibia.[60] Van Wyk reviewed the limited and dispersed historical material related to Khoisan and Cape Dutch medicines and emphasised the small number of formal and informal publications on current medicinal plant-use as related to Cape herbal medicine.[61] Information about the knowledge and practice of healing by indigenous people of the Cape has become scattered over time.[62] One group of people with knowledge of medicinal plants and their usage who are consistently identified are the herbalists or *bossiesdokters* (also called *kruiedokters*),[63] as well as Rastafarian healers.[64] A second

---

53 Green 2012
54 Low 2008; Van Wyk 2008
55 Avula et al. 2009; Johnson et al. 2007; Zhang et al. 2014
56 Gibson 2011
57 Van Wyk 2008; Cohen 2009
58 This is a racially defined category according to the Act. It has been retained by the new government for the purposes of equity. See Carstens 1966
59 Elbourne/Ross 1997
60 Van Wyk et al. 2000; Von Koenen 1996
61 Van Wyk 2008. See also Archer 1990; Cohen 2009; Ferreira 1987; Klaasen et al. n.d.; Montagu Museum 1998; Thring/Weitz 2006; Van Wyk et al. 2000
62 Laidler 1928; Lichtenstein 1812; Paterson 1789; Shapera 1934; Sparrman 1785
63 Archer 1990; Cohen 2013; Gibson 2011
64 In the Western Cape, Rastafarian herbalists represent their plant-related knowledge as strongly linked to their Khoisan heritage. See Oliver 2011 and Philander 2011 for more extensive discussions on this issue.

group are older people,[65] referred to as *die ou mense*. The knowledge of the latter is *oumensraad* (knowledge or advice given by the elders) and forms part of a system of knowledge which transcends the false boundaries of race introduced by colonial authorities, later entrenched in legislation by the apartheid regime and largely kept intact by the post-1994 democratic government.[66] *Oumensraad* is often associated with coloured people whose knowledge of medicinal plants is traceable to their intermixed Khoisan, South East Asian slave, African and European ancestry.[67]

According to Smith the historical emergence of self-treating medicinal knowledge was affected by interaction between Dutch settlers and Khoisan people and the incorporation of their knowledge into a wider Cape pharmacopoeia.[68] Cape herbal medicine knowledge constantly shifts according to the times and the setting, responding to changing physical, and socio-economic environments and selecting whatever proves most efficacious and feasible for a particular moment or need.[69]

The mediation of texts

The above histories, knowledge and politics of plant medicine are intertwined with an array of documents, inscriptions, technologies of translation and mediation, and "mobilisations of the world".[70] The aforementioned draft policy (and others) on TM are valued for their empirical content, but also should be read genealogically and with attention to the documents, as having the historical agency to define, and thus constituting, "subjects, objects and domains".[71] They mediate the relations between these and make the institutionalisation process possible. Thus the policy document, and related policies and legislation that have been signed into law, have to be approached as reports on real events and developments, and concurrently as inscriptions that have their own social and ontological efficacy.[72] In this regard Nimmo writes,

> texts are not dislocated from practice but are intrinsic to practices—indeed there is scarcely a practice in the modern world that does not have its accompanying texts, often a panoply of texts, without which the practice would be deprived of the oxygen of its networks.[73]

---

65 Cohen 2009; Davids 2012; Ferreira 1987; Klaasen et al. n.d.; Nortje 2012
66 Cohen 2009; Levine 2013
67 See Cohen 2009: p. 19
68 Smith 1996
69 Philander 2011; Olivier 2011
70 Latour 1999: p. 99
71 Latour 1999: p. 100
72 Nimmo 2011
73 Nimmo 2011: p. 114

As indicated above, the draft policy and other related documents and texts are accordingly enactments of reality, or ways by which certain things are made current and present. In the process, particular ontologies are performed or enacted into being: for example, medicinal plants as constituents of indigenous knowledge and traditional healing. Texts (such as the draft policy) are hybrids created by this process. The document is a material thing that also mediates relations between subjects, objects and other texts. The draft policy constitutes a particular history in relation to medicinal plants—they are made part of the heritage of TM as a system of knowledge (IKS), which was historically negated or suppressed by the colonial and apartheid governments in South Africa. In the post-apartheid era the document recognises the role such plants historically played as part of the hidden or unofficial health care of disenfranchised South Africans in urban and rural settings. The draft policy can be viewed as a mobile, material inscription, i.e. an active agent that assembles, shapes and connects practices. In doing so it enacts objects, constitutes subjects, and inscribes relations, ontological demarcations and domains.[74]

The draft policy gives us insight into the historical assemblages from which it emerged.[75] These include the presidency of Thabo Mbeki with his attempts to revitalise African pride. For the purposes of developing a draft policy, a range of actors was (briefly) assembled. A presidential task team on African Traditional Medicine (ATM) was appointed in 2006 to make recommendations on national policy and to create "an appropriate, legal framework for the institutionalisation of ATM" (Interview: participant 2).[76] Membership of the task team became increasingly politicised before it was disbanded. Subsequently a Ministerial Task Team under the auspices of the Minister of Health was appointed to consult with stakeholders, and prepare policies and documents on TM.[77]

---

74   Nimmo 2011: p. 114
75   Nimmo 2011
76   Members of the presidential task team included Professor Herbert Vilakazi, special adviser to KZN Premier S'bu Ndebele; University of Johannesburg Botany Professor Ben Erik van Wyk; Medical Research Council President Professor Anthony Mbewu; KZN Health Department official Dr Sibongile Zungu; and Advocate Christine Qunta. This task team was almost exclusively representative of Kwazulu-Natal and Gauteng provinces. Participant 2, Cape Town 13 May 2013, interview by Diana Gibson
77   The task team included professionals (in pharmacy, health care, private health care), representatives of the national departments of Health, of Environment Affairs and Tourism, of Agriculture, of Trade and Industry as well as from committee services and of medicines and regulatory affairs. This Ministerial Task Team is not referred to in the document, even though they produced a report on the restructuring of the Medicines Regulatory Affairs and Medicines Control Council as well as recommendations for the new Regulatory Authority for Health Products of South Africa. The reason for this probably lies in the fact that the Presidential Task Team was closely connected to the Office of President Thabo Mbeki in support of his call for an African renaissance.

According to a participant in the 2006 process:

> The policy document draws on major tenets from national drug policy which in 1996 already was being finalised with the Department of Health and all of its instruments. The tenets of the national drug policy is very strong on Traditional Medicine. To understand this, it is necessary to return to the commissions of the ANC, which determined its policy on health, and helped to shape the future policy. Most of the work flows from the national drug policy. Also, in 2001 the African Union indicated that there should be institutionalisation of TM: it was even termed the Decade of Traditional Medicine.
>
> There were large meetings in Johannesburg, with several hundred traditional healers, academics, experts and such. There were interpreters for four language groups, breakaway groups and commissions, etcetera. It was a challenge. While the idea was to consult everyone, it was also challenging because people there often had very different paradigms, experiences, education etc.[78]

The policy document thus relates objects, texts, and knowledge systems. It makes connections between committees, the African Union, the national health care and legal systems, traditional healers, specialists, academics, interpreters, and an array of documents and referenced academic texts, as well as between the knowledge bodies represented by formal health care, science and traditional knowledge.

African TM is enacted as a hybrid, linking the cosmos, nature and human actors. TM is thus social and natural, involving actors and actants, i.e. the seen and unseen worlds, such as ancestral shades and spirits. It includes indigenous plants—wild-harvested (and cultivated) biological materials and commercially produced traditional plant medicines. In this regard the policy document states that African TM does not regard nature as a neutral entity but as a "living force" and states that TM promotes a "humane relationship and understanding between human beings and nature".[79] This representation of nature may be somewhat romanticised and perhaps even posed as an alternative to the "environmentality" of the state.[80] It also does not take into consideration the historical reality of groups of people in particular parts of the country. In the Western Cape, for instance, Olivier found that Rastafarian healers in Stellenbosch and Paarl made sense of "their being-with-nature as in conflict with, and as a possible alternative to" the emphasis on

---

78 Participant 2, Cape Town 13 May 2013, interview by Diana Gibson
79 Republic of South Africa 2009: p. 9
80 Olivier 2011: p. 43; Alexander 2010

commercialisation of medicinal plants, or its control and regulation through state-driven initiatives.[81] In this regard Petersen argues that national and international conservation objectives concerning the protection of medicinal plants of the Cape floristic region run counter to those of traditional healers and small traders who often harvest illegally.[82]

Although the policy document enacts TM as open and fluid, it also puts boundaries on it. As Latour and Woolgar argue "writing is not so much a method of transferring information as a material operation of creating order".[83] TMs and herbals are enacted as lacking stable, firmly established characteristics or attributes.[84] Because TM knowledge is seen as manifold, discontinuous and dispersed, TM and herbals need to be formalised through institutional processes and scientifically scrutinised.[85] Its margins must be drawn for it to be regulated and protected, but also operationalised in particular ways. Much of the controversy about plants-as-medicines has to do with its naturalness. This is another way in which it is enacted in the national policy. Unlike pharmaceuticals, traditional plant-based medicines are enacted as a kind of pseudo-science, with its use being based in practice and belief and thus open to unintended mistakes and consequences—all the more reason for connecting it to scientific methods and regulation. As one of my research participants pointed out, the National Drug Policy

> is actually quite strong on TM. It defines it in line with WHO guidelines and this informed the draft policy on Traditional Medicine (and other documents), that was gazetted under the auspices of the Department of Health, as well as the Medicines and Related Substances Amendment Act which makes it possible to register such a medicine or to do trials on it. The aim was to advance the rational use of TMs, as advocated by the WHO. I use 'rational' here to mean informed or judicious use, rather than trying to argue that TM is based in superstition. The goal was to focus especially on the quality of plant medicines and to develop 'standards which define their identity, purity and potency' and to formulate and develop policies and guidelines in this regard.[86]

To do so it needs to be documented, systematised, and codified, *inter alia*, so that it can be scientifically studied, as well as protected as part of South Africa's cultural

---

81 Olivier 2011: p. 43
82 Petersen 2014
83 Latour/Woolgar 1979: p. 24
84 Stengers 2010
85 Ellen/Harris 2000
86 Follow-up participant 2 in Cape Town, 5 December 2013, interview by Diana Gibson

heritage and its biodiversity. The document puts the conservation of medicinal plants firmly under the control of the Department of Environmental Affairs.

In the Western Cape, where our research is situated, the protection and permission for the wild harvesting of medicinal plants falls under Cape Nature, which further situates it in the realm of agriculture, forestry and land usage. Our local participants and an array of herbalists stressed the problems of accessing medicinal plants. Petersen writes about the open spaces surrounding Cape Town and the Cape Peninsula with its mountains, beaches, wetlands, marsh areas (*vleie*), agricultural land and conservancy areas, a biome where some 3000 plant species grow, of which 70% are endemic.[87] This plant diversity is promoted for tourism and outdoor activities, as well as its research potential: all middle-class concerns. In contrast, thousands of poor people in townships and informal settlements harvest and informally trade these plants. As Alexander emphasises, even though the current trend is increasingly towards community-based conservation, local people are often either silent about this aspect or not much involved in conservation planning and policy.[88] The latter is left to the jurisdiction of qualified conservation officials and researchers.[89]

Through the policy, medicinal plants are enacted as representative of nature and regarded as being under threat as a result of over-exploitation. In this regard the value of collected and traded medicinal plants from the Cape Floristic Region (CFR) is estimated at R75 million per year.[90] For TMs to survive for future consumption, the increasingly problematic relationship between people, plants and the environment is foregrounded in the policy. Harvesting in the wild is viewed as a potential threat for biodiversity, since it is often done without permits (thus, illegally). As a result of the reduction in wild plants, harvesters are increasingly targeting the plants in protected areas.[91] In the case of Cape Town, Petersen et al. highlight that harvesting of about 70% of plants locally is done so in a non-sustainable way, and 28% of the plant species collected in the city have a status of "vulnerable to endangered" according to the World Conservation Union Red List.[92] Such collection happens most regularly in areas close to local settlements. In the rest of the Western Cape access to wild medicinal plants is fairly (or unfairly) controlled. The lands around towns are mostly farms or conservancy areas and they are restricted, fenced in and not readily accessible.

In places where we have been working intensively in the Western Cape, people utilise plant medicines more frequently if they have easy access to land and plant

---

87 Petersen 2014: p. 1
88 Alexander 2010
89 Alexander 2010: p. 3
90 Peterson 2014
91 Department of Water and Forestry 2005
92 Peterson et al. 2012

resources.[93] If there is a village or town commons, medicinal plants are often more readily available. If there are local *kruiedokters* (herbalists), people will visit them; or if a Rastafarian sells plant medicines people will buy them. If a settlement is surrounded by farms, people are more likely to harvest plant medicines that grow by the roadside. We found that between 65% and 77% of the people surveyed utilise medicinal plants for chronic conditions such as diabetes, high blood pressure, chronic coughing or common colds. They also take it to increase their strength and to enhance resistance to illnesses. Most of the plants are acquired from plant sellers.

Conclusion

By using a material semiotic approach it was possible to illustrate how the policy document as a text (including anyone who reads or writes about it, and the author), weaves various layers of information together to divulge complexities. In doing so it re-enacts subordinated knowledges, such as African traditional healing and TM, and traces relations not only between humans but also the manifold networks and "mediations of a heterogeneous collective" that exists between TM as a commodity but also a product (of particular kinds) of inter-species relations.[94] The medicines are essentially plant material prepared in various ways, mixed together and infused with minerals, water, alcohol and animal matter. They are used principally for humans, sometimes for animals, and to appease or address the ancestors—thus in reality implicated in particular health-promoting and healing-related relationships between species. In this regard, plants are actants in a material semiotic sense.

As this chapter indicates, like the wider process of institutionalisation of plant medicines, the draft policy also has a political dimension. At the same time the exclusion of TM is shifting to its recognition and inclusion. The policies, legislation, academic texts and assortment of documents generated act as technologies of "translation and mediation", which mobilise the world in particular ways.[95]

Thus the concept of TM, *inter alia* as promoted by the government, should be approached with caution, especially if there seems to be an underlying assumption that it is somehow "authentically" originating from a homogenous community or communities. This is important in South Africa where colonisation and apartheid legislation have given way to political and economic change, people have become mobile and communities are more heterogeneous than in the past.[96] This means that TM knowledge has become dispersed and it essentially complicates related issues of intellectual property.[97]

---

93 As indicated above, this research has not been published yet.
94 Nimmo 2011: p. 114
95 Nimmo 2011: p. 114; Latour 1999: pp. 99–100
96 King/Peralvo 2010
97 Gibson/Kilian 2013

The gradual establishment of regulation of TM alongside the emergence of its potential mass commercialisation and contestations concerning its possible incorporation into the health care system, is transforming it. The draft policy, for instance, is a framework to institutionalise TM, and with all its related texts, Acts of Law, state interventions and regulations it is itself an actant within relational environments. It mediates and facilitates the construction of "particular networks". In the process the documents are circulating inscription devices. They are both discursive and material, emerging from and embedded within "multiple ensembles of human-nonhuman relations and practices".[98]

What is currently lacking in South African scholarship are approaches that try to make sense of TM and medicinal plants as a domain of relations, mediated and transformed not only by people but also by molecules, medicinal plants, local legislation, policy and regulatory frameworks, technologies, biological materials, markets and eco-systems.[99]

References

Alexander, J. (2010), Stories from Forest, River and Mountain: Exploring Children's Cultural Environmental Narratives and their Role in the Transmission of Cultural Connection to and Protection of Biodiversity, (MA Thesis, Rhodes University).

Anderson, T., K. Draper, G. Duggan, L. Green, A. Farre, J. Rogerson, S. Ragaller and M. van Zyl (2013), Conservation Conversations: Improving the Dialogue between Fishers and Fisheries Science along the Benguela West Coast. In L. Green (ed.), *Contested Ecologies: Dialogues in the South on Nature and Knowledge*. Cape Town: HSRC Press: 187–201.

Archer, F.M. (1990), Planning with People-Ethnobotany and African Uses of Plants in Namaqualand (South Africa). *Mitteilungen aus dem Institut fuer Allgemeine Botanik Hamburg*, 23: 959–972.

---

98 Nimmo 2011: p. 116

99 I am indebted to the study participants who generously shared their knowledge and ideas with me. Thanks to Denver Davids who managed four randomised surveys on the use of medicinal plants (as well as allopathic medicines) to treat diabetes type 2, high blood pressure and common colds in 1137 households in four towns in the Matzikama district. My gratitude also to Tihana Nathen, Michelle Pasquallie and Hameedah Parker who assisted with the collection of survey data. The results of the surveys are still unpublished. The students are also doing their own individual research projects. I also analysed documents and did my own ethnographic fieldwork with local healers, herbalists, pharmacists, physiologists and botanists. All participants were offered anonymity. The project is registered with full ethical clearance.

Avula, B., Y. Wang, Z. Ali, T. Smillie, V. Filion, A. Cuerrier, A. Arnason and I. Kahn (2009), RP-HPLC Determination of Phenylalkanoids and Monoterpenoids in *Rhodiolarosea* and Identification by LC-ESI-TOF. *Biomedical Chromatography*, 23(8): 865–872.

Beinart, W. and J. McGregor (2003), *Social History and African Environments*. Oxford/Athens/Cape Town: James Currey/Ohio University Press/David Philip.

Carstens, W.P. (1966), *The Social Structure of a Cape Coloured Reserve*. Cape Town.

Carruthers, J. (2014), Environmental History with an African Edge. In C. Mauch and L. Robin (eds.), 'The Edges of Environmental History: Honouring Jane Carruthers', *RCC Perspectives*, 1: 9–16.

Cocks, M. (2006), Wild Resources and Practices in Rural and Urban Households in South Africa: Implications for Bio-cultural Diversity Conservation. *ISER Monograph*, 3.

Cocks, M. and V. Moller (2002), Use of Indigenous and Indigenised Medicines to Enhance Personal Well-being: A South African Case Study. *Social Science and Medicine*, 54(3): 387–397.

Cohen, J. (2009), Medicine from the Father: *Bossiesmedisyne*, People, and Landscape in Kannaland. *Anthropology Southern Africa*, 32(1&2): 18–26.

Cohen, J. (2013), Cultivating Krag, Refreshing Gees: Ecologies of Wellbeing in Namaqualand. In: L. Green (ed.), *Contested Ecologies. Dialogues in the South on Nature and Knowledge*. Cape Town: HSRC Press: 90–109.

Davids, D. (2012), Materia Medica and Care: A Study of the uses of Medicinal Herbs and Remedies as a Form of Treatment and Negotiating Social Relationships in Cape Town and Surroundings, (MA Thesis, University of the Western Cape).

Department of Health, Republic of South Africa (1996), National Drug Policy for South Africa. http://apps.who.int/medicinedocs/documents/s17744en/s17744en.pdf. Accessed 14 February 2008.

Department of Science and Technology, Republic of South Africa (2004), *Indigenous Knowledge Systems Policy*. Pretoria.

Department of Science and Technology, Republic of South Africa (2014), The Bio-economy Strategy. www.innovus.co.za/media/Bioeconomy_Strategy.pdf. Accessed 15 December 2014.

Dold, A. and M. Cocks (2002), The Trade in Medicinal Plants in the Eastern Cape Province, South Africa. *South African Journal of Science*, 98(11&12): 589–597.

Elbourne, E. and R. Ross (1997), Combating Spiritual and Social Bondage: Early Missions in the Cape Colony. In R. Elphick and R. Davenport (eds.), *Christianity in South Africa: A Political, Social and Cultural History*. Berkeley: University of California Press: 31–50.

Ellen, R. and H. Harris (2000), Introduction. In R. Ellen, P. Parkes and A. Bicker (eds.), *Indigenous Environmental Knowledge and its Transformations*. Amsterdam: Harwood Academic Publishers, pp. 1–33.

Ferreira, M. (1987), Medicinal Use of Indigenous Plants by Elderly Coloureds: A Sociological Study of Folk Medicine. *South African Journal of Sociology*, 18(4): 139–143.

Flint, K. (2012), Reinventing "Traditional Medicine" in Postapartheid South Africa. In D. Gordon and S. Krech III (eds.), *Indigenous Knowledge and the Environment in Africa and North America*. Athens, Ohio: Ohio University Press: 259–286.

Gibson, D. (2011), Ambiguities in the Making of an African Medicine: Clinical Trials of *Sutherlandia frutescens (L.) R.Br (Lessertia frutescens)*. *African Sociological Review*, 15(1): 123–136.

Gibson, D. and S. Kilian (2013), The Making of Sutherlandia as Medicine. In L. Green (ed.), *Contested Ecologies. Dialogues in the South on Nature and Knowledge*. Cape Town: HRSC Press: 83–104.

Green, L. (2008a), 'Indigenous Knowledge' and 'Science': Reframing the Debate on Knowledge Diversity. *Archaeologies: Journal of the World Archaeological Congress*, 4(1): 144–163.

Green, L. (2008b), 'Indigenous Knowledge' and the Sciences: Towards a Research Agenda. In N. Shepherd and S. Robins (eds.), New *South African Keywords*. Johannesburg: Jacana Media: 132–142.

Green, L. (2012), Beyond South Africa's 'Indigenous Knowledge – Science' Wars. *South African Journal of Science*, 108(7/8): 44–54.

Haraway, D. (1991), A Cyborg Manifesto: Science, Technology, and Socialist-Feminism in the Late Twentieth Century. In D. Haraway, *Simians, Cyborgs, and Women: the Reinvention of Nature*. New York: Routledge: 149–182.

Hayden, C. (2003), *When Nature Goes Public: The Making and Unmaking of Bioprospecting in Mexico*. Princeton: Princeton University Press.

Johnson, Q., J. Syce, H. Nell, K. Rudeen and W. Folk (2007), A Randomized, Double-blind, Placebo-controlled Trial of *Lessertia frutescens* in Healthy Adults. *PLoS Clinical Trials*. 2(4): e16.

King, B. and M. Peralvo (2010), Coupling Community Heterogeneity and Perceptions of Conservation in Rural South Africa. *Human Ecology*, 38(2): 265–281.

Klaasen, J., F. Weitz, W. Mabusela and Q. Johnson (n.d.), *Medicinal Herbs of the Hardeveld*. Bellville: SA Herbal Science and Medicines Institute, University of the Western Cape.

KZN Midlands Branch Council, SAMA (2009), African Traditional Medicine. *South African Medical Journal*, 99(4): 206.

Laidler, P. (1928), The Magic Medicine of the Hottentots. *South African Journal of Science*, 25: 433–447.

Laplante, J. (2009), South African Roots towards Global Knowledge: Music or Molecules? *Anthropology Southern Africa*, 32(1&2): 8–17.

Laplante, J. (2014), On Knowing and Not Knowing "Life" in Molecular Biology and Xhosa Healing: Ontologies in the Preclinical Trial of a South African Indigenous Medicine (Muthi). *Anthropology of Consciousness*, 25(1): 1–31.

Laplante, J. (2015), *Healing Roots: Anthropology in Life and Medicine*. Oxford/New York: Berghahn Books.

Latour, B. (1993), *We Have Never Been Modern*. Cambridge: Harvard University Press.

Latour, B. (1999), *Pandora's Hope: Essays on the Reality of Science Studies*. Cambridge: Harvard University Press.

Latour, B. (2004), Why Has Critique Run out of Steam? From Matters of Fact to Matters of Concern. *Critical Inquiry*, 30(2): 225–248.

Latour, B and S. Woolgar (1979), *Laboratory Life: The Construction of Scientific Facts*. Princeton and New Jersey: Princeton University Press.

Law, J. (2007), Actor Network Theory and Material Semiotics. http://heterogeneities.net/publications/Law2007ANTandMaterialSemiotics.pdf. Accessed January 2009.

Levine, S. (2013), *Medicine and the Politics of Knowledge*. Cape Town: HSRC Press.

Lichtenstein, M. (1812), *Travels in South Africa in the Years 1803–4–5 and 6*. Translated by A. Plumptree. London: Henry Colburn.

Low, C. (2007), Different Histories of Buchu: Euro-American Appropriation of San and Khoekhoe Knowledge of Buchu Plants. *Environment and History*, 13(3): 333–361.

Low, C. (2008), *Khoisan Medicine in History and Practice*. Köln: R. Köppe.

Lukani, M. (2011), Parliament Spells out Role of Traditional Medicine. http://www.parliament.gov.za/live/content.php?Item_ID=1838. Accessed 1 December 2011.

Malangu, N. and G. Ogunbanjo (2009), A Profile of Acute Poisoning at Selected Hospitals in South Africa. *Southern African Journal of Infectious Diseases*, 24(2): 14–16.

Michael, M. (2000), Reconnecting Culture: Technology and Nature – From Society to Heterogeneity. London. http://www.ukessays.co.uk/essays/geography/material-cultures-of-tourism.php#ixzz3Pw0MPfS2. Accessed 3 March 2014.

Montagu Museum (1998), *Herbal Remedies of Montagu Museum*. Montagu: Montagu Museum.

Motsoaledi, A. (2013), Keynote address NIH–MRC South Africa Research Summit on HIV and TB. http://www.gov.za/keynote-address-health-minister-dr-aaron-motsoaledi-joint-nih-mrc-south-africa-research-summit-hiv. Accessed 17 June 2013.

Nattrass, N. (2008), AIDS and the Scientific Governance of Medicine in Post-Apartheid South Africa. *African Affairs*, 107(427): 157–176.

Nimmo, R. (2011), Actor-Network Theory and Methodology: Social Research in a More-Than-Human World. *Methodological Innovations Online*, 6(3): 108–119.

Nortje, J. (2012), Medicinal Ethnobotany of the Kamiesberg, Namaqualand, Northern Cape Province, (MSc Thesis, University of Johannesburg).

Olivier, L. (2011), Rastafari Bushdoctors and the Challenges of Transforming Nature Conservation in the Boland Area, (MA Thesis, University of Stellenbosch).

Paterson, W. (1789), *A Narrative of Four Journeys into the Country of the Hottentots and Caffraria in the years 1777, 8, and 9*. London: J. Johnson.

Petersen, L. (2014), Cape Town's Trade in Wild Medicines: Ecological Threat or Essential Livelihood Resource? http://www.econ3x3.org/article/cape-town%E2%80%99s-trade-wild-medicines-ecological-threat-or-essential-livelihood-resource#sthash.KosdkM87.dpuf. Accessed 3 January 2014.

Petersen, L., R. Moll and M. Hockings (2012), Development of a Compendium of Local, Wild-harvested Species Used in the Informal Economy Trade, Cape Town, South Africa. *Ecology and Society*, 17(2): 26.

Philander, L. (2011), An Ethnobotany of Western Cape Rasta Bush Medicine. *Journal of Ethnopharmacology*, 138(2): 578–94.

Philander, L., N. Makunga and K. Ester (2014), The Informal Trade of Medicinal Plants by Rastafari Bush Doctors in the Western Cape South Africa. *Economic Botany*, 68(3): 303–315.

Reihling, H. (2008), Bioprospecting the African Renaissance: The New Value of Muthi in South Africa. *Journal of Ethnobiology and Ethnomedicine*, 2008(4): 9.

Republic of South Africa (2008a), Traditional Health Practitioners Act 22, 2007. *Government Gazette*, No. 30660, 10 January 2008.

Republic of South Africa (2008b), Draft Policy on African Traditional Medicines for South Africa. *Government Gazette*, No. 31271, 25 July 2008.

Republic of South Africa (2009). Medicines and Related Substances Amendment Act 72, 2008. *Government Gazette*, No. 32148, 21 April 2009.

Rottenburg, R. (1998), Towards an Ethnography of Translocal Processes and Central Institutions of Modern Societies. In A. Posern-Zielinski (ed.), *The Task of Ethnology: Cultural Anthropology in Unifying Europe*. Poznan: Drawa: 59–66.

Rutert, B. (2010), Bioprospecting in South Africa: New Hopes, Old Troubles. Paper presented at the '11th EASA' conference, Maynooth.

Rutert, B., H. Dilger and G. Matsabisa (2011), Bioprospecting in South Africa: Opportunities and Challenges in the Global Knowledge Economy – a Field in the Becoming. *Center for Area Studies Working Paper*, 1: 1–22.

Shapera, I. (1934), *The Khoisan Peoples of South Africa*. Bushmen and Hottentots. London: Routledge and Kegan Paul Ltd.

Siegfried, N. and G. Hughes. (2012), Herbal Medicine, Randomised Controlled Trials and Global Core. *South African Medical Journal*, 102(12): 912–913.

Smestad Paulsen, B., H. Ekeli, Q. Johnson and K. Norum (2012), *South-African Traditional Medicinal Plants from Kwazulu-Natal*. Oslo: Oslo Academic Press.

Smith, C. (1966), *Common Names of South African plants. Memoirs of the Botanical Survey of South Africa 35*. Department of Agricultural Technical Services, Pretoria.

Sparrman, A. (1785), *A Voyage to the Cape of Good Hope, Towards the Antarctic Polar Circle and Round the World*. Dublin: White, Cash and Byrne.

Stengers, I. (2010), *Cosmopolitics I*. Minneapolis: University of Minnesota Press.

Street, R. and G. Prinsloo (2013), Commercially Important Medicinal Plants of South Africa: A Review. *Journal of Chemistry*, Article ID 205048, http://dx.doi.org/10.1155/2013/205048. Accessed 21 December 2013.

Thornton, R. (2009), The Transmission of Knowledge in South African Traditional Healing. *Africa*, 79(1): 1734.

Thring, T. and F. Weitz (2006), Medicinal Plant Use in the Bredasdorp/Elim Region of the Southern Overberg in the Western Cape Province of South Africa. *Journal of Ethnopharmacology*, 103(2): 261–275.

Van Niekerk, J. (2012), Traditional Healers Formalised? *South African Medical Journal*, 102(3): 105–106.

Van Wyk, B. (2008), A Review of KhoiSan and Cape Dutch Medical Ethnobotany. *Journal of Ethnopharmacology*, 119(3): 331–341.

Van Wyk, B.E., R. Van Oudtshoorn and N. Gericke (2000), *Medicinal Plants of South Africa* (revised edition). Pretoria: Briza.

Viveiros de Castro, E. (1996), Images of Nature and Society in Amazonian Ethnology. *Annual Review of Anthropology*, 25: 179–200.

Von Koenen, E. (1996), *Medicinal, Poisonous and Edible Plants in Namibia*. Windhoek: Klaus Hess Verlag.

Walker, C. (2010), Land Claims, Land Conservation and the Public Interest in Protected Areas. In B. Freund and H. Witt (eds.), *Development Dilemmas in Post Apartheid South Africa*. Durban: University of Kwazulu-Natal Press: 232–244.

Weiner, D. (2005), A Death-Defying Attempt to Articulate a Coherent Definition of Environmental History. *Environmental History*, 10: 404–420.

Whatmore, S. (2002), *Hybrid Geographies: Natures, Cultures and Spaces*. London: Sage.

Wilson, D., K. Goggin, K. Williams, M. Gerkovich, N. Gqaleni, J. Syce, P. Bartman, Q. Johnson and W. Folk (2012), Safety of *Sutherlandia fructescens* in HIV-seropositive South African Adults: an Adaptive Double-blind Randomized Placebo Controlled Trial. http://soafrica.com/events/2012events/HIV/presentation/Tuesday,%2027%20November%202012/Douglas%20Wilson%20-%20Safety%20of%20Sutherlandia%20fructescens%20%2827%20Nov,%2013h30%29.pdf. Accessed 3 March 2012.

World Health Organization (2011), *Progress Report on Decade of Traditional Medicine in the African Region*. AFR/RC61/PR/2, 5 July.

Xaba, T. (2007), Marginalized Medical Practice: The Marginalization and Transformation of Indigenous Medicines in South Africa. In: B. de Sousa Santos (ed.), *Another Knowledge is Possible: Beyond Northern Epistemologies*. London: Verso: 317–351.

Zhang, B., W. Leung, Y. Zou, W. Mabusela, Q. Johnson, T. Michaelsen and B. Smestad Paulsen (2014), Immunomodulating Polysaccharides from *Lessertia frutescens* Leaves: Isolation, Characterization and Structure Activity Relationship. *Journal of Ethnopharmacology*, 152(2): 340–348.

FIGURE 1: On 27 March 2014 protesters gathered for a vigil with flowers outside of St. George's Cathedral in Cape Town (Photographer: M. Boehi).

CHAPTER 8

"Flowers are South Africa's silent ambassadors": flower shows and botanical diplomacy in South Africa

Melanie Boehi

Flowers, posters and clerical garb fused into an impressive display of visual mix-and-match protest poetry when about 50 people gathered for a lunchtime vigil on the steps of St George's Cathedral in central Cape Town on 27 March 2014. Thabo Makgoba, the Anglican Archbishop of Cape Town, initiated the vigil to express support for Public Protector Thuli Madonsela and to call on President Jacob Zuma to respond to her report on disputed public expenditures at his Nkandla homestead. On the previous day, a call to protestors had been made via social media to assemble with "a flower for Thuli" and "a message for the President".[1] In the course of the demonstration the flowers became messages similar to the words written on the posters. They expressed gratitude and support for Madonsela, culturally coded as beautiful and life affirming, but also reminding of the vulnerability and perishability of all life.

The use of flowers in demonstrations has been widespread throughout the 20th century around the globe, ranging from the 1912 "bread and roses" textile workers strike in Lawrence, Massachusetts, to the "flower power" protests against the Vietnam War and Taiwan's sunflower student movement of early 2014. Diverse political movements have used flowers as communicative objects and symbols of peace and hope.[2] However, in South Africa the use of flowers in protest constituted a rather recent phenomenon. The anti-apartheid movement did not prominently

---

1   Bennett 2014: https://www.facebook.com/events/1520102691550031/?ref=notif&notif_t=plan_user_invited (accessed 26 March 2014)
2   For an overview, see McKay 2011

use flowers as symbols. Tellingly, its women's movement deployed symbols such as rocks and stones, which, unlike flowers, were not associated with stereotypes about weak femininity.[3] The only organisation that occasionally used floral symbolism was the Black Sash, a white women's organisation. When unable to wear their signature black sashes, the organisation's members sometimes substituted them with black satin roses.[4]

Historically, flowers and plants have been less associated with protest against than political representations of the state. During apartheid, flowers were, alongside the Kirstenbosch National Botanical Garden (NBG), prominently incorporated in the imaging of a South African botanical complex which worked for the formation of hierarchically ordered subjects and citizens. Plants, in particular when perceived as flowers, were deployed to project positive images to improve the reputation of the state abroad and promote patriotism among white citizens at home.[5]

The Kirstenbosch NBG was established in Cape Town in 1913 and evolved as the centre of a network which today includes ten national botanical gardens dispersed throughout South Africa.[6] Since its establishment, the Kirstenbosch NBG has been one of the key sites where the South African nation was defined through its nature, and where nature was defined through its work in the production of the nation. According to McCracken, the National Botanical Gardens began as a project of "imperial patriotism" and "local nationalism".[7] Van Sittert analysed how the indigenous Cape flora emerged between 1890 and 1939 as "a mark of ethnic, race and class identity as well as regional allegiance within a new and fractious settler national state".[8] The National Botanical Gardens and the Botanical Society of South Africa, which was established simultaneously to provide financial support in addition to the available government funding, were involved in the promotion of nationalism through education programmes, the advancement of "indigenous gardening" and the production of exhibitions.

From the late 1950s onwards, the involvement of the Kirstenbosch NBG in political spectacles increased. While the boycott campaigns of the international anti-apartheid movement targeted South Africa's participation in political meetings, trade, sport, arts and academia, flower shows and scientific botanical

---

3   I thank Bonita Bennett for sharing her memories and interpretation of the absence of floral symbolism in the anti-apartheid movement.
4   Burton 2015: pp. 163–164
5   This chapter focuses on the state's deployment of plants. However, it must be emphasised that black artists have also deployed plants in critical ways, in the visual arts and literature.
6   For an overview of the Kirstenbosch NBG's history see: Compton 1965; McCracken/McCracken 1988; Huntley 2012
7   McCracken 1995: p. 33
8   Van Sittert 2003: p. 125

networks remained open to South African representatives until the late 1980s. The South African government therefore used flower shows and botany to counter international criticism. It practised what can be described as botanical diplomacy based on the continuously reproduced assumption that plants were apolitical and beautiful. The Kirstenbosch NBG emerged as a prominent actor in this alternative form of international relations. The state thereby used the botanical garden to project images of itself as being guided by supposedly universal scientific and aesthetic standards. Government representatives and journalists referred to the Kirstenbosch NBG, Brian Rycroft (the National Botanical Gardens' director for the period 1954–1984) and plants themselves as "ambassadors" of the state.[9] The Kirstenbosch NBG became the main provider of plants for government representations and functioned as a site of production of political narratives and spectacles. After 1994, botanical diplomacy was no longer required as South Africa was welcomed back into the international community. Nonetheless, plants and gardens remained powerful symbols in the post-apartheid era, although now charged with different meanings.

The continuity of the deployment of the seemingly neutral "natureculture" of plants before, during and post apartheid is indeed remarkable.[10] Contrary to the assumption of being apolitical, plants in South Africa have always been politically charged when the state was involved in their representation. This chapter discusses how plants and, in particular, flowers functioned symbolically, how botany was deployed by the state to maintain domestic and international representations and relations, and how the Kirstenbosch NBG functioned as a site of politics.

Botany, power and flowers

Drayton analysed how in Europe the disciplines of plant science have developed in close relationship to power since the mid-16th century.[11] Knowledge of nature was regarded as central to knowledge of government. Rulers surrounded themselves with majestic gardens, displaying plants collected in the colonies and cultivated at high expense, because "power was to be beautiful as well as natural and necessary".[12] Plant beauty and knowledge were produced and displayed in ornamental, agricultural and botanical gardens. European settlers legitimised ownership of colonised land by claiming knowledge about and emotional attachment to its flora. In the late 19th and 20th centuries concerns with nature and nation, particularly

---

9 De Klerk: Gardens Our Finest Envoy, *Cape Argus*, 19 March 1963; Dry 1980: p. 10
10 Science and Technology Studies scholars emphasise that nature and culture don't exist separately. Haraway suggests the term "natureculture" to acknowledge that the material and semiotic always intersect. Haraway 2004: pp. 300–302
11 Drayton 2000: pp. 26–49
12 Drayton 2000: p. 26

with "indigenous" and "exotic" flora and fauna, often intersected with nationalist politics.[13] Nature conservation was a key aspect through which modern states legitimised themselves. In South Africa, the National Botanical Gardens and the Botanical Society were deeply involved in these discourses.

Botanical gardens are archival and museological institutions. They collect, order and keep or discard material. Design is used to produce exhibitions and mediate visitors' experiences in ways similar to activities in museums. Together with other spaces in which plants are collected, ordered and displayed, botanical gardens constitute what can be described as a botanical complex. This complex includes institutions and practices through which social relationships are negotiated by defining relationships between people and plants. Botanical gardens, public parks, nature reserves, private gardens, state-sponsored research institutes, botany departments at universities, flower markets and flower shows are part of this complex. The term 'botanical complex' draws from Bennett's term of the "exhibitionary complex" that he introduced to describe the emergence of the public museum in the late 18th and early 19th century as a vehicle for the exercise of governmental power.[14] The institutions belonging to the botanical complex educated their public about how to internalise discipline by defining relationships to plants, which implied relationships to society, nature and the state. In the botanical garden and the flower shows described below the public was instructed to have knowledge about plants and know their relationship to plants. Through this knowledge formation, publics and social hierarchies were reproduced.

In the activities described in this chapter, the boundary between plants and flowers is a porous one. In botanical terms, 'flower' refers to the bloom or blossom of flowering plants whose function is biological reproduction. However, in the texts discussed in this chapter, the meaning of 'flower' includes dimensions beyond the biological, invoking cultural practices of communication and representation in which flowering plants were involved. Humans have long interacted with flowers in many different ways, including establishing relationships between each other as well as to the environment and to the divine. In many practices, flowers have functioned as symbols and communicative objects.[15] The deployment of flowers by the South African state can be regarded as standing in a genealogy of European practices of flower symbolism and communication. In Europe, flowers have long

---

13 For an introduction to plant discourses and nationalism see: Comaroff/Comaroff 2001; Subramaniam 2001; Ohnuki-Tierney 2002; Van Sittert 2003
14 Bennett 2009: p. 19
15 This chapter focuses on how humans deployed flowers in communication. Plant science showed that also plants themselves communicate and have the abilities similar to seeing, smelling, feeling and hearing. Kranz 2014: p. 6

been associated with meanings in religion, heraldry, painting and literature.[16] As Sartiliot writes, "this floral symbolism was less systematised" while the spheres of the natural and the spiritual were regarded as connected.[17] Systematisation increased at the time of the Renaissance when the naturalist sciences emerged and flowers appeared in paintings and poetry as emblems with fixed meanings. The idea of a language of flowers, called *sélam*, emerged in Orientalist literature. In the early 19th century, books concerned with the language of flowers, which included lists of specific plants and their meanings in the form of dictionaries, became popular first in France, then in Germany, England and North America.

The practicality of floriography, literally meaning writing with flowers, has been criticised for almost as long as literature about it has existed. Floriography has been described as dysfunctional because flowers were arranged in bouquets without syntax, senders and receivers required elaborate botanical knowledge, plants listed in floriography dictionaries were not always in season or universally available and all participants would have needed to use the same code, which was complicated as floriography dictionaries differed greatly. Derrida suggested that "flowers reveal an originless chain of metamorphoses, subverting the neat relationship between signifier and signified, and point to a process of signification that cannot be limited to a single, dominant model".[18] Given the contradictory meanings associated with flowers "they symbolise nothing".[19] According to Goody the "practical language of flowers" diverged substantially from the theoretical language of flowers.[20] The floral symbolism practised was characteristically "fragmentary, localised and complex".[21] Schwan argued that the ambiguities of floral symbolism did not hinder popularity of the language of flowers, in particular for expressing emotions, but opened up ways for creative interpretations.[22] What mattered was not whether particular flowers and particular meanings were firmly linked but the imagination of the possibility of flowers carrying meanings.

Cape Town flower shows and empire

Flower shows were among the main occasions of deploying flowers for communicative and representative purposes. They were major events in the social calendar of Cape Town's white middle and upper class in the first half of the 20th century. Their openings were widely attended and the local press reported about

---

16   For an overview on the language of flowers see Goody 1993: pp. 232–253
17   Sartiliot 1993: p. 3
18   Derrida 1972 quoted in Sartiliot 1993: p. 2
19   Derrida 1974 quoted in Sartiliot 1993: p. 2
20   Goody 1993: p. 251
21   Goody 1993: p. 253
22   Schwan 2014: pp. 218–219

them. A refined taste for plants and membership in the Botanical Society, the Cape Horticultural Society or any specialised horticultural society marked social distinction. Specimens collected on the mountains and in the veld were displayed at wild flower shows. The first wild flower show took place in Tulbagh in 1873, others followed and in the early 1900s half a dozen districts in the Western Cape hosted annual shows.[23] In 1922 the Cape Peninsula Publicity Association began organising a show in Cape Town's City Hall in which the districts competed against each other. These shows took place until 1936 when they were replaced by spring shows with displays of indigenous plants grown in Botanical Society members' gardens. The Kirstenbosch NBG also provided exhibits and its staff identified and judged plants at shows organised by the Cape Peninsula Publicity Association, the Railway Horticultural Society and the Cape Horticultural Society.[24] The supplies from the Kirstenbosch NBG and, from 1921 onwards, its first satellite garden at Whitehill, increased steadily. In 1925 the *Journal of the Botanical Society* reported that "the progress of Kirstenbosch [could] be illustrated by the part it [had] played in the Cape Town Wild Flower Shows".[25]

From 1920 onwards, the Kirstenbosch NBG was also involved in tourism promotion and regularly supplied flower displays to Cape Town's Visitors' Bureau.[26] The Cape Peninsula Publicity Association also organised exhibitions in places further away. During the 1936 Empire Exhibition in Johannesburg, it organised a weekly supply of cut flowers for display for the Cape Pavilion exhibition. The Kirstenbosch NBG provided silver tree leaves (*Leucadendron argenteum*), which were packed in cellophane envelopes as souvenirs for visitors.[27] In 1942 the South African Railways and Harbours agreed to provide a grant for the National Botanical Gardens who, in exchange, would grow and supply indigenous plants to encourage the cultivation of South African flora at railway stations.[28] They also supplied cut flowers for the decoration of the trains that conveyed tourists arriving by ship.[29]

The first major international exhibition in which the National Botanical Gardens participated was the British Empire Exhibition of 1924–1925. Plants from the Kirstenbosch NBG appeared in the Cape Town section, in a display of medicinal and aromatic plants by the Department of Agriculture and in a South African rock

---

23 Wood 1992: p. 38
24 Already in the annual report for 1914, the curator reported that he "acted as judge at numerous shows held by the various Horticultural Societies of the Peninsula". Mathews 1915: p. 7
25 Botanical Society of South Africa 1926: p. 5
26 Botanical Society of South Africa 1920: p. 3
27 Botanical Society of South Africa 1936: p. 4
28 Compton 1943: p. 3
29 Marais 1960: p. 24

Flower shows and botanical diplomacy in South Africa

FIGURE 2: A succulent rockery represented South Africa at the Coronation Empire Exhibition at the Chelsea Flower Show in London in 1937 (Photograph courtesy of the Royal Horticultural Society, Lindley Library).

garden.³⁰ Preparations had begun a year before when the Cape Peninsula Publicity Association sent an "experimental shipment" of cut flowers to England.³¹ The trial proved satisfactory and in 1924 "weekly consignments" sourced from the country districts and the Kirstenbosch NBG were sent "in cool storage".³² About 140 different varieties of seeds and bulbs were sent to the Royal Horticultural Society for cultivation at their garden in Wisley from where plants were transferred to the exhibition ground. The South African Railway horticulturalist, Frank Frith, curated a succulent rock garden. The *Journal of the Botanical Society* reported that thanks to Frith's display "many thousands of people saw there for the first time the amazing plant-forms which are so characteristic a feature of our arid districts".³³ The Royal Horticultural Society awarded Frith's design with a Lindley Medal and Arthur Hill, director of the Royal Botanic Gardens, Kew, was full of praise.³⁴ The life of the plants sent to England for the British Empire Exhibition did not end with the fair's closure but some entered the living or herbarium collection of Kew.³⁵

In 1933, the Kirstenbosch NBG again sent plants for display to London, on the occasion of an art exhibition at South Africa House, and a Royal Horticultural Society show.³⁶ The Botanical Society's *Journal* described the exhibition as an experiment in tourism advertisement.³⁷ However, the article's author was not convinced about the marketing potential of flowers and criticised that tourists might "feel they have been misled" and obtain "a very dubious opinion of our common sense and of our appreciation for the flowers we take such pains to advertise". It was argued that visitors would rarely come at the height of spring and, travelling by road, would see more signs of human destruction than of "our incomparable flora". In 1937 Kirstenbosch participated for the first time in the Chelsea Flower Show during the Empire Exhibition organised in celebration of King George VI's coronation.³⁸ The Chelsea Flower Show was and continues to be the most prestigious of its sort, attended by royals and celebrities, and prominently reported in the British and international media. The Royal Horticultural Society has organised the show on the grounds of the Chelsea Hospital in London since 1913. While most exhibitors were British, foreign participants established a presence early on.³⁹ The Coronation

---

30   Compton 1924: pp. 5–6, 1925: p. 8; Botanical Society of South Africa 1925: p. 4
31   Compton 1924: p. 5
32   Botanical Society of South Africa 1925: p. 4
33   Botanical Society of South Africa 1925: p. 4
34   Royal Botanic Gardens, Kew 1925: p. 40
35   Botanical Society of South Africa 1925: p. 4
36   Mathews 1934: pp. 18–19
37   Botanical Society of South Africa 1933: pp. 2–3
38   Elliott 2014: p. 44
39   Of the about 6000 exhibitors that participated in the Chelsea Flower Show between 1913–2013 over 200 were foreign. Elliott 2014: p. 136

Empire Exhibition was arranged by the curator of Kew. The exhibition consisted of displays of ornamental and economic plants representing the territories belonging to the British Empire. The South African government requested the National Botanical Gardens to take responsibility for its display.[40] Considerable effort was undertaken to reproduce an arid landscape which included about 300 plant species. Succulents were sent from the Karoo Garden at Whitehill and two collecting expeditions were undertaken to gather additional plants.[41] Seeds were sent to an English company to raise plants locally, and English growers and Kew supplied plants. Kew built a rockery resembling Karoo formations and arranged and labelled the plants. Lacking only a painted backdrop, the exhibit resembled a diorama. The design with rockery and separation of the public with ropes gave the plant display the appearance of an island. Visitors were thus taken on an imagined journey through Britain's imperial possessions, represented by their plant world.

According to data gathered from the National Botanical Gardens' annual reports, the *Journal of the Botanical Society of South Africa* and newspaper clippings archived at the Kirstenbosch NBG's Harry Molteno Library, plants were provided on 530 occasions between 1913–1993.[42] Of these occasions, 99 occurred between 1913–1950 and 431 in the period 1951–1993. In the first half of the 20th century exhibitions were limited to South Africa and Britain, while in the second half of the 20th century, destinations included other African countries, the Middle East, Asia and North and South America. Until declared a state-aided institution in 1953, the National Botanical Gardens' financial situation was precarious.[43] It depended largely on financial contributions by members of the Botanical Society and benevolent patrons. The participation in Cape Town's floricultural activities thus provided an opportunity to prove the institution's success to its donors. The participation in international exhibitions strengthened the perception of the Kirstenbosch NBG, both abroad and domestically, as an internationally operating institution. The network which had begun to develop in the first half of the 20th century enabled the rise of botanical diplomacy as an alternative means for the state to maintain international relations and advertise patriotism within South Africa from the 1950s to the 1980s.

---

40 Botanical Society of South Africa 1937: p. 5
41 The Kirstenbosch NBG established the Karoo Garden at Whitehill in 1921 as its first satellite garden. The Karoo Garden was relocated from Whitehill to Worcester in 1945 and was in 2001 renamed "Karoo Desert National Botanical Garden".
42 The existing data do not allow for definite calculation of the number of exhibitions with Kirstenbosch participation. However, the available data show tendencies. Plant displays continued after 1993 though the available records about these are less precise and therefore not included here.
43 Eloff 1988: p. 35

Botanical diplomacy against international isolation

Following the Sharpeville massacre of 21 March 1960 and the banning of the African National Congress (ANC) and the Pan Africanist Congress (PAC), international criticism and the boycott movement, which targeted South Africa's trade as well as participation in academic, art and sport exchanges increased.[44] The deployment of plants by the state began in the late 1950s and its rise paralleled the growth of image campaigns conducted by the apartheid state. While the South African state's activities in setting up media companies and front organisations is well known, the collaborations with botanists and botanical gardens have so far not been addressed. Among the recipients of cut flowers from the Kirstenbosch NBG were state institutions, including the Department of External Affairs, the South African Information Service, the Department of Information, the Union Department of Commerce and Industries, and various South African embassies, and occasionally also private companies who were involved in image campaigns for South Africa.[45] They demanded plants for flower shows, trade exhibitions and displays on state holidays.

FIGURE 3: The South African display at the New York International Flower Show in 1958 featured flowers from the Kirstenbosch NBG (Photograph courtesy of South African National Biodiversity Institute (SANBI), Harry Molteno Library).

The Kirstenbosch NBG participated for the first time in a competitive international exhibition in March 1958. Piet Meiring, the director of the South African Information Service, had suggested displaying a flower exhibit at the International Flower Show in New York.[46] The USA was a particular focus for South Africa's image campaigns as American business investment in South Africa and military collaboration were increasing.[47] The exhibit consisted of cut flowers and foliage of

---

44 Paterson/Malila 2013: p. 1; for an overview of the boycott movement see Kasrils 2012: pp. 98–104
45 Werner 1951: pp. 12–13, 1952: p. 12, 1954: pp. 12–13, 1958: p. 16, Marais 1961: p. 19
46 Botanical Society of South Africa 1958: p. 4
47 Nixon 2015: p. 27

Protea, Erica, Brunia and Leucadendron.[48] Plants of *Protea cynaroides* (giant protea or king protea), which had long, unofficially, and from 1976 onwards, officially, featured as South Africa's national flower, were prominently placed on a pedestal in the centre of the exhibit. The display featured in the international class together with 26 other exhibits from 19 countries. It was awarded a gold medal and the first prize. An exhibit from the nature reserve, The Wilds, in Johannesburg won a bronze medal; and together they won a silver trophy for South Africa. Eric Louw, the Minister of Foreign Affairs, handed over the prizes to Brian Rycroft during a ceremony at Kirstenbosch. Several high-profile office holders, including the Minister and Secretary of Education, Arts and Science, the Director of the South African Information Service and the Speaker of the House of Assembly attended the ceremony.[49] They celebrated the participation as a success both for the Kirstenbosch NBG and the State Information Service "in demonstrating to other countries what South Africa could do".[50] The *Cape Times* went as far as calling it a celebration of the "service that [the South African flora] had done to the country".[51] The South African propaganda machine thus was perceived as one including human and plant actors. The *Cape Times* further commented that the ceremony "was an admirable example of the unifying power of flowers" and that "now that sport is proving a prolific source of quarrels it might indeed be well if people with an urge to peacemaking [sic] brushed up their horticulture and botany".[52]

The success at the New York flower show sparked an increase in cut flower demands from the Kirstenbosch NBG.[53] In the 1960s the demand for cut flowers had grown to an extent that propaganda and propagation got out of balance. According to the Botanical Society's *Journal*, the garden's office was "flooded with correspondence from all parts of the world requesting exhibits of our wild flowers" but most requests had to be declined due to lack of staff.[54] In 1963 the demand for cut flowers began to worry Brian Rycroft and he asked the trustees to lay out a policy of how to deal with these requests.[55] They resolved to give the director permission to reject requests whenever they exceeded the capacity of the garden. The same concerns reoccurred in 1968 when the chief curator expressed concern about the number of flowers cut in the garden. Rycroft replied "that all

---

48 Werner 1958: p. 16
49 Botanical Society of South Africa 1958: p. 4
50 Mr. Louw's Bouquet for Kirstenbosch, *Cape Argus*, 31 July 1958
51 With Flowers, *Cape Times*, 2 August 1958
52 With Flowers, *Cape Times*, 2 August 1958
53 Protea Wins Popularity Abroad, *Cape Argus*, 6 October 1958
54 Botanical Society of South Africa 1958: p. 4
55 Kirstenbosch NBG, Pearson House, Trustees Minutes 1962–1966, Minutes of the Meeting of the Trustees of the National Botanic Gardens Held in the Director's Office at Kirstenbosch on Wednesday, 15 May 1963 at 10.30 a.m.: p. 43

FIGURE 4: Plants from the Kirstenbosch NBG constituted the centre piece of an exhibition for "South Africa Day" in Bournemouth on 20 March 1969. From left to right: F. Stone, I. Baker, M. Botha and H. Uys (Photograph courtesy of the South African National Biodiversity Institute (SANBI), Harry Molteno Library).

these demands were of so much importance that it was very difficult to refuse" and that "in view of the international importance to South Africa and the National Botanic Gardens of South Africa, it [was] very difficult to know where to draw the line".[56] Subsequently a section of the garden was set apart for the cultivation of cut flowers.[57]

While the National Botanical Gardens were involved in the provision of plants, government offices were responsible for organisation and costs. The name of the Kirstenbosch NBG was promoted so that it emerged as a floral representative of the state. In international botanical diplomacy South Africa and Kirstenbosch were perceived as synonyms. A photograph of an event where the Department

---

56 Kirstenbosch NBG, Pearson House, Trustees Minutes 1966–1974, Minutes of the Executive Committee of the Board of Trustees of the National Botanic Gardens of South Africa Held in the Director's Office, Kirstenbosch on Wednesday, 27 November 1968 at 9.30 a.m.: p. 116
57 I thank Julia September for telling me about the existence of the cut flower section. Julia September, Cape Town, 8 October 2014, interview by Melanie Boehi

of Information promoted South Africa in Bournemouth in 1969 exemplifies this well.[58] It shows a display with a protea in the centre, arranged in a flower basket labelled Kirstenbosch, and a direction sign to South Africa pointing at the plants.

International representations were not always requested from the outside but also initiated from within the Kirstenbosch NBG. This was, for example, the case with the restoration of the grave of Christiaan Hendrik Persoon (1761–1836), posthumously declared "a great South African botanist", whose neglected grave at the Père Lachaise Cemetery in Paris was restored by the National Botanical Gardens in 1966.[59]

Reports about plant displays often emphasised the newness of the displayed plants for the international public. The cut flowers sent for displays were mostly of the plant families *Proteaceae* and *Ericaceae*. These plants were rendered as typical representatives of fynbos and many were endemic to the Cape Floristic Region. European naturalists had been studying Cape plants since the 16th century and many were introduced as gardening plants or used for the production of hybrids in Europe. Proteas and ericas were popular gardening plants in England in the late 18th and 19th century but later lost popularity and disappeared from markets and gardens.[60] In South Africa the commercial growing of proteas only developed from the 1950s onwards. These plants were thus not new to Europe but had been out of fashion for over a century. The hype also ignored that other plants from South Africa, in particular pelargonium, had evolved to be the most common and popular ornamental plants.

Actors from within the botanical gardens and the media repeatedly emphasised the communicative capacities of flowers. The South African media described Brian Rycroft as a man versed in the communication with flowers. A portrait in the *Cape Times* stated that "the cliche [sic] 'say it with flowers' [made] sense to Rycroft" who was quoted as having said that there were no politics in the world of botany in which "flowers say it all".[61] In 1975, Rycroft was denied a visa by the Soviet Embassy in London to attend a conference in Russia. He returned to South Africa but sent the flowers to the conference on their own. One newspaper commented that "saying it with flowers could be a new detente [sic] exercise, since it seems to be easier for our proteas to get behind the Iron Curtain, than for one of our eminent horticulturalists".[62]

The 1970s were a time of détente in the foreign policy of apartheid South Africa which conducted discussions with neighbouring countries and had imaginaries of

---

58 Marais 1969: p. 30
59 Off to Paris, *Cape Argus*, 18 July 1966
60 Fraser/Fraser 2011: pp. 153, 162
61 Burnett 1975
62 iKwezi 1976

a constellation of states. In 1980, Rycroft was awarded a decoration of meritorious service to South Africa. *SA Digest*, a publication focusing on spreading positive news about South Africa, reported that Rycroft said on the occasion that "flowers are South Africa's silent ambassadors".[63] The journalist added that "Rycroft has also earned for himself a reputation as one of the country's best ambassadors" as he promoted the image and heritage of South Africa internationally. Rycroft was described as a modest man who let "the flowers do the talking". In 1988 the 75th anniversary of the National Botanical Gardens were celebrated with a conference organised by Kirstenbosch together with the International Union for Conservation of Nature. The *Cape Times* reported that the occasion proved that "the language of flowers is truly universal" and quoted Grenville Lucas, acting director of Kew, saying that "botany doesn't know any political boundaries".[64]

The apartheid government used not only the symbolism of flowers but also of gardening in its political programme. It used the wide acceptance of gardening as a peaceful and healthy activity in the representation of political prisoners. In an attempt to counter rumours about the harsh prison conditions a group of journalists was invited to visit Robben Island in 1977.[65] In reaction to the press visit, Nelson Mandela on behalf of the prisoners wrote a letter of complaint to the Head of Prisons and criticised the invasion of privacy and that they were given "the special work of 'gardening' instead of pulling out bamboo from the sea as we normally do when we go to work".[66] It was ironic that Mandela had indeed through his own initiative become a gardener while imprisoned but this self-determined act of "defiant gardening" was too provocative to be mentioned by the apartheid state.[67] The apartheid government was not the only one to use gardening for image boosting, the Nazis installed gardens in the concentration camps of Dachau and Theresienstadt to convince foreign dignitaries of their supposedly benign motives.[68]

Political spectacles and international visitors at the Kirstenbosch NBG

The Kirstenbosch NBG was not only deployed for image campaigns abroad but also emerged as a site where political spectacles took place within South Africa. These included a celebration of the tercentenary of Van Riebeeck Hedge

---

63 Dry 1980: p. 10
64 Language of Flowers is Truly Universal..., *Cape Times*, 1 September 1988
65 Nelson Mandela Foundation 2013: p. 87
66 Nelson Mandela Foundation 2013: p. 148
67 Mandela 1994: p. 902; Kathrada 1999: p. 78, quoted in Nelson Mandela Foundation 2013: p. 205. Helphand describes gardens built in unfavourable circumstances, e.g. by soldiers and prisoners, as "defiant gardens". Helphand 2006: pp. 1–12
68 McKay 2011: pp. 62–63

and festivities for the institution's 50th anniversary. Both occasions showed resemblances to the Jan van Riebeeck Tercentenary Festival of 1952 which attempted "to display the growing power of the apartheid state and to assert its confidence".[69] The Kirstenbosch NBG had participated in the 1952 Festival with plant displays.[70] In April 1960, the garden celebrated the tercentenary of Van Riebeeck Hedge and literally planted apartheid on to the land. Jan van Riebeeck had initiated the planting of a hedge of *Brabejum stellatifolium* as a frontier between Dutch settlers and Khoikhoi in 1660, parts of which continue to grow on the grounds of Kirstenbosch.[71] Probably inspired by the success of the Tercentenary Festival of 1952, the director of Kirstenbosch had written to public and private owners of land originally covered by the hedge and offered free specimens for replanting and restoration. In the year before, preparations of young *Brabejum stellatifolium* plants for use in the restoration project had begun.[72] Dudley D'Ewes, the president of the Botanical Society, wrote that he doubted "whether the hedge ever actually kept any Hottentot cattle beyond the apartheid line" but that "there is no reason why the original trees plus the young ones handed out today should not still be marking the original bitter-almond apartheid line three centuries from today".[73]

The Van Riebeeck Hedge is a telling example for how politics and horticulture intersected. While the Kirstenbosch NBG almost from the beginning produced historical narratives in the form of displays and monuments in the garden, Van Riebeeck Hedge did not inhabit a special place. The first director of the Kirstenbosch NBG, H.H.W. Pearson, had mentioned the hedge in his address at the annual meeting of the Botanical Society in 1914. Pearson said that the part of the hedge growing within the garden's boundaries was partly burnt and overgrown with weeds, but work was undertaken to carefully preserve it.[74] However, the hedge seems to have been neglected in the years to come. On a "bird's eye view" drawing of the botanical garden published in the Botanical Society's *Journal* in 1917, several other sites are marked due to their historical function but not the hedge.[75] The hedge seemed to have regained importance only in the late 1920s. In 1929, director Compton referred to it as "one of the most interesting antiquities of the Union".[76] According to the annual report, the hedge had previously been

---

69 Rassool/Witz 1993: p. 448; Witz 2003: p. 84
70 Compton 1953: p. 6
71 Rourke 1971: pp. 53–55
72 Werner 1959: p. 13
73 D'Ewes 1960
74 The Botanical Gardens, *Cape Times*, 14 March 1914
75 Goldman 1917
76 Compton 1930: p. 5

difficult to access because of surrounding silver trees. These were now thinned out, wattle, fir and scrub were removed, and various species of *Watsonia* bulbs were planted to provide a colourful display against the dark background.[77] The horticultural interventions continued in the following years. In 1936, Van Riebeeck Hedge was proclaimed a national monument.[78] The monumental gardening with Jan van Riebeeck has continued to this day.

The biggest exercise in botanical diplomacy at the Kirstenbosch NBG was the Golden Jubilee celebrations to mark the 50th anniversary of the National Botanical Gardens and the Botanical Society of South Africa, turning 1963 into "South Africa's Floral Year".[79] For the government, the Jubilee constituted an opportunity to produce images directed at the international community of South Africa as a country of outstanding natural beauty in which scientists and politicians alike cared for the conservation of the floral heritage. By inviting international visitors to the Jubilee the government reassured white South Africans that besides increasing isolation they were still accepted in the global community and that international specialists admired their conservation work. For the National Botanical Gardens and their director Brian Rycroft, the Jubilee was an opportunity to enhance the institution's profile, which at that time still rivalled the National Herbarium in Pretoria.[80] The celebrations were also an important occasion for fundraising.[81]

Preparations for the celebrations began in 1960 when Rycroft started to invite international botanists to visit the country in the anniversary year.[82] The organising committee decided in 1962 to approach government for funding because the festival constituted "one of the great occasions [to] put South Africa on the map, and it should be exploited to the full".[83] It was suggested that the festivities should be held over a whole year and on a national scale. The Minister of Information was interested as the celebrations offered "a wonderful opportunity to bring people here from oversea [sic] to show them something non-political".[84] Other parties interested in uplifting South Africa's image internationally and reassuring white South Africans about the country's place in the world were approached as sponsors, among them the provincial administration, the South Africa Foundation, the Chamber of Mines and the Chambers of Commerce and Industry. The South African state president Charles R. Swart, the Minister of Education, Arts and

---

77 Compton 1930: p. 5; Mathews 1930: p. 16
78 Simmons/Berman 1958
79 Kirstenbosch National Botanic Gardens 1963
80 John Rourke, Cape Town, 8 January 2013, interview by Melanie Boehi
81 Research Institute for Botany Wanted by Kirstenbosch, *Cape Argus*, 13 October 1962
82 Rycroft 1964: p. 11
83 State Aid Sought to Put South Africa on 'Non-Political Map', *Cape Times*, 8 March 1962
84 State Aid Sought to Put South Africa on 'Non-Political Map', *Cape Times*, 8 March 1962

Science, the administrators of the four provinces and South West Africa and the mayor of Cape Town acted as patrons of the celebration.[85]

Over ten months, festivities took place at the Kirstenbosch NBG and in various venues in Cape Town and throughout the country.[86] Among the events that took place in the botanical garden were a party with the state president and his wife as guests of honour, theatre and music performances, historical exhibitions and youth competitions. At the annual social gathering of the Botanical Society, certificates were awarded for long-serving white staff members. A separate dinner was organised for the black staff members where a further nine people were honoured for their long service. External institutions too contributed to the celebratory year. The South African Post Office released a special commemorative stamp. The Cape Horticultural Society organised an international flower show in the City Hall and Old Drill Hall and a wildflower show took place at the Goodwood Showgrounds. About 42,000 visitors attended the shows which staged exhibits from societies, clubs, municipalities and other organisations. An exhibition of medicinal and toxic plants was organised by the University of Cape Town and displayed at the Stuttafords store in Adderley Street. The South African Museum, the National Library, the National Gallery and other institutions showed special exhibitions.[87] The local newspapers reported extensively about the Golden Jubilee and radio programmes and several films were made in relationship to the Jubilee.[88] The publication with the most lasting impact on how the history of the Kirstenbosch NBG was told was the Jubilee book *Kirstenbosch: Garden for a Nation* by former director Robert Compton.[89]

An invitation to an international group of 48 botanists in September and October 1963 constituted the highlight and main publicity act of the Golden Jubilee year.[90] Government representatives framed the botanists' visit as an attempt to counter South Africa's negative international reputation. Nico Malan, Administrator of the Cape Province, said that

---

85 Big Events Planned for Kirstenbosch, *Cape Argus*, 19 July 1962
86 For an overview of the activities, see Rycroft 1964: pp. 11–24
87 Dubow, Flower Exhibition Is Remarkable for its Width of Treatment, *Cape Argus*, 21 August 1963; Capetonians as Trustees of Floral Beauty, *Cape Times*, 15 August 1963; Dubow, Significant, Trivial Flower Paintings, *Cape Argus*, 4 May 1963; Exhibition of Flower Paintings, *Cape Argus*, 19 September 1963
88 Rycroft 1965: p. 8; Botanical Films Are Shown, *Cape Argus*, 24 November 1964
89 The book was supposed to be published in the Golden Jubilee year but was only completed in 1965. Rycroft, 1963, p. 5; Compton 1965
90 The group included botanists from the USA, Germany, Sweden, Denmark, Norway, Austria, Netherlands, Finland, Belgium, France, Italy, Australia, New Zealand, Argentina, Portugal, Rhodesia, Swaziland and South West Africa. Rycroft 1964: pp. 20–22

> with certain elements abroad doing everything in their power to degrade South Africa and her people in the eyes of the world, the decision of the Kirstenbosch Jubilee Council to invite a number of leading scientists from various parts of the world to attend the jubilee celebrations in September and October next year was a most laudable one ... it was not possible to do too much in the direction of publicity for South Africa in present circumstances. A materially wealthy nation should also be rich spiritually and it was right that people should be brought to South Africa to see what was being done in the spiritual field.[91]

It was expected that showing the visiting botanists South Africa's scenic and floral beauty would result in them "on their return, paint a different picture of South Africa than they have believed in in the past" and "put South Africa on the map botanically".[92] Eschel Rhoodie, who was deeply involved in state propaganda as secretary of the Department of Information, claimed that the best way of spreading positive information about the state occurred in the form of "independent opinions", via "independent non-governmental channels, preferably non-South African".[93] Inviting visitors to South Africa was one method used by the Department of Information. Besides the botanists, business people and politicians from the USA and Europe were invited on all-inclusive trips. Private persons acted as hosts to circumvent suspicion or rulings that prohibited politicians from accepting foreign governments' invitations. The Department of Information sponsored and arranged these visits, and organised meetings with politicians during the stays. The Kirstenbosch NBG was one of the destinations on the itinerary during a visit of six US congressmen in January 1975.[94]

The visiting botanists of 1963 first spent two weeks in Cape Town where they were entertained with conferences and local excursions. They were then taken on a month-long botanical tour through the country. Accompanied by South African botanists, they travelled in two buses along the coast as far as Hluhluwe in KwaZulu-Natal, to the Kruger National Park and then via Pretoria and Johannesburg through the Karoo back to Cape Town. A brochure provided the visitors with information about the botanical interests at the various destinations. The itinerary

---

91   S.A. from Spiritual Viewpoint, *Cape Argus*, 18 August 1962
92   An Export Market in Flowers 'Possible', *Cape Argus*, 28 September 1962; Kirstenbosch Fund Drive Has Begun in Earnest, *Cape Argus*, 18 October 1962
93   Rhoodie 1983: pp. 37, 98
94   WikiLeaks, 1975PRETOR00314_b, American Embassy Pretoria Telegram, 28 January 1975, https://wikileaks.org/plusd/cables/1975PRETOR00278_b.html (accessed 17 August 2015)

and photographs of the tour show that the visitors botanised along the route.[95] Private South African companies, national parks, nature reserves, local political authorities and civil groups entertained the group during its tour. Accommodation and food was provided to the tour for free or at reduced rates. Over 60 receptions and functions were given for the group.[96] The botanists' visit was a highly mediated encounter, with a dense travel itinerary that focused on nature conservation sites and meetings with selected scientists and local authorities. Little time was left for spontaneous meetings or for the visitors to spend time outside of the group.

It was arranged that one of the visiting botanists would thank the local hosts at the functions during the tour. White South Africans who encountered the visiting botanists would thus be reassured about their country's standing in the international community. Media reporting ensured that this knowledge also extended to citizens who did not meet the botanists in person. The media widely described the invitation of the botanists as a success. A *Cape Argus* article for example concluded that it was a pity "there [were] not more institutions such as Kirstenbosch to attract visitors with a specialised knowledge and then give them an indirect view of the country as a whole".[97] The *Journal of the Botanical Society of South Africa* made sure that the positive impact of the Golden Jubilee was remembered through several articles published in its 1964 edition and a frontispiece with the signatures of participants of the botanical tour framed by a painted wreath of indigenous plants. The Golden Jubilee attracted the biggest group of botanical visitors; however, smaller groups followed in the years to come. In 1968, a group led by the director of the New York Botanical Garden visited and was taken around by Brian Rycroft. The chairman of the trustees of the National Botanical Gardens praised Rycroft for his contribution "towards a better understanding of South Africa and her people".[98]

The Chelsea Flower Show and contested symbolism

In May 1976, South Africa participated for the first time as an exhibitor on its own in the Chelsea Flower Show. The British flower arranger Pam Simcock had visited Cape Town for a series of lectures and demonstrations in flower arrangement in October 1975.[99] At a function, Simcock met staff members of the Department

---

95 Kirstenbosch National Botanic Gardens (1963); Kirstenbosch NBG, Garden Office, Brian Rycroft photographic collection
96 Rycroft 1964: p. 22
97 Bouquets for a Jubilee, *Cape Argus*, 30 October 1963
98 Kirstenbosch NBG, Pearson House, Trustees Minutes 1966–1974, Minutes of the Executive Committee of the Board of Trustees of the National Botanical Gardens of South Africa Held in the Director's Office, Kirstenbosch on Wednesday, 27 November 1968 at 9.30 a.m.: p. 115
99 Floral Designer for City, *Cape Argus*, 17 October 1975

of Foreign Affairs, including the Secretary of Information, Eschel Rhoodie.[100] During this meeting, the suggestion was made that South Africa should officially participate in the Chelsea Flower Show. The Chelsea Flower Show thus became another image building exercise for the South African state. Pam Simcock was commissioned to design the exhibits and the Kirstenbosch NBG was requested to provide plant material and send staff members to man the exhibition. The botanical garden's representatives were not involved in the design or construction of the exhibition but merely included for providing information and distributing pamphlets to visitors. The Ministry of Foreign Affairs provided the funding and together with the embassy in London organised the exhibitions.[101] It seemed thus that the actors concerned with promoting South Africa had indeed, as the *Cape Times* commentator had suggested almost 20 years earlier, discovered the use of botany and horticulture. In particular, Rhoodie seemed to have come a long way. In his memoir, published in 1983, *The Real Information Scandal*, he harshly criticised his predecessor, Gerald Barrie, for having wasted money on the production of "expensive films on the wild flowers of South Africa", of whose ability to "promote South Africa's image in the post Sharpeville period, only Barrie would ever know".[102] Wild flowers, Rhoodie had concluded, fell in the realm of tourism advertisement, while he preferred "hard-hitting direct information on the problems in South Africa, or on its international standing".[103] Rhoodie did not elaborate whether he underwent a change of opinion to value the soft power of flowers and what would have inspired it. He did not mention any botany or flower-related activities in *The Real Information Scandal*. They might have been minor in comparison to other campaigns, or fallen under the "many projects which will never be disclosed, at least not by me, for they may still be ongoing or they affect the vital interest of other parties which must be protected".[104]

The South African Chelsea exhibits were awarded a gold medal almost every year and in several years won trophies. Indeed, it seems that the flower competitions now substituted for the medals South Africa could not win in sport, due to the international boycott. It mattered little that Chelsea medals were not exclusively limited to the best participants but were mere judgements of a display's quality. While other international exhibitors aimed at advertising their products for export, the declared intention behind the South African exhibit was to "[create] goodwill towards the Republic".[105] South African media reported that "politics may raise

---

100 David Davidson, Cape Town, 1 September 2014, interview by Melanie Boehi
101 Huntley 2012: p. 147
102 Rhoodie 1983: p. 58
103 Rhoodie 1983: p. 41
104 Rhoodie 1983: p. 250
105 Rycroft 1982: p. 10

barriers for South Africa in many fields of endeavour – but not where flowers are concerned. Time and time again, flowers prove, internationally, to be a uniting factor in troubled times".[106] Joan Rycroft, the wife of Brian Rycroft, reported about the 1982 Chelsea Flower Show that "it was good to see how many friends our flowers made in England – and how many friends South Africa still has there".[107] Nonetheless, the media recognised the possibility of tensions around South Africa's public appearance in the world of flowers. When the South African ambassador collected the gold medal and Wilkinson award in 1983 the *Cape Times* reported that "the only protest demo at the start of the show was by garden gnomes" whose ban from the exhibition grounds had been debated for years.[108]

The organisers of the 1963 Kirstenbosch Golden Jubilee celebrations had claimed that "they can boycott anything they want to abroad, but they cannot make the women of the world boycott South African flowers".[109] However, two decades later this was proved wrong when the anti-apartheid movement began targeting the Chelsea Flower Show and the cut flower export industry. Protests against South Africa's participation in the Chelsea Flower Show began in ernest in 1986.[110] One exhibitor, the London borough of Newham, withdrew from the show because of its anti-apartheid policy. Several other exhibitors joined the protest. Initially the Royal Horticultural Society countered that, as a non-political organisation, they would not exclude South Africa. However, in the following year the South African Department of Foreign Affairs was asked not to attend. Unlike the embassy, the Kirstenbosch NBG still received an invitation to participate. The botanical garden's role at the Chelsea Flower Show was not much different to the functioning of the various front organisations set up by the Department for Information. Besides the name of the exhibitor, nothing changed as the embassy continued to organise the displays and the arrangements were undertaken by Simcock. The board of the National Botanical Gardens resolved to support the participation and that "the detail of the planning must be handled very confidentially".[111] Media reports showed that the display was still perceived as South African, as Kirstenbosch and South Africa were used as synonyms.[112] The Department of Foreign Affairs

---

106 Barrett 1981: p. 143
107 Kirstenbosch NBG, Pearson House, Trustees Minutes 1980–1983, Joan Rycroft, Letter to Trustees of the National Botanic Gardens of South Africa, Claremont, 27 May 1982: p. 251
108 SA Flowers Top Show, *Cape Times*, 25 May 1983
109 An Export Market in Flowers 'Possible', *Cape Argus*, 28 May 1962
110 Apartheid Strikes the Chelsea Flower Show, *Cape Argus*, 8 February 1986
111 Chelsea Gold for Kirstenbosch, *Cape Times*, 21 May 1987; Kirstenbosch NBG, Pearson House, Trustees Minutes 1986–1988, National Botanic Gardens Minutes of the Board Meeting Held in Kirstenbosch on 20 February 1987: p. 126
112 SA Wins Gold at Chelsea Flower Show. *Natal Witness*, 3 June 1989

continued to provide funding for the displays at the Chelsea Flower Show until 1994. In 1995, it announced that financial assistance would no longer be provided because the Department's focus would now rather be "on urgent priorities at home".[113] The Kirstenbosch NBG has continued to exhibit at the Chelsea Flower Show to this day, with funding from the private sector.

Besides the Chelsea Flower Show, the cut flower trade also became a target of the international boycott movement in the 1980s. In 1980, the industry publication *International Bulletin* critically reported about destructive harvesting methods and labour exploitation in South Africa, which, according to Middelmann, had a negative impact on the flower export.[114] In May 1986, Dutch anti-apartheid groups launched protests against the trading of South African flowers at the world's biggest flower auction of Aalsmeer.[115] On 17 July 1986, the Aalsmeer flower auction decided to exclude South African products. The industry organisation, SAPPEX, suggested strategies to avoid the boycotts by disguising the plants by avoiding Afrikaans plant names and South African newspapers as packing material.[116] In 1988, the Swiss activist group Erklärung von Bern published an article on the South African export flower industry with the telling title *Blüten der Apartheid* (flowers of apartheid), a reference to Baudelaire's poetry collection *Les Fleurs du Mal* (The Flowers of Evil).[117] However, compared to the boycott of sport, arts and academia, and the iconic use of apples and oranges as symbols in the consumer boycott campaigns, activities related to plants were less strongly targeted. One explanation is that flowers and gardening were primarily of elitist interest and thus not suitable for mass mobilisation campaigns. The Chelsea Flower Show has been and still is a white middle and upper class event where high entrance fees limit access. Tellingly, the Newham Council's protest against the South African exhibit was the only political controversy of its kind that ever occurred in the show's history.[118]

Conclusion

Plants and botanical gardens have been charged with political meaning in South Africa throughout the 20th and 21st centuries. The state participated in a botanical complex in which social hierarchies were negotiated by defining relationships between people and plants. Flower shows in which the Kirstenbosch NBG participated were occasions for local, and later national and international representations, initially of Cape Town, then of South Africa as part of the British

---

113 SA Role at UK Show in Jeopardy, *Cape Times*, 26 January 1995
114 Middelmann 2012: pp. 77–79
115 Fuchs 1988: p. 61
116 Middelmann 2012: p. 81
117 Fuchs 1988: p. 61
118 Elliott 2004: p. 138

Empire and finally the apartheid state. Because of their seemingly apolitical and beautiful natureculture the apartheid state deployed plants, gardens and the discipline of botany to counter international isolation and reassure white South Africans.

The Kirstenbosch NBG emerged as a key actor in this flower diplomacy as the garden provided plants and hosted events in the gardens which allowed the state to project images of itself as scientific, aesthetic and caring. It was mostly due to the perception of flowers as apolitical and beautiful that they could be deployed as communicative objects. This perception also enabled the anti-apartheid movement to mobilise South Africa's "flowers of apartheid", and in March 2014, the vigil holders in Cape Town, to use flowers for expressing concern about the abuse of power by the post-apartheid government. This confirms the findings of the existing floriography scholarship that the ambiguity of floral symbolism does not hinder the deployment of flowers in communication but rather stimulates creative uses in which meanings constantly have to be reaffirmed.

Bibliography

Published literature

Barrett, R. (1981), South Africa – The Winner! *South African Garden & Home*, October: 142–144.

Bennett, B. (2014), A Flower for Thuli, a Message for the President. Facebook. https://www.facebook.com/events/1520102691550031/?ref=notif&notif_t=plan_user_invited. Accessed 26 March 2014.

Bennett, T. (2009, first published 1995), *The Birth of the Museum: History, Theory, Politics*. London: Routledge.

Botanical Society of South Africa (1920), Notes and News. *The Journal of the Botanical Society of South Africa*, 6: 2–4.

Botanical Society of South Africa (1925), News and Notes, *The Journal of the Botanical Society of South Africa*, 11: 2–8.

Botanical Society of South Africa (1926), News and Notes. *The Journal of the Botanical Society of South Africa*, 12: 2–6.

Botanical Society of South Africa (1933), News and Notes. *The Journal of the Botanical Society of South Africa*, 19: 2–6.

Botanical Society of South Africa (1936), News and Notes. *The Journal of the Botanical Society of South Africa*, 22: 2–7.

Botanical Society of South Africa (1937), News and Notes, *The Journal of the Botanical Society of South Africa*, 23: 2–6.

Botanical Society of South Africa (1958), News and Notes. *The Journal of the Botanical Society of South Africa,* 44: 3–8.

Burnett, S., The Plants Are Talking and at Least One Man Is Listening, *Cape Times,* 8 February 1975.

Burton, M.I. (2015), *The Black Sash: Women for Justice and Peace.* Auckland Park: Jacana.

Comaroff, J. and J.L. Comaroff (2001), Naturing the Nation: Aliens, Apocalypse, and the Postcolonial State. *Social Identities,* 7(29): 233–265.

Compton, R.H (1924), *Report of the Hon. Director to the Trustees for the Period January 1st to December 31st, 1923.* Cape Town: National Botanic Gardens.

Compton, R.H. (1925), *Report of the Director to the Trustees for the Period January 1st to December 31st, 1924.* Cape Town: National Botanic Gardens.

Compton, R.H. (1930), *Report of the Director to the Trustees for the Period January 1st to December 31st, 1929.* Cape Town: National Botanic Gardens.

Compton, R.H. (1943), *Report of the Director to the Trustees for the Period 1st January to 31st December, 1942.* Cape Town: National Botanic Gardens.

Compton, R.H. (1953), *Report of the Director to the Trustees for the Period 1 January to 31 December 1952.* Cape Town: National Botanic Gardens.

Compton, R.H. (1965), *Kirstenbosch: Garden for a Nation.* Cape Town: Tafelberg.

Derrida, J. (1972), *La dissémination.* Paris: Seuil.

Derrida, J. (1974), *Glas.* Paris: Galilée.

D'Ewes, D., Apartheid Started With Bitter Almonds, *Cape Argus,* 30 April 1960.

Drayton, R. (2000), *Nature's Government: Science, Imperial Britain, and the 'Improvement' of the World.* New Haven, CT: Yale University Press.

Dry, G., Dedicated to Flowers, *SA Digest,* 22 February 1980: 10–11.

Dubow, N., Significant, Trivial Flower Paintings, *Cape Argus,* 4 May 1963.

Dubow, N., Flower Exhibition Is Remarkable for its Width of Treatment, *Cape Argus,* 21 August 1963.

Elliott, B. (2004), *The Royal Horticultural Society: A History 1804–2004.* Chichester: Phillimore.

Elliott, B. (2014), *Chelsea Flower Show: The First 100 Years: 1913–2013.* London: Frances Lincoln.

Eloff, J.N. (1988), NBG Yesterday, Today and Tomorrow: A Managerial Perspective. *Veld & Flora,* 74(2): 35–41.

Fraser, M. and L. Fraser (2011), *The Smallest Kingdom: Plants and Plant Collectors at the Cape of Good Hope.* Richmond: Royal Botanic Gardens.

Fuchs, E. (1988), *Vorsicht: Blumen. Natur, Kultur, Geschäft.* Zürich: Erklärung von Bern.

Goldman, L.L.B. (1917), Birds-Eye View of the National Botanical Gardens, Kirstenbosch. *The Journal of the Botanical Society of South Africa,* 3: insert.

Goody, J. (1993), *The Culture of Flowers.* Cambridge: Cambridge University Press.

Haraway, D. (2004), *The Haraway Reader.* New York and London: Routledge.

Helphand, K.I. (2006), *Defiant Gardens: Making Gardens in Wartime*. San Antonio: Trinity University Press.

Huntley, B.J. (2012), *Kirstenbosch: The Most Beautiful Garden in Africa*. Cape Town: Struik Nature.

iKwezi, In My Lapa, *The Louvelder*, 20 August 1976.

Kasrils, R. (2012), Sour Oranges and the Sweet Taste of Freedom. In A. Lim (ed.), *The Case for Sanctions against Israel*. London/Brooklyn, NY: Verso: 99–109.

Kathrada, A. (1999), *Letters from Robben Island*. Cape Town: Mayibuye Books.

Kranz, I. (2014), *Sprechende Blumen: Ein ABC der Pflanzensprache*. Berlin: Matthes & Seitz Berlin.

Kirstenbosch National Botanic Gardens (1963), *South Africa's Floral Year* (brochure). Cape Town: National Botanic Gardens.

Mandela, N. (1994), *Long Walk to Freedom: The Autobiography of Nelson Mandela*. Boston: Little Brown and Company.

Marais, J.A. (1960), Report of the Curator of Kirstenbosch Gardens for the Period 1/1/1960–31/03/1960. In H.B. Rycroft, *Report of the Director of the National Botanic Gardens of South Africa to the Board of Trustees for the Period 1 April 1959 to 31 March 1960*. Cape Town: National Botanic Gardens: 22–24.

Marais, J.A. (1961), Report of the Curator of Kirstenbosch Gardens. In H.B. Rycroft, *Report of the Director of the National Botanic Gardens of South Africa to the Board of Trustees for the Period 1 April 1960 to 31 March 1961*. Cape Town: National Botanic Gardens: 15–21.

Marais, J.A. (1969), H.B. Rycroft, *Report of the Director of the National Botanic Gardens of South Africa 1968/69*: 27–31.

Mathews, J.W. (1915), Report of the Curator. In H.H.W. Pearson, *Report of the Honorary Director for the Period January 1–December 31, 1914*. Cape Town: National Botanic Gardens: 5–7.

Mathews, J.W. (1930), Report of the Curator of Kirstenbosch for 1929. In R.H. Compton, *Report of the Director to the Trustees for the Period January 1st to December 31st, 1930*. Cape Town: National Botanic Gardens: 10–21.

Mathews, J.W. (1934), Report of the Curator of Kirstenbosch for 1933. In R.H. Compton, *Report of the Director to the Trustees for the Period January 1st to December 31st, 1933*. Cape Town: National Botanic Gardens: 10–19.

McCracken, D.P. and E.M. McCracken (1988), *The Way to Kirstenbosch*. Cape Town: National Botanic Gardens.

McCracken, D.P. (1995), Kirstenbosch: The Final Victory of Botanical Nationalism. *CONTREE*, 38: 30–35.

McKay, G. (2011), *Radical Gardening: Politics, Idealism and Rebellion in the Garden*. London: Frances Lincoln.

Middelmann, M. (2012), *Proteas: The Birth of a Worldwide Industry*. USA: Xlibris.

Nelson Mandela Foundation (2013), *A Prisoner in the Garden: Opening Nelson Mandela's Prison Archive*. Johannesburg: Penguin Books.

Nixon, R. (2015), *Selling Apartheid: South Africa's Global Propaganda War*. Auckland Park: Jacana.

Ohnuki-Tierney, E. (2002), *Kamikaze, Cherry Blossoms, and Nationalisms: The Militarization of Aesthetics in Japanese History*. Chicago/London: University of Chicago Press.

Paterson, C. and V. Malila (2013), Beyond the Information Scandal: When South Africa Bought into Global News. *Ecquid Novi: African Journalism Studies*, 34(2): 1–14.

Rassool, C. and L. Witz (1993), The 1952 Jan Van Riebeeck Tercentenary Festival: Constructing and Contesting Public National History in South Africa. *The Journal of African History*, 34(3): 447–468.

Rhoodie, E. (1983), *The Real Information Scandal*. Pretoria: Orbis SA.

Royal Botanic Gardens, Kew (1925), Review of the Work of the Royal Botanic Gardens, Kew, during 1924. In *Bulletin of Miscellaneous Information (Royal Gardens, Kew)*, 1925: 37–68.

Rourke, J.P. (1971), Van Riebeeck's Wild Almond: Odd Man out of the South African Proteaceae. *Veld & Flora*, 1(3): 53–55.

Rycroft, H.B. (1963), *Report of the Director of the National Botanic Gardens of South Africa to the Board of Trustees for the Period 1 April 1962, to 31 March 1963*. Cape Town: National Botanic Gardens.

Rycroft, H.B. (1964), Report on Golden Jubilee Celebrations. In H.B. Rycroft, *Report of the Director of the National Botanic Gardens of South Africa to the Board of Trustees for the Period 1 April, 1963, to 31 March, 1964*. Cape Town: National Botanic Gardens: 11–24.

Rycroft, H.B. (1965), *Report of the Director of the National Botanic Gardens of South Africa to the Board of Trustees for the Period 1 April, 1964, to 31 March, 1965*. Cape Town: National Botanic Gardens.

Rycroft, H.B. (1982), *National Botanic Gardens of South Africa Director's Review for the Year Ending 31 December 1981*. Cape Town: National Botanic Gardens.

Sartiliot, C. (1993), *Herbarium/Verbarium: The Discourse of Flowers*. Lincoln, Neb: University of Nebraska Press.

Schwan, A. (2014), Blumen müssen oft bezeigen, was die Lippen gern verschweigen. In V. Räuchle and M. Römer (eds.), *Gefühle Sprechen: Emotionen an den Anfängen und Grenzen der Sprache*. Würzburg: Königshausen & Neumann: 199–221.

Simmons, I. and F. Berman, First Cape Frontier in Living Monument to Van Riebeeck, *Cape Argus*, 4 October 1958.

Subramaniam, B. (2001), The Aliens Have Landed! Reflections on the Rhetoric of Biological Invasions. *Meridians: Feminism, Race, Transnationalism*, 2(1): 26–40.

Van Sittert, L. (2003), Making the Cape Floral Kingdom: The Discovery and Defence of Indigenous Flora at the Cape, ca. 1890–1939. *Landscape Research*, 28(1): 113–129.

Werner, H.F. (1951), Report of the Curator of Kirstenbosch for 1950. In R.H. Compton, *Report of the Director to the Trustees for the Period 1st January to 31st December, 1950*. Cape Town: National Botanic Gardens: 9–13.

Werner, H.F. (1952), Report of the Curator of Kirstenbosch for 1951. In R.H. Compton, *Report of the Director to the Trustees for the Period 1st January to 31st December, 1951*. Cape Town: National Botanic Gardens: 8–13.

Werner, H.F. (1954), Report of the Curator of Kirstenbosch for 1953. In R.H. Compton, *Report of the Director to the Trustees for the Period 1 January to 31 December 1953*. Cape Town: National Botanic Gardens: 9–13.

Werner, H.F. (1958), Report of the Curator of Kirstenbosch Gardens. In H.B. Rycroft, *Report of the Director of the National Botanic Gardens of South Africa to the Board of Trustees for the Period 1 April 1957 to 31 March 1958*. Cape Town: National Botanic Gardens: 13–17.

Werner, H.F. (1959), Report of the Curator of Kirstenbosch Gardens. In H.B. Rycroft, *Report of the Director of the National Botanic Gardens of South Africa to the Board of Trustees for the Period 1 April 1958 to 31 March 1959*. Cape Town: National Botanic Gardens: 13–18.

Witz, L. (2003), *Apartheid's Festival: Contesting South Africa's National Pasts*. Bloomington, Ind: Indiana University Press.

Wood, J. (1992), Spring Wildflower Shows. *Veld & Flora*, 78(2): 38–43.

Newspaper articles without named author
An Export Market in Flowers 'Possible', *Cape Argus*, 28 September 1962.
Apartheid Strikes the Chelsea Flower Show, *Cape Argus*, 8 February 1986.
Big Events Planned for Kirstenbosch, *Cape Argus*, 19 July 1962.
Botanical Films Are Shown, *Cape Argus*, 24 November 1964.
Bouquets for a Jubilee, *Cape Argus*, 30 October 1963.
Capetonians as Trustees of Floral Beauty, *Cape Times*, 15 August 1963.
Chelsea Gold for Kirstenbosch, *Cape Times*, 21 May 1987.
De Klerk: Gardens Our Finest Envoy, *Cape Argus*, 19 March 1963.
Exhibition of Flower Paintings, *Cape Argus*, 19 September 1963.
Floral Designer for City, *Cape Argus*, 17 October 1975.
Kirstenbosch Fund Drive Has Begun in Earnest, *Cape Argus*, 18 October 1962.
Language of Flowers Is Truly Universal…, *Cape Times*, 1 September 1988.
Mr. Louw's Bouquet for Kirstenbosch, *Cape Argus*, 31 July 1958.
Off to Paris, *Cape Argus*, 18 July 1966.
Protea Wins Popularity Abroad, *Cape Argus*, 6 October 1958.
Research Institute for Botany Wanted by Kirstenbosch, *Cape Argus*, 13 October 1962.
SA Flowers Top Show, *Cape Times*, 25 May 1983.

S.A. from Spiritual Viewpoint, *Cape Argus*, 18 August 1962.
SA Role at UK Show in Jeopardy, *Cape Times*, 26 January 1995.
SA Wins Gold at Chelsea Flower Show, *Natal Witness*, 3 June 1989.
State Aid Sought to Put South Africa on 'Non-Political Map', *Cape Times*, 8 March 1962.
The Botanical Gardens, *Cape Times*, 14 March 1914.
With Flowers, *Cape Times*, 2 August 1958.

PART IV

Impoverished Environmentalism

CHAPTER 9

The comprehensive hunting ban: strengthening the state through participatory conservation in contemporary Botswana

Annette LaRocco

Introduction

> It is a simple decision but the ramifications are quite complex.[1]

Contestations over the nature of conservation have emerged as key fault lines between the state and citizens in postcolonial Botswana. In January 2014 the government enacted an indefinite, nationwide ban on hunting, covering both subsistence and commercial practices.[2] This transition from a consumptive-use model of wildlife conservation to a non-consumptive, preservationist approach indicates a significant shift in the country's long-term conservation and rural development strategies.

However, this change in conservation policy is not occurring in isolation, but rather is embedded in a global environmental movement wherein conservation efforts are often constructed as apolitical—a discourse that strips out the ideology and politics of these policies and practices in favour of the appearance of a technocratic approach.[3] Similarly, global- and national-level conservationists often

---

1. Department of Wildlife and National Parks official, Gaborone, 25 September 2013, interview by Annette LaRocco
2. An important caveat to the nationwide nature of the hunting ban is that it does not apply to freehold land—meaning hunting is still permitted on privately-held, independent game farms. Most of these are found in western Botswana. While this is a significant element of the policy that warrants analysis, it is beyond the scope of this chapter, which focuses on Community-Based Natural Resource Management (CBNRM) policy and the hunting ban.
3. Büscher 2010; Ferguson 1990

deploy the politically neutralising rhetoric of the common good in justifying the restrictions and regulations associated with conservation policy.[4] However, as Kelly notes, there are instrumental uses for this kind of discourse as, "the ability of conservationists and participating governments to use environmental arguments to dispossess people of their land and resources has allowed this form of expropriation to rise at an alarming rate".[5] Thus, critically engaging with a seemingly technical policy decision provides great insights into the political nature of these choices.

In fact, a nuanced understanding of the politics of conservation recognises that it may "distribute fortune and misfortune at the same time".[6] As such, access to land and natural resources is mediated through social and political institutions.[7] Grappling with how advantage and disadvantage is meted out provides insight into the working of politics at the local, national and global level.

In Botswana, debates exist regarding the origins of the hunting ban and the long-term environmental implications of the decision. However, it does seem clear that the introduction and implementation of the hunting ban has fundamentally altered the tenets and operation of Community-Based Natural Resources Management (CBNRM) in Botswana, in terms of both policy and process. CBNRM is, at least in theory, grounded in the notion that local knowledge, local management and local buy-in for conservation are necessary and beneficial. Using Botswana and its hunting policy as a case study, this chapter explores how these global and national narratives of participatory conservation mask deeply directive and centre-focused environmental policies and examines the political implications of this tendency.

In this chapter, the hunting ban provides a useful lens through which to interrogate the reproduction and strengthening of the state in rural areas, by considering state-led reorganisation of social-ecological institutions such as CBNRM, local responses to these changes, and the problematic power dynamics that have emerged through the imposition of top-down decisions on what has supposedly been a participatory and bottom-up institutional structure.

The following sections will provide contextual background regarding participatory, community-based approaches to conservation in Southern Africa and then present the specific case of Botswana. From there, the chapter will trace Botswana's history with hunting, describe the policy decision ending hunting throughout the country and then introduce the various ways in which this decision reverberates within communities. It closes by highlighting the unique and illuminating position of elephants in this debate. It ends with a consideration of how the hunting ban

---

4   Brockington 2002
5   Kelly 2011: p. 696
6   Brockington/Duffy/Igoe 2008: p. 73
7   Peluso/Ribot 2003; Twyman 1998

severely limits the participatory element of community-based conservation, which in turn restricts alternative avenues of resource control, thus empowering state-led initiatives over local socio-economic organisation.

Methodology

The scale and nature of the wildlife estate in Botswana makes it a particularly intriguing case study of the politics of conservation policy. Approximately 39 per cent of Botswana's land area is zoned for conservation[8] and it is the second most conserved country in the world, after Tanzania.[9] The government's decision to end hunting is not only noteworthy because of the sheer size of Botswana's conservation estate, but also because this reverses a longstanding policy of sustainable use, otherwise prevalent throughout Southern Africa.[10] This chapter's empirical findings are derived from research conducted in Botswana's Northwest District, a region also referred to as Ngamiland.[11] While the hunting ban has been implemented nationwide—and has national impacts—its ramifications on CBNRM are particularly salient in Ngamiland.

The globally unique Okavango Delta ecosystem is found in northern Botswana and the bulk of Botswana's multi-million dollar commercial safari hunting industry operates in this area.[12] This region is home to the largest concentration of lucrative charismatic megafauna in the country, and also experiences high levels of human-wildlife conflict.[13] For these reasons, CBNRM was seen as a critical conservation and development strategy in Ngamiland. Moreover, the district is home to some the most prominent community-based organisations benefitting from the CBNRM programme in the country.[14]

The findings of this chapter are informed by approximately 130 semi-structured interviews conducted in Botswana between August 2013 and April 2014. Village field sites in Ngamiland were selected on the basis of proximity to the conservation estate and the presence of CBNRM community organisations. Additional interviews were conducted in the district capital, Maun, as well as the national capital, Gaborone. Informants include local residents living in conservation-adjacent communities engaged in CBNRM by means of a community trust. Interviewees in these communities included village and community trust leaders as well as those ordinary residents—men and women with no connection to the official structures

---

8   Barnes 2001: p. 141
9   Director of the DWNP, Gaborone, 28 March 2014, interview by Annette LaRocco
10 Lindsey et al. 2007
11 Tlou 1985
12 Mbaiwa et al. 2011; Thakadu 2005
13 DWNP official, Gaborone, 25 September 2013, interview by Annette LaRocco
14 Lepper/Goebel 2010; Mbaiwa 2004; Mbaiwa et al. 2011

of village life. Also interviewed were government officials from the Department of Wildlife and National Parks, the department tasked with conservation policy at the local level, as well as at the national headquarters in Gaborone.[15] In addition, the author spoke with elected Members of Parliament representing Botswana's conservation-heavy northern constituencies, conservation practitioners, private sector tourism operators (both hunting and photographic), academics, and local conservation and development activists. Interview data was supplemented by analysis of media reports, government documents and academic literature.

Tracing participatory conservation efforts in Southern Africa
What is participatory conservation?
Participatory, or community-based, conservation came into vogue among conservation practitioners in the early 1990s as a reaction to the preservationist and exclusionary, 'fences-and-fines' approach to wildlife conservation, perhaps best described as "fortress conservation".[16] While articulating the shortcomings of fences and fines, conservation practitioners and scholars highlighted the need to incorporate social justice into ecological arrangements.[17] Community-based conservation was the subsequent response to the preservationist, fortress conservation model.[18] As a counter-narrative,[19] community-based conservation emphasises a people-centred approach and seeks to consider economic and social development needs alongside biodiversity conservation. Community-based conservation was conceived as an attempt to reintegrate the previous dichotomisation of human society and environment, thus bridging the nature/culture divide

The ethos behind participatory conservation is that those communities closest to protected areas bear the most significant costs of conservation, and thus should see direct benefits from these efforts. Moreover, the theory suggests once these communities begin to see economic and social benefits from conservation policies, they will invest in and protect their surrounding natural capital. These initiatives were viewed as win-win—both as conservation policies and rural development programmes that allowed community participation in decisions regarding land-use, resource-use and conservation beneficiation.[20]

---

15   The author was fortunate to gain access to a wide swathe of DWNP employees, from the Director of the department to middle management, all the way to the frontline public servants working in Ngamiland. This spectrum allowed for an in-depth understanding of the department's thinking with regard to the issues of hunting and CBNRM.
16   Brockington 2002
17   Brechin et al. 2003; Brosius et al. 2005; Ghimire/Pimbert 1997; Hulme/Murphree 2001
18   Adams/Hulme 2001
19   Leach/Mearns 1996; Roe 1991
20   Brosius et al. 2005; Fabricius et al. 2004; Hulme/Murphree 2001; Western/Wright 1994

The notion of community involvement in resources management quickly spread across Southern Africa. With its genesis primarily identifiable in Zimbabwe's Communal Areas Management Programme for Indigenous Resources (CAMP-FIRE) (which is itself a highly distinct and richly studied programme),[21] other initiatives began to sprout in neighbouring countries, including Botswana, Zambia, Namibia, and South Africa, often under the auspices of western donor funds.[22] However, acknowledging the problems of fortress conservation does not mean that community-based conservation initiatives are inherently the right answer. The last two decades have illustrated that these programmes have had mixed and varied results, often tied deeply to the local and regional political contexts into which they were embedded. Many have fallen far short of the theoretical ideal of participatory conservation.[23]

Problems of participatory conservation in practice
Many scholars have examined the problematic assumptions and shortcomings of community conservation in practice.[24] In particular, community conservation requires the local application of global concepts, ideologies and policies. This involves the deployment of a set of assumptions and practices, as well as regulatory and disciplining strategies to bring behaviour in line with these positions. Twyman suggests that even with the use of participatory language, the top-down approach to conservation and development prevails, creating a situation where wildlife management becomes, in fact, "people management" and centrally determined priorities continue to be enacted upon rural populations.[25] Moreover, CBNRM has most frequently been promoted in communities with a history of dispossession and land alienation, which often exist in a fraught relationship to the central state.[26] In these instances, participatory processes are highly problematic—characterised by paternalistic programmes focused on gaining compliance to state-level prerogatives rather than genuine input from local constituencies.[27]

Additionally, the totalising and essentialising concept that communities are organic, homogenous units and representative of the interests of conservation-

---

21 While beyond the scope of this paper, for further discussion of CAMPFIRE and its complexities see Alexander/McGregor 2000; Child 1996; Duffy 2000; Murombedzi 1999, 2001; Murphree 1995, 2001, 2005; Rihoy et al. 2010; Taylor 2009
22 Murombedzi 2004
23 Nelson/Agrawal 2008; Murombedzi 2004; Nelson 2010; Rihoy/Maguranyanga 2010
24 Alexander/McGregor 2000; Agrawal/Gibson 2001; Blaikie 2006; Duffy 2000; Nelson 2010; Ribot 2004; Twyman 1998
25 Twyman 1998
26 Bolaane 2004, 2013; Magole 2009; Taylor 2001a
27 Twyman 2000a, 2000b

adjacent residents has been scrutinised. In fact, so-called communities[28] are diverse, dynamic, complex and often highly stratified.[29] As such, access to resources within them is socially differentiated.[30] Despite the widespread characterisation of these rural communities as inherently local and bounded in a singular, often remote place, they are demonstrably connected to a global system.[31] Moreover, the conventional, depoliticised discourse of CBNRM fails to address the importance and power of the local political and historical contexts into which CBNRM programmes are introduced, and occludes the potentialities of elite capture of benefits that is commonplace in many CBNRM programmes.[32]

Participatory conservation emerged from within a historical moment characterised by shifts in development policy toward participatory, decentralised approaches emphasising capital and global markets. This aligned with the widespread ideological positions of the northern donor community; reduction of the state, economic incentives for behavioural change and local governance were all commonplace buzzwords of the 1990s. In the years since, significant critical engagement has shown that much of the logic underpinning community-based conservation was highly theoretical and idealised, often bearing little actual correlation to the way such schemes operated in the real world.[33] Indeed, from within the context of CBNRM policy, rural people are often blamed when projects fail, despite the structural and institutional barriers to success that are prefigured by those in power.[34]

Whether along strictly preservationist lines or as part of a community-centred approach, conservation processes create people and spaces that are highly dependent on the commodification of natural resources through capitalised global industries, most notably ecotourism.[35] In a sense, conservation brings the rural to the global market, and vice versa.[36] From within this context, presenting CBNRM initiatives as win-win for all those stakeholders involved becomes suspect.

---

28 Bearing this important critique in mind, for brevity's sake throughout this chapter I will use the word 'community' to refer to those villages engaged in CBNRM initiatives. This recognises that these communities are inherently complex and imbued with rich social, political and cultural contexts that cannot adequately be done justice in such a short piece.
29 Agrawal/Gibson 2001; Leach et al. 1999; Twyman 1998, 2000b
30 Leach et al. 1999; Peluso/Ribot 2003
31 Agrawal/Gibson 2001; West 2007
32 Alexander/McGregor 2000; Murombedzi 2004
33 Swatuk 2005
34 West/Igoe/Brockington 2006
35 Duffy 2002; Kelly 2011
36 West 2007

Community conservation in Botswana

Botswana's conservation estate has proven to be a very lucrative national resource, as wildlife tourism is the second largest economic sector in the country, behind diamonds.[37] Aligning with the broader regional trend towards community-based conservation identified above, since the early 1990s conservation policy in Botswana has incorporated a participatory approach in the form of CBNRM. Yet, throughout CBNRM's two-decade history, meaningful participation and decentralisation have often been found lacking.[38]

There are a variety of mechanisms whereby significant decentralisation can be stymied by those in power, many of which are apparent in this case.[39] Unlike other local level conservation arrangements in Southern Africa, CBNRM in Botswana has never been afforded a permanent legal status enshrined in law. In fact, the programme operated for nearly two decades without even a policy framework, as the official CBNRM policy only came into force in 2007.[40] As such, since brought into practice in the early 1990s, CBNRM has remained subject to ongoing top-down restructuring of the terms of governance. Communities have little legal recourse to contest *ad hoc*, top-down alterations to the conditions of conservation systems in the country. Thus, scholars have suggested the central government's rhetoric with regard to community-based conservation has never met the on-the-ground reality of top-heavy conservation decision-making and centralised beneficiation from conservation resources.[41] Magole argues that CBNRM in Botswana has more in common with statist conservation approaches than the participatory rhetoric implies, noting "in its current format, CBNRM stands to benefit the government much more than the people it claims to support".[42]

In fact, if fully participatory CBNRM were implemented in Botswana it would have the potential to challenge the central state's ability to collect revenue from productive conservation areas for the national coffers, and set a precedent for community-level beneficiation and management of resources, at the expense of national level institutions.[43] Natural resource policy in Botswana broadly considers three categories of resource: minerals, land and wildlife. By law, all natural resources are national resources, held in trust by the government on behalf of all citizens.[44]

---

37 Atlhopeng/Mulale 2009; Thakadu 2005
38 Blaikie 2006; Madzwamuse 2010; Magole 2009; Poteete/Ribot 2010; Rihoy/Maguranyanga 2010; Swatuk 2005; Twyman 2000a
39 Poteete/Ribot 2010
40 DWNP 2007; Rihoy/Maguranyanga 2010
41 Blaikie 2006; Poteete/Ribot 2010; Swatuk 2005
42 Magole 2009: p. 608
43 Poteete 2009; Rihoy/Maguranyanga 2010
44 Molomo 2008

This was crucial in Botswana's early postcolonial development, as the nation's mineral reserves were used to drive growth across the state, not just in the areas home to the most lucrative mineral deposits.[45] Thus Botswana's hegemonic control of conservation practices is in line with the state's unitary approach to development and pro-growth economic orientation.[46] This nationalised discourse is then deployed in the state-building project, which seeks to transcend regional and ethnic identities.

As Poteete notes, CBNRM policy, which implies superior local rights to benefit from a locally-derived resource, exposes an incongruity with potentially problematic repercussions.[47] As communities adjacent to Botswana's diamond mines adopted the language of CBNRM in pursuit of greater income remaining in their areas, the decentralisation of wildlife revenues began to threaten the centralised model on which the Botswana state had been built.[48] As such, the series of manoeuvres that have led to the recentralisation of CBNRM appear to have little to do with environmental management but are in fact in response to political imperatives as "at least some BDP [ruling party] politicians would rather dismantle CBNRM than compromise on mineral policy, despite the risk of antagonising wildlife communities".[49]

The historical trajectory of Botswana's conservation policies illustrates a tendency toward centralisation often in spite of CBNRM initiatives, and a reluctance to relinquish meaningful responsibility to rural dwellers, despite participatory rhetoric.[50] Perhaps what holds the hunting ban to be particularly noteworthy amidst even the *longue durée* of Botswana's state-led conservation is its sweeping scope—covering the entire country without any particular regard to local context in rural spaces, or the vast variety in cultural and economic practice of rural dwellers.

A brief history of hunting in Botswana

Hunting in Africa has long been stratified—with the sporting activities of colonial whites viewed as hunting proper while black African subsistence hunting for the pot was constructed as poaching.[51] The creation of this artificial distinction allows for the structuring of one behaviour as deviant while the other is deemed acceptable.[52]

Historically, Botswana is the only country in Southern Africa to have national legislation regarding subsistence hunting. While always proscribed in various ways,

---

45 Molomo 2008; Tlou et al. 1995
46 Magole 2009; Rihoy/Maguranyanga 2010
47 Poteete 2009
48 Poteete 2009; Good 1996, 1999, 2008; Rihoy/Maguranyanga 2010
49 Poteete 2009: p. 298
50 Madzwamuse 2010; Taylor 2001a
51 Adams 2009; Adams/Hulme 2001; Dickson/Hutton/Adams 2009
52 Anderson/Grove 1987; Brockington/Duffy/Igoe 2008; MacKenzie 1988

hunting had existed as a customary right among the largest Tswana-speaking groups in the precolonial era. With colonisation, the colonial authorities *and* traditional leaders slowly began to hem in hunting rights.[53] However, hunting remained an important part of cultural heritage, particularly among some of Botswana's smaller and non-dominant ethnic groups such as the San.[54] For the San, hunting was viewed as both an economic and a cultural activity, as hunting occupied an important place in social ceremonies and meat exchange was as an important tradition.[55]

Under the 1979 Unified Hunting Regulations, Special Game Licences (SGL) were introduced.[56] These licences permitted their holders to practise subsistence hunting. The main objectives of the SGL were two-fold: to legalise hunting among the poorest segments of Botswana's population and to provide food security to rural people through the consumption of meat or sale of meat to increase cash income. While some in government suggested that the SGLs were always meant to be a temporary poverty-eradication measure,[57] by the mid-1990s there were over 2,000 SGLs issued throughout Botswana's remote areas. Some recipients had been receiving them every year for nearly two decades.

Despite this, the SGL programme faced significant headwind. Some politicians argued that SGLs were conferring special rights to a specific class of people at the expense of all citizens, thus invoking Botswana's statist development approach to highlight the incompatibility of SGLs with the country's modern and difference-blind orientation.[58] Others invoked moral and animal rights-based arguments suggesting that the hunting authorised by the SGL system was inhumane. Another commonly-held view in government circles was that hunting was a primitive activity, the practice of which reflected badly on Botswana's reputation as a developmental darling.[59] Importantly, there are ongoing semiotic struggles involved in conservation wherein a whole host of values, normative positions and symbolic meanings are attached to particular resources or environmental practices, such as with hunting.[60]

---

53 Spinage 1991
54 The term 'San' refers to the diverse group of indigenous, traditionally, hunter-gatherers living across Southern Africa. The terms 'Bushmen' and 'Basarwa' are often used in Botswana, but both terms are fraught. I opt to use 'San' in this chapter as this was the term most of my self-identified San informants asked me to adopt when referring to them in English texts.
55 Hitchcock 2001; Madzwamuse 2010; Taylor 2001a, 2001b
56 This section relies heavily on the work of Hitchcock 2001.
57 A view still commonly expressed in my interviews with government officials circa 2013–2014.
58 Molomo 2008; Saugestad 2001; Solway 2002
59 In interviews with government wildlife officials, hunting was frequently referred to as primitive, backward and as a relic of another time before Botswana became a middle-income country.
60 Taylor 2002

Therefore, within government, the reliance on wildlife for subsistence is associated with backwardness and hunting is seen as primitive, undeveloped and cruel. By 1996 the SGL system had fallen out of favour. In Ngamiland in particular, CBNRM was introduced as an alternative mechanism through which communities in Botswana could benefit from the consumptive use of wildlife.[61]

Special Games Licences, which legitimised subsistence hunting, were swapped out for CBNRM and a quota system beginning in 1996. This meant individual hunting rights were exchanged for communal access to wildlife resources through community trusts.[62] In addition to the problems of sublimating an individual right to a wider corporate body, the amount of meat available under the new quota system decreased significantly, leaving many unable to meet subsistence needs.[63]

After the transition from the SGL system to a quota system, commercialised safari hunting became a key economic feature of CBNRM communities. From the early stages of CBNRM in northern Botswana, communities worked in cooperation with a safari hunter to utilise and monetise a hunting quota. In these communities, CBNRM as a concept became associated with hunting and the distribution of hunting quotas as commodities.

Hunting ban and its political implications

The hunting ban is all the more intriguing in Botswana because the consumptive use of wildlife has been the norm throughout Southern Africa for decades. Brockington, Duffy and Igoe observe:

> the international hunting fraternity remains a powerful force behind conservation today. Countries that prohibit hunting (Kenya and India) are unusual for doing so.[64]

Thus, the decision to *end* hunting, rather than maintain the status quo, can provide a glimpse into how the state goes about controlling and governing its people, territory and resources, and how those citizens respond. The hunting ban in Botswana was enacted through a presidential directive. It was not brought to a vote in parliament, nor was it processed through the cabinet. It was a decision made with relative opacity. In fact, several of the elected Members of Parliament representing areas with high densities of wildlife conservation and commercial

---

61 In Ghanzi and Kgalagadi Districts the dispensation of a small number of Special Game Licences continued until the advent of the hunting ban in 2014. Regional Wildlife Officer for Ghanzi and Kgalagadi, Ghanzi, 11 February 2014, interview by Annette LaRocco
62 Taylor 2002
63 Taylor 2002: p. 478
64 Brockington/Duffy/Igoe 2008: p. 47

safari hunting were unaware of the decision until after it was announced by the president in *kgotla* meetings[65] in their constituencies.[66]

The official justification for the hunting ban is that Botswana has seen a steady and unexplained decrease in wildlife populations. As one senior member of the Department of Wildlife and National Parks notes:

> Well the hunting ban was taken in with solid reasons behind it. As I indicated we have these [wildlife population] declines that have been picked up. In many of those cases we are not really sure why there are these. But we always are on side of caution in Botswana. I think the precautionary principle is what guided the hunting ban. We felt there was a need to understand what was happening to our wildlife populations, in an atmosphere free of the challenge of having to manage legal hunting.[67]

However, this claim has been vehemently contested by many members of the academic community, as well as in the public debate playing out in the media. In fact, scepticism regarding the supposedly scientific basis for the hunting ban featured prominently across a wide variety of stakeholders, including even private sector operators working in the non-consumptive tourism sector,[68] those standing to gain access to more wildlife concession areas with the end of hunting. Thus many respondents view the official justification as obscuring political motives for the ban.

While perhaps the most sweeping environmental regulation to come about in this manner, the implementation and execution of the hunting ban show remarkable continuity in the way state deals with CBNRM-related issues. In fact, the hunting ban is the latest in a series of decisions aimed at redefining the terms of governance in rural Botswana in favour of the central state and away from local level resource users. Other changes include: the introduction of a 65 per cent/35 per cent sharing scheme for all community-based conservation funds wherein the bulk of the profits go to the central government, the imposition of template constitutions on

---

65 *Kgotla* meetings are traditional town-hall type meetings held throughout Botswana. For a detailed description of how *kgotla* meetings operate, and how they may be used strategically by the government see Gulbrandsen 2012. For further information regarding the questionable "participatory" nature of *kgotla* meetings, see Mompati/Prinsen 2000
66 Member of Parliament, Gaborone, 23 September 2013, interview by Annette LaRocco; Member of Parliament, Gaborone, 26 September 2013, interview by Annette LaRocco
67 Deputy Director of the DWNP, Gaborone, 14 October 2013, interview by Annette LaRocco
68 Photographic tourism operator, Maun, 16 November 2013, interview by Annette LaRocco

all community-based conservation organisations throughout the country, and the increased role of the Botswana Tourism Organisation in the tendering process for community conservation concessions.[69]

The hunting ban and the façade of CBNRM

The hunting ban is significant in demonstrating that the rhetoric of participation belies the top-down nature of CBNRM in Botswana. Putting aside the debates regarding the impetus for the ban, the manner in which it was enacted sharply departs from the stated tenets of CBNRM both in the way it came about—top-down rather than consultative—as well as its predicted impacts—increasing apathy and potential environmental degradation among conservation-adjacent communities.

Among impacted communities, responses to the hunting ban in the initial months following its introduction were varied. While most individuals were unhappy with the incumbent loss of income, employment and game meat, occasionally respondents viewed the hunting ban more generously, hoping that it was undertaken in their best interest in the long term. Yet, an interesting caveat to this divide is nearly all respondents, even those willing to give the ban the benefit of the doubt, took issue with how the decision was announced, enacted and implemented. One man insisted:

> We were not consulted. We heard over the radio where they mentioned something like we were causing a decline in animal population. We were not informed about the animals which were endangered and the ones which were not. The ban was a top-down decision.[70]

Concerns were not limited to the lack of consultation at the beginning of the process. There was a consistent, pervasive belief that the ban would lead to more arrests and incarcerations in their area due to increased poaching activity and a heightened presence of law enforcement in place to monitor the ban. This is indicative of the way in which conservation-adjacent communities perceive their interactions with state authority, particularly with regard to wildlife. Specifically, policies limiting hunting have the impact of criminalising an activity viewed as a safety net and, for some, an important aspect of cultural identity, further marginalising hunting communities and reducing the regularity of game meat. Moreover, since January 2014, it appears that hunting continues regardless of the regulation, albeit in a

---

69 DWNP official, Gaborone, 25 September 2013, interview by Annette LaRocco; Photographic tourism operator Maun, 9 November 2013, interview by Annette LaRocco

70 Local resident, Boro, 25 November 2013, interview by Annette LaRocco, translation by Emmanuel Mogende

more clandestine, less socially controlled manner.[71] Taylor (2002) describes that in these instances of increased regulation and restriction, hunting becomes "hidden",

> making hunting a hidden activity encourages wasteful practices, such as leaving the skins in the bush to hide incriminating evidence, or leaving some of the meat if it is too much for a lone hunter to carry. It simultaneously acts to undermine the ability of the village as a whole to regulate such hunting practices, as keeping activities out of the public arena makes it all the harder to exercise accountability in restricting abuse.[72]

Taylor's study took place over a decade before the hunting ban but his analysis continues to reverberate in the contemporary Okavango Delta. One informant involved with commercial hunting and tourism suggested it was "naïve" to believe that poaching levels would not be exacerbated by the decision to end hunting, which bars conservation-adjacent people from benefitting from wildlife legally.[73] Furthermore, beyond increased illegal hunting, the ban disconnects people from surrounding resources. Addressing this, an MP from Ngamiland directly engaged with the language of CBNRM to suggest that it is the failure to involve communities in environmental decisions and management—not the continuation of hunting—that will lead to environment catastrophe for Botswana's wildlife populations:

> You're going to encourage disorder because you are not allowing or empowering the owner [sic] of these products to manage and to have determination of it ... So even if they don't shoot themselves, they'll turn a blind eye if they see someone with a gun going into the bush because it's a source of bitterness for them.[74]

The informant referred to communities as the owners of natural resources, while in fact, all natural resources are legally owned by the state. However, this discursive choice is interesting because it indicates a tension surrounding notions of ownership and the rights of citizens within the state. The erosion of collective environmental controls in communities ostensibly engaged in CBNRM is both counter-intuitive to

---

71 Local resident, Mababe, 4 December 2013, interview by Annette LaRocco, translation by Emmanuel Mogende; DWNP Anti-Poaching official, Gaborone, 31 March 2014, interview by Annette LaRocco. This is still relatively anecdotal because enough time has not elapsed to conduct a rigorous survey.
72 Taylor 2002: p. 485
73 Hunting tourism operator, Maun, 13 November 2013, interview by Annette LaRocco
74 Member of Parliament, Gaborone, 26 September 2013, interview by Annette LaRocco

the programme and pernicious. While once empowered to believe CBNRM gave them some modicum of local control, the hunting ban deepens processes of alienation of people from the land and resources that surround them, fuelling the source of bitterness as noted above.[75] Moreover, the hunting ban is a sweeping nationwide policy with no consideration of local contexts, specific environmental imperatives or historical social-ecological arrangements, negating all the benefits intended to result from CBNRM. Contrary to the tenets of CBNRM, the implication of the hunting ban is that it will operate the same way across the country, encompassing highly varied ecosystems and without regard to local perspectives.

There is a belief among those rural and remote populations that the terms of participatory conservation in Botswana have been fundamentally disrupted without their input. As noted earlier, with the advent of CBNRM, the vast majority of the Special Game Licences were revoked with the tacit understanding that rural communities (as opposed to rural individuals) would be able to benefit from wildlife through the CBNRM programme. By selling a community hunting quota to a hunting operator, the village would have access to money, employment and game meat. Among the rural dwellers interviewed, this was seen as a compromise with the government. As they understood it, at the government's request they agreed to relinquish their Special Game Licences, which had empowered individual citizens to take advantage of wildlife resources, in exchange for a system that would allow meat and monetary benefits to accrue to the community at large. However, with the implementation of the hunting ban, these rural citizens felt that the terms of this compromise had been altered without their consent or knowledge. Not only have their individual rights to meat utilisation been prohibited, but communities no longer receive either monetary or caloric benefits from safari hunting. As with the transition from SGLs to the quota system, the hunting ban placed increasing limits on local residents' ability to benefit from wildlife, especially direct consumption of game meat. For many conservation-adjacent citizens, the steady removal of hunting rights ignores the historical environmental stewardship they believe they had practised for generations, often using discourse about future use and sustainability that would be recognisable to any typical conservationist. As a *kgosana* said:

> We suspect that tourists and the Department of Wildlife acted in concert to have hunting banned. To me, wildlife is like cattle; they are kept to sustain our livelihood. But we consume our domestic animals sparingly with our future needs in mind. The same goes for wild animals.[76]

---

75 Molomo 2008
76 *Kgosana* (Headman), Boro, 25 November 2013, interview by Annette LaRocco, translation by Emmanuel Mogende

Conservation practices and discourses can become part of the framework through which people imagine themselves within their environment. These shifts in environmental subjectivities are important in the study of the political impacts of conservation policies.[77] Conservation policies work to shape and position people's perceptions of belonging relative to land, territory, resources and the authority invoked over them. Emerging from the research is local communities' reliance on various repertories to protest perceived top-down conservation decisions like the hunting ban, which they viewed as allied with the interests of tourists rather than local people. In particular, claims of autochthony, for example, the invocation of the status of being a "Son of the Delta"[78] and rhetorics of belonging and indigeneity call on local ethnic identities and histories and are juxtaposed against the dominant national paradigm of a homogenous state presented by the central government.[79]

This invocation is particularly noteworthy on the part of San communities and is encapsulated in this statement from a resident of a conservation-adjacent village in northern Botswana: "Those who make policies don't know how we interact with the animals … We, the San, know about conservation. We come from far living … together with animals and other resources we need."[80] This worldview is attempting to weaken the state's unequivocal claim over conservation enactments such as the hunting ban by appealing to logics of local history and ethnic identity, and the rights of local people to assert authority over their surrounding environment.

Additionally, these rhetorical imaginaries of resistance to the hunting ban utilise the fundamental premise of participatory conservation. They also use historical and contemporary proximity to wildlife to argue that they, conservation-adjacent communities, are more fit to determine how resources are used than decision-makers in far-off, urban Gaborone:[81]

> Instead of banning hunting, government should engage us to solve any problems concerning hunting activities. We live alongside these animals, we know them better than people from Gaborone or further afield who want to tell us how to live with them.[82]

---

77 West/Igoe/Brockington 2006
78 Local resident, Boro, 25 November 2013, interview by Annette LaRocco, translation by Emmanuel Mogende
79 Nyamnjoh 2004; Saugestad 2001; Solway 2002
80 Local resident, Mababe, 3 December 2013, interview by Annette LaRocco, translation by Emmanuel Mogende
81 One respondent suggested that those decision-makers from Gaborone were "as good as tourists" because they understood so little about life in the rural areas of Botswana.
82 *Kgosana* (Headman), Boro, 25 November 2013, interview by Annette LaRocco, translation by Emmanuel Mogende

This localised rhetorical resistance is interesting when considered with the longer term tendency of the state to limit or not fully enable CBNRM. However, the deployment of identity and regional politics is a particularly fraught strategy because of Botswana's postcolonial nation-building project around Tswana identity, and the state's reluctance to accept notions of indigeneity for discrete populations.[83]

CBNRM does political work; it empowers centrifugal forces in society. As such, there are structural, state-enhancing incentives to limit its robust implementation. From its introduction to its current manifestation relative to the hunting ban, many of the features of CBNRM—the consultation of communities, the notion of local stewardship being suited to conservation, and the role of social control against poaching—are lacking in Botswana. Furthermore, despite these lacunae, the discourses invoked around CBNRM linger, as various stakeholders including local residents themselves continue to deploy the discourses of participatory conservation in order to voice objections to the hunting ban and to the manner in which state authorities interact with communities and environments.

Photographic or hunting tourism? Trade-offs and the state
The hunting ban takes the question of sustainable use of wildlife completely out of the realm of participatory, community conservation and places it squarely as the purview of the government. In practice, the decision to end all hunting in Botswana is deeply intertwined with CBNRM policy because the community trusts, which form the backbone of the CBNRM conservation approach, owe most of their income to safari hunting. After the ban was implemented, and hunting quotas were no longer able to be sold, the majority of community trusts in Ngamiland faced financial hardship requiring retrenchment of staff and cutting of services.[84] This has led many community members, as well as conservation activists and academics, to claim that the decision to end hunting has favoured non-consumptive tourism operators at the expense of local Batswana communities. One such conservation activist noted, "what is clear and what is irrefutable is that [the] hunting ban will benefit photographic tourism, and a lot of these photographic tourism investors are very politically connected".[85] While hunting tourism made up a smaller percentage of the overall size of the industry, it directly benefitted CBNRM communities to

---

83 Specifically, the government of Botswana does not recognise claims of indigeneity from citizens, especially from San peoples, stating that all citizens of Botswana are indigenous. For a more in-depth explanation of how this has presented difficulties for San populations, see Saugestad 2001; Nyamnjoh 2007; Zips-Mairitsch 2013
84 *Kgosi* (Village Chief), Sankuyo, 19 November, interview by Annette LaRocco; DWNP Community CBNRM liaison, Maun, 7 November 2013, interview by Annette LaRocco
85 Conservationist activist, Maun, 24 October 2013, interview by Annette LaRocco

a greater extent than photographic-only operations.[86] Thus, the perception, as the above quote suggests, is that the decision to end hunting favours large, corporate photographic tourism rather than communities attempting to benefit from the nearby resources.[87] Furthermore, this view considers the ban not as a technical solution to an environmental problem,[88] but rather a measure meant to be attractive to a particular Western clientele to whom hunting is both odious and considered anathema to a conservation ethos,[89] and upon whom the photographic tourism industry depends.

CBNRM refracts the unequal power relations between the state, safari companies and rural communities, rendering the characterisation of participatory conservation problematic. In these struggles, the Botswana state, within its pro-growth development agenda, tends to act on behalf of private capital, which in the process undermines social justice.[90] Decisions made regarding conservation, and CBNRM, are decisions that determine which institutions, individuals, and organisations may benefit from tourism and wildlife resources found throughout the conservation estate. In Botswana, conservation decisions dictate who controls the productive resources of wildlife and land. Thus, statements such as this emanating from CBNRM communities may give pause to the government:

> Ngamiland with that rich natural resources is the poorest compared to other areas [in Botswana] where they don't have natural resources. It means that everything that is done in Ngamiland, goes to the Government coffers which is shared to the whole nation. I think there must be a percentage that stays in Ngamiland.[91]

---

86 Lindsey et al. 2007. See also Mbaiwa 2004, 2005 for further discussion of the dynamics surrounding the photographic and hunting tourism industry in Botswana.
87 Most photographic tourism in Botswana adheres to the government's high value, low volume tourism strategy, which puts an emphasis on luxury high-end lodge experiences and clients. This strategy makes it very difficult for communities to compete in such a market, and partnering with private sector companies to run such ventures on community concessions often creates tensions, acrimonious relationships, and unhappiness for both parties. Hunting provided a somewhat different economic model, wherein the community could earn millions of pula directly from selling its animal quota, separate from other joint ventures like lodges. Thus, in interviews, the relationships between a safari hunting operator and a community, and a photographic operator and a community, were often articulated as significantly different from the point of view of local residents.
88 Conservation practitioner, Maun, 1 November 2013, interview by Annette LaRocco
89 Conservationist activist, Maun, 24 October 2013, interview by Annette LaRocco; Photographic tourism operator Maun, 30 November 2013, interview by Annette LaRocco
90 Molomo 2008
91 *Kgosi* (Village Chief), Sankuyo, 19 November, interview by Annette LaRocco

The idealised discourse of CBNRM seeks to devolve this decision-making power. Therefore statements such as the one above—which draws upon the rhetoric of CBNRM—directly challenges the central state's hegemony over the second largest economic sector in the country, wildlife tourism. Thus, it is not surprising that CBNRM, in practice, has been greatly contested by the central authorities, as it diffuses the decision-making process that dictates control and beneficiation over resources. Interestingly, while many non-consumptive tourism operators will benefit from the ban by gaining access to some new, lucrative wildlife concessions,[92] quite frequently these informants expressed concerns that ending hunting in wildlife areas unsuitable for photographic tourism would leave these tracts of land vulnerable to poachers and encroachment from cattle.[93] This sentiment is often echoed in aggrieved CBNRM communities. Despite calls for a one-to-one exchange of hunting operations for photographic tourism, hunting concessions cannot be repackaged that easily. Consumptive-use tourism can occur in less aesthetically pleasing areas unsuitable for attracting photographic tourists, making such a seamless transition impossible in many areas.[94] Mbaiwa estimates that a greater percentage of the profits derived from hunting remain with communities, as compared to photographic tourism ventures, though there are significant leakages in both cases. Thus, he views hunting and photographic tourism not as in opposition but rather as complementary economic activities, each suited to different local contexts and community preferences.[95] Though importantly he notes that both kinds of tourism are plagued by similar problems that vex CBNRM initiatives—racial, gender and class hierarchies, catering to western audiences above and beyond local needs and perpetuating particular notions of environment, wildlife and landscape.[96]

However, the somewhat simple question of whether hunting or photographic tourism is better for communities economically presents a false choice. These two options require different inputs, produce different outcomes and are differentially beneficial to a variety of stakeholders, one of which is the central government. It is not that either hunting or photographic tourism is better or worse, but that the choice to favour one economic activity represents the pre-eminence of one set of interests over another. The question also masks some of the similarities and continuities that exist between both forms of tourist-driven exploitation. One informant in a CBNRM community noted:

---

92 Photographic tourism operator, Maun, 16 November 2013, interview by Annette LaRocco
93 Photographic tourism operator, Maun, 6 November 2013, interview by Annette LaRocco
94 Photographic tourism operator, Maun, 9 November 2013, interview by Annette LaRocco; DWNP official, Gaborone, 11 October 2013, interview by Annette LaRocco
95 Mbaiwa 2003
96 See Mbaiwa 2005 for a discussion of what he characterises as "enclave tourism" in Botswana.

Tourism generates a lot of revenue thus growing Botswana's economy. Hence they [government] seek to make economic fortunes at the expense of the people. It shows that a person's life is insignificant; animals are more valued. I believe that in the beginning, when the universe was created, a human being was given control over all living things. Nowadays it beats me that all of a sudden an animal takes priority over human being.[97]

Neither approach to utilising wildlife is inherently good or bad but rather exists within a matrix of policies, ideologies and positionalities, often reflecting the political atmosphere in which these decisions are made. The discourses, then, used to resist and make sense of the hunting ban reveal how, through the very language of CBNRM, the government created a space in which rural dwellers were allowed to imagine a state-sanctioned right to influence and participate in conservation. Yet, this space has been periodically hemmed in as the state struggles to reclaim control over these processes. At a local level, resentment has grown around a perceived state bias toward photographic tourism actors at the expense of CBNRM communities, many of which had expressed a preference to continue hunting operations, or at least viewed hunting and photographic tourism as compatible activities. The feeling that Ngamiland, despite its natural wealth, had been left behind in favour of a national development to which they are alienated, characterised rural dwellers' orientation toward the central state.

Hunting and elephants – a call for a compromise

Despite misgivings, communities engaged in CBNRM appeared willing to go very far in accepting the premise of the hunting ban, invoking strongest resistance only in the context of particular, acute affects on everyday livelihoods—specifically, from elephants. In fact, many informants have suggested they would be willing to accept the hunting ban if only the government would carve out an exception for elephants. One local resident noted, "the law is not good, it should have excluded problem animals such as elephants which destroy our fields, crops, and even homesteads. They should have allowed these animals to be hunted."[98] DeMotts and Hoon highlight the unique political salience of elephants in northern Botswana.[99] Over 200,000 elephants live in the two northern-most districts in Botswana[100]—

---

97 Local resident, Xuoxao, 27 November 2013, interview by Annette LaRocco, translation by Emmanuel Mogende
98 Local resident, Mababe, 3 December 2013, interview by Annette LaRocco, translation by Emmanuel Mogende
99 DeMotts/Hoon 2012
100 Department of Wildlife and National Parks 2012: p. 31

the single largest African elephant population on the continent.[101] And despite elephants often being construed by Western audiences as gentle, charismatic giants, for conservation-adjacent communities elephants are pests at best and life-threatening hazards at worst. Elephants destroy crops and property, and in extreme though not uncommon cases, kill humans. This perpetual destruction wrought on poor, conservation-adjacent communities exacerbates local–national tensions, as people never feel adequately compensated for hardship. A local resident living next to the Okavango Delta noted:

> Just recently, elephants made their way into my garden and destroyed lettuce, green pepper and other vegetables. That dealt a heavy blow to my life. However, I have no problem with living alongside animal but an issue of concern is that we are not adequately compensated for wild animal damages. There is a huge difference between the compensation and damages incurred. Like I already mentioned, I don't have a problem with wild animals mainly because they boost the national economy.[102]

Elephant trophy hunting had, in a small way, helped to ameliorate some of the antagonisms between communities, elephants and the government. One informant, discussing the legalised sale of elephant hunts, noted that "what it did was pay for tolerance".[103] Others remarked, "with a hunting quota for an elephant alone you can sustain a community".[104] The negotiating tactic of asking—or pleading—for the continuation of elephant hunting at a minimum, may seem infinitely reasonable in the local context. However, when this runs up against the Western moral and ideological backlash against big trophy hunting,[105] as well as the potential for capital accumulation that elephants, as one of the species most revered by tourists, bring to the wealthy elites of Botswana's photographic tourism industry, it is easy to see why the government of Botswana is unlikely to consider these local demands.

---

101 Director of the DWNP, Gaborone, 28 March 2014, interview by Annette LaRocco
102 Local resident, Boro, 25 November 2013, interview by Annette LaRocco, translation by Emmanuel Mogende
103 Hunting tourism operator, Maun, 13 November 2013, interview by Annette LaRocco
104 DWNP official, Gaborone, 25 September 2013, interview by Annette LaRocco. See for example: "We'd shoot an elephant and bring it to the village and within two hours the whole elephant had disappeared. They eat the meat, boil down the bones for lard, and use the hide, too. They had 23 elephants a year [from a quota]. One elephant approximates about 10 domestic cows. It's equivalent to the community losing 230 domestic cows a year. Who is going to drop off 230 cows for the community to access the same kind of red meat?" Hunting tourism operator, Ghanzi, 24 February 2014, interview by Annette LaRocco
105 See Wemmer/Christian 2008 for further reading regarding western views of elephant hunting.

In particular, people in the Global North are often primarily exposed to Africa's charismatic megafauna like elephants through popular culture including children's stories, zoos and wildlife documentaries.[106] These representations are highly stylised and emotive, and more often than not remove any mention of the daily human interactions with African fauna. Garland suggests that this perpetuates an attachment to these animals on the part of Western societies, one that is often in tension with the stark realities required to live alongside wildlife. Indeed, African animals are perceived as important members of a global faunal kingdom that belongs to all humanity as a kind of international natural heritage. Yet as Garland eloquently notes:

> It is in Africa, however, that wild animals actually live, and on African shoulders that the primary responsibility for maintaining this "global" inheritance falls. The burden that this responsibility represents is substantial, and the terms on which it is undertaken are seldom, if ever, determined by African people or nations alone. On the contrary, African actors participate in the provision of wildlife to the world from a global vantage point deeply compromised by the continent's history of colonization and association with nature in Western systems of thought.[107]

Elephants are a significant touchstone in the debate over the hunting ban. This is exacerbated further by the government's, and especially the current president Lt General Ian Khama's, significant efforts to cultivate the image of Botswana as a haven for elephants amidst a time of historical levels of poaching for their ivory. Elephants are central to Botswana's "marketing of the nation state" in the context of ecotourism,[108] and feature prominently in the country's international conservation profile. President Khama, who is often personally engaged in setting conservation priorities, is well-known for his aversion to hunting and allegiance to a preservationist style of environmental policy.[109] This has created tension and even backlash in a country with a strong tradition of sustainable use. A prominent community conservation activist noted, "our president is a board member of Conservation International, so you can imagine what kind of 'insights' he is receiving from the old bearded white men in California".[110] The attempt to harmonise an international wildlife conservation perspective with the realities of

---

106 Garland 2008
107 Garland 2008: p. 52
108 Duffy 2002
109 Director of the DWNP, Gaborone, 28 March 2014, interview by Annette LaRocco
110 Conservation activist, Maun, 24 October 2013, interview by Annette LaRocco

human–wildlife conflict on the ground illuminates the tensions between local and global environmental perspectives.[111] These are contradictions that a functioning CBNRM programme is meant to address. Furthermore, this highlights the global inequalities inherent in conservation, brought to the fore once again through the hunting ban. The question of who the ban is for—the international community or for Batswana—lingers. This tension is very apparent to local communities dealing with the limited CBNRM system, as one young man noted:

> They [the government] always concern themselves with what the international community says about Botswana. They don't pay attention to how the ordinary Motswana is impacted. I am of the view that the lives of people, who live in a tourism area that generates a lot of money like ours, should be better. The financial success of the wild animal tourism industry in this area should be reflected through the standard of living of its residents. There shouldn't be a mismatch.[112]

Conclusion

> Conservation to them [the government] is a tool to asserting their power base. It's not conservation for the sake of preserving biodiversity or empowering the local communities.[113]

This chapter examined the politics of Botswana's hunting ban in the context of participatory conservation, in this case, CBNRM. The impact of the hunting ban across the country, especially with regard to CBNRM, is complex and varied. However, a common theme which unifies many of the responses to this newly-implemented policy is the role of the state vis-à-vis the rural and remote areas of its territory. The question of how the environment is governed, especially from within an ostensibly participatory approach has emerged as a key site of negotiation of state practices. All of this serves to probe the deep questions surrounding the participatory nature of CBNRM in Botswana, which still claims to put communities and community consultation at the centre of its conservation policy. It also probes whether tenets of the programme have ever been actualised in practice. Under the hunting ban, in fact, communities can no longer chose to interface with conservation and the related tourism industry in one of two ways—

---

111 Mbaiwa 2003; Gressier 2012
112 Local resident, Xuoxao, 27 November 2013, interview by Annette LaRocco, translation by Emmanuel Mogende
113 Opposition MP from Ngamiland, 26 September 2013, Gaborone, interview by Annette LaRocco

either consumptive or non-consumptive use—but rather must adhere to state-level mandates, which are seen to promote a preservationist approach favoured by many photographic tourism operators and their international clients.

Drawing from extensive data collection this chapter illustrated just how far the state in Botswana has moved from a genuine CBNRM approach, even when considered across a long trajectory of recentralising tendencies. It is clear that analysis must move away from thinking about CBNRM in Botswana as if it exists in any way except on paper. The hunting ban is fundamentally contrary to the ethos of CBNRM—it eschewed local consultation and marginalised local resource-use preferences—but yet is closely aligned with the way conservation policy is enacted in Botswana. The hunting ban may be contradictory to the tenets of CBNRM but it is not aberrant; it is in keeping with the historical trajectory of Botswana's state-building process, overall political economy, and the manner in which authority is enacted and perceived in rural areas.

Yet importantly, CBNRM also retains some clout in how it shapes imaginaries and resistance to state-centred priorities on the part of conservation-adjacent citizens. And while it does not really exist in practice in Botswana, participatory conservation is still used and deployed as a site of contestation and opposition. CBNRM and the discourses used to embed communities in conservation decisions provide a means for local residents to reject what they view as over-extensions of state authority and capital extraction from the areas where they live, as they articulate grievances related to the hunting ban through the language of participation and local control.

However, the myth that participation—a space for a say in how lives and livelihoods are governed—continues to do useful political work in pacifying discontent in conservation adjacent areas is highly controversial. CBNRM becomes a platform upon which rural communities are expected to place all of their development hopes, regardless of the extreme top-down limitations they face in tapping the benefits of their areas. This chapter demonstrates that the state works to restructure and repossess devolved conservation and resource beneficiation institutions found within the participatory paradigm. Decisions such as the hunting ban that deeply impact on rural dwellers are made by a small elite in the capital, while lip service is paid to the norms of community involvement. As it stands now, it is unclear if the hunting ban is permanent. It is evidently indefinite but the structure of the ban and its *de facto*, rather than *de jure*, process of implementation leave it open to reversal if the political winds change in Botswana.

References

Adams, W.M. (2009), Sportman's Shot, Poacher's Pot: Hunting, Local People and the History of Conservation. In B. Dickson, J. Hutton and W.M. Adams (eds.), *Recreational Hunting, Conservation, and Rural Livelihoods*. Oxford, UK: Blackwell: 127–140.

Adams, W.M. and D. Hulme (2001), Conservation and Community: Changing Narratives, Policies and Practices in African Conservation. In D. Hulme and M.W. Murphree (eds.), *African Wildlife and Livelihoods: The Promise and Performance of Community conservation*. Portsmouth, NH: Heinemann.

Adams, W.M. and M. Mulligan (2004), *Decolonizing Nature: Strategies for Conservation in a Post-colonial Era*. London: Earthscan.

Agrawal, A. and C.C. Gibson (2001), *Communities and the Environment: Ethnicity, Gender, and the State in Community-based Conservation*. New Brunswick, NJ: Rutgers Univ. Press.

Alexander, J. and J. McGregor (2000), Wildlife and Politics: CAMPFIRE in Zimbabwe. *Development and Change*, 31(3): 605–627.

Anderson, D. and R. Grove (1987), *Conservation in Africa: People, Policies, and Practice*. Cambridge, UK: Cambridge University Press.

Anderson, D.G. and K. Ikeya, (2001), *Parks, Property, and Power: Managing Hunting Practice and Identity within State Policy Regimes*. Osaka: National Museum of Ethnology.

Atlhopeng, J. and K. Mulale (2009), Natural Resource-based Tourism and Wildlife Policies in Botswana. In J. Saarinen (ed.), *Sustainable Tourism in Southern Africa: Local Communities and Natural Resources in Transition*. Bristol, UK: Channel View Publications: 134–149.

Barnes, J.J. (2001), Economic Returns and Allocations of Resources in the Wildlife Sector of Botswana. *South African Journal of Wildlife Research*, 31(3&4): 141–153.

Blaikie, P. (2006), Is Small Really Beautiful? Community-based Natural Resources Management in Malawi and Botswana. *World Development*, 34(11): 1942–1957.

Bolaane, M.M.M. (2004), Wildlife Conservation and Local Management: The Establishment of Moremi Park, Okavango, Botswana in the 1950s–1960s, (PhD Thesis, Univ. of Oxford).

Bolaane, M.M.M. (2013), *Chiefs, Hunters and San in the Creation of the Moremi Game Reserve, Okavango Delta: Multiracial Interactions and Initiatives, 1956–1979*. Osaka: National Museum of Ethnology.

Brechin, S.R., C.L. Fortwangler, P.R. Wilhusen and P.C. West (2003), *Contested Nature: Promoting International Biodiversity Conservation with Social Justice in the Twenty-first Century*. Albany, NY: State University of New York Press.

Brockington, D. (2002), *Fortress Conservation: The Preservation of the Mkomazi Game Reserve, Tanzania*. Oxford, UK: James Currey.

Brockington, D., R. Duffy and J. Igoe (2008), *Nature Unbound: Conservation, Capitalism and the Future of Protected Areas*. London: Earthscan.

Brosius, J.P., A.L. Tsing and C. Zerner (eds.) (2005), *Communities and Conservation: Histories and Politics of Community-based Natural Resource Management*. Walnut Creek, CA: AltaMira Press.

Büscher, B. (2010), Anti-Politics as Political Strategy: Neoliberalism and Transfrontier Conservation in Southern Africa. *Development and Change*, 41(1): 29–51.

Child, B. (1996), The Practice and Principles of Community-Based Wildlife Management in Zimbabwe: The CAMPFIRE Programme. *Biodiversity & Conservation*, 5(3): 369–398.

DeMotts, R. and P. Hoon (2012), Whose Elephants? Conserving, Compensating, and Competing in Northern Botswana. *Society and Natural Resources*, 25(9): 837–851.

Department of Wildlife and National Parks (2012), *Aerial Census of Animals in Botswana: 2012 Dry Season*. Gaborone: Government Printer.

Department of Wildlife and National Parks (2007), *CBNRM Policy*. Gaborone: Gov. Printer.

Dickson, B., J. Hutton and W.M. Adams (2009), *Recreational Hunting, Conservation, and Rural Livelihoods*. Oxford, UK: Blackwell.

Duffy, R. (2000), *Killing for Conservation: Wildlife Policy in Zimbabwe*. Oxford: James Currey.

Duffy, R. (2002), *A Trip too Far: Ecotourism, Politics, and Exploitation*. London: Earthscan.

Fabricius, C., E. Koch, S. Turner and H. Magome (eds.) (2004), *Rights, Resources and Rural Development: Community-based Natural Resource Management in Southern Africa*. London: Earthscan.

Ferguson, J. (1990), *The Anti-Politics Pachine: "Development", Depoliticization, and Bureaucratic Power in Lesotho*. Cambridge: Cambridge University Press.

Garland, E. (2008), The Elephant in the Room: Confronting the Colonial Character of Wildlife Conservation in Africa. *African Studies Review*, 51(3): 51–74.

Ghimire, K. and M.P. Pimbert (1997), *Social Change and Conservation: Environmental Politics and Impacts of National Parks and Protected Areas*. London: Earthscan Publications.

Good, K. (1996), Authoritarian Liberalism: A Defining Characteristic of Botswana. *Journal of Contemporary African Studies*, 14(1): 29–51.

Good, K. (1999), Enduring Elite Democracy in Botswana. *Democratization*, 6(1): 50–66.

Good, K. (2008), *Diamonds, Dispossession and Democracy in Botswana*. Suffolk, UK: James Currey.

Gressier, C. (2012), An Elephant in the Room: Okavango Safari Hunting as Ecotourism? *Ethnos: Journal of Anthropology*, 1(1): 1–22.

Gulbrandsen, Ø. (2012), *The State and the Social: State Formation in Botswana and its Precolonial and Colonial Genealogies*. New York: Berghahn Books.

Hitchcock, R.K. (2001), 'Hunting is Our Heritage': The Struggle for Hunting and Gathering Rights among the San of Southern Africa. In D.G. Anderson and K. Ikeya (eds.), *Parks, Property, and Power: Managing Hunting Practice and Identity within State Policy Regimes*. Osaka: National Museum of Ethnology: 139–156.

Hulme, D. and M.W. Murphree (2001), *African Wildlife & Livelihoods: The Promise and Performance of Community Conservation*. Portsmouth, NH: Heinemann.

Kelly, A.B. (2011), Conservation Practice as Primitive Accumulation. *The Journal of Peasant Studies*, 38(4): 683–701.

Leach, M. and R. Mearns (1996), *The Lie of the Land: Challenging Received Wisdom on the African Environment*. Oxford: James Currey.

Leach, M., R. Mearns and I. Scoones (1999), Environmental Entitlements: Dynamics and Institutions in Community-Based Natural Resource Management. *World Development*, 27(2): 225–247.

Lepper, C.M. and J.S. Goebel (2010), Community-based Natural Resource Management, Poverty Alleviation and Livelihood Diversification: A Case Study from Northern Botswana. *Development Southern Africa*, 27(5): 725–739.

Lindsey, P.A., P.A. Roulet and S.S. Romanach (2007), Economic and Conservation Significance of the Trophy Hunting Industry in Sub-Saharan Africa. *Biological Conservation*, 134(4): 455–469.

Madzwamuse, M. (2010), Adaptive or Anachronistic? Maintaining Indigenous Natural Resource Governance Systems in Northern Botswana. In F. Nelson (ed.), *Community Rights, Conservation and Contested Land: The Politics of Natural Resource Governance in Africa*. London: Earthscan: 241–268.

MacKenzie, J.M. (1988), *The Empire of Nature: Hunting, Conservation, and British Imperialism*. Manchester, UK: Manchester University Press.

Magole, L.I. (2009), Common Pool Resource Management among San Communities in Ngamiland, Botswana. *Development Southern Africa*, 26(4): 597–610.

Mbaiwa, J.E. (2003), The Socio-Economic and Environmental Impacts of Tourism Development on the Okavango Delta, North-Western Botswana. *Journal of Arid Environments*, 54(1): 447–67.

Mbaiwa, J.E. (2004), The Socio-Economic Benefits and Challenges of a Community-Based Safari Hunting Tourism in the Okavango Delta, Botswana. *Journal of Tourism Studies*, 15(2): 36–50.

Mbaiwa, J.E. (2005), Enclave Tourism and its Socio-Economic Impacts in the Okavango Delta, Botswana. *Tourism Management*, 26(1): 157–72.

Mbaiwa, J.E., A. Stronza and U. Kreuter (2011), From Collaboration to Conservation: Insights From the Okavango Delta, Botswana. *Society and Natural Resources*, 24(4): 400–411.

Molomo, M. (2008), Sustainable Development, Ecotourism, National Minorities and Land in Botswana. In K. Amanor and S. Moyo (eds.), *Land and Sustainable Development in Africa*. London: Zed Books: 159–183.

Mompati, T. and G. Prinsen (2000), Ethnicity and Participatory Development Methods in Botswana: Some Participants Are to Be Seen and Not Heard. *Development in Practice*, 10(5): 625–637.

Murombedzi, J.C. (1999), Devolution and Stewardship in Zimbabwe's CAMPFIRE Programme. *Journal of International Development*, 11(2): 287–293.

Murombedzi, J.C. (2001), Committees, Rights, Costs and Benefits: Natural Resource Stewardship and Community Benefits in Zimbabwe's CAMPFIRE Programme. In D. Hulme and

M.W. Murphree (eds.), *African Wildlife and Livelihoods: The Promise and Performance of Community Conservation*. Portsmouth, NH: Heinemann: 244–255.

Murombedzi, J. (2004), Devolving the Expropriation of Nature: The 'Devolution' of Wildlife Management in Southern Africa. In W.M. Adams and M. Mulligan (eds.), *Decolonizing Nature: Strategies for Conservation in a Post-colonial Era*. London: Earthscan: 135–151.

Murphree, M.W. (1995), *The Lesson from Mahenye: Rural Poverty, Democracy and Wildlife Conservation*. London: IIED.

Murphree, M.W. (2001), Community, Council and Client: A Case Study in Ecotourism Development in Mahenye, Zimbabwe. In D. Hulme and M.W. Murphree (eds.), *African Wildlife and Livelihoods: The Promise and Performance of Community Conservation*. Portsmouth, NH: Heinemann: 177–194.

Murphree, M.W. (2005), Congruent Objectives, Competing Interests, and Strategic Compromise: Concept and Process in the Evolution of Zimbabwe's CAMPFIRE, 1984–1996. In J.P. Brosius, A.L. Tsing and C. Zerner (eds.), *Communities and Conservation: Histories and Politics of Community-based Natural Resource Management*. Walnut Creek, CA: AltaMira Press.

Nelson, F. (2010), *Community Rights, Conservation and Contested Land: The Politics of Natural Resource Governance in Africa*. London: Earthscan.

Nelson, F. and A. Agrawal (2008), Patronage or Participation? Community-Based Natural Resource Management Reform in Sub-Saharan Africa. *Development and Change*, 39(4): 557–585.

Nyamnjoh, F.B. (2004), Reconciling 'the Rhetoric of Rights' with Competing Notions of Personhood and Agency in Botswana. In H. Englund and F.B. Nyamnjoh (eds.), *Rights and the Politics of Recognition in Africa*. London: Zed Books: 33–63.

Nyamnjoh, F.B. (2007), 'Ever-Diminishing Circles': The Paradoxes of Belonging in Botswana. In M. Cadena and O. Starn (eds.), *Indigenous Experience Today*. Oxford: Berg: 305–332.

Peluso, N.L. and J.C. Ribot (2003), A Theory of Access. *Rural Sociology*, 68(2): 153–181.

Poteete, A.R. (2009), Defining Political Community and Rights to Natural Resources in Botswana. *Development and Change*, 40(2): 281–305.

Poteete, A.R. and J.C. Ribot (2010), Repertoires of Domination: Decentralization as Process in Botswana and Senegal. *World Development*, 39(3): 439–449.

Roe, E. (1991), Development Narratives, or Making the Best of Blueprint Development. *World Development*, 19(4): 287–300.

Ribot, J.C. (2004), *Waiting for Democracy: The Politics of Choice in Natural Resource Decentralization*. Washington, DC: World Resources Institute.

Rihoy, L., C. Chirozva and S. Anstey (2010), 'People are Not Happy': Crisis, Adaptation and Resilience in Zimbabwe's CAMPFIRE Programme. In F. Nelson (ed.), *Community Rights, Conservation and Contested Land: The Politics of Natural Resource Governance in Africa*. London: Earthscan: 174–201.

Rihoy, L. and B. Maguranyanga (2010), The Politics of Community-Based Natural Resource Management in Botswana. In F. Nelson (ed.), *Community Rights, Conservation and Contested Land: The Politics of Natural Resource Governance in Africa*. London: Earthscan: 55–78.

Saugestad, S. (2001), *The Inconvenient Indigenous: Remote Area Development in Botswana, Donor Assistance and the First People of the Kalahari*. Uppsala: Nordic Africa Institute.

Spinage, C.A. (1991), *History and Evolution of the Fauna Conservation Laws of Botswana*. Gaborone: Botswana Society.

Solway, J.S. (2002), Navigating the 'Neutral' State: 'Minority' Rights in Botswana. *Journal of Southern African Studies*, 28(4): 711–729.

Swatuk, L.A. (2005), From 'Project' to 'Context': Community Based Natural Resource Management in Botswana. *Global Environmental Politics*, 5(3): 95–124.

Taylor, M.J. (2001a), Life, Land and Power: Contesting Development in Northern Botswana, (PhD Thesis, University of Edinburgh).

Taylor, M.J. (2001b), Narratives of Identity and Assertions of Legitimacy: Basarwa in Northern Botswana. In D.G. Anderson and K. Ikeya (eds.), *Parks, Property, and Power: Managing Hunting Practice and Identity within State Policy Regimes*. Osaka: National Museum of Ethnology: 157–181.

Taylor, M.J. (2002), The Shaping of San Livelihood Strategies: Government Policy and Popular Values. *Development and Change*, 33(3): 467–488.

Taylor, R. (2009), The Performance of CAMPFIRE in Zimbabwe 1989–2006. In H. Suich, B. Child and A. Spenceley (eds.), *Evolution and Innovation in Wildlife Conservation: Parks and Game Ranches to Transfrontier Conservation Areas*. London: Earthscan: 201–222.

Thakadu, O.T. (2005), Success Factors in Community Based Natural Resources Management in Northern Botswana: Lessons from Practice. *Natural Resources Forum*, 29(3): 199–212.

Tlou, T. (1985), *A History of Ngamiland, 1750 to 1906: The Formation of an African State*. Gaborone: Macmillan Botswana.

Tlou, T., N. Parsons and W. Henderson (1995), *Seretse Khama, 1921–80*. Braamfontein: Macmillan.

Twyman, C. (1998), Rethinking Community Resource Management: Managing Resources or Managing People in Western Botswana? *Third World Quarterly*, 19(4): 745–770.

Twyman, C. (2000a), Participatory Conservation? Community-based Natural Resource Management in Botswana. *The Geographic Journal*, 166(4): 323–335.

Twyman, C. (2000b), Livelihood Opportunity and Diversity in Kalahari Wildlife Management Areas, Botswana: Rethinking Community Resource Management. *Journal of Southern African Studies*, 26(4): 783–806.

Wemmer, C.M. and C.A. Christen (2008), *Elephants and Ethics: Toward a Morality of Coexistence*. Baltimore, MD: Johns Hopkins University Press.

West, P. (2007), *Conservation is Our Government Now: The Politics of Ecology in Papua New Guinea*. Durham: Duke University Press.

West, P., J. Igoe and D. Brockington (2006), Parks and Peoples: The Social Impact of Protected Areas. *Annual Review of Anthropology*, 35: 251–277.

Western, D. and R.M. Wright (1994), *Natural Connections: Perspectives in Community-based Conservation*. Washington, D.C: Island Press.

Zips-Mairitsch, M. (2013), *Lost Lands?: (Land) Rights of the San in Botswana and the Legal Concept of Indigeneity in Africa*. Copenhagen: IWGIA.

CHAPTER 10

Land relations and property rights in central-north Namibia's communal areas

Romie Vonkie Nghitevelekwa

Introduction

People relate to land, and to each other, over land in varied ways. I include both relationships under the broad term of 'land relations'. In societies in which land use is the basis of people's livelihoods, land further plays an important role in the creation and maintenance of relations between people. Very often, land is controlled or administered by one set of actors ("level of socio-political authority"), and it is used and exploited by a different set of actors ("level of use and exploitation").[1] In this context, the relationships between actors in the two levels are reciprocal. Sikor and Lund elaborate that actors at the level of use and exploitation seek to have their "access claims recognized as legitimate property by a politico-legal institution" and that at the same time this process "works to imbue the institution that provides such recognition with the recognition of its authority".[2] The two authors define these reciprocal relationships as "the 'contract' that links property to authority".[3]

Besides these reciprocal relationships, actors ascribe different meanings to land. While some actors seek to gain control over land, others seek to derive material and economic benefits for their basic livelihoods or for capital accumulation, and others seek to define their social identities. According to Parker and Goheen, this triangulation underscores three kinds of human ambition—"power, wealth and meaning".[4] Because different actors have varied aspirations for land, land is a highly contested resource—contested between and within the two levels of actors.

---

1 Conceptions borrowed from Von Benda-Beckmann 1979
2 Sikor/Lund 2009: p. 1
3 Sikor/Lund 2009: p. 1
4 Shipton/Goheen 1992

This chapter explores land relations and property rights in communal areas in central-north Namibia. It conceptualises communal land as a complex and contested terrain comprising of different social actors, who manoeuvre and struggle to control and use land, and ascribe different meanings to land.[5] The totality of these activities shape land relations and property rights. The actors at the level of socio-political authority are the state and state institutions in the form of communal land boards (CLBs) and the customary authorities in the form of traditional authorities (TAs) in their hierarchical structures. The level of use and exploitation comprises of varied land users who derive benefits from land through different mechanisms of access. The chapter examines the complexities and contestations within the context of the ongoing communal land reform, a broad-based programme being implemented through the Communal Land Reform Act, 2002 (Act No. 05 of 2002).

The socio-economic context

The geographical region herein referred to as central-north Namibia is made up of the four political and administrative regions Ohangwena, Omusati, Oshana and Oshikoto. It is further made up of seven different polities: Ombalantu, Ondonga, Ongandjera, Oukwanyama, Uukolonkadhi, Uukwaluudhi and Uukwambi, collectively referred to as the *Aawambo* societies. They are politically organised through TAs, which in some cases overlap between the four regions. The societies share many socio-economic, cultural and political traits.[6] Central-north Namibia's lifeworlds include rural and urban settings characterised by different forms of land tenure. Namibia at large has a dual structure of land tenure systems composed of freehold and communal land, reminiscent of the colonial past.[7] The rural setting in central-north Namibia is all communal land, which is the focus of this chapter.

Central-north Namibia is a densely populated expanse with an estimated population of 850,000 people, the majority of which lives in rural areas.[8] Spatially, it accounts for less than seven per cent of the country's total surface area.[9] Putting the estimated population statistics in the context of the approximate size of the area, one notes a relatively high population density that is considered to be "greater than in other rural areas in south-western Africa".[10] Like many other societies living on

---

5   I use the notion of social actors within the theoretical context of a field of power. In a field of power, social action is defined by converging or contrasting interests but also by power differentials. In this context the respective actors manoeuvre to have their interests realised or even legitimised.
6   Dobler 2014: p. xix
7   Werner 1993
8   This is about 40% of Namibia's total population (2,1 million), Namibia Statistic Agency 2011
9   Siiskonen 2009, Namibia's total surface area is about 825,000 km²
10 Mendelsohn 2006

communal land in Namibia, central-northern Namibian societies are predominantly agrarian. Agriculture constitutes the basis of people's livelihoods, and therefore, land "is the most important form of property and productive resource".[11] In this context, people are "in constant search of good cultivating and grazing land".[12]

According to the Namibian constitution, all natural resources, including land, that are not held under freehold titles belong to the state.[13] Communal land cannot be privately owned, meaning "no right conferring freehold ownership is capable of being granted or acquired by any person in respect of any portion of communal land".[14] Caution should be exercised in treating communal land as a homogenous unit, which is instead a terrain comprising of varied land uses that inform the different kinds of tenure arrangements. I follow Cousins who states that it is a *"mixed tenure regime, comprising of individual, family, sub-group and larger group rights and duties in relation to a variety of natural resources"*.[15] In the central-northern Namibian context, *mixed* tenure regimes refer to individualised landholdings used for residence and cropping, commonage used for common grazing, individualised large tracts of fenced-off land, and emerging groups' fenced-off commonage used for individualised and group grazing.

Land for residence and crop production is individualised. Here a specific piece of land is allocated for the sole use by a specific family unit called *eumbo*. Land for livestock farming is traditionally commonage, although this too has seen an increasing rate of individualisation, whereby large tracts of land are appropriated and fenced-off by individuals.[16] The size of the respective land used for the different purposes varies substantially. The average size of the land used for residence and crop production is between five and ten hectares, while individualised fenced-off grazing land can be as vast as 4000 hectares. People produce a variety of crops on their land. *Omahangu* (pearl millet) is the most important crop grown, and serves as staple food. Other cultivated crops are sorghums, beans, pumpkins, watermelons and groundnuts. For livestock farming people keep cattle, goats, and donkeys, notwithstanding the "high levels of variations in … ownership".[17]

The agrarian economy as a traditional base of livelihoods in central-north Namibia faces frequent external threats and shocks in the form of droughts and floods. Consequently, supplementary sources of livelihoods have become increasingly important. It is noted that "an average of 73% of the total household income come

---

11 Siiskonen 2009: p. 5
12 Cited in Williams 1994: p. 36
13 Article 100 of the Constitution of the Republic of Namibia. Republic of Namibia 1990: p. 47
14 Republic of Namibia 2002: p. 10
15 Cousins 2000: p. 154
16 *Eumbo* sing. (*omaumbo* pl.) is the basic unit of social organisation in central-north Namibia
17 Mendelsohn 2006: p. 35

from non-farming activities of pensions, business earnings, wages and remittances".[18] National statistics also point to this diversity of income streams with contributions being derived from farming (16,4%), wage and salaries (47,7%), cash remittance (5,4%), business non-farming (11,6%), pensions (14,2%), retirement fund (0,8%), orphan's grant (1,3%), disability grant (0,7%) and other (1,9%).[19] Despite there being a wide range of sources from which people derive their livelihoods, I share Mufune's sentiments that it is "impossible to imagine rural livelihoods in Southern Africa without some kinds of access to land".[20] Furthermore, while recognising the diversity of livelihood sources, we should also recognise the variations among *omaumbo* as there are "many very poor households indeed largely rely[ing] on farm and commonage resources".[21]

This section concludes with a note on the methodology used. The data for this chapter are drawn from thirteen months of fieldwork carried out between 2013 and 2015 in central-north Namibia. The core areas of fieldwork were the villages of Ondobe, Omunyekadi, Efidi, Ohengobe and Etope in the western Ohangwena Region, and Onghalulu, Okambali and Onane to the east of the region. The research participants included actors from central and regional state institutions, the hierarchical TAs (queen, senior traditional councillors, traditional councillors/village headmen and *kapatashu*) and the land users.[22] The data were collected by means of interviews and participant observations of the land users' daily activities, village and district meetings, land board meetings and field visits. Attending land board meetings allowed for further enrichment of data since cases addressed there are not confined to the above villages, but the Ohangwena Region as a whole. Data representing other regions were drawn from visits to the Ministry of Land Reform's regional offices and from media reporting.

Land relations and property rights

Different meanings ascribed to land shape the complex land relations and property rights in central-north Namibia. Actors variously seek to establish an active presence in the power relationships in the control of land, to retain an autonomous position in the control of land, to maximise production output targeted towards commercialisation, and to derive basic livelihoods from the land. Land is also be used to define social identities.

---

18 Mendelsohn 2006: p. 39; Mendelsohn et al. 2012: p. 4
19 Namibia Statistic Agency 2011: p. 66
20 Mufune 2011: p. 54
21 Mendelsohn et al. 2012: p. 4
22 The *kapatashu* are representatives of village headmen in the different parts of villages. They assist the village headmen in land allocation and village level dispute resolutions.

Among the *Aawambo* societies the control of land is one of the main factors which played a role in the foundation of independent kingdoms. The powers of kingdoms were measured in terms of land, cattle and people.[23] Referring to the early 1940s, Williams noted that:

> During the coronation of King Sheepo [also known as Kambonde kaNamene] the son of Namene, while others inherited the rest of the property of their deceased uncle Martin the son of Kadhikwa, Sheepo (knowing that he was the heir) exclaimed: 'The land is mine! That is what I have inherited; I have nothing to do with cattle and other things.' Sheepo knew that with the heritage of land he would be able to control and rule those who inherited other property since they would be on his land. The one who controlled land, ultimately controlled everything on it.[24]

Today, communal land belongs to one set of actors (the state) and it is administered by another set of actors (the hierarchical TAs), and the advisory and oversight functions are vested in the CLBs. These institutions are mandated with their respective functions and powers by different sets of legal frameworks: the state by the constitution; the TAs by the Traditional Authorities Act, 2000 (Act No. 25 of 2000) and their respective customary laws; and the CLBs by the Communal Land Reform Act. Both the state and TAs are further mandated by the Communal Land Reform Act, which vests the land in the former in trust for the benefit of the people and for the purpose of promoting economic and social development and in the latter with the primary powers to administer communal land.[25]

Communal Land Boards—the new actors in the communal land question
Land boards are relatively new actors in the contested terrain of communal land. Their membership is a combination of representatives of state institutions, who are nominated from ministries responsible for regional government, land, environment and agriculture; and TAs that fall within the respective regional boundaries. Other members are representatives of farming associations, two women engaged in farming operations in the respective boards' areas from the respective CLB jurisdictions and two women who have expertise relevant to the functions of a board.[26] The representation of women on the land boards is a deliberate effort

---

23 Williams 1994
24 Williams 1994: p. 95
25 Republic of Namibia 2002
26 Republic of Namibia 2002: p. 5

as part of Namibia policy to advance gender equality in governance structures. The overall representation is mandatory and, as such, CLBs represent all actors at the level of socio-political authority and at the level of use and exploitation. The functions of CLBs are as follows:

> To exercise control over allocation and the cancellation of customary land rights by traditional authorities; to consider and decide on applications for rights of leasehold; to establish and maintain a register and a system of registration for recording the allocation, transfer and cancellation of customary land rights and rights of leasehold; and to advise the Minister in connection with the making of regulations or any other matter pertaining to the Act.[27]

The establishment of CLBs, their roles and mandates were received with mixed reactions, especially by TAs who are concerned that the boards would reduce their powers, functions and status with regard to land matters.[28] The Communal Land Reform Act itself resulted from processes of back-and-forth contestations between the state and the TAs. At the Consultative Conference on Communal Land Administration held in 1996 the seven TAs from *Owambo* opposed the provision in the draft bill, which stated that "land boards should be vested with powers to exercise control over the occupation and use of communal land".[29] They felt the draft bill reduced them to "the back-yard boys of what should be technical and advisory bodies, namely the Regional Land Boards".[30] TAs saw themselves as having "a long standing responsibility and ... therefore more authoritative than appointed land professionals and technicians".[31]

At a meeting organised by the Ministry of Land Reform, which occurred during the fieldwork of this study, one TA called for the state to dissolve CLBs on the basis that they were conflicting with their mandates. Some TAs, however, welcome CLBs as a structure that helps TAs to survey land parcels and to register land rights.[32]

The Namibian government regards the CLBs as a crucial institution for the implementation of the Communal Land Reform Act, and for the "improve[ment of] security of tenure of customary land rights holders".[33] The establishment of these boards enables the state to eventually exercise an active presence in the

---

27 Republic of Namibia 2002: p. 5
28 Hinz et al.2010: p. 120, Mendelsohn 2008
29 Owambo Traditional Leaders 1997: p. 69
30 Owambo Traditional Leaders 1997: p. 69
31 Owambo Traditional Leaders 1997: p. 69
32 Werner 2008
33 Werner 2008: p. 16

power relationships associated with communal land administration. They play an important role for spearheading the process that integrates customary forms of land rights into national legal frameworks. Rather than conflicting with the mandates of TAs, land boards are herein viewed as important actors in ensuring good governance and accountability in communal land administration. Their functions are purely of oversight and advisory nature, with a long-term view of improving transparency in land administration. Land boards oversee the functions of other actors involved, and do not undertake these functions themselves. This represents a change in land relations, especially at the level of land administration. Before CLBs were in place, the decisions of TAs were final. It did not matter whether these decisions were to the disadvantage of the rural poor or not, and no checks and balances existed. With the establishment of land boards, land rights conferred and/or their cancellation by TAs are no longer final nor have they legal effect unless ratified by the boards.[34]

I have participated in CLBs' meetings, and my overall impression is that they provide a platform for land users to hold TAs accountable for their functions. Land users are, in particular, found to constantly seek audiences with the CLBs, reporting cases of allocations by their TAs, which do not consider existing landholders. One particular case involved a headman who is said to have allocated land to people not originally from the village, without consulting members of the village. In this case, those born in the village felt that they should have a say in how their village land is allocated, especially when it comes to outsiders.[35] In such cases, CLBs provide platforms for people to complain about alleged injustices experienced through their TAs. Having CLBs providing oversight functions means that TAs' actions can be questioned, brought under dispute and objected.

The state—the executive power holder

The Namibian state has been involved in the contested terrain of communal land since independence in 1990, when legislation that vested land in the South African apartheid regime was repealed. On the basis of Article 100 of the constitution, the state stands at the highest level of the gradation in terms of property rights over communal land and plays the role of outward-representation.[36] Outward-representation means representation against foreign actors.[37] For example, foreign nationals (either as individuals or companies) are restricted from acquiring customary land rights in communal areas.[38] "A foreign national who wishes to acquire customary land right or right of leasehold must first obtain written authorisation

---

34 Republic of Namibia 2002
35 Anonymity is maintained in these cases.
36 Von Benda-Beckmann 1979
37 Republic of Namibia 2002: p. 10
38 Republic of Namibia 2013: p. 2

from the Minister before he or she applies for such rights."[39] This ensures protection of customary land rights which are a safety net for the rural poor. All acquisitions of communal land by foreign nationals (especially in the case of companies) are therefore confined to commercial use, thus being granted rights of leaseholds.

While customary land rights are a safety net for the rural poor, rights of leaseholds on the other hand are market-oriented forms of security of tenure for commercialised land-based production.[40] The state approves acquisitions of communal land by foreign companies in the context of its responsibility to promote social and economic development as required by Section 17 (1) of the Communal Land Reform Act. Therefore, foreign investors' acquisitions of communal land are approved if assurances are given that they will contribute to employment creation and poverty reduction. The extent to which these projects realise these goals is another question that can be investigated in the future as it is relevant to the rest of Africa.[41]

Further, the state has powers to designate parts of communal land for the purpose it deems fit. Proclamation of local authority areas, defining areas for public use such as building social services facilities like schools, hospitals, clinics, agricultural extension services, and construction of infrastructure such as roads and railway lines and designation of areas for commercialisation of land-based production are some examples. These are also contextualised within the socio-economic development goals. A caveat to bringing about socio-economic development especially through proclamation of local authority areas involves alienating parts of communal land. Section 15 (2) of the Communal Land Reform Act provides that:

> Where a local authority area is situated or established within the boundaries of any communal land area the land comprising such local authority area shall not form part of that communal land area and shall not be communal land.[42]

This provision further involves a shift in the administration and governance responsibilities, in particular a shift of jurisdiction from the traditional to the local

---

39 Republic of Namibia 2013: p. 3
40 Nghitevelekwa 2015
41 For Namibia not much in-depth research has done except by Odendaal 2011. The discussion is contextualised within the ongoing discourse which surrounds the conception of 'land grabbing' in other parts of Africa. The impacts of land grabbing are argued to be "threatening millions of rural producers, marginalising small-medium scale farming into enclaves or as appendages to large-scale, industrial agriculture; at worst, it is erased; and further deepening inequalities associated with globalisation". Peters 2013: p. 538
42 Republic of Namibia 2002: p. 9

authority, very often resulting in feelings of animosity and opposition by the TAs towards this process. Traditional authorities lose their powers over the alienated land. It is however important to underline that the decisions of the actors (e.g. of the state as presented above) are not unilateral. Consultations with other actors do take place and consent is sought. In practice, such consultations are ambiguous and often contested, as some actors especially at the lowest level of the TAs feel left out. Communal land boards come into play here in that they have to grant the rights of leasehold. It is important to note that projects suggested by whichever actor may not always be conceded by everyone, and will have to be discussed and negotiated.

Traditional Authorities—the long standing actors in the terrain

Traditional authorities are hierarchical institutions. The supreme leader is a king/queen (locally referred as *ohamba/omukwaniilwa*). The king/queen appoints senior councillors (*elenga lakula/elenga enene*) who preside over districts (*oikandjo*).[43] The third hierarchical level of TAs comprises of village headmen or traditional councillors (*mwene womukunda*) who preside over villages (*omikunda*) and report directly to their respective senior councillors. In addition to headmen, within villages there are actors locally referred to as *kapatashu* (*ookapatashu* pl.). *Kapatashu* are representatives of headmen in the different sections of the respective villages. One of the research participants explained this hierarchy:

> The kingdom (*ouhamba*) is big; therefore the king or queen cannot lead alone. The hierarchy follows that: the king/queen delegates senior councillors, senior councillors delegate village headmen and village headmen delegate *ookapatashu*. The senior councillors form the cabinet of the traditional authority and they report to the king/queen as in the ministers reporting to the president of a country.[44]

All actors in the TAs' hierarchical structures have specific powers and functions, which they exercise at their respective levels. These are not only derived from the Traditional Authorities Act, but also from the Communal Land Reform Act and customary law.[45] The Traditional Authorities Act for example is silent on the

---

43 *Elenga* (sing), *omalenga* (pl.)

44 AH. Omunyekadi, May 2013, interview by Romie Nghitevelekwa

45 The Traditional Authorities Act, 2000 defines customary law as the "norms, rules or procedure, traditions and usages of a traditional community in so far as they do not conflict with the Namibian constitution or with any other written law applicable in Namibia". Republic of Namibia 2000: p. 3. National laws or statutory laws on the other hand are national or state laws respectively. The customary laws of the *Owambo* societies were ascertained and published in Hinz/Namwoonde 2010.

functions of TAs in regard to land, except for Section 3(1)(b) which states that, a member of a TA shall

> ensure that all members of his or her traditional community use the natural resources at their disposal on a sustainable manner that conserves the environment and maintains the ecosystems for the benefit of all persons in Namibia.[46]

Customary law and the Communal Land Reform Act define the roles of TAs in land administration. The Communal Land Reform Act vests the primary power of land allocation in the chiefs, but it further leaves it open for the chiefs to decide whether to delegate this function to other actors within the TA hierarchical structure. Section 20 (a & b) of the Act states that

> the primary powers to allocate or cancel any customary land rights in respect of any portion of land in the communal area of a traditional authority vests (a) in the Chief of that traditional community; or (b) *where the Chief so determines*, in the Traditional Authority of that traditional community.[47]

In the context of customary law, and within this hierarchical structure, it is the village headmen and *ookapatashu* that are directly involved in land allocation, not the king/queen nor the senior councillors. Village headmen and their *kapatashu* regulate access to land and are responsible for legitimising property to land users in their respective villages. These include customary rights to residence, crop land and other land uses. In the far eastern areas of Ohangwena Region, complaints have been noted where senior councillors had bypassed the role of the village headmen by allocating land, a function not falling under their mandate. Here, senior councillors are said to have allocated large tracts of land often favouring the elites, and therefore resulting in land disputes.

The mandates of the king/queens and senior traditional councillors include all matters concerning the designation and re-designation of communal land for the various purposes within the respective territorial unit, as well as the function of maintaining a direct link between people on the ground and the state. For example, when the state designated land for agricultural purposes, it consulted with senior traditional councillors and the kings/queens, and not the village headmen. In one of the areas designated for agricultural purposes, village headmen showed animosity

---

46 Republic of Namibia 2000: p. 5
47 Emphasis added, Republic of Namibia 2002: p. 11

to the designation, claiming that they had not been consulted. They argued that the state only consulted the senior traditional councillors and the queen, and not the headmen although this land falls under their jurisdiction.[48] This shows that, although the differentiation in the powers and functions of the actors in the hierarchical structure of TAs seems clear, power remains contestable at the implementation phase.

Despite having the socio-political authority which presides over control of access, landholders and land users who are actors at the level of use and exploitation are equally important in the question of land relations in central-north Namibia. In this context Williams convincingly argues that "despite the fact that the king controls land and continues to receive tribute yearly from the usufructury, the homestead [*eumbo*] remained the most effective landholding unit over whose production the king has no control".[49] This argument is still valid today in that actors at the level of socio-political authority control access to land but use and exploitation of land is determined at other levels. This complicates emergent land relations.

Landholders and land users
In central-north Namibia, people derive benefits from land through different mechanisms of access. These are categorised into property relations and other relations of access (i.e. non-property relations). I follow a conceptual distinction between property and access adopted by Ribot and Peluso, which locates property as one of many access relationships or mechanisms of access to resources.[50] In this section, a distinction is drawn between property relations and access in the context of customary tenure. The different mechanisms of access reflect processes of social differentiations in access to land characterised by inequalities and uneven power structures.

Property relations are the formal mechanisms of access to land. They are constituted through the legitimising authorities i.e. TAs, and are given statutory legal effect by the CLBs. As Sikor and Lund argue, "property is only property if socially legitimate institutions sanction it".[51] The following processes and elements have to be in place in order to legalise landholding. The first step is the identification of an available piece of land, followed by visits to the TA to ascertain its availability. Ascertaining whether the land is available involves the TA consulting with the future neighbours of the incoming landholder. This is in line with the communality of land, if we are to follow its definition to mean "a degree to which community control

---

48 PN. Okambali, April 2015, interview by Romie Nghitevelekwa
49 Williams 1994: p. 4
50 Ribot/Peluso: 2003
51 Sikor/Lund 2009: p. 1

over who is allowed into the group, thereby qualifying for an allocation of land for residence and cropping, as well as rights of access to and use of the shared, common pool resources used by the group".[52] While this is an ideal scenario, in reality only some TAs follow it, others do not. If the land is available, negotiations on the boundaries follow and eventually *ombadu yekaya* is given, a form of tribute to the village headman. For an individual landholding, a once-off amount of N$600 or one head of cattle is given.[53] Thereafter, the landholder makes an annual payment of N$10.00 as land tax (locally referred to as *iifendela yedu*), which goes into the respective TA's fund. In other words, *ombadu yekaya* is an important element in legitimising property relations, while the land tax is an important element in maintaining property relations.

After *ombadu yekaya* has been given, rights to the respective landholdings are legitimised. Here the respective landholders attain what Schlager and Ostrom refer to as management and exclusion property rights for their respective landholdings. This means landholders can regulate internal use patterns and transform the land by making improvements and investments and they can determine who will have access rights.[54] Furthermore, the landholders have the rights to relinquish and/or transfer management and exclusion rights or all rights in totality. These are property rights assigned to the landholder in the formation of the *eumbo* unit. The unit of *eumbo* comprises of different members who cannot be regarded as homogenous, and neither are their respective relationships to the landholding egalitarian. Different power relations exist between different users within the unit, with some actors being mere users while others users and rights holders.

However, all users have some form of claims on the respective landholding, some of which may have been transferred across generations. For instance, some users may relate to the landholding through its founder, i.e. the person who cleared the land. In such a case, a person would justify his/her claim in a sentence like 'it was our great-grandparents land, this is our roots'. These justifications determine how and to whom the rights will be transferred. For example, when the land is linked to the great-grandmother or the grandmother, the rights are kept within the maternal family line. Different people, who may or may not be residing on the landholding, may have claims because of its history.

The picture becomes even more complex when considering that bundles of claims on a respective landholding may be extended beyond members within the unit of *eumbo*. Non-members of the unit, for instance neighbours, may also have claims or

---

52 Cousins 2000: p. 152
53 The current customary value of a head of cattle is N$600. This is however not a market related value which is more than that.
54 Schlager/Ostrom 1992

even hold certain rights. This is quite common for claims of and rights over fruit trees on the landholding, for seasonal rights of use or for rights of way with regard to certain routes or paths. These arrangements are maintained and cultivated through social relations and hence support the argument that social relations are pivotal to access to resources. In other words, people do not only derive benefits from land through property relations constituted through socio-political authorities, but also through social relations. In short, landholders or rights holders may have rights of exclusion but these rights are neither private nor absolute as the landholding is situated within a communal set-up. Certain parts of rights of exclusion are exercised in consideration of others. For example, if a landholder puts up a fence blocking routes, other members of the village who use that particular route can object. Other rights that may exist are seasonal, for example, livestock belonging to other village members may graze on one's landholding after the harvest season. The latter practice is however decreasing because of fencing. Even if landholdings may be open for routes, they might not be open for grazing of neighbours' and other villagers' livestock as was common in the past.

My empirical data have shown that property relations are the most sought-after form of mechanism of access to land. However, the important argument here is that property relations are not the only mechanism through which people derive benefit from resources but that other mechanisms are also at play. These other mechanisms of access are however still linked to property relations. In fact they operate in parallel with property relations and come into being through property relations. Here I concur with the argument that "those deriving benefits from land through property relations 'mediate others' access".[55]

Other mechanisms of access are land banking, sub-divisions of landholdings, inheritance and land sales. These are arrangements and transactions that take place between land users or at the level of use and exploitation. In the beginning or even the whole duration of the agreement, actors at the level of socio-political authority are not involved. The only time they get involved is when agreements have to be formalised and therefore legalised. While some of these mechanisms or arrangements may end in constitution of property relations, others may remain just that, informal agreements.

A person, for instance, can be the legitimate rights holder, but not the direct user of part or the entire landholding. This is particularly evident in cases of multiple landholdings and sub-division of landholdings. Landholders with multiple landholdings give reasons like "the other land is for my children when they grow up", "keeping the land for future use" or "when I retire, I would like to return to my village". Meanwhile, other people will be using the 'banked land'. For example,

---

55 Ribot/Peluso 2003: p. 158

one can come across a landholding that seemingly has two independent *omaumbo*, with independent homesteads and clear boundaries of cropland. One of the two might be the actual legitimate property rights owner whereas the other may only consist of mere users.[56] In other cases, the users or occupants of a landholding are not necessarily the 'owners' or the rights holders even when they have lived there for more than a decade. Cases of land banking, sub-divisions of landholdings and land markets are increasing as a result of the scarcity of land. In one of the villages where this research was undertaken, the village secretary shared that the village leadership had not registered any newly cleared land during the thirteen months of this research's fieldwork. The headman or the secretary has only registered landholdings which have been sub-divided from existing landholdings or landholdings that have been inherited.[57]

Sale of communal land is prohibited. However this practice has been identified and is on increase. Land sales take various forms and include either alienating part or the entire landholding in return for monetary reward. Cases of landholders selling land they once used for trading and cropland have been noted during the fieldwork. Monetary transactions noted involve sales in return of N$12,000, 10,000, 8000, 6000, 4000 and 2000. I see this as a form of emerging speculation and commodification of land. There are no specific guidelines for these exchanges since the practice is legally prohibited. This prohibition is intended to protect land users who dispose of their land and are left landless and poorer. With land sales, landholders are likely to sell their land hastily, and thus lose their family homes and security, usually for a pittance. This not only affects landholders, but secondary rights holders as well. Besides, this kind of mechanism of access to land causes contestations with TAs, especially in cases where they do not benefit from the monetary exchange. However, it remains a mechanism through which people are able to derive benefits from land.

On the death of the rights holder, the rights revert to the chief or the TA for re-allocation. Today, both statutory and customary law protects the rights of widows: they can now inherit land and are entitled to keep the land rights they enjoyed before their husbands' deaths.[58] These changes came into effect after the state promulgated laws, and TAs updated their customary laws to protect the rights of widows, especially on land inheritance.[59] Before, land and other assets were often seen as belonging to the matrilineal relatives of the husband. While widows' rights are now protected by both statutory and customary law, whether they should pay

---

56   *Omaumbo* is plural for *eumbo*.
57   LH. Omunyekadi, May 2013, interview by Romie Nghitevelekwa
58   Republic of Namibia 1998; 2002
59   The TAs of Owambo have updated their laws published in Seven Traditional Authorities of Owambo 2014

the customary *ombadu yekaya* for rights re-allocation is still contested. There have been calls to end this practice, based on the argument of the economic position of women, as "women have less access to resources such as cash or cattle than men; they tend to lack the means for paying for the land, and thus may be discriminated against indirectly".[60] Traditional leaders had committed to have *ombadu yekaya* by widows done away with, but this practice has continued.

Traditional authorities, especially at the village level, argue that *ombadu yekaya* is their source of income. Widows not paying *ombadu yekaya*, they argue, would result in a substantial loss of income. They insist on payment of *ombadu yekaya* for every allocation or re-allocation of rights. In spite of calls to end this practice, without clear provision in the national statutory law to strictly forbid this practice, widows continue to pay. While TAs have no powers to chase widows off the land in the case of non-payment of *ombadu yekaya*, this research noted several forms of 'punishments' endured by widows and other landholders. These include the land remaining in the name of the deceased person for years until such payment is made—in one case, a research participant shared that her land remained in the name of the deceased person for three years until she was able to pay.[61] Other participants pointed to headmen refusing to give forms and consent letters for land rights registrations. A research participant recounts her experience:

> Most people in this village have received forms to apply for their land rights; we have not received one because I did not give *ombadu yekaya*. When I ask the headman about the form, he says I should go and collect it myself from the main office of our traditional authority. But others received their forms from him. He says he cannot give assistance to those who did not pay *ombadu yekaya*.[62]

The quote echoes the ongoing centrality of *ombadu yekaya* in constituting and legitimising property relations under customary systems, and the politics behind it. These contestations are part of the broader discourse on contradictions and conflicts at the intersection between customary and statutory land law and the challenges that come with legal pluralism. The said contestations also highlight the politics around property rights and divergent interests between different actors within the customary socio-political authority. While it is at the highest level within the customary socio-political authority where decisions were taken to meet, for instance, the demands of the state, it is usually at the lowest level, at the level

---

60 Becker 1997: p. 57
61 AK. Omunyekadi, September 2013, interview by Romie Nghitevelekwa
62 MN. Etope, May 2013, interview by Romie Nghitevelekwa

of the headman, where these decisions are supposed to be implemented. The case discussed shows the interconnectivity between the *ombadu yekaya* paid to a village headman for individual land allocation and the *ombadu yekaya* the village headman has to pay to the next level of the TA. It becomes clear that any attempt to successfully put an end to the former practice also needs to question the latter.

Differentiating property relations from other relations of access brings to our attention a wide range of "social relationships that enable people to benefit from resources" and to the fact that people do not only benefit from land through property relations, but that other relations of access are equally important.[63] Understanding the complexities of the varying relations also enables us to map dynamic processes of access to resources, as well as to understand the social positions of different actors by separating those who "control resources access from those who maintain their access *through* those who have control".[64] Most importantly, these differences point us to the embedded social differentiations characterised by inequalities in access to resources. The main question that arises here is: who benefits from statutory protected security of tenure?

Changing land relations in the context of communal land reform

The sections above touched on the politics around the establishment and functions of the CLBs, and how these relate to other actors involved in communal land administration. The following sections address the changing land relations in the context of communal land reform at the level of use and exploitation. Namibia's ongoing communal land reform was instituted after the Communal Land Reform Act came into force in 2003. Communal land reform addresses the fundamental issue of security of land tenure, which is central to land relations in Namibia's communal areas. Under the act, the following rights are secured; customary land rights, rights of leasehold and occupational land rights. Customary land rights are rights to a residential and farming unit. Rights of leaseholds are divided into two categories, namely, general rights of leaseholds and rights of leaseholds for agricultural purposes. Lastly, occupational land rights are granted to institutions providing public services, such as churches, schools etc. All these land rights are allocated by the TAs and ratified by the CLBs, in so doing, establishing the dual system of customary and statutory land rights. For customary land rights, this is manifested through two types of proof: a green card provided by the TAs and a land rights registration certificate provided by the CLBs.

Questions to ponder here are: does registration of land rights change land relations, and if so, how? These changes are not so obvious, perhaps because this

---

63 Ribot/Peluso 2003: p. 158
64 Ribot/Peluso 2003: p. 154

process has only been in place in Namibia for about 14 years. The process started slowly, picked up around the year 2008, and still has a long way to go. The main problem is that it is difficult to pinpoint the supposed changes as they take place within complex customary tenure regimes. As Werner argues, "the Communal Land Reform Act will take some time to permeate customary tenure regimes".[65] What one can observe are the emerging politics in the events as they unfold, and the positions of land users in relation to the process. Land disputes as they unfold are not necessarily emanating from land rights registration, but are caused by existing complex deep-rooted matters and/or long standing intra-community injustice. These are issues that have long existed in society, but there was no platform on which they could be raised. The registration process and the CLBs provide an enabling platform where these matters are now brought to light. However, this is not to deny that there are those that emanate directly from land rights registration itself, especially if the existing nature of bundles of claims and rights over land are not considered in the registration model as we will see below.

Mechanisms of access, bundles of claims and rights in the context of security of tenure

In the above sections, I argued that people derive benefits from land through varied mechanisms of access, categorised into property and access relations. I have further elaborated on the bundles of claims and rights over land. A piece of land is often not attributed to one individual, but to a variety of actors who attach different meanings to it and may relate to it through historical claims. In other words, we are dealing with a setting comprising of primary and secondary rights holders. Mapping mechanisms of access to land as well as the bundles of claims and rights allow us to understand who benefits from resources and through what kinds of relationships. They also allow us to understand who benefits from security of tenure and, more politically, who is excluded from it.

The current model of security of tenure that Namibia is pursuing largely leans towards property relations and primary rights holders at the exclusion of other relations of access. This is evident in the granting of statutory land registration certificates. For instance, it is the actor whose name is noted in the books of the TAs that is registered for customary land rights, irrespective of whether this actor is the primary or direct user of the land. The actors who relate to land through other relations of access or non-property relations do not benefit from security of tenure. Mechanisms of access to land under customary tenure regimes point to social differences characterised by inequalities. The process of providing security of tenure nonetheless reveals social exclusions.

---

65 Werner 2008: p. 17

Security of tenure and the two economies

As far as land as a production asset is concerned, two types of economies are apparent in north-central Namibia: crop and cattle economies. Inherently, the two are interdependent but benefit from different land rights. The crop economy takes place in individualised property and is secured through customary land rights. The cattle economy, however, takes place in three categories of land, namely the commonage, individualised large fenced landholdings and areas designated for agricultural purposes. Land rights in the last two categories are secured through customary law or leases. These arrangements do not apply to the commonage. The Communal Land Reform Act does not make provision to protect the commonage. This raises important policy questions regarding why legal protection is only provided for individualised properties under which the crop economy takes place, and not the commonage which is essential for the cattle economy.

In north-central Namibia the cattle economy found in areas designated for agricultural purposes gives a different picture. Land users/primary rights holders are granted market-oriented land rights and rights of leasehold. Here, land users/secondary rights holders who derive benefits from the same land through other relations of access are also secured. For example, in a particular landholding (e.g. 4000 ha), there may be ten land users—a combination of primary and secondary rights holders. The primary rights holder (whose rights are legitimised by TAs) is the leaseholder (legitimised by CLBs), and other land users/secondary rights holders, who came there through informal arrangements are now benefiting from statutory protection (also legitimised by CLBs). Such is the model that should be applied across the spectrum to secure all rights to resources, and to ensure broad-based inclusivity.

The politics around the process of providing security of tenure: the sceptics and the optimists

Upon being conferred property rights by the TAs, land users receive a green card that certifies their membership to the village, that they have paid *ombadu yekaya* and do pay the land tax. In going to *omaumbo* and asking about people's land rights, one is often shown the green card. On the question of how people understand their land rights, one of the research participants replied:

> What is she asking about? Is she asking about the green card that we have from the headman? I have my land rights, because I have paid my *ombadu yekaya* and my annual N$10.00 to the headman. I am not in arrears, and therefore I have my land rights.[66]

---

66   KL. Omunyekadi, 8 August 2013, interview by Romie Nghitevelekwa

Such kinds of responses come from research participants that I categorise as participants who did not identify with the statutory protected land rights upfront. Their first point of reference in regard to their land rights is the green card and therefore customary tenure. Some people falling into this category could not locate where they put their certificates, but were reminded by the research assistant of this study, who was actually one of the *kapatashu* in one of the villages "that the land rights certificate is an important document and it should be where people's national identity cards are stored".[67]

Others are more sceptical about land rights registration, as one of the research participants showed:

> Those are just rich people who think they are clever. The problem is not in communal areas, the problem is in freehold areas. They have thousands hectares of land, and they want to squeeze us into twenty hectares landholdings. Now they want to shift the problem, to say that we need security. We were never insecure in our land. Maybe the insecurity was about inheritance by widows, but that was addressed immediately after independence when the laws on gender equality were passed. The problem we have in Namibia is unequal distribution of land between those in the communal and freehold areas.[68]

The statement comes out of a group which I categorise as the sceptics. Some of them feel that registration is changing their culture, as one of the research participants puts it in relation to areas designated for agricultural purposes. It is understood that the beneficiaries receive rights of leasehold and that there will be no more addition or subtraction from the list of beneficiaries:

> Your registration is changing our culture. Do you want to say that, if I have my nephew whom I want to give part of my land, I will not, just because you people have registered names of the beneficiaries already? This is an old practice that we have inherited from our forefathers; it cannot end because of your registration.[69]

Similarly, others put it that certificates should not change relations in their *omaumbo*. This was raised during a CLB field visit, about a land dispute where a land user has erected a fence, which blocked a road. During the meeting, a member

---

67 EW. Omunyekadi, 8 August 2013, discussion with Romie Nghitevelekwa
68 AH. Omunyekadi, 28 May 2013, interview by Romie Nghitevelekwa
69 K. Ohangwena Communal Land Board meeting

of the CLB stated that "according to the law, you actually have no right to put up this fence, because this land belongs to your mother, it is her name on the land rights certificate".[70] The woman, responsible for putting up the fence responded:

> You do not have any right to decide on what happens in our house—your certificate does not change relations in our house. Do you know how our responsibilities are allocated? It does not mean that if it is my mother's name on the certificate, that I have no say on what happens on the land. Will your certificate also stop me to plough the land, just because it is not on my name?[71]

While there are doubts about the process, there are many others who identify with their statutory land rights certificates. This third group is optimistic about the process, and in particular in relation to a reduction in boundary disputes, and land inheritance.

One of the research participants shared that

> my certificate shows me the boundaries of my landholding. This is very good because in cases of boundary disputes with my neighbours, I will show them the map at the back of my certificate. My boundaries are clear.[72]

Among this group are also those who feel that, with a certificate, they are secure, unlike in the past. One participant said:

> When I was a young man, I worked in Outjo and Omaruru. My father died when I was on my last contract, which was the longest one. In fact, he died when I still had six months before the end of my contract. I had to finish my contract; I did not mourn my father at home. When my contract finished, I went home. When I got home, my mother had already gone to her family in Angola. My father's land was already in the hands of my uncle. In fact, my mother was chased away. That is different now. With this certificate, I am now at peace that when I am no more, my wife and my children are safe. This certificate is their protection ticket for the future.[73]

---

70 M. Ohangwena Communal Land Board meeting
71 M. Onanadi, Ohangwena Communal Land Board, dispute meeting
72 JN. Omunyekadi, 5 August 2013, interview by Romie Nghitevelekwa
73 JN. Omunyekadi, 5 August 2013, interview by Romie Nghitevelekwa

These are all dynamics that were noted in relation to providing security of tenure. Some are rather sceptical while others are optimistic about the process. But the fundamental argument it comes to is that the current model of security of tenure needs to be redefined to provide legal protection to commonage in the open and to land users who use land through other mechanisms of access beside property relations. This is to prevent social exclusion and to ensure inclusivity in the process.

Conclusion

Land relations and property rights in north-central Namibia are complex. Different social actors have different roles to play in communal land. The level of socio-political authority consists of different actors and is characterised by contestations among them, e.g. between TAs and the state and/or the CLBs, and within the different institutions, e.g. contestations within the institutions of TAs. The bases of contestations often concern power relations, raising questions of who has the power to do what. As such it is argued that property rights are about power relations between different actors. It has been noted that there is a sense of feeling of being undermined on the part of TAs as a result of the establishment of CLBs. This chapter concludes that having different actors within the socio-political authority actually prevents monopoly of control and hegemony. It also ensures checks and balances on the different parties in land administration.

At the level of use and exploitation of land, we are able to identify and/or to categorise different actors. These categories are not only framed in terms of classes but also in terms of complex webs. Primary rights holders, land users and secondary rights holders/claimants are all conceptualised to benefit from land either through property relations or through other relations of access. These show us socially embedded differences characterised by inequalities in access to land. These differences allow the process and outcome of providing tenure security to be visible. They make it clear that eventually only those who benefit through property relations are able to benefit from security of tenure, and not those benefiting through other mechanisms. Those deriving benefits from land through individualised property benefit from legal protection of land rights. Those deriving benefits from land through undivided shares in commonages remain without legal protection. This picture reveals a social field characterised by social exclusion. I conclude that the model of providing security of tenure perhaps needs to be redefined, because in its current form, it does not provide mechanisms for distributing benefits from land.[74]

---

74 This research was funded through the SNSF-DFG project: Communal Land Reform in Namibia: Implications of Individualisation of Land Tenure.

References

Becker, H. (1997), Women and Land Rights. In J. Malan and M. Hinz (eds.), *Communal Land Administration: Second National Traditional Authority Conference: Proceedings*. Windhoek: Centre for Applied Social Sciences (CASS).

Cousins, B. (2000), Tenure and Common Property Resources in Africa. In C. Toulmin and J.F. Quan (eds.), *Evolving Land Rights, Policy and Tenure in Africa*. London: DFID/IIED/NRI: 151–180.

Dobler, G. (2014), *Traders and Trade in Colonial Ovamboland*. Basel: Basler Afrika Bibliographien.

Hinz, M.O., C. Mapaure, N.E. Namwoonde and N.P. Anyolo (2010), The Protection of Natural Resources and Biodiversity: Work in Progress in Three Master's Theses in the Faculty of Law of the University of Namibia. *Namibia Law Journal*, 2(1): 116–120.

Hinz, M. and N.-E. Namwoonde (2010), *Customary Law Ascertained (Vol. 1): The Customary Law of the Owambo, Kavango and Caprivi Communities of Namibia*. Windhoek: Namibian Scientific Society.

Mendelsohn, J. (2006), *Farming Systems in Namibia*. Windhoek: Research and Information Services of Namibia.

Mendelsohn, J. (2008), *Customary and Legislative Aspects of Land Registration and Management on Communal Land in Namibia*. Windhoek: RAISON.

Mendelsohn, J., L. Shixwameni and U. Nakamela (2012), *An Economic Overview of Communal Land Tenure in Namibia: Unlocking its Economic Potential*. Windhoek: RAISON.

Mufune, P. (2011), *The Rural in Namibia: An Introduction to Concepts and Issues*. Windhoek: Solitaire Press.

Namibia Statistic Agency (2011), *Namibia 2011 Population and Housing Census Main Report*. Windhoek: Namibia Statistic Agency.

Nghitevelekwa, R. (2015), Identifying, Streamlining and Harmonizing Existing Land Rights and Access Arrangements to Provide Security of Tenure in Areas Designated for Commercialization of Land-based Production: Case study: Okongo Designated Areas, Ohangwena Region. Windhoek: Ministry of Land Reform.

Odendaal, W. (2011), Land Grabbing in Namibia: A Case Study from the Omusati Region, Northern Namibia. Paper presented at the International Conference on Land Grabbing, 6–8 April 2011, University of Sussex.

Owambo Traditional Leaders (1997), Statement: Seven Traditional Authorities from Owambo. In J. Malan and M.O. Hinz (eds.), *Communal Land Administration: Proceedings of the Consultative Conference on Communal Land Administration, 26–28 September 1997*. Windhoek: Centre for Applied Social Sciences: 68-69.

Peters, P.E. (2013), Land Appropriation, Surplus People and a Battle over Visions of Agrarian Futures in Africa. *The Journal of Peasant Studies*, 40(3): 537–562.

Republic of Namibia (1990), *The Constitution of the Republic of Namibia*. Windhoek: Government of the Republic of Namibia.

Republic of Namibia (1998), *National Land Policy*. Windhoek: Ministry of Lands, Resettlement and Rehabilitation.

Republic of Namibia (2000), *Traditional Authorities Act, 2000 (Act No. 25 of 2000)*. Windhoek: Republic of Namibia.

Republic of Namibia (2002), *Communal Land Reform Act, 2002*. Windhoek: Republic of Namibia.

Republic of Namibia (2013), *Communal Land Reform Amendment Act, 2013 (No. 13 of 2013), Pub. L. No. 353*. Windhoek: Republic of Namibia.

Ribot, J. and N. Peluso (2003), A Theory of Access. *Rural Sociology*, 68(2): 153–181.

Schlager, E. and E. Ostrom (1992), Property-Rights Regimes and Natural Resources: A Conceptual Analysis. *Land Economics*, 68(3): 249–262.

Shipton, P. and M. Goheen (1992), Introduction: Understanding African Land-Holding: Power, Wealth, and Meaning. *Africa: Journal of the International African Institute*, 62(3): 307–325.

Siiskonen, H. (2009), Land Use Rights and Gender in Ovamboland, North-Central Namibia, Since the 1930s. *Fennia*, 187(1): 5–15.

Sikor, T. and C. Lund (2009), Access and Property: A Question of Power and Authority. In T. Sikor and C. Lund (eds.), *The Politics of Possession: Property, Authority, and Access to Natural Resources*. London: Blackwell Publishing Ltd.: 1–22

Von Benda-Beckmann, F. (1979), *Property in Social Continuity: Continuity and Change in the Maintenance of Property Relationships through Time in Minangkabau, West Sumatra*. The Hague: Martinus Nijhoff.

Werner, W. (1993), A Brief History of Land Dispossession in Namibia. *Journal of Southern African Studies*, 19(1): 135–146.

Werner, W. (2008), *Protection for Women in Namibia's Communal Land Reform Act: Is It Working?* Windhoek: Legal Assistance Centre.

Williams, F.-N. (1994), *Precolonial Communities of Southwestern Africa: A History of Owambo Kingdoms 1600–1920* (2nd edition). Windhoek: National Archives of Namibia.

CHAPTER 11

Local community disempowerment at the (trans)frontier

Ndidzulafhi Innocent Sinthumule

> Primary stakeholders/affected persons should be empowered to sustain development impacts of the project. This will ensure that project interventions and their benefits are sustainable over a longer time and motivate future development and further popular initiatives at the grassroots level where communities can make critical decisions affecting the quality of their everyday life.[1]

Introduction

The above quotation summarises the importance of empowering local communities in development projects. The goal of empowering local communities is to ensure that they participate and influence decisions on issues that affect them. The concept of empowerment in development and as a political process gained prominence during the American civil rights movement, which sought to put political power in the hands of its followers.[2] Empowerment in the community development context is defined as "the creation of sustainable structures, processes, and mechanisms, over which local communities have an increased degree of control, and from which they have a measurable impact on public and social policies affecting those communities".[3] Thus, empowerment is associated with feelings of high self-efficacy and higher levels of performance.[4] In nature conservation projects, empowering local communities has become important and, in some cases, a prerequisite for donors funded projects.[5] In

---

1 Maiti 2006: p. 294
2 Toomey 2008: p. 23
3 Craig 2002: p. 3
4 Eylon/Bamberger 2000: p. 358
5 Sarin 2001a: p. 341

this study, empowerment is understood as the process that opens up opportunities for marginalised communities and includes participation and engagement in local environmental matters. Whereas local communities are increasingly targeted as primary beneficiaries of nature conservation projects, recent literature has shown that they are often left disempowered by the projects that are supposed to empower them, as suggested by the epigraph.[6] Disempowerment is defined as any intentional or unintentional, verbal or nonverbal behaviour that can be interpreted as hostile, offensive, intimidating, demeaning, or threatening to individuals or communities.[7] Thus, disempowerment of local communities weakens the self-efficacy beliefs and perceived personal control or power,[8] and diminishes the sense of credibility.[9] At its worst, disempowerment results in perceived abusiveness, which may lead to a reduced level of performance.[10]

Whereas a number of definitions have been used to explain disempowerment, in this study, disempowerment can be defined as an act of preventing or depriving local communities from having power, influence or authority over development projects. In nature conservation projects, there are a number of ways in which local communities are disempowered. These include marginalisation of local communities[11] and the eviction from and dispossession of their ancestral land to promote nature conservation projects.[12] The end results of disempowering local communities in nature conservation projects include loss of access to or restriction of livelihood opportunities or future income related to environmental resources.[13] This chapter builds on these bodies of work to bring disempowerment of local communities to the forefront in transfrontier conservation areas (TFCAs). The main research question guiding the discussion of this chapter is how and why local communities are disempowered in the creation of TFCAs. Answers to these questions are drawn from Greater Mapungubwe Transfrontier Conservation Area spanning Botswana, South Africa and Zimbabwe.

Empowerment and/or disempowerment in nature conservation projects

Historically, nature conservation projects have shown little or no concern for the interests and humanity of local people. Common practice in conservation attempts

---

6   See among others, Kellert et al. 2000; Sarin 2001b; Byers et al. 2001; Marcus 2007; Spierenburg et al. 2008
7   Young et al. 2003: p. 163
8   Conger/Kanungo 1988: p. 473; Eylon/Bamberger 2000: p. 355
9   Young et al. 2003: p. 163
10 Laband/Lentz 1998: p. 594
11 Byers et al. 2001: p. 210; Sarin 2001a: p. 341; Marcus 2007: p. 205
12 See among others, Cernea 2005; Brockington/Igoe 2006; Agrawal/Redford 2009
13 For a more nuanced picture, see Cernea 2005; Brockington/Igoe 2006

to preserve species from extinction by separating humans from non-humans through, among other things, the creation of nature reserves and national parks. Thus, local communities were disempowered in the establishment and management of protected areas. Most often, in the United States (US), India, Thailand, Brazil and many parts of Africa, communities were forcibly removed from national parks and other protected areas in order to make way for recreational tourism.[14] As a result of these practices, local communities who depended entirely on natural resources were systematically alienated from ownership, participation and control over these resources. This resulted in communities being denied access to basic resources for their livelihoods and cultural needs.[15] As documented by many scholars, in Southern Africa, these practices were common in the colonial and apartheid eras.[16] This exclusionary model of wilderness preservation was based on very wrong assumptions that local people were only helpful as labourers and viewed as agents of environmental destruction who should be removed from protected area at the earliest opportunity.[17]

Over the past three decades, there has been a paradigmatic shift in global nature conservation approaches from strict preservation that excluded local people to a broader community conservation in which all sectors of the population have a stake.[18] Thus, the old narrative of 'fortress conservation' was largely displaced by the counter-narrative of development through community conservation and sustainable use of biodiversity to achieve socio-economic objectives.[19] This paradigmatic shift in nature conservation was influenced by both conservation science and political changes. Scientifically, there has been a growing concern by conservation biologists that, although protected areas are vital for the maintenance of biodiversity, they are not a sufficient solution for biodiversity conservation despite adequate management within their borders.[20] Thus, additional land is required for conservation of biodiversity. This is because genetic, taxonomic and ecological diversity manifests itself throughout the whole system and not only in protected areas.[21]

---

14 For more details on how local people were forcibly removed for conservation purpose, see Dowie 2009
15 See De Villiers 2008 for more details
16 For a more nuanced picture, see Metcalfe 2003; Ramutsindela 2003; Magome/Murombedzi 2003; Kepe 2004
17 See De Villiers 2008; also see Carruthers 2009: pp. 35–50
18 Jones/Murphree 2004: pp. 63–103; Carruthers 2009: pp. 35–50
19 Kellert et al. 2000: p. 706; Jones/Murphree 2004: pp. 63–103. Hutton et al. 2005 have shown that conservationists are moving back to 'fortress conservation'.
20 Trisurat 2006: p. 268; Hilty et al. 2006: p. 22; Hansen/DeFries 2007: p. 974; Muchapondwa et al. 2009: p. 1; DeFries et al. 2010: p. 2870
21 See among others, Miller 1996; Hilty et al. 2006; Hansen/DeFries 2007; DeFries et al. 2010

Consequently, changes in land use outside protected areas can alter ecological functions inside protected areas and result in biodiversity loss, given that protected areas are almost always parts of larger ecosystems.[22] These limitations of protected areas form a compelling argument for community conservation which encourages protection of biodiversity even beyond protected areas. The paradigmatic shift to community conservation was also due to political changes from colonial governments to independent states, particularly in Southern Africa. After independence, there was a political demand for the transference of economic success on private (white-owned) land to communal (black-owned) land.[23] The idea was to allow local black communities on communal land to benefit economically from natural resources, particularly wildlife, as had their white counterparts on private land. Zimbabwe and Namibia were in the forefront of this type of community conservation policy development.

This policy shift, which was swayed by conservation science and political changes, has led to the development of Community-Based Natural Resource Management (CBNRM) as an approach to conservation. Although there is no single definition of CBNRM, the premise underlying CBNRM is that sustainable management is most likely where local users are able to manage and extract benefits from natural resources.[24] The CBNRM approach seeks to encourage better resource management outcomes with full participation of local communities and resource users in decision-making activities. CBNRM is also a response to the limitations of a resource management paradigm emphasising technical expertise, a focus on Western forms of science, and bureaucratic centralisation.[25] Of relevance to the discussion of this chapter is the empowerment of local communities who have been disempowered for centuries. This chapter argues that local communities who are increasingly targeted as primary CBNRM beneficiaries, are often left marginalised and disempowered. In Ambovombe-Androy in southern Madagascar, political decentralisation associated with community water resource management and implemented as part of an untested perception that budding democracies are enhanced by local empowerment, has led to a disengagement of the state and disempowerment of local communities. Rural communities are suddenly faced not with increased opportunities for institutional participation, transparency, or oversight, but with having to pay exorbitant costs for water delivered in irregular intervals.[26] There local communities are of the view that they have been marginalised by their government and as a result they are unable to get water supply. Similarly, in

---

22 Hansen/DeFries 2007: p. 976; DeFries et al. 2010: p. 2870
23 See Jones/Murphree 2004: pp. 63–103 for more details
24 Jones/Murphree 2004: pp. 63–103
25 Armitage 2005: p. 703
26 Marcus 2007: p. 206

north-eastern Madagascar, the imposition of an ill-suited model of CBNRM led to community-based institutions becoming instruments of coercion in the periphery of the Makira Natural Park rather than a route to empowerment for community members.[27] Consequently, the virtualising vision of CBNRM led to the further marginalisation of people already on the periphery.

Furthermore, a shift to CBNRM in Nepal, Kenya and the US (Washington and Alaska) has shown that, despite sincere attempts and some success, serious deficiencies are widely evident.[28] The study revealed that CBNRM in the North American case study was more successful than in Nepal and Kenya, where it had hardly made any difference to more equitable distribution of power and economic benefits. Nor had CBNRM reduced conflict, increased consideration of traditional or modern environmental knowledge, protection of biological diversity, or sustainable resource use, thus disempowering local communities in Nepal and Kenya. The evidence accumulated in the case studies examined in these three countries on three continents suggests the reality often falls far short of the rhetoric and promise of CBNRM.

Empowerment in TFCAs

The challenges faced with CBNRM prompted another paradigmatic shift to the establishment of TFCAs as the 21st century approach for managing contiguous protected areas. TFCAs are defined as "large conservation areas that straddle the political borders between two or more countries, and cover natural systems that include one or more protected areas".[29] The concept of TFCAs is not new—it dates back to the creation of the first binational park on the United States–Canadian border, the Water–Glacier International Peace Park established in 1932.[30] However, in Southern Africa the courageous dream of cross-border protected areas was only realised in the early 1990s when Anton Rupert, a South African business tycoon, made formal proposals for TFCAs with the support of his long-time friend, the Prince Bernhard of the Netherlands.[31]

The sudden shift of conservation approach to TFCAs in the region is due to several reasons and claims by the supporters of TFCAs. The most cited reasons for establishing TFCAs are to conserve biodiversity, social harmony, and the promotion of peace and security.[32] Of relevance to the discussion of this chapter is the claim

---

27 Cullman 2015: p. 30
28 Kellert et al. 2000: p. 705
29 Sandwith et al. 2001: p. 3
30 Mayoral-Phillips 2002: p. 3; Van Amerom 2002: p. 265; Duffy 2006: p. 90
31 Spierenburg/Wels 2010: p. 661; see also Ramutsindela et al. 2011
32 For a more nuanced picture, see Griffin 1999; De Villiers 1999; Sandwith et al. 2001; Van der Linde et al. 2001; Hanks 2003

that TFCAs takes the interests and livelihoods of local residents seriously. Thus, protected areas were no longer supposed to marginalise and disempower local communities living within or around conservation areas. Proponents of TFCAs insist that people living in or close to TFCAs will benefit from the opportunities for economic growth that these areas offer, and that they will participate in the establishment and management of TFCAs as captured in the following quotation:

> The essential action that need [sic] to be taken to lay the foundations for effective community involvement in transfrontier conservation areas include to engage early in the discussion with indigenous peoples and local communities inhabiting all jurisdictional zones of transfrontier conservation areas, or using their resources. Dialogue should be about the concept, process and implications of transfrontier conservation areas establishment and management.[33]

The above comment reveals not only the importance of informing and involving local communities in TFCAs but also the stage at which local communities should be informed and involved. Thus, empowerment in TFCAs is supposed to happen through notifying and involving local communities from the beginning so that they can participate and influence decisions in the establishment and management of TFCAs. In addition, TFCAs are also increasingly promoted as a vehicle for local economic development.[34] Ecotourism development is seen as the main vehicle for economic growth, especially in areas which have marginal value for agriculture.[35] It is believed that TFCAs will stimulate such growth as well as empower local communities.[36] Furthermore, proponents claim that TFCAs will create employment opportunities in distressed rural areas.[37] Employment is seen as a form of empowerment, particularly in poor rural communities which face poverty, starvation and high unemployment. Consequently, the major indicators for empowerment in TFCAs include, but are not limited to, informing and involving local communities, poverty alleviation through employment opportunities, influence of communities on policy-making, and access to land and its resources by local communities. The principal claims of empowering local communities by proponents of TFCAs should be subjected to empirical scrutiny. The purpose of this chapter is to assess the validity of these claims in the Greater Mapungubwe TFCA.

---

33 Sandwith et al. 2001: p. 20
34 See among others, Griffin 1999; Van der Linde et al. 2001; Sandwith et al. 2001; Hanks 2003 for details
35 Sandwith et al. 2001: p. 7; Van der Linde et al. 2001: p. 15
36 Van der Linde et al. 2001: p. 15; see also Katerere et al. 2001
37 See among others, Van der Linde et al. 2001; Sandwith et al. 2001; Hanks 2003

Study area and notes on methodology

The Greater Mapungubwe TFCA, which is one of the TFCAs in Southern Africa, is located at the confluence of the Limpopo and Shashe Rivers, on the international boundaries between Botswana, South Africa and Zimbabwe (Figure 1). The idea of establishing this TFCA was realised with the signing of the Memorandum of Understanding (MoU) by the ministers of the three countries on 22 June 2006.[38] The MoU designates areas that each country should release into the TFCA. For example, Botswana committed the Northern Tuli Game Reserve (NOTUGRE)— which extends over an area of approximately 75,000 ha to the Greater Mapungubwe TFCA.[39] On the South African side, the land committed to the TFCA is made up of Mapungubwe National Park, contracted freehold land that is not owned by South African National Parks (SANParks) but found within Mapungubwe National Park and World Heritage Site, and Venetia Limpopo Nature Reserve, which together constitutes 55,000 ha.

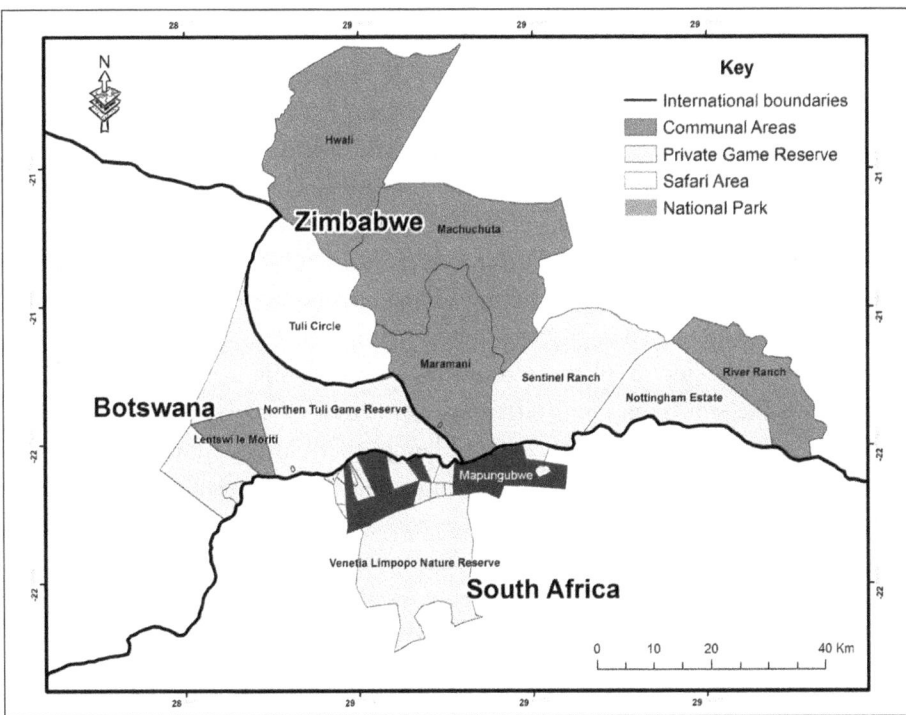

FIGURE 1: Greater Mapungubwe TFCA (Source: N.I. Sinthumule).

---

38 Greater Mapungubwe TFCA TTC 2006: http://iea.uoregon.edu/pages/view (accessed 11 May 2011)
39 De la Harpe/De la Harpe 2004; Grafhorst 2012 describe it as one of the largest game sanctuaries in Africa.

In Zimbabwe, the land committed to the TFCA is made up of the Tuli Circle Safari Area (part of the Zimbabwean national conservation estate), the western portions of the Machuchuta Wildlife Management Areas (WMA) along the Shashe River, the western and eastern portions of the Maramani WMA, River Ranch WMA, Sentinel Ranch and Nottingham Estate which together constitute 130,000 ha.[40] Thus, the contribution of the three countries combined constitutes a total of 260,000 ha which forms the core area of Greater Mapungubwe TFCA. Below is a brief description of how data were collected in the study area.

This chapter draws on fieldwork carried out in Botswana, South Africa and Zimbabwe between February 2011 and June 2013. The fieldwork involved semi-structured interviews with 131 key informants, selected to include government officials, conservation non-governmental organisations (NGOs) directly involved in the creation of the TFCA, communities within and around the TFCA, and private land owners. Authorisation to conduct research was granted by the Department of Wildlife and National Parks in Botswana, SANParks in South Africa and Beit Bridge Rural District Council in Zimbabwe. This study was also discussed in the Trilateral Technical Committee (TTC) meeting of 8 June 2011 and was approved by committee members from Botswana, South Africa and Zimbabwe. The TTC comprises delegates from Botswana, South Africa and Zimbabwe who discuss progress, take decisions and make recommendations to the Trilateral Ministerial Committee (TMC) on issues related to Greater Mapungubwe TFCA. Permission to interview key stakeholders at local level was obtained from the district council, municipalities, chiefs and headmen. Communities were asked for their permission before they were interviewed and only those who were interested in participating were interviewed.

Data were collected in all three countries by asking similar questions in order to compare the similarities and differences of activities taking place across their borders. A methodological approach and design that pays attention to both sides of the TFCA was necessary for making informed conclusions about these cross-border conservation schemes. As noted previously, the focus of the study is how and why local communities have been disempowered in the creation of Greater Mapungubwe TFCA. The main indicators of disempowerment in this study include lack of ownership of land, inability to participate and make decision, the lack of political power and the lack of influence on policy-making by communities.

Local community disempowerment at Mapungubwe

In the MoU signed by the ministers of Botswana, South Africa and Zimbabwe on 22 June 2006, objective number (d) states that TFCA "will develop frameworks and strategies whereby local communities will participate in, and tangibly benefit from,

---

40 Greater Mapungubwe TFCA TTC 2010: p. 64

the management and sustainable use of natural and cultural resources that occur within the proposed TFCA".[41] In other words, the establishment of Mapungubwe TFCA will empower local people by allowing them to participate and derive benefits from the TFCA. In order to test the validity of this claim in the creation of Greater Mapungubwe TFCA, I first discuss the situation in Lentswe Le Moriti, Motlhabaneng and Mathathane villages in Botswana.

Community experiences in Botswana

Lentswe Le Moriti village is within NOTUGRE whereas Motlhabaneng and Mathathane communal land are the last two settlements on the western side before entering the NOTUGRE main gate. The main land use activity in all three villages is livestock farming; crop farming is also practised in Motlhabaneng and Mathathane villages. The livestock, important for the community's food security, are also an important source of income. People sell their livestock when there are funerals, parties, and weddings. Butcheries also source their meat products from local communities. Livestock include cows, goats and sheep that depend on grazing within and around NOTUGRE. In addition, since the idea of a TFCA emerged in Mapungubwe, there is poor maintenance of the electric border fence on the western side of NOTUGRE. This reluctance to maintain the fence is in line with the idea of creating a borderless landscape for ecological reasons. Consequently, wildlife has free access to Motlhabaneng and Mathathane villages, leading to the killing of livestock by wildlife as the following comment makes clear:

> My whole life depends on livestock as they are my main source of income. However, the problem in this area is wildlife from Tuli Block.[42] Wildlife, particularly lion, leopards, hyena and jackals, kill our livestock regularly and sometimes we are not compensated for the damage caused by wildlife. The management of Tuli Block even accuses us of poisoning wildlife but it is not true that we poison wildlife that feed on dead carcass of our livestock. We like wildlife but the only problem is that they kill our livestock which is our only source of income. We like wildlife when they are away from our livestock but when they start feeding on our livestock they become our enemies because they leave us with nothing.[43]

---

41 Greater Mapungubwe TFCA TTC 2006: http://iea.uoregon.edu/pages/view (accessed 11 May 2011)
42 Depicted as Northern Tuli Game Reserve in Figure 1
43 Mashape Nkoloi Kobe, Lentswe Le Moriti, 19 September 2012, interview by Innocent Sinthumule, translation by Isaac Mampane

In addition, agriculture is practised in Motlhabaneng and Mathathane villages along the NOTUGRE fence; the main crops that are planted include maize, groundnuts, beans, watermelon and sorghum. However, poor maintenance of the electric fence surrounding NOTUGRE allows wildlife, particularly elephants and baboons, to roam freely in the villages and to raid crops that serve as a source of food, as made clear by the following comment in Mathathane:

> We have a nine hectare farm near Tuli Block. We use our farm for cultivation and the main crops that are planted include maize, watermelon, pumpkin, beans and groundnuts and we rely on rainfall. Our farm is our main source of food as we do not work. However, we harvest very little and the biggest chunk of the crops we plant is eaten by wildlife particularly baboons and elephants. Although we have erected a fence to protect our crops from destruction, we have realized that we have wasted our time because elephants always destroy fence and get into our farm anytime they want. During the day, our energy is wasted on shouting when elephants are feeding on our crops.[44]

Women also make an income out of weaving baskets and mats from ilala palms which are sold to tourists and other people who visit the three villages. In Motlhabaneng village, others make a living out of brewing ilala palm wine which is normally sold to villagers and tourists who visit the area. Ilala palm wine is produced by cutting the stem of the ilala palm and channelling the drips of water that come out into a container. After fermentation, the water becomes wine. The palm wine brewers also complain that elephants that roam all over in Motlhabaneng village put their life at risk and they also drink their wine as the following comment makes it clear,

> Brewing palm wine is all I do on a daily basis and the money generated help me to support my family. In recent years, elephants have become the biggest threat in this area. They not only threaten me but also drink wine which I produce from ilala palms and this has negative implications on the income I generate in a month.[45]

The increased presence of wildlife, particularly elephants and baboons, in communal land of Botswana has disempowered local communities socially and economically.

---

44   Hubonetsi Maemo and Kelennetse Maemo, Mathathane, 13 June 2013, interview by Innocent Sinthumule, translation by Isaac Mampane
45   Thetshelesani Seshoka, Motlhabaneng, 18 September 2012, interview by Innocent Sinthumule, translation by Isaac Mampane

The claim that local communities living in or close to TFCAs will be empowered by participating and benefiting from the establishment of TFCAs has become an important argument to support their establishment in post-apartheid Southern Africa. In Botswana, the study found that though Lentswe Le Moriti is within the TFCA and Motlhabaneng and Mathathane villages are near NOTUGRE and the TFCA, these villages do not form part of the TFCA, despite the popular claim that local communities living within or near the jurisdiction of the TFCA would be included in the establishment and management of TFCAs.

While the idea of a TFCA is to expand conservation land by integrating communal, private and state land, in Botswana, only private land (NOTUGRE) forms part of the Greater Mapungubwe TFCA. It is important to note that communal land in Botswana remains the property of the state. Unlike private land holders in NOTUGRE, communities in communal land do not have the freedom to incorporate their land into the TFCA or to negotiate the conditions under which they can be involved in such a conservation project. As a result, community participation is limited.

This division of residents in terms of participation shows that lack of property rights contributes to disempowerment in conservation and also limits their potential to extract benefits from tourism in the area, despite the popular TFCA narrative that communities stand to benefit from nature-based tourism that the TFCA brings. The community was unable to participate and influence decisions relating to the creation of Mapungubwe TFCA, but bear the cost of conservation which includes destruction of crops and killing of domestic animals by wildlife.

Furthermore, local communities of Lentswe Le Moriti, Motlhabaneng and Mathathane villages knew nothing about the TFCA in the region. This lack of knowledge could be attributed to the fact that their land is not part of the TFCA. Interviews with community members confirmed that communities were not informed by government about the establishment of the TFCA. Of the 19 community members interviewed in Botswana, only two (the headman of Motlhabaneng and the secretary of the Zion Christian Church in Lentswe Le Moriti village) knew about the TFCA; the other 17 villagers had no knowledge of the creation of Greater Mapungubwe TFCA. The two knew about the TFCA because they were invited to attend the signing of the Memorandum of Understanding in 2006 held at the confluence of Limpopo and Shashe Rivers. However, they did not understand what it was all about and how they would benefit from the creation of the TFCA.

Since the signing of Memorandum of Understanding was a formal ceremony, they did not get an opportunity to ask questions about the TFCA. As a result, they were unable to give feedback to their communities. It can be said that they were only invited because they are leaders and the idea was to gain support from such influential people in the communities.

Local community experiences in South Africa

On the South African side of the TFCA, there are no villages within or near Mapungubwe National Park. The area is dominated by private game farms and commercial agricultural farms. Some of the farmworkers are permanent residents in the area because they were born on the farms, while others have lived on the farms for decades. These farmworkers are considered local communities on the South African side of the TFCA. They work on farms within the Mapungubwe National Park but not part of the park. The farmworkers who have neither property rights nor control over the land have not been informed and nor been involved in the establishment of the TFCA as made clear by one farmworker in Samaria farm:

> I have been working in Mapungubwe for the past 10 years. My boss has not informed us about the TFCA and I am not sure how I will be affected or benefit. I am just a farm worker who is a foreigner and maybe TFCA does not involve foreigners.[46]

The study found that the majority of farmworkers in Mapungubwe are Zimbabwean and Mozambican nationals. None of the farmworkers interviewed (both South African and non-South Africans) had any knowledge of the Greater Mapungubwe TFCA.

To consolidate the core of the TFCA, SANParks has bought farms from private land owners, which has led to forced removals and disempowerment of many farmworkers. For instance, when Rhodesdrift, a commercial farm, was incorporated into Mapungubwe National Park and the TFCA, 50 permanent employees living on the farm were forced to vacate the land as their services were no longer required by the new owners. One informant expressed her feelings by saying:

> When Rhodesdrift farm was sold to SANParks, we were given six month to demolish all houses and vacate the farm. It was hard and difficult to believe that the farm has been sold. I was forced to move out of the farm and I did not know where to go because all my life was based in the farm. Our boss Wellie Syman gave us transport to remove all our belongings to our homes but I did not have a home outside the farm. Fortunately, I got a stand in Alldays and I used the Zink of my demolished house to build a two room house. Since then, I never had an interest to work again in the farm. It is something that I will never forget in my life.[47]

---

46 Joseph Samu, Samaria farm, 17 January 2012, interview by Innocent Sinthumule
47 Sophie Tshifhumulo Mmbadaliga, 17 January 2012, interview by Innocent Sinthumule

Thus, through the buying of farms by SANParks, farmworkers lose their jobs and places to stay because they do not have property rights in land. The buying of irrigation farms for conservation purposes is considered as "displacement without resistance".[48] The ultimate intention of SANParks is to buy all the commercial farms in the area to allow free movement of wildlife. If this ambitious dream becomes a reality in future, more farmworkers will lose jobs and be forced to relocate from the Mapungubwe area, despite the claims of job creation through TFCAs.

Land claimants also form part of local communities in the Greater Mapungubwe TFCA. The Machete and Sematla clans are not farmworkers but land claimants who were forcibly removed as a result of racially discriminatory laws and practices in the late 1960s. Those who remained in the Mapungubwe area became labour tenants of white farmers in return for staying on their land. Den Staat farm is within the borders of Mapungubwe National Park but is not part of the park or the TFCA. The land claimants moved back to the farm in 2009. The study found that the land claimants have heard about the TFCA but they are not part of the TFCA and they are not interested in being part of the TFCA. In other words, there is resistance by land claimants to release their land for conservation purpose. Land claimants prefer to use their land for farming rather than conservation. During the time of fieldwork, Den Staat farm was used mainly for citrus and crop farming.

As in Botswana, the study found that the knowledge of TFCA is skewed towards powerful private land owners who support conservation and government officials. Whereas some private land owners volunteered to be part of the TFCA, others were approached by SANParks to be part of Greater Mapungubwe TFCA. The study found that those private land owners who released their land to be part of the TFCA are happy with the establishment of the park. However, there are other private land owners, including game as well as irrigation farmers, who refused to release their land for conservation purposes because they would prefer to farm. At the time of conducting the study, there were ten large-scale commercial irrigation farms and ten game farms within the borders of Mapungubwe National Park and World Heritage Site but not part of the park or the TFCA. Thus, resistance by farmers to release land for conservation has created some challenges and this has serious implications on the consolidation of the land in the Mapungubwe TFCA.

The Zimbabwean experience

The Zimbabwean portion of the TFCA is largely dominated by communal lands, namely, Maramani, River Ranch and Machuchuta. These communal lands to the western side of Beit Bridge Rural District are among the poorest in Zimbabwe.[49]

---

48   See Turner 2006 for details
49   CESVI 2003: http://www.cesvi.eu/ (accessed 12 May 2010)

There is no tourist infrastructure in these communal areas. Agriculture is the main source of food for these communities. People who live in these communal areas depend on intensive crop production as well as extensive livestock production. The main crops that are cultivated include maize in summer and wheat in winter, but unfortunately communities are often unable to harvest because their crops are destroyed mainly by wildlife. As in Botswana, the creation of the TFCA has allowed wildlife, particularly elephants, to roam freely across national borders with devastating effects on agriculture as made clear by one community member in Maramani village:

> We live with wildlife in this area but elephants are the most problematic animals. Elephants own this area and as a result they are all over this village land. Some of them come from Botswana via Shashe River. You won't like them when you see big herds of elephants with their young ones in this area. They are more aggressive when they walk around with their young ones. Though we have fenced our farms with poles and branches of trees, it is like we have done nothing. This is because they break the fence and when they get into our agricultural field, they eat whatever they want from maize to watermelon and you cannot control them. We put a lot of effort cultivating in our farms but we do not harvest anything.[50]

Livestock farming is dominated by domestic animals such as cows, goats, sheep and donkeys. As in Botswana, livestock is the most important component of food security for communities because livestock owners are able to generate income to feed their families from selling some of their domestic animals. However, there are conflicts between wildlife and domestic animals, leading to the death of domestic animals. The killing of domestic animals by wildlife has already created some antagonism and hatred towards wildlife.

While there has always been wildlife on communal land, the study found that the conflict was not intense because of a limited amount of wildlife in the area. However, the increased presence of wildlife, particularly elephants coming from Botswana and South Africa, because of the creation of the TFCA across borders has intensified land-use conflict in the area. Other community members in Maramani, River Ranch and Machuchuta make a living by making brooms from ilala palm leaves or by brewing palm wine.

Unlike in Botswana where communal lands were not integrated into the TFCA, a large area of Zimbabwe's contribution to the TFCA is dominated by communal

---

50   Belida Mbedzi, 14 May 2011, Maramani, interview by Innocent Sinthumule

land. As in Botswana and South Africa, people living on communal land in Zimbabwe were not consulted about the creation of the Mapungubwe TFCA. This could be because communal land in Zimbabwe remains the property of the state. In other words, a project can be undertaken by government in communal land without the knowledge of communities as confirmed by this study. During fieldwork, communities from all communal lands that form part of the TFCA were interviewed to get their views and knowledge regarding the TFCA. Key informants included the headman, ward councillors, Communal Areas Management Programme for Indigenous Resources (CAMPFIRE) committee members, and individuals in households and on irrigation farms. Of the 39 community members interviewed, 36 people had never heard about the concept of TFCA and only three people knew about it. The three people who had heard about the TFCA were the headman, a counsellor and one community member but they could not remember how they heard about the idea of a TFCA in the area. Community members who have direct interests in the resources within the areas earmarked for the creation of Greater Mapungubwe TFCA have been disempowered as made clear by one informant in Maramani Village:

> We have never been informed about the TFCA and we don't know what it is about. Our chief and councillors have not informed us about the TFCA. Even our government officials have not informed us about the TFCA. Maybe they are still going to inform us. We don't know how we will be affected and how we will benefit if there will be any benefits. We only wish that they don't remove us from our forefather's land.[51]

As in Botswana, those who heard about the concept do not know what it entails and how they will benefit from it. The respondent above stated that he does not wish to leave the land—perhaps there can be no benefits if the land is taken from him for purposes of conservation.

Communities do not have representatives at the TTC meetings.[52] They are instead represented by the chairperson of the Community Development Working Group (CDWG) in Zimbabwe, who is also the Chief Executive Officer of Beit Bridge Rural District Council. Thus, they are represented by a government official who does not reside within the community. Although there is a firm TTC decision that communities should represent themselves and the Peace Parks Foundation has offered to carry the additional costs for transport and accommodation, this

---

51 Zakaria Ndou, Maramani, 14 May 2011 and 20 August 2011, interview by Innocent Sinthumule
52 Observation by Innocent Sinthumule during the TTC meeting of 8 June 2011 in Pretoria

has not yet happened in Zimbabwe. The bulk of Zimbabwe TTC working group representatives are from Harare and Beit Bridge.[53] Whilst the Beit Bridge Rural District Council claims that it informs communities about the TFCA, on the ground communities are ignorant of the concept of TFCA. It is therefore clear that TTC representatives from Zimbabwe decide what is best for the resident communities. The decisions about the idea and plans for the TFCA are taken at a higher level without consultation with communities on the ground. The dissemination of information and decisions to communities is also weak despite the popular TFCA narrative that local communities will be involved and informed about the establishment and management of TFCAs. As a result there is a serious lack of information about the TFCA in the communities. Without this knowledge, local communities are unable to participate and influence decisions and policies regarding the establishment of a TFCA in the region. Whereas on one hand the communities are not involved in the establishment of the TFCA, on the other hand the powerful white private land owners in Nottingham and Sentinel (see Figure 1) are members of the TFCA and the TTC. As in Botswana and South Africa, the study found that the knowledge of TFCAs is skewed towards government officials and the private sector.

The idea behind establishing the TFCA is to transform space by removing state borders that are seen as fragmenting habitats and entire ecosystems. In the case of Mapungubwe, the purpose of creating the Greater Mapungubwe TFCA is to remove state borders separating Botswana, South Africa and Zimbabwe. Whilst there is substantial border transformation for purposes of conservation, local communities in the Mapungubwe region remain divided by the same borders that have been rendered ineffective for wildlife. In other words, state borders were removed only for wildlife and not for local communities within and around the Greater Mapungubwe TFCA. For instance, Tshivenda-speaking communities on the southern side of Zimbabwe and northern side of South Africa remain separated by the international border (i.e. Limpopo) that has been rendered ineffective for conservation purposes. Zimbabwean residents from Maramani, Machuchuta and River Ranch who are seen crossing the border to visit their relatives in South Africa are criminalised as poachers whereas the crossing of the same border by wildlife is seen by conservationists as a natural way of life. Thus, Zimbabweans passing through the Greater Mapungubwe TFCA are seen as illegal or 'border jumpers' who should be arrested at the earliest opportunity and extradited to their home country whereas animals are encouraged to roam freely across the borders. Similarly, local communities from Botswana going to South Africa and Zimbabwe and vice versa are also required to have proper documentation before crossing

---

53 Observation by Innocent Sinthumule during the TTC meeting of 8 June 2011 in Pretoria

the borders. This situation perseveres in Mapungubwe regardless of the claim that TFCAs will re-unite communities that had been divided by colonial borders.

Conclusion

This chapter has sought to understand disempowerment of local communities in the context of nature conservation projects. It has demonstrated that conservation science and political changes have led to a paradigmatic shift in nature conservation projects in order to integrate communal land into conservation and to allow communities to participate and benefit from conservation projects. In other words, the aim is to empower local communities whilst increasing conservation land for wildlife. Thus, this shift towards TFCAs is meant to take the interests and livelihoods of local communities seriously. However, the evidence from the Mapungubwe TFCA suggests that the reality falls far short of the promises of the TFCAs. Rather than shifting towards empowering local communities, the TFCA has led to disempowerment of local communities. There are a number of ways in which local communities are disempowered in the creation of the Mapungubwe TFCA. These include local communities not being informed and involved by both government and non-governmental organisations in the process leading to the establishment of a TFCAs. Consequently, communities are unable to participate and influence decisions. In addition, the increased presence of wildlife on communal land because of the creation of a TFCA also leads to the disruption of the livelihoods of local communities. Contrary to the claim that TFCA will empower local communities, the study found that the TFCA does not live up to its promises of empowering local communities. Some scholars have argued that proponents of TFCAs have included the notion of community participation, empowerment and local economic development in the packaging and design of TFCAs in order to win the support of government and donor agencies.[54] Whereas proponents of TFCAs claim that the paradigmatic shift epitomised by conservation in the form of TFCAs will empower local communities, in the Greater Mapungubwe TFCA, the study found that there is no empowerment of local communities within and across national borders.

---

54 Ramutsindela 2004: p. 63

References

Agrawal, A. and K. Redford (2009), Conservation and Displacement: An Overview. *Conservation and Society*, 7(1): 1–10.

Armitage, D. (2005), Adaptive Capacity and Community-based Natural Resource Management. *Environmental Management*, 35(6): 703–715.

Brockington, D. and J. Igoe (2006), Eviction for Conservation: A Global Overview. *Conservation and Society*, 4(3): 424–470.

Byers, B.A., R.N. Cunliffe and A.T. Hudak (2001), Linking the Conservation of Culture and Nature: A Case Study of Sacred Forests in Zimbabwe. *Human Ecology*, 29(2): 187–218.

Carruthers, J. (2009), National Parks in South Africa. In H. Suich, B. Child and A. Spenceley (eds.), *Evolution and Innovation in Wildlife Conservation: Parks and Game Ranches to Transfrontier Conservation Areas*. London: Earthscan: 35–50.

Cernea, M. (2005), Restriction of Access is Displacement: A Broader Concept and Policy. *Forced Migration Review* 23: 48–49.

CESVI (2003), Review of Land Use and Resource Management Options in the Zimbabwe Component of the Proposed Shashe/Limpopo TFCA, Prepared for Beit Bridge Rural District Council, Beit Bridge, http://www.cesvi.eu/. Accessed 12 May 2010.

Conger, J.A. and R.N. Kanungo (1988), The Empowerment Process: Integrating Theory and Practice. *Academy of Management Review*, 13(3): 471–482.

Craig, G. (2002), Towards the Measurement of Empowerment: The Evaluation of Community Development. *Community Development*, 33(1): 124–146.

Cullman, G. (2015), Community Forest Management as Virtualism in Northeastern Madagascar. *Human Ecology*, 43(1): 29–41.

DeFries, R., K.K. Karanth and S. Pareeth (2010), Interactions between Protected Areas and their Surroundings in Human-dominated Tropical Landscapes. *Biological Conservation*, 143(12): 2870–2880.

De la Harpe, R. and P. de la Harpe (2004), *Tuli, Land of Giants*. Gaborone: Sunbird Publishing (Pty) Ltd.

De Villiers, B. (1999), *Peace Parks: The Way Ahead*. Pretoria: Human Sciences Research Council Publishers.

De Villiers, B. (2008), *People and Parks: Sharing the Benefits*. Johannesburg: Konrad Adenauer Stiftung.

Dowie, M. (2009), *Conservation Refugees: The Hundred-year Conflict between Global Conservation and Native People*. Cambridge: The MIT Press.

Duffy, R. (2006), The Potential and Pitfalls of Global Environmental Governance: The Politics of Transfrontier Conservation Areas in Southern Africa. *Political Geography*, 25(1): 89–112.

Eylon, D. and P. Bamberger (2000), Empowerment Cognitions and Empowerment Acts Recognizing the Importance of Gender. *Group and Organization Management*, 25(4): 354–372.

Greater Mapungubwe TFCA TTC (2006), Memorandum of Understanding to Facilitate the Establishment of the Limpopo/Shashe Transfrontier Conservation between the Government of the Republic of Botswana, South Africa and Zimbabwe. http://iea.uoregon.edu/pages/view. Accessed 11 May 2011.

Greater Mapungubwe TFCA TTC (2010), *Greater Mapungubwe Transfrontier Conservation Area Integrated Development Plan*, First edition.

Grafhorst, V. (2012), *Northern Tuli Game Reserve: A Walk on the Wild Side.* Botswana: Discover Botswana.

Griffin, J. (1999), *Study of Development of Transboundary Natural Resource Management Areas in Southern Africa.* Washington DC: Biodiversity Support Programme.

Hansen, A.J. and R. DeFries (2007), Ecological Mechanisms Linking Protected Areas to Surrounding Lands. *Ecological Applications*, 17(4): 974–988.

Hanks, J. (2003), Transfrontier Conservation Areas (TFCAs) in Southern Africa: Their Role in Conserving Biodiversity, Socioeconomic Development and Promoting a Culture of Peace. *Journal of Sustainable Forestry*, 17(1–2): 127–148.

Hilty, J.A., W.Z. Lidicker Jr. and A.M. Merenlender (2006), *Corridor Ecology: The Science and Practice of Linking Landscapes for Biodiversity Conservation.* Washington DC: Island Press.

Hutton, J., W.M. Adams and J. Murombedzi (2005), Back to the Barriers? Changing Narratives in Biodiversity Conservation. *Forum for Development Studies*, 32(2): 341–370.

Jones, B.T. and M.W. Murphree (2004), Community-based Natural Resource Management as a Conservation Mechanism: Lessons and Direction. In B. Child (ed.), *Parks in Transition: Biodiversity, Rural Development, and the Bottom Line.* London: Earthscan: 63–103.

Katerere, Y., R. Hill and S. Moyo (2001), *A Critique of Transboundary Natural Resource Management in Southern Africa.* Regional Office for Southern Africa: IUCN.

Kellert, S.R., J.N. Mehta, S.A. Ebbin and L.L. Lichtenfeld (2000), Community Natural Resource Management: Promise, Rhetoric, and Reality. *Society and Natural Resources*, 13(8): 705–715.

Kepe, T. (2004), Land Restitution and Biodiversity Conservation in South Africa: The Case of Mkambati, Eastern Cape Province. *Canadian Journal of African Studies/La Revue canadienne des études africaines*, 38(3): 688–704.

Laband, D.N. and B.F. Lentz (1998), The Effects of Sexual Harassment on Job Satisfaction, Earnings, and Turnover among Female Lawyers. *Industrial and Labor Relations Review*, 51(4): 594–607.

Maiti, P. (2006), Democracy versus Development: New Urban Debates. *The International Journal of Sustainable Development and World Ecology*, 13(4): 289–294.

Magome, H. and J. Murombedzi (2003), Sharing South African National Parks: Community Land and Conservation in a Democratic South Africa. In W.M. Adams and M. Mulligan (eds.), *Decolonizing Nature, Strategies for Conservation in a Post-colonial Era.* London: Earthscan: 108–134.

Marcus, R.R. (2007), Where Community-based Water Resource Management has Gone Too Far: Poverty and Disempowerment in Southern Madagascar. *Conservation and Society*, 5(2): 202–231.

Mayoral-Phillips, A.J. (2002), Transboundary Areas in Southern Africa: Meeting the Needs of Conservation or Development? 'The Commons in an Age of Globalization', Ninth Conference of the International Association for the Study of Common Property, Victoria Falls, Vol. 1721.

Metcalfe, S. (2003), Impacts of Transboundary Protected Areas on Local Communities in Three Southern African Initiatives. In Workshop on Transboundary Protected Areas, Governance Stream of the 5th World Parks Congress, 12–13 September, Durban, South Africa.

Miller, K. (1996), Balancing the Scales: Guidelines for Increasing Biodiversity's Chances through Bioregional Management. In R. Breckwoldt (ed.), *Approaches to Bioregional Planning*. Proceedings of the Conference, 30 October to 1 November, Melbourne.

Muchapondwa, E., H. Biggs, A. Driver, F. Matose, K. Moore, E. Mungatana and K. Scheepers (2009), Using Economic Incentives to Encourage Conservation in Bioregions in South Africa. *Economic Research Southern Africa (ERSA) working paper*, 120.

Ramutsindela, M. (2003), Land Reform in South Africa's National Parks: A Catalyst for the Human–Nature Nexus. *Land Use Policy*, 20(1): 41–49.

Ramutsindela, M. (2004), Glocalisation and Nature Conservation Strategies in 21st-Century Southern Africa. *Tijdschrift voor Economische en Sociale Geografie*, 95(1): 61–72.

Ramutsindela, M., M. Spierenburg and H. Wels (2011), *Sponsoring Nature: Environmental Philanthropy for Conservation*. Earthscan: London.

Sandwith, T., C. Shine, L. Hamilton and D. Sheppard (2001), *Transboundary Protected Areas for Peace and Cooperation*. Gland: IUCN.

SANParks (2010), *Mapungubwe National Park Management Plan, South African National Parks*, Pretoria: SANParks.

Sarin, M. (2001a), Empowerment and Disempowerment of Forest Women in Uttarakhand, India. *Gender, Technology and Development*, 5(3): 341–364.

Sarin, M. (2001b), Disempowerment in the Name of 'Participatory' Forestry? Village Forests Joint Management in Uttarakhand. *Forests, Trees and People Newsletter*, 44.

Spierenburg, M., C. Steenkamp and H. Wels (2008), Enclosing the Local for the Global Commons: Community Land Rights in the Great Limpopo Transfrontier Conservation Area. *Conservation and Society*, 6(1): 87–97.

Spierenburg, M. and H. Wels (2010), Conservative Philanthropists, Royalty and Business Elites in Nature Conservation in Southern Africa. *Antipode*, 42(3): 647–670.

Trisurat, Y. (2006), Transboundary Biodiversity Conservation of the Pha Taem Protected Forest Complex: A Bioregional Approach. *Applied Geography*, 26(3): 260–275.

Toomey A.H. (2008), A Transition to Sustainable Development: Empowerment and Disempowerment in a Nicaraguan Community, (MA Thesis, American University).

Turner R.L. (2006), *Farming to Nature: Displacement without Resistance in Northernmost Limpopo?* Prepared for Delivery at the 2006 Annual Meeting of the African Studies Association November 16.

Van Amerom, M. (2002), National Sovereignty and Transboundary Protected Areas in Southern Africa. *GeoJournal*, 58(4), 265–273.

Van der Linde, H., J. Oglethorpe, T. Sandwith, D. Snelson and Y. Tessema (2001), *Beyond Boundaries: Transboundary Natural Resource Management in Sub-Saharan Africa.* Washington DC: Biodiversity Support Program.

Young, A.M., C.M. Vance and E.A. Ensher (2003), Individual Differences in Sensitivity to Disempowering Acts: A Comparison of Gender and Identity-Based Explanations for Perceived Offensiveness. *Sex Roles*, 49(3–4): 163–171.

CHAPTER 12

On identities, ways of knowing and interactions across difference in collaborative urban nature conservation at Macassar dunes, Cape Town

Marnie Graham

Introduction: Heritage Week overnight camp, 2012
We form an attentive, jovial and relaxed circle with our twenty or so human bodies, standing together in the Macassar Dunes Conservation Area. Most in our circle come from the persistently racially segregated Cape Flats' townships of Khayelitsha, Macassar and Mitchell's Plain, which adjoin the dunes in which we now stand.[1] The nature conservators who manage these dunes have brought us together in the hope that we will share our diverse relationships to nature, and thus learn more about and from each other than has been possible in the divisive apartheid and colonial pasts. Ultimately, they also hope that through this sharing and learning we will be united by the need to conserve these dunes and the rich biodiversity they hold.

The slender, smooth body of a harmless common corn snake is gently passed on to the next willing taker in our circle until it is placed in a bucket in the middle of us all. It is to the snake's petite and now motionless, coiled body that the conservators direct our attention, prompting us to share our personal and cultural relationships

---

1 Participants are anonymous in this study to protect their identities, though occasionally pseudonyms are used to animate the dialogue. Heritage Week participants include on-ground nature conservators and residents of Macassar, Khayelitsha and Mitchell's Plain who are together engaged in collaborative conservation arrangements at Macassar Dunes Conservation Area/Wolfgat Nature Reserve. These arrangements involve environmental and conservation education and on-reserve conservation activities. Heritage Week is one of these activities, and is the primary interaction whereby local community participants are actively and explicitly encouraged to speak of their own understandings of nature (see Graham 2015a).

to snakes. Some Mitchell's Plain residents describe fearfully fleeing from accidental encounters with the creatures in the shrubby vegetation that borders their township. Others from Khayelitsha tell of growing up in rural Xhosa villages, some 1,000 kilometres away in the Eastern Cape, and being taught that the highly venomous snakes of the area were dangerous pests to be killed on sight.

When it is his turn to speak, Declan, a nature conservator, indicates that actually we rather need to be respectful of the snake and of all creatures, because they provide us with ecological services—helping, for example, to keep rodent pests away from crops and dwellings. Whilst the Cape Flats was largely neglected in terms of nature conservation during apartheid, today the conservation community understand Macassar Dunes as an area of "critical biodiversity"—such that Declan's comment leaves hanging in the air the perception that the local township residents largely do not value or respect Macassar Dunes in this way.[2]

After a short while contemplating, Dembeza, a young isiXhosa-speaking man from Khayelitsha responds:

> Declan, did you know the snake is also important for us Xhosa people? In my culture, my clan name is Majola—it means the snake. And we have a story that when a baby is born, within a few months when the baby is still very small then a snake will come visit the mother and baby of Majola, and that is where we get our clan name from, from the snake—that is, we Majola.

The isiXhosa-speaking contingent of the circle nods their heads in confirmation of this story. Declan nods his head in response too: "That was very interesting, Dembeza, thanks for sharing that with us. And do you, or does anyone know why the snake visits the mothers?" Declan pauses for effect and then points to his chest: "This is why: when mothers breastfeed, the snake can actually smell the woman lactating, he can sense it with his powerful sense of smell. So when he smells the milk, he knows the young are near …"

Exclamations of surprise mixed with nervous laughter erupt from the circle at this fascinating yet horrifying notion of snakes sensing human milk and babies. Before long, however, Akhona, an older Xhosa-speaking woman also originally from the Eastern Cape, takes the floor. Everyone listens intently as she questions the validity of Declan's response:

> Declan—yes, I understand this explanation from you. But no—it doesn't provide all the answers. If this what you tell us is true, the snake would

---

2 Stipinovich/Holmes 2009: p. 15

visit every mother. But the snake *don't* visit every mother—he only visit the Majola—this is why they get their clan name—MA-JO-LA. Why the snake only visiting them? You see! Do you have an explanation for that?!

Akhona erupts into a beaming smile as she poses this question for which she knows there will be no explanation. Everybody is delighted at this interjection and we all laugh, including Declan, who briefly searches the circle for help in responding, but then grins good-naturedly, shrugs in concession and responds: "No, I don't have an explanation for that ..."

Post-apartheid social reconciliation and collaborative nature conservation
The Heritage Week participants mentioned above were already familiar to each other, because together they engage in collaborative conservation arrangements at Macassar Dunes Conservation Area. These arrangements encompass activities facilitated and convened by the nature conservators, like alien vegetation removal and local environmental education campaigns. Macassar Dunes Heritage Week, however, differs from these conservator-controlled interactions in that it is much more democratic, and is therefore significant from a nature conservation perspective. As an annual celebration, the event is specifically intended for all collaborators to openly and actively explore and share their diverse understandings of and relationships with nature. In 2012 the Heritage Week celebrations involved a long-weekend overnight camp where participants shared their relationships towards the dunes' flora and fauna species, and this event—in which I, as a foreign researcher from Australia was fortunate enough to participate—is the focus of this chapter.

Macassar Dunes Heritage Week celebrations are also symbolically significant in terms of social reconciliation in post-apartheid South Africa. Like many South Africans, the participants have not spent time learning deeply about each other across intense and persistent colonial and apartheid racial, economic and class divisions. Located in the peripheral spaces of the city—some 30 kilometres southeast of the centre and adjacent to the False Bay coast—the Cape Flats were developed during apartheid, as gradually much of the city centre was declared for the residence of whites only.[3] The area was not only purposely ghettoised (with grossly inadequate housing, amenities and services), but was also spatially ordered along the lines of apartheid's hierarchical statutory racial categories.[4] Mitchell's Plain and Macassar townships were developed in the 1960s and 1970s for those designated 'coloured' or 'mixed race', and involved many forced removals of city

---

3   Western 1996; Bickford-Smith et al. 1999
4   Seekings 2011

residents.⁵ Khayelitsha, which sits in between them, was developed as a worker dormitory suburb in 1983 to spatially consolidate and control black labourers from around the city.⁶ Whilst the ecologically sensitive area was essentially bulldozed in order to create the Cape Flats (which is today home to the majority of the city's population), remnant green spaces between township areas were planned as buffers to enforce racial segregation, and several large sandy, vegetated areas still separate them.⁷ Acutely politicised and frequently provocative racialised and ethnicised relations transpire today, amidst the persistent race-based residential segregation that still characterises the area.⁸

More than two decades after apartheid's demise, the tensioned situation on the Cape Flats is perhaps unsurprising. Enforcing racial and ethnic boundaries, apartheid policies worked "through explicit territorial and residential segregation to spatially delimit the nature of identity, drawing ever tighter the boundaries separating self from other".⁹ Alongside residential segregation, strict prohibitions on inter-racial sex and marriage "remov[ed] the possibility of assimilation or other forms of boundary-crossing".¹⁰ Such boundaries were fundamental to white minority-rule through the perpetuation of a "caste-like system" of inequality—with whites above coloureds, and then Africans at the bottom—with "largely impermeable boundaries" that determined one's available life options.¹¹

Indeed, social, material, and psychological divisions were created on the basis of the apartheid race categories, and they continue to impact South Africans' lives.¹² Today racialised and ethnicised identities in South Africa remain not only pervasive, but appear to be actually *strengthening*.¹³ Even in desegregated public

---

5 Western 1996; Besteman 2008
6 Besteman 2008. The Population Registration Act (No. 30 of 1950) required all South Africans to be classified according to statutory racial categories—White (for those deemed to be of European descent), Black (sometimes also referred to as African, Native and/or Bantu) and Coloured (which was further subcategorised into Cape Malay, Griqua, Indian, Chinese and Cape Coloured). The Group Areas Act (No 41 of 1950) legally enabled spatial segregation according to these categories.
7 See Seekings 2011 on the contemporary Cape Flats population, and Western 1996 on apartheid-era planning for the development of the Cape Flats.
8 See Besteman 2008 and Seekings 2011 for information on racialised and ethnicised tensions in Cape Town. Persistent segregation of the study area along apartheid-era racial categories is reflected in the 2011 Census. 90.8 per cent of Mitchells Plain's 310,000 residents and 88.6 per cent of Macassar's 32,356 residents self-identified as Coloured, while 96.8 per cent of Khayelitsha's 391,748 residents identified as Black African.
9 Popke/Ballard 2004: p. 99
10 Seekings 2011: p. 532
11 Seekings 2011: p. 533
12 Wale 2014
13 Wale 2014—based on comparisons of a decade of annual post-apartheid national reconciliation surveys.

spaces like malls, beaches and restaurants, post-apartheid studies reveal racial mixing largely does not occur.[14] And, furthermore, it is the poorest (generally black) South Africans—like many of the Cape Flats' population—who appear increasingly excluded from inter-racial socialisation.[15]

Hailing from diverse racial backgrounds and tensioned political spaces, the significance of Heritage Week becomes apparent. Here participants actively engage in steps to address these fraught relations—by voluntarily sharing, learning, and trying to understand more about each other and about each other's histories, cultures, places and relations of care. Importantly, the Week offers ample opportunities to *transgress* the boundaries separating self from other that so permeated apartheid relations, and which evidently appear to infuse post-apartheid relations too.[16] Time and space are enabled for significant informal conversations, and as well deeply intimate interactions are facilitated—sleeping side-by-side in tents, making up songs together, sharing meals, tea breaks, ablution facilities and evenings by the campfire, and helping each other navigate moonlit midnight hikes through the steeply undulating and darkly shadowed dunes.

This chapter focuses on Heritage Week in 2012 as a site of cross-social interaction by attending to the importance of post-apartheid identities. Analytical concentration on identities is imperative in the context of post-apartheid social reconciliation processes, because firstly, claiming and asserting post-apartheid identities is an "inherently political" process in South Africa.[17] Secondly, the Cape Flats' history is of spatial exclusions and tensions based on racialised and associated ethnicised identities, making attention to contemporary identities pertinent in any decisions over how best to use, value and manage urban space in the post-apartheid city. In the context of the significant social inequality of the Cape Flats, a focus on identities is also critical, thirdly, for addressing issues of power in nature conservation as a spatial and social practice.[18] This is tackled by exploring "the myriad ways" in which social identities "are at stake in the daily discourses, practices, and performances of natural resource management, struggles over access and control, as well as the very definition of whose environmental knowledge counts".[19] Such exploration is particularly pertinent in Cape Town more broadly, where academic and policy literatures frequently represent urban conservation areas as apolitical spaces of nature, unrelated to apartheid and colonial histories,

---

14 Dixon et al. 2008
15 Wale 2014
16 Popke/Ballard 2004: p. 99 write on the boundaries separating self from other. See Wale 2014 on post-apartheid relations.
17 Battersby 2005
18 Sundberg 2004
19 Sundberg 2004: p. 44

and managed as "historically, culturally, and spatially distinct entities" from the urban scape.[20]

In this chapter I specifically consider how participants who identify as Xhosa, Majola, Rastafari and as nature conservators asserted diverse ways of knowing urban nature at Heritage Week, thus actively reworking, reconfiguring and contesting historically racialised and ethnicised identities. Through these participants, I explore how race and ethnicity remain pervasive though flexible identifiers in post-apartheid South Africa, and how the pursuit of meaningful post-apartheid identities that break free of colonising bounds is a highly complex, dynamic process.[21] Focused to date on the perspectives of ecologists and on the management of nature as separate from people, there is an imperative to *politicise* urban nature conservation in Cape Town, to which this chapter makes three contributions:[22]

1. By bringing attention to the ways that historically-entrenched racial, ethnic and cultural identity stereotypes are manifest within urban nature conservation practices, ideas and collaborations;
2. By considering how sharing openly and intimately about diverse ways of knowing urban nature can challenge these long-held conceptions of each other; and can open challenging questions of who gets to speak for urban nature and conservation practice in Cape Town.
3. By considering how urban nature conservation and Heritage Week specifically are implicated and limited in questions of social reconciliation and conservation justice in Cape Town—a city of huge economic and social inequalities.[23]

Collaborative nature conservation and colonial, apartheid and post-apartheid identities

The Heritage Week participants from Khayelitsha identify as Xhosa people, originally hailing from and/or maintaining ancestral and familial linkages to the largely rural Eastern Cape[24], and for whom isiXhosa (Xhosa language) is first and

---

20 See Graham 2015a for discussion of the depoliticisation of spaces of nature in Cape Town; See Olwage 2013: p. 79 on the separation of cities and nature, colonialism/apartheid histories and contemporary conservation practice, within current management practices and ideologies in Cape Town.
21 Battersby 2005
22 Graham 2015a, 2015b; see also Katzschner 2014
23 Conservation justice as described by Ferketic et al. 2010: p. 1168 is "the logical extension of community-based conservation ... [such that] achieving justice in conservation requires working toward procedural and distributional fairness in planning and implementation. Conservation planners should accordingly meet standards of conservation justice". See Besteman 2008 on the social and economic inequalities in Cape Town.
24 Parnell/Crankshaw 2013: p. 600 note South Africa's transition to an overwhelmingly urban society dates from the mid-1970s, such that many urban South Africans are "first generation migrants with strong rural consciousness and enduring rural linkages".

English their second (or third) languages. Some have lived in the greater Cape Town area their entire lives and for several generations, others for decades, and a few have recently arrived from the Eastern Cape. Meanwhile—reflective of the wider post-apartheid Cape Town situation discussed herein—Heritage Week participants from Mitchell's Plain and Macassar variously embrace and reject the notion of a coloured identity, and others still reflect on the term ambiguously—for example, the participants in this study who identify as Rastafari.[25] Many have strong historical and familial linkages to the greater Cape Town area, and typically have Afrikaans and English as their first and/or second languages.

Participants also come from a range of socio-economic situations—some live in middle-class private dwellings, others in low-income Reconstruction and Development Programme (RDP) housing provided by the state, whilst others live in shacks erected in backyards and informal settlements. A few have regular or irregular jobs, most are either searching for employment, or volunteering or interning at workplaces; the participants also run or contribute to community-based organisations, the majority of which operate on little or no funding.[26] Of the 20 of us involved in Heritage Week, most were somewhere between 20 and 50 years of age, a couple were older. Importantly, the conservators on the ground participating in this study are also residents of, or live nearby the local township areas, and/or identify racially, linguistically or ethnically with residents (explored further herein).

Throughout this text I use the terms 'black', 'white' and 'coloured' as used by participants to refer to themselves and to others, reflecting the persistent use of apartheid racial categories in South Africa and the persistence of race as a signifier of social differentiation.[27] Following Hammett, I understand these terms as contested, their use herein as problematic, and hope to not perpetuate an understanding of racial signifiers as "static, exclusionary social constructs".[28] Indeed, the opposite motivation is true. This chapter seeks to draw out the diversity, dynamism and nuances in how Heritage Week participants perform and assert aspects of their identities and ways of knowing Macassar Dunes.

Identity as a theoretical concept is perhaps necessarily ambiguous to reflect the complexities of the many ways and means by which humans identify. Defined as

---

25 See Ruiters 2009
26 Graham 2015c
27 Teppo 2009: p. 38. My own identity also came into play during the interviews and participant observations that constitute this chapter. Participants frequently referred to me either explicitly or implicitly as white, and also as an Australian, such that I was rendered insider/outsider in some subtle and some more acute ways. Still, participants always welcomed me to actively participate and share my thoughts and feelings, and I am indebted to them for sharing their perspectives with me in English, which is also by necessity engaged as lingua franca during Heritage Week.
28 Hammett 2008: p. 653

"a set of socially constructed traits around which members of a group organize a sense of belonging", feminist and postcolonial scholars have theorised extensively on how the identities we embrace are multiple and relational.[29] Theorists assert our identities are always in transition, never maintaining essentialised characteristics, and are formed through relations of power, contestation, and intersecting discourses.[30] Discussion of the processes of identity-formation and associated identity politics are particularly relevant in post-apartheid South Africa, given that in the colonial and apartheid eras racialised and related ethnicised identities were imposed on South Africans with varying degrees of violence, and for differential reasons[31]—but always to compel segregation, and resulting in the simplification of complex social relations.

In contemporary South Africa, citizens variously seek to rework and move beyond the confines and brutalities of identity signifiers imposed through apartheid and colonialism, and yet also to respect and celebrate diverse heritages and histories and identities of shared significance and experience.[32] This reworking involves complex, contested, and often uncomfortable negotiations in a society that still largely operates in terms of race.[33] As Ruiters writes:

> Apartheid legislation created correlations between race, space, language and class, and communities who struggle for meaning in the new South Africa continue to cling to these familiar configurations ... People's reconstructions of their ethnic and, by extension, racial identities in the post-apartheid period point to the process of creating their own self-understanding because of a shared history and space, and their own version of identity. This process, however, is affected by prior constructions of identities and the power relationships that undergird that structure, therefore the new constructions need to negotiate a space for themselves within a structure that still functions along the lines of race and ethnicity.[34]

Indeed, the historical configurations of racial and ethnic identities in South Africa cannot be ignored in discussions of post-apartheid cross-social relations and social reconciliation. The coloured apartheid statutory racial category, for example, was

---

29 Kobayashi 2009: p. 282; see Rose 1997 on feminist and postcolonial scholars.
30 Gibson-Graham 1996 on dynamic identities, and Rose 1993: pp. 5–6 on identities and power.
31 See Kobayashi 2009: p. 282 on identity politics within human geography.
32 Battersby 2005
33 Ahluwalia/Zegeye 2003; Battersby 2005; Ruiters 2009
34 Ruiters 2009: p. 110

preceded by a derogatory mixed race category, used by colonial authorities to instil notions of racial purity and to maintain separate races.[35] This term was used to describe what colonists saw as the alarmingly creolised progeny of the diverse populations who inhabited the Cape Colony—including European residents, indigenous KhoiKhoi whose lands were dispossessed and substantial slave populations brought from Asia and elsewhere in Africa.[36] Later, during apartheid, Cape Town's majority coloured population played an important role within the regime's divisive racialised social strategies—allowed some urban-based privileges above blacks, and thus used as a "social and political buffer between the black majority and white minority".[37] Erasmus has written of the difficult mixed feelings that post-apartheid reflections on coloured identities elicit, including feelings of shame around this historically denigrated racialised ethnicity.[38]

Recognised historically and contemporarily as darker-skinned and culturally-distinct to indigenous KhoiKhoi, those Bantu-speaking people who at colonisation farmed areas to the east and north of present-day Cape Town were later defined in apartheid parlance as blacks.[39] For blacks, the spatial delimitation of racialised and ethnicised identities was profoundly based on a rural/urban distinction.[40] That is, segregationists framed urban centres like Cape Town during apartheid as white space, with blacks both formally excluded and concomitantly essentialised as rural peoples.[41] This occurred despite blacks outnumbering whites in many urban areas.[42]

Devised in 1913 and legally established by 1950, bantustans were developed ostensibly as self-governed black ethnic homelands.[43] Designed to dispossess black people of their lands and resources by containing them within these remote, rural reserve areas, the bantustans equated to just 13 per cent of South Africa's land mass.[44] They served to delineate not only the spatial territories of the black inhabitants, but each bantustan was also associated with particularised ethnic identities and languages—which remain highly pervasive ethnicity signifiers today.[45] For example,

---

35 Ahluwalia/Zegeye 2003
36 See Adhikari 2011 on the history of Khoi dispossession.
37 Hammett 2010: p. 253
38 Erasmus 2001
39 Western 2002; Magubane 2003
40 See Popke/Ballard 2004 on spatialised identities.
41 See Parnell/Crankshaw 2013 on cities as white space, also Popke/Ballard 2004. See Maylam 1982 in Ballard 2005 on the exclusion of blacks from urban space, and Mbembe/Nuttall 2004 on the essentialisation of blacks as rural people in historical and contemporary discourse.
42 Lemon 1991 in Parnell/Crankshaw 2013
43 Bennett 2010
44 Bennett 2010
45 See Ballard 2005 on the association of bantustans with ethnic identities, and Battersby 2005 on the persistence of these identity signifiers.

Transkei and Ciskei bantustans, now incorporated into the Eastern Cape province, were associated with Xhosa ethnicity.[46]

In Cape Town today the demographic situation is rapidly changing, with implications for cross-social relations and racial politics.[47] Significant black rural-urban migration has occurred since the end of apartheid, resultant of poverty and historical disinvestment in the Eastern Cape.[48] Indeed, Parnell and Crankshaw remark how South African cities are today "quintessentially African spaces" in terms of population numbers—despite the continued social and economic inequalities between formerly white and black areas, as evidenced in Cape Town.[49] This demographic change has exacerbated racial tensions in Cape Town, where contemporary political divides have been characterised as persistently determined by race.[50] Worden notes that the need for black/coloured unity against apartheid has dissolved post-1994, and: "in particular the politics of the new dispensation resulted in awareness of a distinctly coloured identity and heritage".[51] Furthermore, an oft-cited sentiment is of coloured residents claiming under apartheid that they were "not 'white enough' to enjoy the benefits of citizenship, and now in the post-apartheid era they claim that they are not 'black enough' to access programmes that address social inequalities".[52] The Cape Flats in particular sees frequent protests and racial tensions flaring over perceptions of politically motivated racial preferencing in the national, provincial and municipal governments' provision

---

46 In the anonymously authored academic chapter 'Ethnicity and Pseudo-Ethnicity in the Ciskei' (in *The Creation of Tribalism in Southern Africa*, edited by Vail 1989), the author notes "it is impossible to say with any certainty why the Xhosa-speaking people have been divided between the two rival Bantustans of Ciskei and Transkei. The most common popular explanation is that this is an example of 'divide and rule' ..." (p. 398). The author, however, has a different interpretation, understanding the two bantustans were created because of the different political realities for the apartheid government represented by the Transkei and Ciskei territories. The Transkei consisted of an ethnically homogenous, large, rural, contiguous territory governed by "hard-line pro-government chiefs" (p. 396)—thus making it perfect for the creation of apartheid-era independent Bantustan, with self-government granted in 1963 and independence in 1976. The Ciskei, however, consisted of black reserves interspersed with white-owned farms and towns, and black leaders who "wanted nothing to do with the so-called Bantu Authorities" (p. 397)—and thus was much more problematic for the apartheid government (not gaining independence until 1982). (The chapter is anonymously authored because of the politically sensitive and potentially dangerous nature of writing about race and politics at the time of publication in 1989 under the apartheid government).
47 See Parry/van Eeden 2015 on rapidly changing demographics
48 Western 2002
49 Parnell/Crankshaw 2013: p. 591; see Sinclair-Smith/Turok 2012 on persistent inequalities.
50 Bickford-Smith 2009: p. 1775
51 Worden 2009: p. 27
52 Ruiters 2009: p. 104

of housing, education, economic development opportunities, and amenities and services like water, sanitation and electricity. In summary, the intense residue of colonial, apartheid and post-apartheid policies and relations manifests in Cape Town today in persistently racialised communities remaining highly suspicious of each other.[53]

Attending to the importance of post-apartheid identities within collaborative urban nature conservation and social reconciliation, I now focus on Heritage Week as a site of cross-social interaction through which participants actively rework and contest racial, ethnic and cultural identity stereotypes by performing diverse ways of knowing the urban nature of Macassar Dunes. As outlined, such performances raise important political questions around who speaks for urban nature and conservation in Cape Town, as well as raising important questions of the role and limitations of Heritage Week in social reconciliation and conservation justice on the Cape Flats.

Heritage Week in focus
The politics of sharing and knowing

Conservation advocates understand the challenges of contemporary nature conservation on the Cape Flats include local communities perceiving conservation as an elitist white endeavour, accompanied by the "widespread feeling that the privileged classes believe animals and plants are more important than people".[54] These sentiments are symptomatic of the systematic neglect of nature conservation on the Cape Flats during apartheid (with efforts directed rather towards the iconic nature near to white areas), and the racially exclusionary nature of conservation practice.[55] Another pervasive discourse within the conservation literature suggests Cape Flats' communities do not care for sites of nature, because they perceive them negatively and use them unwisely—for example, as sites for waste dumping, criminal activities, illegal harvesting of flora and fauna, drug-taking, rape and prostitution.[56]

The conservators at Macassar Dunes Conservation Area therefore use the collaborative conservation arrangements to promote biodiversity protection within local communities. They also use the arrangements to confront the difficult racialised relations between Macassar, Mitchell's Plain and Khayelitsha communities, which

---

53 Ahluwalia/Zegeye 2003; Besteman 2008
54 See Davis 2005 and Layne 2013 on perceptions of nature conservation as elitist, and Katzschner et al. 2005: p. 95 on the perception of plants being placed above the welfare of local communities.
55 Davis 2005; Layne 2013; Graham 2015a, 2015b
56 Graham 2015c; Graham/Ernston 2012; see e.g. Rebelo et al. 2011; Walters 2011

inhibit conservation efforts and cross social-interactions.[57] This senior conservator describes some of these tensions, whereby black people are still rendered as rural newcomers who don't actually have a say about the dunes:

> [Apartheid worked] not just spatially, but also in terms of the mindset ... And the whole success of it was that because the coloured people were perceived to be better than black people it was their obligation to oppress the black people, because otherwise they would lose the privilege. And you still see this distinction happening now, where you have an influx from the rural areas into urban areas and people are saying "Well you historically don't belong here. There were no black people in Cape Town historically, so you don't actually have a say." And you know, you still have that tension ... especially within your poorer coloured communities. You'll find it a lot in the Mitchell's Plain area, where they feel the tension between Khayelitsha.[58]

Heritage Week is therefore specially facilitated by the conservators as a process working towards integrating these communities, who face racialised, linguistic and social barriers alongside political tensions:

> One of our objectives of the reserve is to integrate these communities. It is a challenge because [Mitchell's Plain] is basically a coloured area in which people speak Afrikaans and English. Khayelitsha is Xhosa speaking people, and then Macassar is again Afrikaans ... But with our programs, what we do, especially like the Heritage [Week] camp, we integrate them together—and I see that they do integrate.[59]

Conservators view the sharing of personal and cultural relationships to nature through the intimate interactions of Heritage Week as part of this integration process. As such the camp involves many hours to talk, to wander together in the dunes and beach areas, and to share time in each other's presence talking about plants, animals and nature. They learn about conventional nature conservation practices and imperatives, and about each other's relationships to nature and conservation. Nonetheless, given the racial, political and spatial politics of this area, such processes of sharing with each other are also potentially fraught—liable to open a Pandora's box of difficult historical and political relations, and racial

---

57 Graham 2015b
58 Interviewee Q, senior nature conservator, 2013
59 Interviewee C, nature conservator 2012

tensions about who belongs in the area—who has been there the longest, and thus who can legitimately speak for the dunes.

In order to avoid these historical and contemporary tensions, the conservators therefore employ a strategy of essentially divorcing the material space of Macassar Dunes from any particular racial, ethnic or cultural identities or heritages at Heritage Week. As such, the cultural diversity within the nearby communities is acknowledged as coming from the environment, but this environment remains nameless—existing somewhere out there, not here, at the dunes:

> We are not saying that there is heritage here [at the dunes], we are saying that there are communities around these sites that have their own heritage and all of them have come from the environment, there is an environmental aspect of it. So let's use that and do something about it. So we've done that [with Heritage Week].[60]

This strategy renders the dunes as an ostensibly neutral political space, and enables the conservators to deflect concerns and potential tensions over who has a say about the dunes. Indeed, it enables the conservators to assert their own ways of knowing the dunes as a space of critical biodiversity, requiring and legitimising conventional conservation management practices as the appropriate management strategy to speak for the dunes. Certainly in Cape Town, nature conservators as regulators of conservation law and holders of science-based conservation knowledge are represented within nature conservation policy and academic literatures as legitimately determining the course of nature conservation practice in the city's urban nature reserves.[61] This is reflective of nature conservation practice in South Africa more broadly, which remains embedded in a Western scientific framework, with very little attention given to African approaches towards conservation.[62]

Put another way, the conservators at Heritage Week effectively acknowledge a diversity of cultural relationships to nature encompassed by the diversely identifying local communities. These relationships, however, are ultimately subsumed under the importance of uniting the local communities around the need to conserve the dunes as a space of critical biodiversity. This situation is reflective of Battersby's argument that the post-apartheid South African state embraces cultural and ethnic identities, but seeks to control or shape these identities as merely seasoning to the higher order of producing a cohesive national identity.[63] Yet importantly—and

---

60 Interviewee P, senior nature conservator, 2012, interview by Marnie Graham
61 Graham 2015a, 2015b
62 Cocks et al. 2012 on South African conservation remaining embedded in a Western framework; see Cocks/Wiersum 2014 on African approaches to conservation.
63 Battersby 2005

perhaps inevitably, as this chapter highlights—the sharing of diverse relationships to nature through Heritage Week also results in the performance and articulation of diverse ways of knowing Macassar Dunes—*including* by the conservators. These performances contest historically racialised and ethnicised identity stereotypes, and furthermore challenge this notion of the dunes as an apolitical space of nature—thus opening more contested questions of who might legitimately speak for the urban nature and conservation of the dunes.

To demonstrate, I return now to the light-hearted opening exchange between Declan, Dembeza, and Akhona at Heritage Week to explore how some participants expressed aspects of their Xhosa identities through their ways of knowing snakes. This exchange is indicative of the complex ways that racialised and ethnicised identities were reworked and challenged through Heritage Week, and indicates how the celebration is implicated in powerful and hopeful social reconciliation processes that contest conventional nature conservation processes and ideas.

Diversifying a Xhosa identity

Dembeza and Akhona expressed their cultural connection to the snake through sharing the important and specific human-animal relationship between the snake and the Majola clan. This documented relationship is based on tradition and spirituality, and connects Majola mothers, children and kinship networks to the snake.[64] Dembeza asserts through his narrative not only his Xhosa identity as distinguished from the homogeneous black racialised category that is associated with Khayelitsha's residents. In explaining Majola-snake relationships he also sensitises participants to the complexity of identities enrolled within the conception of Xhosa ethnicity. Indeed, patrilineal clan names (called *isiduko* in isiXhosa) like Majola are fundamental to Xhosa identity.

Breidlid notes how: "the holistic nature of the interrelationship between nature, human beings and the supernatural is foundational in the Xhosa knowledge system", and for Akhona the complex Majola-snake interrelationship is one that she is not willing to have explained away by Declan's rationalised, conservation science mode of knowing human-snake relationships.[65]

By drawing on Xhosa and Majola connections to the snake, she asserts the importance of Xhosa ways of knowing and spiritual relationships to the natural world, which have been silenced in conventional nature conservation practices through apartheid processes of dispossession. Cocks et al. suggest that, despite such histories of dispossession from ancestral lands and being pushed into bantustans and urbanised spaces, for urban Xhosa dwellers "a variety of manifestations of

---

64 Manxaile 1998: pp. 37–38
65 Breidlid 2009: p. 141

biocultural values are still prevalent", which provide "untapped opportunities for conservation".[66]

Still, Akhona discerns also the potential to co-construct *new* ways of knowing Macassar Dunes through learning about and from each other. Despite living in Khayelitsha for decades, she had not walked in the dunes prior to Heritage Week and did not consider them a space of nature requiring her attention or protection. Indeed, Akhona recognises her understandings of nature are embedded in her upbringing and relations to the Eastern Cape, and that the nature of Macassar Dunes also *challenges* her ways of knowing nature. She suggests, however, that this does not preclude her from learning to care about and identify with the nature of the dunes—even the snakes she grew up fearing. She later relates to me how she understands the point Declan was trying to make in asserting his way of knowing snakes as beings to be respected and conserved. This information enabled a transformation in how Akhona sees snakes in the everyday:

> The snakes, we used to kill them; but now the information I receive from [the nature conservators] is you can't—you must be calm. Because our parents used to say to us 'if the snake bite you, then you will die, instant!', you understand? But now with the information I receive [I] know you should be calm when we see the snake, they won't bite you. To me it was very important because I didn't know.[67]

At present largely excluded from educational policy, Breidlid also makes the case for endeavouring to constructively complement African cultures and knowledge systems with Western science-based environmental knowledges to achieve "a more sustainable future".[68] Asserting her identity as an urban resident, Akhona contests the historical and politicised essentialising of Xhosa as rural people, and furthermore the stereotype of black township residents as ignorant and uncaring degraders of Macassar Dunes, perpetuated through conservation literature in Cape Town.[69] For Akhona, the value of her knowledge for urban conservation thus lies not only in her "African culture and knowledge", but also in her experiential knowledges of Cape Town township life.[70] Akhona completed education only to primary level, and describes her experiential knowledge gained from everyday life as uneducated. Like Declan's narrative about caring for snakes, Akhona indicates Heritage Week enables the possibility for new relationships and ways of

---

66 Cocks et al. 2012 in Cocks/Wiersum 2014
67 Interviewee R, Khayelitsha resident, 2012, interview by Marnie Graham
68 Breidlid 2009: p. 147
69 Graham 2015a, 2015c; Graham/Ernstson 2012
70 Breidlid 2009: p. 147

knowing Macassar Dunes to be co-constructed, providing potential for "a more sustainable future"[71]:

> Akhona: I take the education from [the nature conservators] because they've got Masters degrees, [and] I don't have those things, you understand ... [But] if you take an 'uneducated' information, then you mix it with Masters [education] or whatever, then you will do something! ... If we mix that knowledge, we will make something new![72]

It is in these possibilities—of complex identity-making processes informing the co-construction of new ways of knowing and being—through which Heritage Week can become a space of social reconciliation in collaborative conservation practice. The following section discusses how Rastafari Heritage Week participants also contested racial and cultural identity stereotypes. And by performing their ways of knowing Macassar Dunes as a space of healing and spiritual connection, they assert their claim as legitimately speaking for the urban nature of Macassar Dunes.

Rastafari participants' relationships to Macassar Dunes

The Cape Flats' many urban plant harvesters such as traditional healers are negatively represented within nature conservation discourses as environmental degraders who damage the remnant sites of urban nature on the Cape Flats. Petersen et al. for example describe these harvesters as individuals who "appear to be justified by culture but motivated by cash income".[73] At Heritage Week in 2012, however, Rastafari participants self-identified as 'nature people', intimately and spiritually connected to nature and to the dunes specifically. The Afrocentric Rastafari movement encompasses "an ecological conscientiousness", which in Cape Town is syncretised with KhoiSan traditional healing practices based in "core values of dignity and self-sufficiency for people of color".[74] (See Gibson in this volume). In asserting their identity as nature people and sharing their ways of knowing Macassar Dunes as a space where they harvest medicinal and traditional-use plants, the Rastafari participants talked back to the negative representation of plant harvesters by explaining and demonstrating to Heritage Week participants:

---

71 Breidlid 2009: p. 147
72 Interviewee R, Khayelitsha resident, 2012, interview by Marnie Graham
73 Petersen et al. 2012: p. 7
74 Aston Philander 2012: p. 138. Drawing on Salter/Tafari (2005), Aston Philander (2012: 358) notes Rastafari in South Africa was introduced via reggae music in the 1970s, and is "a Jamaican-spawned global spiritual movement dedicated to returning to, retrieving, or reinventing African heritage and identity". Rastafari reject modernity as the product of colonial oppression.

> We don't go there [to the dunes] to destroy the plants. There are certain ways that we are harvesting plants, so that we can make sure that we are not hurting it, and it's gonna grow again. We are not destroying the nature ... We just come take a little bit, a piece of the creation and let the others grow; we don't come pick it out with the roots and everything.[75]

The Rastafaris also contested the portrayal of the dunes as apolitical space, disassociated from their heritage and spirituality, and the notion of conservation science as the only appropriate way of knowing and caring for Macassar Dunes. Learned from their own fathers, passed down through oral tradition, and infused with spiritual and cultural relationships that legitimate this knowledge, the Rastafaris judge their own knowledges and relations to the dunes as being inherent, and as deeper, more holistic and robust than the nature conservators' textual-based and abstracted conservation science knowledge, obtained through formal conservation education:

> Author: Being nature people—do you have the same understanding of nature as the people in the [nature conservation authority]?
>
> Interviewee Z: No. We don't think so. Because our knowledge is beyond the books that are written, that is written, you see. They are only educated in ... relation to the subjects they are taught. Whereas we've been taught in a much broader aspect, you know. So our knowledge is more deeper than what they know. 'Cause they concentrate only on a few stuff, where we concentrate on all, on the bigger picture ... and it's knowledge that's been passed on from generation to generation. Because we are people like that; we pass it on like that because you can destroy books and papers, you know, but you can't destroy the mind of a person ... They have a different way of seeing things according to the books that they learn and go to study, even go to colleges ... to study as conservation officers ... But we as Rastafarians we never went to training and colleges. It's just something that you've been raised up in—it's within you, that you live for and strive for.[76]

Whilst those identifying as Rastafari in Cape Town are a diverse group drawing on different heritages, they are united in cultural beliefs that reject practices of racial

---

75 Interviewee M, Mitchell's Plain resident, 2012, interview by Marnie Graham
76 Interviewee Z, Mitchell's Plain resident, 2012, interview by Marnie Graham

oppression embedded in mainstream practices and processes, such as formalised education, capitalism, Western medicine and religious systems.[77] As such, a dominant and powerful social discourse found across all racial groups presents those who identify as Rastafari in Cape Town as existing very much on the fringe of societal norms, with the pervasive stereotype as "ganja smoking, dreadlocked dropout[s]".[78] Through sharing with Heritage Week participants their knowledges of different plants found in the reserves and their spiritual uses, the Rastafari participants challenged these stereotypes of Rastafari culture. After three days of talking, laughing and sharing with the Rastas at Heritage Week, a young Xhosa woman reflected the feelings of many when she described what these interactions had sensitised her to:

> I have learned the Rastas are not just "Rastas". 'Cause [before] when I see Rastas I think just 'ah, they're just dagga smoking guys on the side of the road, selling the dagga'. But now I learn they know lots about the plants, about their relationship to the plants. Before I didn't know … and I'm really impressed.[79]

Indeed, the Rastafari participants actively engaged in Heritage Week specifically to change those stereotypes that "discount … Rastafari values and ethos".[80] Also, they wanted to be actively seen as Rastafari, to initiate a conversation on breaking free of racially-based identity codes that persistently lump Mitchell's Plain residents into the 'coloured' box. After their Heritage Week experiences, which were sometimes challenging but always respectful, these Rastafari participants note:

> Interviewee 1: We can see truly the people they have understanding now about Rastafar; because some of those people tell me: 'oh man, when I see a Rasta man I just think dagga, dagga, dagga—but now I see [there's] another side too'. Then … I feel great, … I'm achieving something. Because the people are seeing Rastafar in a different way than they have seen [us] before …
>
> Interviewee 2: Ja, they see us in a non-racial and a non-partial way.[81]

---

77 Aston Philander 2012; Olivier 2010
78 Ganja is marijuana, also known in South Africa as dagga; see Aston Philander 2012: p. 139 on this stereotype, and also Tolsi 2011.
79 Interviewee L, Khayelitsha resident, 2012, interview by Marnie Graham
80 Aston Philander 2012
81 Interviewees 1, 2, Mitchell's Plain residents, 2012, interview by Marnie Graham

Heritage Week facilitated a space for the Rastafari participants to perform their ways of knowing nature, and to assert identities that exist as part of, contradictory to, and in defiance of apartheid racial categories and racialised identities.[82] Next I discuss how conservators too were deeply affected by the ways that the Rastafari and Xhosa participants openly shared their knowledge and elaborated their ways of knowing Macassar Dunes at Heritage Week.

Exploring conservators' identities

During apartheid, traditional healing practices and medicines were perceived as a threat to colonial politics, and thus were denigrated and suppressed under Witchcraft Suppression Acts of 1957 and 1970.[83] (See Gibson in this volume). Whilst the conservator below is schooled in conventional conservation knowledge based on conservation science, learning about Rastafari and Xhosa relations to nature reconfigured his understanding of what constitutes legitimate ways of knowing Macassar Dunes:

> Some of these plants is part of their cultures, where they believe that this plant has maybe got a healing power for certain sickness and they use it maybe as part of their initiation ... And that is quite interesting [because] we know plants and animals with the scientific names ... [but the] Rastafarians, they brought plants through in a different way. They brought in the spirits of the plants and to them plants have a different dimension ... Like you cannot put, like, certain plants together in a bag ..., because the spirits of the plants will not agree, and it will maybe have an effect on you. Now all these different types of knowledge that [community participants] bring—like the Rastafarians, they completely live off the plants and they can educate other members of the community. Like me! I haven't used tablets this year. I've used the [medicinal] plants and I've tried it and it worked.[84]

The conservator's narrative importantly also brings forth the multiplicity of his own identity—as both a municipal nature conservator and as a member of the community, with whom he engages and interacts. This narrative unsettles the pervasive conception of conservation as a monolithic activity peopled by a homogeneous group of conservation professionals who share a core set of values and goals, "regardless of the social and economic contexts in which they are embedded

---

82 Besteman 2008
83 Devenish 2005; Flint 2008 in Aston Philander 2012
84 Interviewee C, nature conservator, 2012, interview by Marnie Graham

and the experiences that have shaped their conservation interests".[85] Indeed, many of the Cape Flats conservators are also members of the local township communities, thus making the interactions on the ground between conservators and local communities in Cape Town incredibly complex and often ethically challenging.[86]

These challenges are described by this conservator who is presented with the ethical challenge between upholding his authority to prosecute conservation offences like illegal plant harvesting, with his sensitisation to the need to negotiate law, culture and spirituality in his interactions with local community members:

> For me it is a little conflict of interest because I work with these communities and they are the communities that break the law as well ... If I get a Rastafarian and he's got a bag of plants with him, I cannot just arrest him ... because he is going to tell me that it is part of his religion, that all plants are free and it doesn't belong to us—it belongs to God. And that is his religious belief so I cannot basically arrest him. But what I can do is I can educate him and tell him: "Listen here, but I understand that this is your religion but you have also broken the law." So I can explain to him that part of it. Then he can maybe understand ... But I am not interested in arresting people in that business unless it is maybe somebody that makes a habit of it ... that we have maybe caught 3, 4 or 5 times.[87]

And this conservator:

> When I meet people in the Reserve sometimes they are aggressive and asking me why I am doing this. For example, the Rastas say: "nature belongs to nobody, you can't tell me what I can and cannot do". But I [also] think nature belongs to everybody—it is written in the Bible, God says that we have dominion over the Earth, the plants and animals—so we have the same understanding as Rastas. But Rastas also believe that nobody should be able to tell them what to do, because they do not like the system of rules and regulations that tell people what they must do. I tell them "I understand where you are coming from, but this is my job—I do not make the rules and regulations, but you must abide by them, because it is the law, and it is my job to enforce the law."[88]

---

85 Sandbrook et al. 2010: p. 292
86 Graham 2015b
87 Interviewee C, nature conservator, 2012, interview by Marnie Graham
88 Interviewee H, nature conservator, 2013, interview by Marnie Graham

These analyses indicate how different aspects of conservators' identities co-exist, and the ethical challenges that result. Another important component of recognising the diversity of conservators' identities is in further disrupting notions of who speaks for urban nature, the articulation of which is enabled through the openness of Heritage Week. This conservator, for example, disrupts the false distinctions made between universalised, science-based Western knowledge and localised indigenous knowledge that are perpetuated through development discourses.[89] Although schooled in conventional conservation science, he rather charts his conservation knowledge and relations to nature as stemming from a Xhosa conservation ethic. Indeed, his Xhosa identity, culture and knowledge are embedded in his background and experiences growing up in the Eastern Cape, and he chose to share these at Heritage Week. These experiences actually motivate him to conserve nature, and to communicate in relatable ways to township residents who share his background and language:

> Even in the Eastern Cape we were doing conservation indirectly. We did not know while we were still young that we were 'doing conservation'. Even our forefathers and grannies they were doing 'sustainable harvesting', only they were using [Xhosa language] terms ... Our parents would always encourage that you just pick the leaf and don't uproot the entire vegetation, because we still want to live with that [plant]. So it is conservation that we were doing [then], and we are still doing it. But when you use those [English conservation] terms, some of the people [in Khayelitsha] will ask: "What do you mean?", and then [I can] explain to them.
>
> So maybe if I never grew up in the Eastern Cape, it would have been difficult for me to explain to them ... It is easy for me to translate some of the materials that are in English into Xhosa, just because of the background that I've been exposed to while I was still young. It's my background, it's part of my identity. Yeah, part of the work that I am doing is being, like, motivated by my background.[90]

Beyond Heritage Week

I now explore what these sharing activities might mean beyond the confines of Heritage Week. Heritage Week is revealed as working to reconfigure how participants relate to each other and to nature. And as opening challenging questions of whom and what kinds of ways of knowing might legitimately speak

---

89 Agrawal 1995
90 Interviewee Y, nature conservator, 2012, interview by Marnie Graham

for the urban nature of Macassar Dunes. The symbolic and political significance of this event is further evidenced in that participants expressed desires to make the celebration bigger and better, and to embrace other ways of sharing and knowing that might increase understanding and bridge historical divides—for example, through sharing food and language.[91] Indeed, whilst English as the lingua franca serves to open linguistic space for communication and sharing at Heritage Week, the varied English skill-levels of participants makes sharing more difficult for some than others, and limits the kinds of relationships to nature and to Macassar Dunes that people might articulate. Certainly a greater focus on the sharing of relationships to nature through language is an important arena through which the social reconciliation possibilities of Heritage Week might be strengthened in future.

These outcomes suggest Heritage Week is implicated in processes of social reconciliation in Cape Town—certainly in terms of the ways that participants learn about and from each other by transgressing some of the long-formed boundaries that have historically separated self from other on the Cape Flats and in South Africa more generally. Yet Heritage Week is only one week a year and is the primary space for the open and active sharing of diverse relationships to nature. Thus, in considering social reconciliation processes, the real significance of Heritage Week lies in the ways these sharing interactions are implicated in everyday conservation and collaborative practices. Negotiating if and how those diverse ways of knowing Macassar Dunes that emerge during Heritage Week can be recognised, negotiated and incorporated within everyday conservation practices is an important component of social reconciliation. Such negotiations recognise the value and importance of diverse ways of knowing urban nature and conservation, thus making collaborative nature conservation a site of dialogue and of co-production of new understandings across historical divides.[92]

Understanding social reconciliation from this perspective, a fundamental concern lies at the heart of Heritage Week. In sharing, acknowledging and even respecting diverse ways of knowing nature, conflicting priorities are introduced to the conventional biodiversity conservation mandate. For the conservation authority in Cape Town, a problematic question arises: is it implied to communities that those diverse ways of knowing and caring for nature will be actively incorporated into management practices? One senior nature conservator explains this conundrum in relation to Heritage Week:

> It is an area that we haven't actually fully explored and I think that there is reluctance from the conservation sector to ... engage in that,

---

91 See also Graham/Ernstson 2012
92 Graham/Ernstson 2012

> because of their perceptions that people are looking and eyeing the conservation areas for opportunities—whether it is for initiation sites, or bush meat, and the guys like your Rastas harvesting ... And especially in the context of Cape Town where you've got this finite resource in terms of your natural areas, there is [the question] when people are looking at Heritage [Week]: is it just around 'sharing' or is it around actively practising? ... So can you accommodate those [other] practices within the conservation area? And are we prepared to compromise? And are the user groups also prepared to compromise?[93]

Indeed, this concern sets the limitations of Heritage Week as it now stands as a space of social reconciliation in conservation practice. Currently there is no process for negotiating compromises or trade-offs around conventional conservation practices and ideas, and the different ways of knowing and caring for Macassar Dunes elicited through Heritage Week. At present many participants have learned about the importance of nature conservation from the perspectives of both conventional biodiversity conservation and other ways of knowing, yet they are not united by what conservation means, how it should be practised, nor who legitimately has a say in the management of Macassar Dunes.

In this respect, Heritage Week is therefore also fundamentally limited from a conservation justice perspective. That is, whilst Heritage Week creates dialogue and understanding across persistent social and racial barriers, there is at present no mechanism for negotiating how the dunes should be used and who should benefit from their use. The powerful representation within the academic and policy literature of the dunes as a space purely for biodiversity protection, rather than as a space for community or economic development remains entrenched and normalised through the Heritage Week interactions. In the context of the huge poverty, social inequalities and under- and unemployment of residents of the Cape Flats, this is a complex yet profoundly important arena that remains unaddressed through the current manifestation of Heritage Week.

It is furthermore also important to acknowledge that those productive relations and social reconciliation processes that do emerge through Heritage Week are also vulnerable. The celebrations at present are reliant on the openness and resource capacities of nature conservators to externally fund and facilitate the interaction, involving commitments to work over long-weekend holidays and above and beyond their nature conservation mandate. For community participants too, their

---

93 Interviewee Q, senior nature conservator, 2013, interview by Marnie Graham. 'Bush meat' is a term commonly used in South Africa and more widely throughout parts of Africa to refer to wildlife caught by local people for eating purposes.

participation involves a commitment to sharing and learning beyond historical boundaries, and the inherent risks involved in doing so in this potentially fraught context.

Conclusion

Conservators on the ground engage collaborative conservation participants in Heritage Week activities to share diverse personal and cultural relationships to nature, in order to integrate the historically divided communities of Macassar, Khayelitsha and Mitchell's Plain, and unite them around the common goal of conserving the dunes. I argue conservators present Macassar Dunes and conservation practice as apolitical at Heritage Week, in order to avoid the tensioned racialised relations evidenced amongst these communities, and the political tensions around who has a say about the dunes area. This analysis indicates how historically racialised, ethnicised and cultural stereotypes are perpetuated not only through colonial, apartheid and post-apartheid social and political processes, but also through nature conservation discourses, practices and ideas. Nonetheless, this chapter demonstrates how through the Heritage Week interactions, the participants—including the nature conservators—perform diverse ways of knowing the Macassar Dunes, and assert a range of post-apartheid identities that contest, rework and reconfigure such historically imposed racialised and ethnicised identity stereotypes.

In doing so, Heritage Week is clearly not a panacea for addressing post-apartheid social reconciliation, and the deeply entrenched divisions and political tensions between the communities of Macassar, Khayelitsha and Mitchell's Plain. Where urban nature conservation intersects with poverty, informality and structural and everyday violence, such contestation is perhaps inevitable.[94] Heritage Week is also not a panacea for exploring the complex questions of conservation justice that pervade the Macassar Dunes area. Yet whilst there are fundamental limitations in the premise of Heritage Week in social reconciliation processes and in transforming conventional conservation practices and theories, I argue these interactions are nonetheless important in terms of social reconciliation and in co-constructing new relations to nature and to each other.

Indeed, Heritage Week enables participants to enter an uncensored yet respectful space to share their lives, histories and cultures with each other, and facilitates their engagement in deeply intimate interactions. These interactions indicate participants are taking an important and significant step towards co-constructing new understandings of the dunes, of these Cape Flats townships, and of Cape Flats residents as open to reconciliation and learning about each other. What emerges through these interactions are the complex identities of community participants

---

94   Graham/Ernstson 2012

and of nature conservation staff, and the challenges and politics of asserting these identities. The focus on participants' post-apartheid identities in this chapter most importantly indicates important disruptions to notions of stakeholder groups as singular, cohesive entities, including local communities and nature conservators.

In light of these limitations and possibilities of Heritage Week, steps need to be enabled to move beyond only sharing and into processes that enable negotiating and co-constructing new ideas around what conservation means; who has a say in conservation management and decision-making; and in what kinds of conservation imperatives justice might be negotiated through collaborative nature conservation. Without such steps, conservation management in Cape Town more broadly will remain focused on top-down management processes. Furthermore, continuation of the significant social reconciliation successes of Heritage Week are rendered vulnerable in the future. And that would be a shame in so many ways.

References

Adhikari, M. (2011), *The Anatomy of a South African Genocide: The Extermination of the Cape San Peoples*. Ohio: Ohio University Press.

Agrawal, A. (1995), Dismantling the Divide Between Indigenous and Scientific Knowledge. *Development and Change*, 26: 413–439.

Ahluwalia, P. and A. Zegeye (2003), Between Black and White: Rethinking Coloured Identity. *African Identities*, 1(2): 253–280.

Anonymous (1989), Ethnicity and Pseudo-Ethnicity in the Ciskei. In L. Vail (ed.), *The Creation of Tribalism in Southern Africa*. Berkeley/Los Angeles/Oxford: University of California Press.

Aston Philander, L.E. (2012), Hunting Knowledge and Gathering Herbs: Rastafari Bush Doctors in the Western Cape, South Africa. *Journal of Ethnobiology*, 32(2): 134–156.

Ballard, R. (2005), When in Rome: Claiming the Right to Define Neighbourhood Character in South Africa's Suburbs. *Transformation: Critical Perspectives on Southern Africa*, 57(1): 64–87.

Battersby, J. (2005), Re-inscribing Race and Ethnicity in Post-apartheid South Africa. In P. Gervais-Lambony, F. Landy and S. Oldfield (eds), *Reconfiguring Identities and Building Territories in India and South Africa*. Delhi: Manohar Publishers: 85–97.

Bennett, B.M. (2010), Reading the Land: Changing Landscapes and the Environmental History of South Africa. In M. Godby, C. Walker, S. Klopper and B.M. Bennett (eds), *The Lie of the Land: Representations of the South African Landscape*. Cape Town: Pinewood Studios: 46–59.

Besteman, C. (2008), *Transforming Cape Town*. Berkeley: University of California Press.

Bickford-Smith, V. (2009), Creating a City of the Tourist Imagination: The Case of Cape Town, 'The Fairest Cape of Them All'. *Urban Studies*, 46(9): 1763–1785.

Bickford-Smith, V., E. Van Heyningen and N. Worden (1999), *Cape Town in the Twentieth Century: An Illustrated Social History*. Cape Town: New Africa Books.

Breidlid, A. (2009). Culture, Indigenous Knowledge Systems and Sustainable Development: A Critical View of Education in an African Context. *International Journal of Educational Development*, 29(2): 140–148.

Cocks, M.L., T. Dold and S. Vetter (2012), "God is My Forest": Xhosa Cultural Values Provide Untapped Opportunities for Conservation. *South African Journal of Science*, 108(5/6): 1–8.

Cocks, M.L. and F. Wiersum (2014), Reappraising the Concept of Biocultural Diversity: A Perspective from South Africa. *Human Ecology*, 42(5): 727–737.

Davis, G. (2005), Biodiversity Conservation as a Social Bridge in the Urban Context: Cape Town's Sense of the "Urban Imperative" to Protect its Biodiversity and Empower its People. In T. Trzyna (ed.), *The Urban Imperative*. Sacramento: California Institute of Public Affairs: 96–104.

Devenish, A. (2005), Negotiation Healing: Understanding the Dynamics amongst Traditional Healers in Kwazulu-Natal as They Engage with Professionalisation. *Social Dynamics*, 31(2): 243–284.

Dixon, J.A., C.G. Tredoux, K. Durrheim, G. Finchilescu and B. Clack (2008), "The Inner Citadels of the Color Line": Mapping the Micro-ecology of Racial Segregation in Everyday Life Spaces. *Social and Personality Psychology Compass*, 2(4): 1547–1569.

Erasmus, Z. (2001). Introduction: Re-imagining Coloured Identities in Post-apartheid South Africa. In Z. Erasmus (ed.), *Coloured by History, Shaped by Place: New Perspectives on Coloured Identities in Cape Town*. Cape Town: Kwela Books and SAHO.

Ferketic, J.S., A.M. Latimer and J.A. Silander (2010), Conservation Justice in Metropolitan Cape Town: A Study at the Macassar Dunes Conservation Area. *Biological Conservation*, 143(5): 1168–1174.

Flint, K.E. (2008), *Healing Traditions: African Medicine, Cultural Exchange and Competition in South Africa 1820–1948*. Athens: Ohio University Press.

Gibson-Graham, J-K. (1996), *The End of Capitalism (As We Knew It): A Feminist Critique of Political Economy*. Oxford: Blackwell.

Graham, M. (2015a), Postcolonial Nature Conservation and Collaboration in Urban Protected Areas: Everyday Relations at Macassar Dunes/Wolfgat Reserves, Cape Town, South Africa, (PhD Thesis, Macquarie University).

Graham, M. (2015b), Postcolonial Nature Conservation in Practice: The Everyday Challenges of On-ground Urban Nature Conservation, Cape Town, South Africa. *Geojournal*, August: 1–20.

Graham, M. (2015c), Everyday Human (In)securities in Protected Urban Nature – Collaborative Conservation at Macassar/Wolfgat Dunes Nature Reserves, Cape Town, South Africa. *Geoforum*, 64: 25–36

Graham, M. and H. Ernstson (2012), Co-management at the Fringes: Examining Stakeholder Perspectives at Macassar Dunes, Cape Town, to Understand Contestations and Common Ground at the Intersection of Remnant Biodiversity, Informality, and Urban Poverty. *Ecology and Society*, 17(3): 1–34.

Hammett, D. (2008), The Challenge of a Perception of "Un-entitlement" to Citizenship in Post-apartheid South Africa. *Political Geography*, 27(6): 652–668.

Hammett, D. (2010), Ongoing Contestations: The Use of Racial Signifiers in Post-apartheid South Africa. *Social Identities: Journal for the Study of Race, Nation and Culture*, 16(2): 247–260.

Katzschner, T. (2014), State of Bordering in Urban Nature. In M. Ramutsindela (ed.), *Cartographies of Nature: How Nature Conservation Animates Borders*. Newcastle: Cambridge Scholars Publishing: 141–168.

Katzschner, T., G. Oelofse, K. Wiseman and J. Jackson (2005), The City of Cape Town's Biodiversity Strategy. In T. Trzyna (ed.), *The Urban Imperative*. Sacramento: California Institute of Public Affairs: 91–95.

Kobayashi, A. (2009), Identity Politics. In R. Kitchen and N. Thrift (eds.), *International Encyclopedia of Human Geography*. Oxford: Elsevier: 282–286.

Layne, T. (2013), Ordinary Magic: The Alchemy of Biodiversity and Development in Cape Flats Nature. *Solutions*, 4(3): 84–92.

Lemon, A. (ed.) (1991), *Homes Apart: South Africa's Segregated Cities*. London: Paul-Chapman.

Magubane, Z. (2003), Simians, Savages, Skulls, and Sex: Science and Colonial Militarism in Nineteenth-Century South Africa. In D.S. Moore, J. Kosek and A. Pandian (eds.) (2003), *Race, Nature, and the Politics of Difference*. Durham: Duke University Press: 99–121.

Manxaile, A. (1998), *Xhosa Peri-urban Women's Views on Abortion as a Human Right: Implications for a Pro-impilo Theological Discourse on the Choice of Termination of Pregnancy Act No. 92 of 1996, South Africa*, (PhD Thesis, University of Natal Pietermaritzburg).

Maylam, P. (1982), Shackled by the Contradictions: The Municipal Response to African Urbanization in Durban, 1920–1950. *African Urban Studies*, 14: 1–18.

Mbembe, A. and S. Nuttall (2004), Writing the World from the African Metropolis. *Public Culture*, 16(3): 347–72.

Olivier, L. (2010), Racial Oppression and the Political Language of Rastafari in Stellenbosch. *South African Review of Sociology*, 41(2): 23–31.

Olwage, E. (2013), *"Growing Together": Exploring the Politics of Knowing and Conserving (Bio)diversity in a Small Conservancy in Cape Town*, (MA Thesis, Univ. of Cape Town).

Parnell, S. and O. Crankshaw (2013), The Politics of 'Race' and the Transformation of the Post-apartheid Space Economy. *Journal of Housing and the Built Environment*, 28(4): 589–603.

Parry, K. and A. van Eeden (2015), Measuring Racial Residential Segregation at Different Geographic Scales in Cape Town and Johannesburg. *South African Geographical Journal*, 97(1): 31–49

Petersen, L.M., E.J. Moll, R. Collins and M.T. Hockings (2012), Development of a Compendium of Local, Wild-harvested Species Used in the Informal Economy Trade, Cape Town, South Africa. *Ecology and Society*, 17(2): 1–26.

Popke, E.J. and R. Ballard (2004), Dislocating Modernity: Identity, Space and Representations of Street Trade in Durban, South Africa. *Geoforum*, 35: 99–110.

Rebelo, A.G., P.M. Holmes, C. Dorse and J. Wood (2011), Impacts of Urbanization in a Biodiversity Hotspot: Conservation Challenges in Metropolitan Cape Town. *South African Journal of Botany*, 77(1): 20–35.

Rose, G. (1993), *Feminism and Geography: The Limits of Geographical Knowledge*. Minneapolis: University of Minnesota Press.

Rose, G. (1997), Situating Knowledges: Positionality, Reflexivities and Other Tactics. *Progress in Human Geography*, 21(3): 305–320.

Ruiters, M. (2009), Collaboration, Assimilation and Contestation: Emerging Constructions of Coloured Identity in Post-apartheid South Africa. In M. Adhikari (ed.), *Burdened by Race: Coloured Identities in Southern Africa*. Cape Town: UCT Press: 104–133.

Salter, R.C. and I. Tafari (2005), Rastafarianism. In L. Jones (ed.), *Encyclopedia of Religion*. Farmington Hills: Macmillan Reference 11: 7622–7629.

Sandbrook, C., I.R. Scales, B. Vira and W.M. Adams (2010), Value Plurality among Conservation Professionals. *Conservation Biology*, 25(2): 285–294.

Seekings, J. (2011), Race, Class, and Inequality in the South African City. In G. Bridge and S. Watson (eds.), *The New Blackwell Companion to the City*. Malden, MA: Wiley-Blackwell: 532–546.

Sinclair-Smith, K. and I. Turok (2012), The Changing Spatial Economy of Cities: An Exploratory Analysis of Cape Town. *Development Southern Africa*, 29(3): 391–417.

Stipinovich, A. and P. Holmes (2009), *City of Cape Town's Biodiversity Network C-Plan & Marxan Analysis 2009: Methods & Results*. Cape Town: City of Cape Town.

Sundberg, J. (2004). Identities in the Making: Conservation, Gender and Race in the Maya Biosphere Reserve, Guatemala. *Gender, Place and Culture*, 11(1): 43–66.

Teppo, A.B. (2009), "My House Is Protected by a Dragon": White South Africans, Magic and Sacred Spaces in Post-apartheid Cape Town. *Suomen Antropologi: Journal of the Finnish Anthropological Society*, 34(1): 19–41.

Tolsi, N. (2011), The Rise and Rise of the Rastafari, *Mail and Guardian*, 14 October. http://mg.co.za/article/2011-10-14-the-rise-and-of-rastafari. Accessed 13 September 2013.

Wale, K. (2014), *Reflecting on Reconciliation: Lessons from the Past, Prospects for the Future*. Cape Town: The Institute for Justice and Reconciliation (IJR). http://reconciliationbarometer.org/wp-content/uploads/2014/12/IJR-SA-Reconciliation-Barometer-Report-2014.pdf. Accessed 12 December 2014.

Walters, L. (2011), *Draft Management Plan for Wolfgat Nature Reserve*. Cape Town: City of Cape Town.

Western, J.C. ([1981] 1996), *Outcast Cape Town*. Berkeley/Los Angeles: University of California Press.

Western, J. (2002), A Divided City: Cape Town. *Political Geography*, 21(5): 711–716.

Worden, N. (2009), The Changing Politics of Slave Heritage in the Western Cape, South Africa. *The Journal of African History*, 50(01): 23–40.

CHAPTER 13

Fragile ground, contested soil: dynamics of tenure and policy in the Bamenda wetlands

Sandro Simon

Introduction

Wetlands, occurring in various settings around the globe, represent on the one hand important ecological resources and, on the other hand, offer an array of functions to a multitude of actors. Those actors, however, can compete over management and use. They are for instance informed by conservation discourses or economic interests and determined by legal changes or bargaining power—which are again embedded in historical developments of land tenure and policy and must hence be assessed in relation to them. As I will show in this chapter, conservation initiatives, reaching back to the colonial-era perception of local users as threats to pure nature, and processes of privatisation, nationalisation and industrialisation in post-colonial times have weakened existing governing structures around wetland use and also altered ecological conditions. In the worst cases, this has led to transformation, exclusion or overuse with negative impacts on local livelihoods.

The chapter begins by looking at the different forms of wetlands, their services and their value as well as the threats they face according to wetland science, UNESCO and the International Union for Conservation of Nature (IUCN). An assessment of the developments from commons and customary tenure to nationalisation and privatisation then follows. Finally, a case study explores the changing and overlapping tenure and management regimes of competing authorities in the urban wetlands of Bamenda, Cameroon, and how the affected farmers deal with these situations of legal and normative pluralism.

Defining and valuing wetlands for policy design
The Convention on Wetlands (better known as the Ramsar Convention), a UNESCO-based intergovernmental treaty on wetlands adopted in Ramsar, Iran,

in 1971, provides a broad but widely-used definition of wetlands.[1] In Article 1.1, wetlands are characterised as

> areas of marsh, fen, peatland or water, whether natural or artificial, permanent or temporary, with water that is static or flowing, fresh, brackish or salt, including areas of marine water the depth of which at low tide does not exceed six meters,

and in Article 2.1 it is pointed out that wetlands may also incorporate

> riparian and coastal zones adjacent to the wetlands, and islands or bodies of marine water deeper than six meters at low tide lying within the wetlands.[2]

Wetland science has ordered wetlands into natural and artificial or constructed wetlands, although many natural wetlands are used by diverse people for activities such as agriculture, fishing, hunting or herding and are therefore natural-anthropogenic ecosystems shaped through recursive co-evolution.[3] Because local resource users who co-shape a resource need to negotiate and coordinate their use, the institutional context cannot be separated from the ecosystem context.[4] Nevertheless, distinctions between the hydrological, biological and geological set-up, and the origin of a wetland can help to assess its diverse functions. For natural wetlands, Shine and De Klemm differentiate between marine and coastal wetlands and wetlands-in-dryland.[5] The case study focuses on a wetland-in-dryland that is strongly interlinked with precipitation. It can be characterised as a riverine wetland with a natural origin and a long history of human influence.

---

1 While the definition can be universally applied to any given wetland, the Ramsar Convention seeks to define and protect specific areas of special global relevance under the concept of 'wise use' i.e. the sustainable utilisation of wetlands so that they yield the greatest continuous benefit for present generations and maintain at the same time their potential for future generations (Smardon 2009: 9). Wise use is however widely left to the national governments; it is highly contested and difficult to achieve in various contexts (Richardson 1993; Ramsar Convention on Wetlands 1996a, 2002, 2008, and 2015; Earle/Bazilli 2013). Up to today, 169 countries have signed the convention and 2227 sites of international importance in terms of the significance of their ecology, botany, zoology, limnology or hydrology have been designated with a total area of 214,875,598 hectares (Ramsar Convention on Wetlands 2016).
2 Wetlands are hence neither clearly terrestrial nor clearly aquatic, making a determination where they begin and where they end sometimes problematic (see Hammer/Bastian 1989).
3 Farrell 2007
4 Haller et al. 2013: p. 3
5 Shine/De Klemm 1999: pp. 5, 6

In the case of artificially-created wetlands, they are usually created and designed for specific purposes like agriculture or energy production and do not have the full range of wetland functions and values of their natural counterparts.[6] Moreover, their establishment might even involve the destruction or degradation of natural wetlands, for instance, when mangroves are transformed into aquaculture ponds.[7] While there is consensus that constructed wetlands cannot replace natural ecosystems (or do in fact even damage existing ones), their creation (besides restoration) has become increasingly popular in industrialised countries where natural wetlands have undergone degradation for decades, and where constructed wetlands—sometimes with the idea of relieving natural wetlands—promise to be effective for wastewater treatment.[8]

Since the 1960s, under the auspices of the IUCN, the International Wildfowl Research Bureau (IWRB), and UNESCO scientists (e.g. environmental economists), the assessment and inventory of wetland services determine direct-use, indirect-use and non-use values in managing and conserving the wetlands.[9] Direct-use values involve recreation, transport and research, and also extractive and consumptive use of wetland products; indirect use values could be flood and storm control, groundwater recharge, carbon storage or retention of nutrients.[10] Especially in semi-arid areas, wetlands constitute important engines of natural resource reproduction and resilience in adjacent ecosystems.[11] This makes them ecosystems of major importance for protection and conservation. Their high productivity and the recycling of nutrients can contribute to the livelihoods of local communities and allow them to practise subsistence as well as commercial activities of various kinds—as, for example, on African floodplains.[12] Goods deriving from the wetlands range from fish and timber, wildlife and wild plants to agriculture, water supply for extra-wetland purposes such as irrigation or drinking water, housing materials and peat.[13]

Non-use values (also called existence, passive or intrinsic values) relate to contemporary or prospective values and are subjective as they reflect the individual or collective willingness to invest in the continued existence and/or the safeguarding of options for future generations.[14] Hence, biodiversity, recreation, diversity in the

---

6 Shine/De Klemm 1999: p. 6
7 Shine/De Klemm 1999: p. 6
8 Shine/De Klemm 1999: p. 7; see Hammer/Bastian 1989
9 Constanza et al. 1997: p. 253; Matthews 1993: pp. 5, 9; Shine/De Klemm 1999: pp. 10, 11; Ramsar Convention on Wetlands, Fact Sheet 2015b; Heimlich et al. 1998: p. 13
10 Shine/De Klemm 1999: p. 10; Boyer/Polasky 2004: p. 747; Ramsar Convention on Wetlands, Fact Sheet 2015a
11 Haller 2010a: pp. 7, 8
12 Haller 2010a: pp. 7, 8; Shine/De Klemm 1999: p. 7
13 Shine/De Klemm 1999: pp. 7, 8
14 Shine/De Klemm 1999: p. 10

landscape, hereditary perpetuation, etc.—all provided by wetlands—are differently valued by the social actors without attaching a price tag on them.[15] Greater scientific research helps to increase the appreciation, especially of non-use values, and to make public policy increasingly directed at protecting wetlands instead of draining them.[16] Nevertheless, wetland loss remains a top concern of the Ramsar Convention as, on a global scale, 64 per cent of wetlands has disappeared in the last 115 years.[17] The threats to wetlands can thereby be categorised into loss of wetland area, changes to the water regime, changes in water quality, overexploitation of wetland products and introduction of alien species.[18] Causes can be changes in land use (especially an increase in agriculture and grazing animals), water diversion through dams, dikes and canalisation, infrastructure development (particularly in coastal areas and river valleys, as we will also see in the case study), air and water pollution, excess nutrients and change in rainfall patterns through climate change.[19]

From wetland commons and customary tenure to wetland nationalisation and privatisation

Tenure regimes of common (wet-)land use that had been established long before colonialism and continued in post-colonial times, favoured the intrinsic nature of the habitat. This posed difficulty in defining the boundaries and allocating resources.[20] However, they were often conflated with pre-property or non-property forms of managing land.[21] Or they were assumed to be open access instead of shared private property.[22] In an act of disqualifying local users' creative interrelatedness with their environment, colonial powers understood this form of resource use within what they perceived as the natural landscape as a threat to 'pure nature' and its governmental ownership.[23] In post-colonial times, the idea of the *tragedy of the commons* suggested that a lack of formal property rights led to unsustainable use and degradation and the World Bank proclaimed the necessity to press ahead with the establishment of private property.[24] As the result, many post-colonial

---

15 Carlsson et al. 2003; Boyer/Polasky 2004
16 Boyer/Polasky 2004; Heimlich et al. 1998
17 Ramsar Convention on Wetlands, Fact Sheet 2015a
18 IWRB 1993, cited after Shine/de Klemm 1999: p. 15
19 Ramsar Convention on Wetlands, Fact Sheet 2015b; Haller 2010a: p. 14
20 Adger/Luttrell 2000: pp. 79, 80, citing McCay 1978; Feeny et al. 1990; Vondal 1990; McGrath et al. 1993
21 See Peters 1996
22 Haller 2010a
23 Haller et al. 2013: pp. 2, 4. The authors call this the 'colonial gaze' which is usually taken as a starting point to refer to sustainability. Hence, on most African floodplains nowadays, protected areas exist, many of which reach back to colonial times (Haller 2010a: pp. 23, 24).
24 Hardin 1968; World Bank 1981, 1989

governments then took away resource rights and responsibilities from local groups with the argument that the existing overuse of these resources was the result of an assumed non-management and open access situation.[25] Hence, common tenure regimes are today missing partly due to institutional change, e.g. were 'legislated out of existence' when not further formalised, when their existing institutions were not recognised or when the common resources became nationalised or privatised.[26]

Today, ecosystems and natural habitats like wetlands have lost their inclusive status and are parcelled out under separate laws dealing with water, forests, minerals, wildlife, fisheries and so on, although these resources themselves are not partitioned physically.[27] Wetlands, with their seasonal changings and connectivity to larger hydrological cycles, can hence fall into different types of tenancy that might overlay each other—apparent for instance in the case of seasonal floodplains that are divided into individual plots for crop cultivation once the water recedes—and therefore require holistic and situationally adequate management approaches that reach beyond boundaries or specific habitats.[28]

Authorities can apply ideas imported from very different contexts (e.g. laws from the colonial motherland or today's global conservation discourse) for property right structures as well as for property management, but then actively employ and 'idiomatise' them.[29] The Ramsar Convention, for instance, influenced policy-makers around the globe as it provided the first basic tools for governmental wetland management.[30] However, in its initial stages, it lacked appreciation of the value of wetlands to local communities and did not aim to bridge the conflicting practices of customary and non-customary users.[31] This negligence of the local resource users in the Ramsar Convention framework was particularly acute for

---

25 Haller 2010a: p. 26. Common property was hence misinterpreted as an open access system and the particular local and historical reasons for overuse, such as demographic, technological, economic and political factors within colonisation and post-colonial state building were often left unnoticed (Haller 2010a: p. 26). This is not to say that heterogeneity of interests/users as well as the value of future vs current use will not in fact lead to overuse of resources (Becker/Ostrom 1995, cited in Haller 2010a: pp. 35, 36).
26 Haller 2010a: pp. 25, 33
27 Richardson 1993; Adger/Luttrell 2000
28 Richardson 1993; Risser 1990
29 Lund/Sikor 2009: p. 7
30 Adger/Luttrell 2000: p. 79
31 Adger/Luttrell 2000: p. 79. In 1996, parties to the Convention were urged "to develop appropriate national and local mechanisms, drawing from any existing models, to ensure consultation with local and indigenous people with a view to reflecting their needs and values, traditional and other knowledge and practices in national wetland policies and programmes, and in management planning for Ramsar sites and other significant wetlands" (Ramsar Convention on Wetlands 1996b: p. 2). Three years later, Ramsar acknowledged that "very little guidance on this topic is available to the Contracting Parties" (Ramsar Convention on Wetlands 1999: p. 5).

tropical wetlands that were heavily utilised by subsistence users.[32] The large-scale and universalised approach therefore initially failed to provide a comprehensive and adaptable framework for local circumstances in the global South. Moreover, the Ramsar Convention's focus on conservation, based on biodiversity ethic alone, often conflicted with local economic interests.[33] From the 1980s onwards, although this problem was increasingly recognised, including by Ramsar, and approached through the creation of commons and co-management initiatives, the involvement of local people in such initiatives was often marginal and did not meet their needs, and protected areas continued to be enlarged at the cost of local users.[34]

The influence of conservation efforts such as the Ramsar Convention on the different levels of governance fostered disparity not only horizontally between the institutionalised and the customary actors, but also vertically between different governmental actors—for instance, between the realm of the local and the national or international.[35] A local government could thus be caught between conservation intentions of the central government (e.g. influenced by the Ramsar Convention) and the economic interests and political demands of local users. Furthermore, with the growing grip of the post-colonial state on land management matters, the fragmentation of responsibility within the state grew, so that different departments had responsibility for different lands and land uses.[36] However, such a fragmentation of responsibilities, often combined with limited capacity for coordination and the outparcelling of resources, neither provided integrated management approaches to multiple use nor flexibility towards the biological, geological and hydrological dynamics of wetlands and ultimately made collective action more costly by increasing transaction costs at both the state and the local level.[37] Moreover, when governmental takeovers failed to exert full control, institutional fit decreased, situations of legal and normative pluralism emerged and resources factually turned into no one's or everyone's property.[38]

In customary systems, by contrast, transactions were embedded within cultural and religious belief systems, which were again based on rules of reciprocity with other user groups, allowing for the flexible adaptation of use regimes of limited resources when economically and ecologically necessary.[39] Customary authorities

---

32 Bailey 1988, cited after Adger/Luttrell 2000: p. 79
33 Adger/Luttrell 2000: p. 79
34 Haller 2010a: p. 24
35 Adger/Luttrell 2000: p. 78
36 Haller et al. 2013: p. 11
37 Haller et al. 2013: pp. 4, 11
38 Von Benda-Beckmann et al. 2006: pp. 19, 24; Haller 2002: p. 32; Haller et al. 2013: pp. 3, 4
39 Haller et al. 2013: p. 4; Peters 2000: p. 11; Van den Berg 1992: pp. 23, 24. Adger and Luttrell (2000: p. 80) specify that common property works best when there are "relatively

were hence often well able to mediate, manage, monitor and sanction the different users' interests—due also to their local socio-religious embedding—but these functions were increasingly dismantled through state interventions, first by the colonial and then by the post-colonial state.[40] A further threat to those authorities arose when the natural systems to which they were tailored and to whose changing nature they had reacted over a long time, themselves experienced fundamental threat.[41] The threats accrued from technological changes like dams or urbanisation, or from neglect and abandonment or overuse of the resources, which again reflected changes in the political environment, such as changed property rights systems, state regulations for the access to pasture and transformation of space for agriculture or conservation.[42] This was often also interlinked with the increasing economic and monetary value of these resources.[43] Such a commoditisation became effective at different levels.

The state's interest in integrating producers into a market economy could change the demand and relative prices for land and hence also the composition of users and the local accountability for use.[44] Furthermore, tax payments to the state as well as private purchase could undermine the responsiveness between users and customary authorities and the existing common property regimes.[45] As a result, users searched for the authority that served their interests best.[46] One strategy of 'disconnected' users was thereby to refer to the state and their citizenship rather than to local customary authorities and to group membership.[47] This again played together with intra-family conflicts through land sales that allowed actors to act beyond the consent and control of their kin.[48] Customary authorities, for their part, did stand or fall by their ability to adapt their services to the new circumstances—those who could be monetarised stayed in place, while those that impeded or hindered the adaptation of the local users to earn cash with these resources, fell away.[49] Within this quest for gains from natural resources, people with higher bargaining power and economic resources also exercised influence on the existing institutions, and

---

    small groups with shared needs and norms; clear boundaries for resource management; stability in the group undertaking management; and relatively low costs of enforcement".
40 Haller et al. 2013: pp. 11, 12
41 Haller et al. 2013
42 Haller et al. 2013
43 Haller 2002: p. 32
44 Haller 2013: p. 11
45 Haller 2013: p. 11
46 Von Benda-Beckmann 1981
47 Haller 2010a: p. 3
48 Haller 2002; Colin 2008; Colin/Woodhouse 2010
49 Haller 2002: p. 33. This cash is needed not only for consumer goods of the globalised world, but also for the construction of social networks (cf. Berry 1989, 1993; Haller 2002).

FIGURE 1: Panorama of the study site as seen from the Below-Foncha quarter, March 2014 (Photographer: S. Simon, March 2014).

might even have eradicated them or created new ones, and in this way gained access to resources.[50] However, it was not always the most effective institutions that emerged from this process but the ones that suited the needs of the more powerful, which could again bring negative outcomes for the resource itself, such as overstocking, soil erosion, reduction of grass cover and quality, and might thereby again lead to conflicts between users.[51] This makes clear why conversion to private or state *de facto* property needs to be assessed critically as it might negatively impact the distribution of wealth and livelihood security.[52]

An overview of the Bamenda wetlands and their use

Situated in the north-east of the city of Bamenda, the capital of the North-West province in Cameroon, the Below-Foncha part of the Bamenda riverine wetlands constitutes one of the last larger open spheres remaining within relative proximity

---

50 Haller 2002: p. 32; Ensminger 1992, cited after Haller 2010a: p. 40. Bargaining power stems from social status, wealth or the ability to manipulate ideology and is non-static (Ensminger 1992, cited after Haller 2010a: p. 39). It is reciprocally interlinked with the other three endogenous spheres (ideology, institutions and organisation) while also being influenced by external factors such as social and physical environment, demography and technology (Haller 2010a: p. 39).
51 Haller et al. 2013: p. 3
52 Guha 1989, cited after Adger/Luttrell 2000: p. 80

to the urban centre. It marks the boundary between the Fondoms (customary kingdoms) Nkwen and Mankon as well as between the governmental subdivisions Bamenda II and Bamenda III. Declared as governmental land and selected to become the city's second centre in the medium-term future, the wetlands are today used by male herders and fishermen and cultivated by a multitude of predominantly female farmers during the dry season and parts of the rainy season.

The people who first settled in the area towards the middle of the 20th century were of both intra- and extra-Fondom origin. The population in the quarters around the wetlands were thus from the beginning of mixed origins but under the formal rule of the two Fondoms.[53] From the 1960s, however, migration to Bamenda and urbanisation started to increase significantly.[54] Therefore, the heterogeneity of the population around the wetlands also increased and privatisation and commoditisation processes took off, while the land-membership nexus declined. Within the more and more individualised processes of production, management, transmission and alienation, a differentiation of the user group emerged. The first

---

53 My informants refer either to their grandfathers or to their fathers as among the first ones to settle in the area. For instance, the Quarterhead of Mulang states, that his grandfather, some sixty years ago, was the first one to settle, and after driving away the hunters of the Fon of Mendankwe, established the quarter and "was here alone without any disturbances". (Mulang Quarterhead, Bamenda, March 28 2014, interview by Sandro Simon). Some of the forefathers had an extra-Fondom origin but were nevertheless able to become part of the local nobility through time.
54 Kometa/Akoh 2012: p. 65

user group, 'early-comers', married into a family on site and obtained rights of use within the family or were passed a plot by their fathers, e.g. via the widowed mother. In any case, they understood themselves as 'owners' and solidified their rights by cultivating ancestral land to which strong non-use values were attached. The second group, 'late-comers', consists of farmers with a more recent history of rural-urban migration who perceive themselves as 'care-takers' rather than owners. These include people who rented land from the owners without being affiliated to their families and who lived either in the quarter they farmed or in a neighbouring one, and other late-comers who bought land without first renting it.[55]

The difference in the histories of early- and late-comers is reflected in land cultivation, tenancy, technique adaptation, plant selection, the degree of commercial production and land alienation. All this took and still takes place in a space that has changed from dry- to wetland and, in a strictly legal sense, from customarily-controlled over individually-held, but customarily-embedded, to governmentally-owned land within the last 50 years. Today, users face on the one hand the danger of displacement or expropriation and the ambiguities of legal and normative pluralism and, on the other hand, the early or even permanent flooding of the area and increasing water pollution.

While farming in the dry season and part of the rainy season is an opportunity for agriculturalists to generate income, the whole valley is prone to floods and ponding during the rainy season. This not only restricts agricultural practice during that period, but has also led to the destruction of houses. In response to this, artificial riverbeds and bridges were constructed in 2007 to secure a steady runoff. The Programme *D'Appui Aux Capacites Decentralisees De Developpement Urbain* (PACDDU) resulted in the construction of two drainages and two box culverts, funded 85 per cent by the European Union and 15 per cent by the Bamenda City Council. The project was executed by the local company Edge. While some hydrological investigations were undertaken, no socio-economic and health impact assessment was made.[56] As beneficial as this construction was, apart from the problems of its sustainable maintenance, they also led to the destruction of yields, cut some farms in two or reduced part of the acreage, led to a renegotiation and the fixing of Fondom boundaries and triggered conflicts over land.

The basis for the project fell under the 1974 land law which considered all wetland as governmental property, together with other possibly hazardous zones such as slopes. However, this has not discouraged people from settling on slopes

---

55 The users' varying needs, affiliations and attachments to the land as well as a certain fluctuation among them disadvantage a more institutionalised common use (see Adger/Luttrel 2000) but must be understood within the local context of overlapping and competing authorities.

56 PACDDU 2005; Edge 2008

FIGURE 2: A rusting sign announces the PACDDU Project of 2007 (Photographer: S. Simon, March 2014).

and farming, herding or fishing wetlands. Tolerance of these practices around Below-Foncha might nevertheless come to an end in the not-so-distant future. The area has been targeted for development, and could become the city's second centre. It is not much of a surprise that the Urban Planning Office sees plenty of potential in the still 'undeveloped' wetlands, the only place inside the city where there has been no building activity so far. As for the planners, the advantages of the wetlands, especially for farmers, are substantial: through the availability of water, nearly exclusively through shallow wells and hand-watering, it is possible to plant in the dry season and produce foodstuffs that have a higher market price due to generally low supply. Additionally, for those who do not sell much of their produce, the wetlands still offer the possibility to lower household expenditure and for those who hold the land to rent out or even sell it to others. The wetlands are thus a place of cultivation in many ways, be it consumable or marketable goods, relationships, well-being or socio-economic status. Furthermore, the wetlands have a significant gender dimension: As the book title *Men Own the Fields, Woman Own the Crops* of Goheen indicates, women used to be in charge of the production of food for the family.[57] In the wetlands, however, not only cultivation, but also management and ownership, albeit in informal tenure, are to a large degree vested in the hands of women.

---

57 Goheen 1996

From dry- to wetlands, from 'bush' to city: ecological and demographic change

At the time when many of today's early-comer families settled in the Below-Foncha area, the land was dry around the river and palmwine tapping as well as agriculture, herding and fishing were performed.[58] Settlement and resource use were bound to the rule of the Fons of Mankon and Nkwen, represented by trustees and members of the nobility on site today called Quarterheads.[59] Embedded firmly in the community they supervised and often users themselves, these regimes allowed for adaptability and flexibility of management, although most of the time, they were concerned with dryland matters rather than wetlands and their different users.

No exact date exists for the change from dry- to wetlands. The process might have started as early as the 1960s while continuing to expand through the early 1990s, but in the last 20 years, the place has become considerably wetter.[60] While the change to wetland in ecological terms was obviously a long-term process, there was a threshold where farming started to shift from dry- to wetland and from rainy- to dry-season cultivation. Within the period of this change towards more lucrative cultivation, new actors were attracted and further blended the composition of the cultivators and crop choices in the area, also influenced by the general urbanisation that started in the 1960s.[61] Gloria, a female farmer in her mid forties, hence stated "when I grew up, there was only bush. With time, the city came to us."[62]

While ecological change— e.g. through the anthropogenic influence on water patterns—might have been interlinked with immigration and urbanisation, both of them fostered new incentives for farming and new demand for land and are composed of an array of factors. Different to the early-comers, for many late-

---

58 Before the settlement, the Mankon side was used by hunters of the Mendankwe Fondom and called *nta mandam* (meaning the hill where people from Mendankwe usually visit for hunting) by the Mankon people. The Nkwen side used to be the hunting ground of the Nkwen Fon and was called Ntenefor by its residents. However, I could not find out exactly why and when it changed to the name of national politician and Nkwen prince John Ngu Foncha, who was given a large piece of land by the Fon and set up a cacao plantation and a fish pond in the 1960s. To add to the confusion, the map from 2002 shows, that officially, it is (still) part of Ntenefor or Lower Bayelle while an informal wetland sale agreement from 1998 shows Nekume/Below-Foncha.
59 Conversion of food crop land into cash crop land was for instance perceived as a 'taboo', punishable by the customary authorities (Below-Foncha Quarterhead, March 23 2014, Bamenda, interview by Sandro Simon).
60 Kometa and Akoh (2012: p. 65) note: "Many of the farmlands, wetlands, and forests that existed in the 1950s have over the past decades been transformed into urban settlements." In the Below Foncha Part of the wetlands, however, the opposite accounts: they evolved along with the increase in immigration and urbanisation.
61 Woodhouse et al. 2000, Kometa/Akoh 2012: p. 65
62 Gloria, Bamenda, 22 February 2013, Bamenda, interview by Sandro Simon. Name of interviewee changed.

comers, *Njama Njama* (*Solanum scabrum*), a crop that grows especially well in the wetlands, represents one of the basic ingredients of their 'traditional' dish.[63] These different food patterns might thus have played a role in the choice of crop. Further, the city's growing demand for food set an incentive for more market-oriented cultivation—something the fruitful wetlands offered.[64] Also, the late-comers, predominantly female as mentioned before, did not have much capital, their husbands had yet to establish themselves on the job market and they were farming on sharecropped or rented plots which forced them to redeem their expenditure (firstly only gifts, later monetarised rents and sales) through direct marketing.[65] It might therefore have been a mixture of existing and accessible arable land, economic pressure, adaptable farming skills and general demand that induced late-comers to cultivate mainly off-season *Njama Njama* and to become quite commercially oriented farmers of the wetlands.

For the increasingly independent early-comers (from the customary authorities), some of whom might have had too much land to cultivate or been in financial distress, leases and sales were a chance to earn money. Furthermore, they might also have been able to afford a less commercial approach and slow adaptation because of having acquired capital, for instance, through dry- or wetland sales and advanced establishment on the urbanising job market. There is, however, also some evidence that the early farmers adapted their techniques and crops more slowly to the new circumstances than late-comers, as underlined for instance by the quote: "I was still burning the ankara when people started digging wells around me to water their farms."[66] Additionally, there were narratives circulating that the early-comers

---

63 Like all other crops cultivated in the wetlands today, it stems from rain-fed dryland cultivation, where it yields considerably less harvest. Various people, both women and men from different intra-and extra-Fondom origins claim to be the pioneers of transferring it to the Below-Foncha wetlands after seeing it planted in other wetlands.

64 For another example concerning the relationships between crop choice, food patterns and commoditisation see Lahiff 2000: p. 175.

65 Today, all of my late-comer female informants, of whom none finished basic levels of school, see resale marketing (Buyam-Sellam), cooking and agriculture with the possibility for direct marketing as their only available job options. Furthermore, entry costs are perceived as an obstacle for resale-marketing. Agriculture with direct marketing is seen as a way to obtain the capital needed to enter into such resale marketing, although it remains unclear whether the gains from resale marketing are indeed higher than those from agriculture with direct marketing.

66 Emma, 30 March 2014, Bamenda, interview by Sandro Simon. Name of interviewee changed. Ankara is a heap of plant matter covered by soil. It is lit and burns for several days but is rarely applied in the wetlands. Today's wetland farmers widely perceive this technique as not sustainable because it only gives good soil for one year and after that, the soil is leached. The practice has been declared illegal but neither my informants nor I knew of any case where the state enforced this law.

did not 'understand' the value of their own (wet)land.[67] By the time of this research, while there are differences in commerciality of production or the needs beneath it, and—probably influenced by this commerciality—the differing crop preferences and uses of fertilisers, the techniques, e.g. the appliance of tools or the usage of wells, were quite uniformly distributed among both early- and late-comers.

Even though the female wetland farmers remained dependent on their families and were dominated by male family heads and the customary authorities in various aspects and to varying degrees (e.g. the delivery of profits from rentals and sales to the husband or lineage head, and in cases of conflicts and their mediation), they gained more and more room for manoeuvre and were able to consolidate their formerly weak use rights towards more permanent rights.[68] Within this process, the access to wetland and, to a lesser degree, the sustaining of it in terms of both rights and ecological circumstances became increasingly vested in the hands of women who took advantage of family or individual rights and existing laws governing land acquisition. These opportunities were further expanded by the availability of land suitable for farming, and by women's increased independence from male domination.[69] As a result, there are various examples where women resolved conflicts, sold or leased out land without family consent, negotiated prices for sales, leases and produce between themselves and disposed of the revenue from leases, sales and marketing independently from their kin.

Over time, the increase in the number of farmers also contributed to the commoditisation of the plots as well as to the reduction in their size. They were considerably smaller than their dryland counterparts. This again affected the sociality of the farmers beyond the wetlands (e.g. less help needed, fewer 'buffers' for other women), and also the cultivation (e.g. intensity, crop choice). The possible ecological damage and the associated health risks (e.g. leaching) stemming from one sort of use (e.g. agriculture) posed a threat to other users (be it other agriculturalists

---

67 Sandro Simon, field notes 2014. For similar expressions on the Maasai's assumed inability to "understand the value of wetland" and their actual, far more successful participation in the commoditisation process, see Southgate/Hulme 2000: p. 89.

68 This is for instance visible by the means of fallowed land: while formerly, legitimacy of tenure was reciprocally interlinked with productive use, today, leaving land unused does not lead to expropriation through any authority. Consequently, the (former) temporal transfer of use rights can increase the efficiency (see Colin/Woodhouse 2010) and allows flexible access according to peoples' changing needs, while leaving land fallow to be able to quickly sell it if an opportunity shows up, can lead to poorer land use and exclusion (Atwood 1990, cited after Lund 2001: p. 16).

69 Historically, plots might have been situated in proximity to bodies of water, but it was the emergence of the wetlands that brought about a specific 'off-season' cultivation within its irrigation schemes. This does not mean, however, that there are no customs (or non-use values) that evolved around dryland cultivation and were then 'transferred' to the wetlands (or maintained in a place that changed ecologically).

FIGURE 3: A snapped banana stem lies in a bed of freshly transplanted *Njama Njama* and a row of gathered waste ready to be burned (Photographer: S. Simon, March 2014).

or fishers and herders) but went largely unpunished in an environment where different authorities compete against each others—as the next section will show.

From customary tenure to governmental acquisition and legal pluralism

Besides ecological and demographic change, the third overarching factor shaping the wetlands was the declaration of all wetlands as state land in 1974. Since the Below-Foncha wetlands probably took shape after 1974, they virtually grew into the law, which would actually enable owners to search for compensation. This, in turn, complicated the role of the state in mediating conflicts over the wetlands.

The government formally took over some responsibilities that had been vested in the customary authorities, for instance, the allocation of land (e.g. city planning) and the provision of infrastructure (e.g. canal building). However, this did not obstruct open access (the way described before) and one institution did not replace the other. Quite the opposite: their grips were partly overlapping, conflicting and coexisting as they both offered their individual 'shopping forums'.[70] The success or failure of their interventions was reciprocally interlinked with their acknowledgement by the people.[71] Indeed, they have very different spheres of power. While the government was able to execute top-down projects without much involvement of the people

---

70 Von Benda-Beckmann 1981; Lund 2001
71 Juul/Lund 2002

on site (as the PACDDU project showed), the Quarterheads, who do not dispose of the same means of enforcement and economic resources, need to be acknowledged by the quarter members in order to recruit them as members of a work force for community work. These quarter members in turn need to come to terms with their Quarterheads, since they are not elected but installed by the Fons. In contrast, some of the governmental authorities were elected. However, the decentralisation process is far from complete, as delegates, e.g. for land tenure, are still installed by the central government and the access to police or legal procedure is highly dependent on the bargaining power and/or wealth of those who search for support. Farmers' access to both authorities thus has distinct hindrances.

Through the declaration of the wetlands as governmental land and the reestablishment or reconfirmation of the Fondom boundary along the now straightened river in governmental land in the course of the PACDDU project (before that, the river was meandering and served as an orientation line rather than a fixed boundary), layered territory (state–customary authorities) and layered property (individuals–state) manifested. As a consequence, both authorities now search to exercise their potency over property and territorial matters, be it as infrastructure-providers (government), conflict mediators (customary authorities) or infrastructure-maintainers (customary authorities).[72]

Users, in turn, do 'forum shopping' according to their individual aims and situations.[73] Those aims and situations could thereby vary greatly: while all farmers were cultivating governmental property, some late-comers were additionally cultivating land that was territory of the traditional authority of their quarter to which they were affiliated to a certain degree, but to which they had no hereditary connection. Other late-comers were farming on land that was neither territory of their affiliated quarter nor kin. None of these late-comers were openly resisting customary authorities by referring directly to their national citizenship and the government as the territorial authority or the owner, but there were examples of early-comers with strong bargaining power and economic resources who turned to the government to press their claims.[74] Still, late-comers were reluctant to call in the customary authorities for conflict mediation, condemn the Country Sundays or even hid on the farms when being called for community work.[75] On the one hand, they tried to circumvent and

---

72   Similar to roads (again governmentally owned) which are sometimes maintained by (customary) community work, governmental property is partly territorially 'overlayered' by the customary authorities—tolerated or even encouraged by the state.
73   Von Benda-Beckmann 1981
74   For users referring to their national citizenship in order to 'overcome' kinship affiliations, see Haller 2010b: p. 429.
75   The 'traditional' week has eight days of which two are the big and the small Country Sunday. On the former, no work on the land is allowed; on the latter, no iron blade (e.g.

avoid, but not openly contest the customary authorities to a certain degree while, on the other hand, they still relied on them because they were perceived as the ones generally in charge (e.g. to organise community work) and the ones that were best able to bring in the government when it came to the establishment and maintenance of the canal.

Similar to the late-comers, early-comers preferred to solve problems bilaterally, probably again out of practical reasons (time, cost, the prevention of 'bad talk') and saw their customary leaders as responsible for carrying their claims to the government. However, they had low trust in their ability to get the government to act on the water problem or to organise effective community work and criticised the minimal cooperation across Fondom boundaries. Their relationship was furthermore strained through the customary authorities' inability to secure their subjects' lands against governmental acquisition or expropriation. This privation and uprooting is fundamental and engendered the feeling and narrative amongst early-comers of having lost their ancestral land, which is so central for their belonging and progeneration—although they were still able to negotiate *de facto* access to and control over it to a large extent (e.g. through leases and sales).

Unlike the early-comers who saw their ancestral land become wet and subsequently declared governmental land, late-comers established relationships with their farms that were from the beginning influenced by the feeling of being strangers and caretakers, not owners, both because it was governmental land and because they did not have a hereditary connection to it. The sense of a real threat of loss among both groups arose with the specific plans for a second city centre. It was linked to their experiences with the PACDDU project, when farmers lost harvests

FIGURE 4: A guava tree was introduced as a boundary marker by the customary authority after a boundary conflict, serving today as an orientation rather than a strict demarcation marker (Sandro Simon field notes 2014, Photographer: S. Simon, March 2014).

---

a hoe) shall enter the soil. Since they're tied inseparably to the land rather than to the people, farmers, no matter where they come from and with whom they are affiliated, stick to the Country Sunday rules of the palace on which territory they work.

and parts of plots but kept quiet because they had farmed on governmental land and were happy that "something was done at all" to control the water.[76] Farmers therefore appeared to be confronted with over-challenged customary authorities and a certain marginalisation by the government that had been condoning but not supporting the informal agricultural use of the wetlands so far. This affected their acknowledgement of both governmental and customary authorities. The former were seen as quite effective but the farmers' access to them was generally restricted by their informal tenure and bound to their individual bargaining power and/or economic resources. The latter appeared as less powerful but more accessible. However, the less the farmers were acquainted with the corresponding customary authority on whose territory they farmed, the more they hesitated to turn to it for support.

From intra-governmental contestation to effective policy

While the government has so far been assessed as an actor and as the counterpart to customary authorities and users, this section aims to provide insight into the government as an arena where competing departments, concerned with different aspects and features of the wetlands and agriculture within the city, exert influence. In this competition, the wetlands and urban agriculture became segmented by the various interests, roles and viewpoints represented by the departments of Urban Planning, Health and Sanitation, Environment, Land Tenancy, and Agriculture.[77] Ideologies, bargaining power and organisation played their part in this process, for instance, the current global conservation discourse or the access to the central government and its financial resources.[78] For the Below-Foncha area, Urban Planning, with the go-ahead from the central government that supervises and approves local planning, seems to have gained the upper hand. Concerns over forced changes in the larger hydrological and biodiversity set-up were largely brushed aside for both the canal building and the planned second city centre.

Agriculture within the city also came under attack when, in 2009, the city council released a press statement that prohibited agricultural cultivation, especially along major streets and encouraged citizens to plant flowers and ornamental trees instead.[79] In essence, it was forbidden to cultivate foodstuffs along major streets, in front of public offices and on the edges of roads.[80] Driven by Urban Planning that planned to push urban agriculture and especially livestock farming to the city's border,

---

76 Sandro Simon, field notes 2014
77 Within the different departments, there are processes of consensus building, but their analysis is beyond the scope of this chapter.
78 Haller 2010a
79 Ojong 2011: pp. 16, 17
80 Ojong 2011: pp. 16, 17

these measures earned criticism from the departments of Agriculture, Environment and Health and Sanitation who insisted on the importance of cultivation of food around the house and in free zones inside the city. They described the flowers and ornamental trees policy as a misleading attempt to copy northern cityscapes. While, on the one hand, agriculture was practised all across the town, on the other hand, it found little appreciation in the policy-making of the city—as described for many African cities.[81]

Materialisation and visualisation of the states' claim to govern the wetlands

As one faction of the governmental apparatus and its logic gained control over the prospective configuration of the wetlands, other voices concerned with ecological or livelihood issues became more and more marginalised. Consequently, the management of the Below-Foncha wetlands became strongly directed towards a successful prospective implementation of the plan to build a second city centre. The state increasingly undertook efforts to defend and display its power to govern the access to and control over the land.

For decades, the state's claim to govern the wetlands has been limited to written law and a circulating narrative but excluded the actual enforcement of this claim. With the construction of the canal in 2007, the government and its power to act became present and tangible—but only for a moment, because this 'interruption' remained rather isolated as the maintenance was not comprehensively carried out. In 2013, however, a more permanent display of power was established: signboards stating 'No Land Reclamation' and listing the different laws, ordinances and decrees concerned with the management of wetlands were put up.[82]

For a more in-depth understanding of the intentions of the signboards, we must ask what the motivation or the trigger for their installation was. It turns out that they were put up after some people started filling the ground that was intended for the construction of the second city centre and were thereby increasing susceptibility to flooding in the area. The signboards were hence not put up as a forewarning of the planned infrastructure project but rather as a reaction to activities of citizens that counteracted those plans. The public only had a rudimentary knowledge of the plans; there was no public participation in their design because the details were confidential and yet to be approved by the central government.

Another important question is the effect of the signboards on the social life in the wetlands and the relationships between the different actors. Although being

---

81 Prain et al. 2010
82 A municipal order on the regulation of health hazards and a law on the framework relating to environmental management are listed, although they were not taken into account for the canal construction and so far have not been taken into account for the establishment of the second city centre.

painfully reminded that they had lost the land or were caretakers, not owners, few informants saw the signboards as binding for farmers and stated, for instance, that people had become reluctant to buy plots in the wetlands. Most farmers, in contrast, were confident that the signposts only referred to land reclamation for building purposes and not to agricultural activities. They hence made a distinction between those who were already there and those who intended to come and, accordingly, between two different property claims. This corresponded with the perception of farming as temporary and continuously needing care, while infrastructural measures endured without the same amount of maintenance. The signboards, however, reinforced a previous claim and translated this into a tangible fact. They symbolised a claim that might gain social relevance. However, the signboards did not seem to evoke an acknowledgement of binding obligation amongst farmers; they merely functioned as floating or ambiguous signifiers.

The intentions of those who produced the signboards and encoded a meaning were thus not read or decoded in the same way by those who encountered them. The signboards were intended to transport territorial claims based on laws aimed at rendering space politically, but "words gather their meaning from the relational properties of the world itself" and not from their attachment to abstract concepts imposed upon a meaningless world of entities and events 'out there'.[83] Consequently, the signboards effectively created overlapping and contradictory rules with differently structured effects on access and property because different people had different relations to and with them but no 'common reading' since they lacked common experience.[84] 'No Land Reclamation' was thereby read as 'Governmental Land' by the farmers in reference to their ongoing practice and discourse and in the absence of governmental enforcement, although there was a growing anticipation for such an enforcement. For the signboards this meant that they could change their meaning according to the sedimentation of the actors' lived experience with them as they 'stand alone without assistance' (i.e. enforcement of what they claim).

Strikingly, the city council also did not envisage the signboards as binding on the farmers but as aimed solely at deterring aspirant house owners. The government's claims via the signboards were thus selective in their target group—although the signboards themselves did not make such a division. This hinted at the fact that the wetland law itself did not foresee a temporal use of the wetlands for agricultural or other resource-use based purposes (different to state-governed "common pools" as described by Haller et al. 2010). Although there was no legal basis that corresponded with the actual doings of the farmers, the government tolerated

---

83 Ingold 2000: p. 409
84 Lund/Sikor 2009: p. 5; Ingold 2000: p. 409

Dynamics of tenure and policy in the Bamenda wetlands

FIGURE 5: Signboards with the declaration "No Land Reclamation" were put up in 2013 (Photographer: S. Simon, March 2014).

FIGURE 6: The straightened canal divides farm land on the right and a site that was levelled for construction on the left before the "No Land Reclamation" signboards were put up (Photographer: S. Simon, March 2014).

them. It thereby both disallowed and allowed certain claims of land use and access to its territory and its property—without adjusting the law accordingly. The local governmental authorities thus circumvented what they did not see as appropriate or suitable just like the farmers did. For the government, the installation of the signboards was not only an act of power but must also be understood as a risk. Similar to the canal, whose construction was a demonstration of power but then lacked further comprehensive maintenance, signboards must be taken care of to retain their effect. However, materials undergo continual transformation—metal rusts, paint bleaches, the visual can be manipulated etc.—and hence always win out over form in the long term as they are 'ongoing historicity', immersed in the currents of time.[85]

Conclusion

Just as the wetlands have different functions and offer an array of services, the possible users and governing institutions have different perceptions of them, according to their various needs and wishes, i.e. the wetlands' perceived direct-use values like extraction, indirect-use values like groundwater recharge or non-use values like the safeguarding of biodiversity for future generations or the progeneration of a hereditary attachment. Wetlands have hence always been influenced by people and the institutions they established around them and must be understood as natural-anthropogenic ecosystems.[86] Within this reciprocal relationship, wetlands, on the one hand, can provide users with goods but also deprive them of goods, for instance in the case of ecological change while, on the other hand, users can overexploit, pollute or otherwise harm the wetlands. In the African context, the latter has been hastily interpreted in the way that colonial subjects generally threaten pure nature (colonial state) and that only private or national, but not common property, provides a framework for sustainable use (post-colonial state).

This strand of analyses overlooked and ignored that the drivers for degradation were often demographic, technological, economic and political factors within colonisation and post-colonial state building.[87] Hence, the often flexible and therefore fitting local customary institutions that were established around common use but not recognised by the colonial and post-colonial state or the advocates of the *tragedy of the commons* have not been a hindrance for sustainable wetland use. Rather, incomplete governmental acquisitions leading to the dismantling of the established authorities on site and to open access, or privatisation processes in which bargaining power and wealth might shape or produce unfitting institutions

---

85 Barad 2003, cited after Ingold 2012: p. 439
86 Haller et al. 2013
87 Haller 2010a

have been responsible. The initial motivation for such acquisitions often stemmed from conservation intentions, which, in turn, were influenced by global discourses and their specific initiatives. However, not only the state's inability to completely fill the governing role it proclaimed for itself, but also the implementation and adaptation of such generalised conservation approaches to the local circumstances were often incomplete and excluded the affected from participation. Furthermore, different governmental units, established around the parcelled-out environment, and/or different governmental levels can come into conflict with each other as they pursued different ideologies and interests.

This is the case for the Bamenda wetlands where the Department of Urban Planning, with the support of the central government, gained the power to map out and partly implement a planning policy that did little to take into consideration questions of ecology, sustainability and livelihood, as represented by other governmental departments. The consequent marginalisation of wetland farmers took place in an environment of legal and normative pluralism where customary and governmental authorities' services coexisted, overlapped and contested each other. As a result, farmers searched for a fitting authority, but their access was hindered by their informality, bargaining power, wealth (state) and affiliation (customary authority), so that they tried to circumvent both authorities to a large degree. Hence, conflict resolutions often took place bilaterally as far as possible. If no agreement could be reached, the customary authority of the concerned territory was called in, since the farmers had not established specific wetland institutions or committees able to punish any counteracting to the rules or enable common action against risks like flooding, animals or theft. However, the customary authorities themselves were not omnipresent. While they were able to mediate boundary conflicts etc., they lacked the economic resources and the fellowship to comprehensibly tackle issues, such as flooding.

Furthermore, the users had different degrees of affiliation and 'proximity' to the land. Because access and control was largely privatised and commoditised, they also did not have control over a (common) sustainable use of the wetlands, where the users kept their resource extraction in balance with each other, whether farmers, fishers or herders.

The difficulties of enforcement together with the heterogeneity of the users also disadvantaged more institutionalised common property regimes.[88] The state has been a 'present absentee' for a long time. Because the wetlands were labelled governmental property, the activities taking place there and the challenges, such as sustainable use that arise with them, could literally 'not be' according to the law. As a consequence, possibly contaminated wetland produce was sold on the market and

---

88 See Adger/Luttrel 2000

the users' possible influence on biodiversity or water patterns was left unattended. Every intervention that aimed to better this would equal the legitimisation of the informal use. Thus, only the enforced prohibition of any wetland activities would match *de jure* law with *de facto* practice. While this looks more and more like a future fact in the course of the consolidation of the plans for the second city centre, the government currently has restricted its claim to the safeguarding of the opportunity to use the wetlands. Farming, fishing or herding have not been perceived as threats. With regard to the costliness of any bigger intervention, signboards that discourage land reclamation were set up as a preventive measure. Aimed at discouraging prospective land-filling and especially construction and not farming, fishing or herding, and 'read' like this by the majority of users, the signboards highlighted the discrepancy between law, which was fixed and generalised and on which management and policy so strongly built, and social practice, which was continuously changing and particular.[89]

References

Adger, W.N. and C. Luttrell (2000), Property Rights and the Utilisation of Wetlands. *Ecological Economics*, 35(1): 75–89.

Atwood, D.A. (1990), Land Registration in Africa: The Impact on Agricultural Production. *World Development*, 18(5): 659–671.

Bailey, C. (1988), The Social Consequences of Tropical Shrimp Mariculture Development. *Ocean Shoreline Management*, 11(1): 31–44.

Barad, K. (2003), Posthumanist Performativity: Toward an Understanding of How Matter Comes to Matter. *Signs*, 40(1): 801–831.

Becker, C.D. and E. Ostrom (1995), Human Ecology and Resource Sustainability: The Importance of Institutional Diversity. *Annual Review of Ecology and Systematics*, 26: 113–133.

Berry, S. (1989), Social institutions and access to Resources in African agriculture. *Africa*, 59(1): 41–55.

---

[89] This chapter draws on fieldwork undertaken in 2013 and 2014 during a total of 15 weeks. Parts of the findings were presented at the workshops on The Politics of Nature and Science in African History (Basel, 15–16 May 2014) and Visuality and Policing (Basel, 10 October 2014). I would like to thank participants of these two workshops as well as Elísio Macamo, Piet van Eeuwijk, Lucy Koechlin, Till Förster, Jean Comaroff, and Pauline Peters for their helpful comments and their supervision. I am grateful to all my informants, my assistant Akumbu Jones, and the external reviewer for their feedback.

Berry, S. (1993), *No Condition is Permanent: The Social Dynamics of Agrarian Change in Sub-Saharan Africa*. Madison: University of Wisconsin Press.

Boyer, T. and S. Polasky (2004), Valuing Urban Wetlands: A Review of Non-Market Valuation Studies. *Wetlands*, 24(4): 744–755.

Carlsson, F., P. Frykblom and C. Liljenstolpe (2003), Valuing Wetland Attributes: An Application of Choice Experiments. *Ecological Economics*, 47(1): 95–103.

Colin, J.-P. (2008), Disentangling Intra-kinship Property Rights in Land: A Contribution of Economic Ethnography to Land Economics in Africa. *Journal of Institutional Economics*, 4(2): 231–254.

Colin, J.-P. and P. Woodhouse (2010), Interpreting Land Markets in Africa. *Africa 80*, 1–13.

Constanza, R, R. d'Arge, R. de Groot, S. Farber, M. Grasso, B. Hannon, K. Limburg, S. Naeem, R.V. O'Neill, J. Paruelo, R.G. Raskin, P. Sutton and M. van den Belt (1997), The Value of the World's Ecosystem Services and Natural Capital. *Nature*, 387(15): 253–260.

Earle, A. and S. Bazilli (2013), A Gendered Critique of Transboundary Water Management. *Feminist Review*, 103(1): 99–119.

Edge (2008), *Programme D'Execution Des Travaux* (Company report without publisher).

Ensminger, J. (1992), *Making a Market: The Institutional Transformation of an African Society*. Cambridge: Cambridge University Press.

Farrell, K. (2007), Living with Living Systems: Co-Evolution with Values and Valuation. *International Journal of Sustainable Development & World Ecology*, 14(1): 14–26.

Feeny, D., F. Berkes, B. McCay and J. Acheson (1990), The Tragedy of the Commons: Twenty-Two Years Later. *Human Ecology*, 18(1): 1–19.

Goheen, M. (1996), *Men Own the Fields, Women Own the Crops: Gender and Power in the Cameroon Grasslands*. Madison: University of Wisconsin Press.

Guha, R. (1989), *The Unquiet Woods: Ecological Change and Peasant Resistance in the Himalaya*. Oxford: Oxford University Press.

Haller, T. (2002), Common Property Resource Management, Institutional Change and Conflicts in African Floodplain Wetlands. *The African Anthropologist*, 9(1): 25–35.

Haller, T. (2010a), Institutional Change, Power and Conflicts in the Management of Common-Pool Resources in African Floodplain Ecosystems: An Introduction. In T. Haller (ed.), *Disputing the Floodplains: Institutional Change and the Politics of Resource Management in African Wetlands*. Leiden: Brill: 1–76.

Haller, T. (2010b), Between Open Access, Privatization and Collective Action: A Comparative Analysis of Institutional Change Governing Use of Common-Pool Resources in African Floodplains. In T. Haller (ed.), *Disputing the Floodplains: Institutional Change and the Politics of Resource Management in African wetlands*. Leiden: Brill: 413–44.

Haller, T., G. Fokou, G. Mbeyale and P. Meroka (2013), How Fit Turns Into Misfit and Back: Institutional Transformations of Pastoral Commons in African Floodplains. *Ecology and Society*, 18(1): 1–15.

Hammer, D.A. and R.X. Bastian (1989), Wetlands Ecosystems: Natural Water Purifiers. In D.A. Hammer (ed.), *Constructed Wetlands for Wastewater Treatment*. Chelsea: Lewis: 5–19.

Hardin, G. (1968), The Tragedy of the Commons. *Science*, 162(3859): 1243–1248.

Heimlich, R.E., K.D. Wiebe, R. Claassen, D. Gadsby and R.M. House (1998), *Wetlands and Agriculture: Private Interests and Public Benefits*. Resource Economics Division, Economic Research Service, U.S. Department of Agriculture. Agricultural Economic Report No. 765.

Juul, K. and C. Lund (2002), Introduction: In K. Juul and C. Lund (eds.), *Negotiating Property in Africa*. Portsmouth: Heinemann: 1–10.

Ingold, T. (2000), *The Perception of the Environment: Essays on Livelihood, Dwelling and Skill*. London/New York: Routledge.

Ingold, T. (2012), Toward an Ecology of Materials. *The Annual Review of Anthropology*, 41: 427–442.

IWRB (1993), Conclusions of a Workshop on Measuring Ecological Change in Wetlands. Symposium held in St. Petersburg, Florida, November 1992.

Kometa S.S. and N.R. Akoh (2012), Hydro-geomorphological Implications of Urbanisation in Bamenda, Cameroon. *Journal of Sustainable Development*, 5(6): 67–73.

Lahiff, E. (2000), The Mutale River Valley: An Apartheid Oasis. In: P. Woodhouse, H. Bernstein and D. Hulme (eds.), *African Enclosures: The Social Dynamics of Wetlands in Drylands*. Oxford: James Currey: 155–194.

Lund, C. (2001), *African Land Tenure: Questioning Basic Assumptions*. London: IIED.

Lund, C. and T. Sikor (2009), Access and Property: A Question of Power and Authority. *Development and Change*, 40: 1–22.

Matthews, G.V.T. (1993), *The Ramsar Convention on Wetlands: Its History and Development*. Gland: Convention on Wetlands of International Importance especially as Waterfowl Habitat, Ramsar Convention Bureau.

McCay, B. (1978), Systems Ecology, People Ecology and the Anthropology of Fishing Communities. *Human Ecology*, 6(4): 397–422.

McGrath, D., F. de Castro, C. Futemma, D. de Amaral, and J. Calabria (1993), Fisheries and the Evolution of Resource Management on the Lower Amazon Floodplain. *Human Ecology*, 21(2): 167–186.

Ojong, N. (2011), Livelihood Strategies in African Cities: The Case of Residents in Bamenda, Cameroon. *African Review of Economics and Finance*, 3(1): 8–25.

PACDDU (2005), Rapport D'Avant Projet Sommaire.

Peters, P.E. (1996), Failed Magic or Social Context? Market Liberalization and the Rural Poor in Malawi. *Harvard Institute for International Development, Harvard University, Development Discussion Paper*, No. 562.

Peters, P.E. (2000), Grounding Governance: Power and Meaning in Natural Resource Management. Keynote Address to International Symposium on Contested Resources: Challenges to Governance of Natural Resources in Southern Africa, Cape Town, October, 2000.

Prain, G., N. Karanja and D. Lee-Smith (eds.) (2010), *African Urban Harvest: Agriculture in the Cities of Cameroon, Kenya and Uganda*. Ottawa: Springer.

Ramsar Convention on Wetlands (1996a), Strategic Plan 1997–2002. http://ramsar.rgis.ch/pdf/key_strat_plan_1997_e.pdf. Accessed 25 February 2016.

Ramsar Convention on Wetlands (1996b), Recommendation 6.3: Involving Local and Indigenous People in the Management of Ramsar Wetlands. http://ramsar.rgis.ch/pdf/rec/key_rec_6.03e.pdf. Accessed 25 February 2016.

Ramsar Convention on Wetlands (1999), Resolution VII.8. www.ramsar.org/sites/default/files/documents/library/key_res_vii.08e.pdf. Accessed 25 February 2016.

Ramsar Convention on Wetlands (2002), Strategic Plan 2003–2008. http://ramsar.rgis.ch/pdf/key_strat_plan_2003_e.pdf. Accessed 25 February 2016.

Ramsar Convention on Wetlands (2008), Strategic Plan 2009–2015. http://ramsar.rgis.ch/pdf/strat-plan-2009-e-adj.pdf. Accessed 25 February 2016.

Ramsar Convention on Wetlands (2015), Strategic Plan 2016–2020. www.ramsar.org/sites/default/files/documents/library/4th_strategic_plan_2016_2024_e.pdf. Accessed 25 February 2016.

Ramsar Convention on Wetlands, Fact Sheet (2015a), Wetlands: Why Should I Care. www.ramsar.org/sites/default/files/documents/library/factsheet1_why_should_i_care_0.pdf. Accessed 19 February 2016.

Ramsar Convention on Wetlands, Fact Sheet (2015b), Wetlands: Wise Use Basics on Site. www.ramsar.org/sites/default/files/documents/library/factsheet2_wise_use_basics_0.pdf. Accessed 19 February 2016.

Ramsar Convention on Wetlands, Ramsar List (2016), The List of Wetlands of International *Importance*. www.ramsar.org/sites/default/files/documents/library/sitelist.pdf. Accessed 19 February 2016.

Richardson, B.J. (1993), Environmental Management in Uganda: The Importance of Property Law and Local Government in Wetland Conservation. *Journal of African Law*, 37(02): 109–143.

Risser, P.G. (1990), The Ecological Importance of Land-Water Ecotones. In R.J. Naiman and H. Decamps (eds.), *Ecology and Management of Aquatic-Terrestrial Ecotones*. Paris: UNESCO: 7–21.

Shine, C. and C. de Klemm (1999), *Wetlands, Water and the Law. Using Law to Advance Wetlands Conservation and Wise Use*. Gland: IUCN Environmental Policy and Law Paper No. 38.

Smardon, R.C. (2009), *Sustaining the World's Wetlands: Setting Policy and Resolving Conflicts*, New York: Springer.

Southgate, C. and D. Hulme (2000), Uncommon Property: The Scramble for Wetland in Southern Kenya. In P. Woodhouse, H. Bernstein and D. Hulme (eds.), *African Enclosures: The Social Dynamics of Wetlands in Drylands*. Oxford: James Currey: 73–118.

Van den Berg, A. (1992), *Women in Bamenda: Survival Strategies and Access to Land*. African Studies Centre Leiden, Research Report 50.

Von Benda-Beckmann, K. (1981), Forum Shopping and Shopping Forums: Dispute Processing in a Minangkabau Village in West Sumatra. *Journal of Legal Pluralism*, 13(19): 117–159.

Von Benda-Beckmann, K., F. von Benda-Beckmann and M.G. Wiber (2006), *Changing Properties of Property*. Oxford: Berghahn.

Vondal, J. (1990). The Common Swamplands of Southeastern Borneo. In B.J. McCay and J.M. Acheson (eds.), *The Question of the Commons: The Culture and Ecology of Communal Resources*. Tucson: University of Arizona Press: 231–249.

Woodhouse, P., P. Trench and M.D.M. Tessougué (2000), A Very Decentralized Development: Exploiting a New Wetland in the Sourou Valley, Mali. In P. Woodhouse, H. Bernstein and D. Hulme (eds.), *African Enclosures: The Social Dynamics of Wetlands in Drylands*, Oxford: James Currey: 29–72.

World Bank (1981), *Accelerated Development in Sub-Saharan Africa: An Agenda for Action*. Washington: World Bank.

World Bank (1989), *Sub-Saharan Africa: from Crisis to Sustainable Development*. Washington: World Bank.

PART V

Interventions

CHAPTER 14

Hidden struggles in conservation: people's resistance in Southern Africa

Frank Matose

Introduction

Over many years I have been puzzled about why local people have not risen up against the state in many local settings in Southern Africa, where the state has not only dispossessed them of their land and forest resources but also of other natural resources and property rights. Why have they not bothered to take on states by engaging in revolutionary activities in a Marxist sense of the oppressed will rise against their oppressors? How and why do they cope with being dispossessed of their forests, their land and their rights? At the core of this chapter is an analysis of how the dispossessed are not quiet but wage struggles that are mostly hidden and only surface on occasionally. 'Hidden' is used in the Foucaultian sense of the exercise of power relations between state actors (using hegemonic power) and local people who exercise their power through mostly covert ways.[1] Such exercise of power by both state and local actors is often hidden from the public gaze and these are the politics referred to in the chapter.[2] So then, how are these forms of struggle waged, by whom, where, and under what circumstances?

This contribution offers an analysis of forest conservation conflicts, the quotidian politics and practices of different villagers challenging the status quo and the current laws by their everyday actions in order to gain access to and benefit from forests from which they have been dispossessed for more than a century. This analysis is done across two sites in Southern Africa, namely Dwesa-Cwebe in South Africa and Mapfungautsi in Zimbabwe. The conquest and dispossession that took place in the 19th century was accompanied by a distortion of existing common property relations

---

1 After Foucault 1991
2 Scott 1990

through privatisation by the state.³ As a result of these structural changes over property around forests, the two states of South Africa and Zimbabwe attempted to stem conflicts through collaborative arrangements with dispossessed communities. Through conservation, protected forest areas become protected spaces for the state to exercise forms of government that are routinely resisted through everyday practices that take different forms across different spaces and people.⁴ While co-management is often used by the state to resolve conflicts in conservation, this contribution makes the claim that without resolving property rights in the form of rights *and* access for local people at the same time, such projects do not yield the intended outcomes.⁵ For both cases, the state's co-management projects that are meant to retain the state's hegemony over protected forests are found wanting and rendered ineffectual through the resistance of local people. In the Dwesa-Cwebe case, the state restores rights to the forest reserve through the restitution programme but takes away access to resources in anticipation of tourist revenue. In the Zimbabwean case, rights to forest land and resources are denied while access is provided through the co-management project. The choice of the two is to contrast whether giving rights versus providing access for resources through co-management arrangements respectively would offer any different insights into the nature of hidden struggles by local people.

My interest in hidden politics in conservation dates back to the early 1990s and 2000 (for the two cases, respectively) when I sought to understand the strategies that local people deploy whilst living under the state's failure to make collaborative projects work in both settings. Joint management of protected forests has not changed property relations obtained under colonial and apartheid rule. Local people engage in resistance that hardly comes into the open, yet are criminalised when they do.⁶ The paper is organised as follows: first, a typology of resistance is given. Second, the empirical evidence of resistance from the two selected cases is examined, followed by a discussion section before some conclusions are drawn.

Typology of resistance around forest conservation

In examining the resistance strategies deployed by local people in preference to collaborative arrangements around protected forests, I developed a typology whose terms I borrow from Sitas et al.⁷ The typology is underlain with different power relations (hidden politics) that are deployed by the various actors embedded

---

3   Beinart 1989
4   Government in the sense of Foucault 1991
5   Borrini-Feyerabend et al. 2000; Carlsson/Berkes 2005; Ramutsindela 2004. See also Ribot/Peluso 2003
6   Kull 2002
7   Sitas et al. 2014

in the resistance strategies. So the typology represents particular ways of exercising power through the acts that are deployed. The terms used in the typology evolved from words and meanings that were articulated to me by the various performers across different localities. Through their use, the attempt is not to denigrate terms already in existence in resistance literature, including those defined by Scott, Kull and Holmes, but to try and perhaps make sense of local people's own practices of their engagements.[8] In my typology, the first form of resistance is what I refer to as 'articulatory' resistance. This is characterised by an act that articulates or signifies intention either through the language used or some performance that is deliberate in communicating the fight for rights over or access to resources. The acts or struggles that I categorise as such are often more overt as they are intended to articulate the actors' position regarding the political battles with the state as well as the trajectories at play. For example, occupation or squatting inside a state forest clearly articulates peoples' contestation of rights over land and resources. At the same time, such squatting represents the exercise of 'mass' power by the dispossessed in regaining lost rights and access. The overall impact of this set of acts is to communicate to the state about intent by the performers and an indirect assertion of rights over resources denied by the state.

The second form of resistance in my typology, 'existential' resistance, refers to acts that are associated with the performer's assertion of the meaning of life or existence (*impilo yam'*).[9] Existential acts are less about the exercise of power than the first type of resistance as often people in forested landscapes use materials around them for their day-to- day lives and existence. The main challenge for such people is having access to and rights over such resources that are being denied by the state's own exercise of power over the same resources. Performers of these acts undertake them as part of their overall existence regardless of whether such acts are prohibited or not. 'Poaching' of timber from protected forests is an activity which illustrates this resistance. People use timber for the construction of their houses and need to do so because otherwise they would not have shelter and having shelter is just the way life is – a part of human existence in forested landscapes in which people depend on resources around them. Such forms of resistance therefore form part of the repertoire of hidden politics that local people deploy against the more powerful states.[10] Moreover, they are not mutually exclusive but tend to overlap; each act may illustrate both forms of resistance and is used to differentiate the intended outcomes of those performing them and as heuristic devices.

---

8   Scott 1985; 1990; Kull 2002; Holmes 2007
9   Literal translation from isiXhosa *impilo yam'*: "that's the way I live" in other words 'that's what life is all about'.
10 After Poteete/Ribot 2011

Case studies of resistance against collaborative projects

This section provides evidence of the resistance drawn from the two case studies that were examined over many years. For the Zimbabwe case, data were initially collected for my doctoral studies in the late 1990s, with subsequent research being undertaken from time to time and for shorter periods between 2000 and 2013.[11] For the South African case, an initial research exercise was undertaken in 2000 with subsequent work being undertaken between 2010 and 2014.[12] For each narrative, a brief background to the conservation project is given in order to situate the resistance that takes place. The resistance narratives presented here are more recent and represent the current trajectories of the nature of local people's struggles against their respective states.

Dwesa-Cwebe Nature Reserve, Eastern Cape, South Africa

Dwesa-Cwebe Nature Reserve is located in the Amathole District Municipality on the Wild Coast in the Eastern Cape Province of South Africa. Dwesa-Cwebe's total land area of approximately 235 square kilometres consists of both state and communal lands. The Dwesa-Cwebe community comprises of seven communal villages. The population density in the area is low, with an estimated 15,000 people, consisting of approximately 2,400 households, and poverty levels are high. The community which was removed from part of its ancestral land in the late 1800s now co-manages the Dwesa-Cwebe Nature Reserve following successful land restitution in 2001.

The nature reserve is managed jointly by the Eastern Cape Parks and Tourism Agency (ECPTA) and the community through the Dwesa-Cwebe Land Trust. The nature reserve is just under 6,000 ha and occupies a small coastal strip approximately 14 km long and extends from 3 to 5 km inland. The nature reserve conserves the largest tracts of indigenous coastal forest in the Eastern Cape.

The Dwesa-Cwebe Settlement Agreement of 2001 gives the communities ownership of the conservation areas, with resource access being managed through a co-management committee in conjunction with the state. Dwesa-Cwebe residents depend on forest resources for many of their livelihood needs.[13] When the ECPTA took over the running of the reserve from the Forestry Department in 2007, the access rights regime changed. Access to resources became restrictive, denying people access to several resources for their livelihoods such that by 2010, relations worsened and many people were arrested, assaulted and shot at because

---

11 Matose 2002
12 Grundy et al. 2004
13 Palmer et al. 2002; Timmermans 2004

they entered the Dwesa-Cwebe Nature Reserve.[14] The level of conflict to date has escalated as local people are frustrated by the failure of the co-management arrangements to assist them access forest resources as well as lack of revenue returns that were expected from ecotourism receipts.[15] While the Dwesa-Cwebe Nature Reserve formally belongs to local people under the 2001 settlement of the land claim, in practice, local people have little say in the management of the reserve, hence resistance to the co-management arrangements in which the state has retained hegemony.

While people around Dwesa-Cwebe are denied access to forest resources in order to preserve a pristine environment for discerning ecotourists, such commodification has barely produced tangible benefits in the form of revenue for the locals. The following narrative was extracted from several interviews of people in the Cwebe area between July and September 2011 after the fatal shooting of a man who was harvesting poles inside the reserve to meet his family's needs.

CASE STUDY 1: THE SHOOTING INCIDENT OF JUNE 2011

In June 2011, John (not his real name) was shot by a forest ranger when he was harvesting construction poles inside the Cwebe area of the reserve. According to witnesses, John bled to death and his body was taken to the nearest town of Elliotdale without consultation of his family or the local chief, as should have been done. The ranger was never arrested because the family did not lay charges. John's family said that the ranger shot John in the leg close to the waist and that he bled to death. The ranger who shot John is known to the family. The family states that John had left his home early in the morning and entered the Cwebe part of the reserve to cut poles for fencing his home. At around midday, the chief was visited by police and taken to where John had been shot while felling trees. The chief revealed that he could not tell what had really happened at the site in the reserve. The ranger who shot John said that he had confronted John for felling trees inside the reserve (an activity prohibited by the state). John had indicated that he had no intention to stop cutting timber. The ranger then went back to the office for assistance in dealing with this situation. With another ranger, he went back into the reserve to confront John. When confronted again, John got agitated and threatened the ranger with his axe. In order to protect himself, the ranger took out his gun and shot John. Many Cwebe residents did not believe the ranger's version of the story as they had not seen John's body. John's family, the local chief and the entire Cwebe community were very upset by the fact that when they visited the site of the incident, the body had already been taken away by the police without their

---

14   Ntshona et al 2010
15   Paterson 2011 and Fay 2007; 2012

consent or witnesses. The only evidence they saw were the poles that John had felled. The shooting incident and subsequent death had ramifications across all the surrounding villages for the Dwesa-Cwebe Nature Reserve.[16]

Whereas John had overtly articulated his need for construction materials from the reserve, with fatal consequences, the ECPTA, through the rangers, had in turn articulated its authority over the reserve. John's case represented local people's need for resources from the reserve following its restoration to community ownership in 2001 but managed through co-management. However, access continues to be denied by the state through the ECPTA much to the disgust of communities surrounding the reserves. At the same time, John's incident also illustrates existential resistance through the shelter materials that were being harvested from the forest. Such materials formed part of John's family's life. Overall, people surrounding Dwesa-Cwebe pointed out that even though some of them had been shot at, killed, and assaulted, "we will continue fighting for our own rights as legitimate owners of the land to access and use natural resources within the protected area".[17]

Mapfungautsi Forest, Gokwe, Zimbabwe

Mapfungautsi State Forest lies in Gokwe South District, Midlands Province in north-western Zimbabwe. It is the third largest protected state forest in Zimbabwe and is almost entirely surrounded by communal areas. When it was first demarcated as a state forest in 1953, the forest was 101,000 ha in size. In 1972, the northern part of the forest was reclassified as a communal area, due to rampant squatting. In exchange, the state took over some former communal areas in the south and proclaimed them as state forest, leaving a total of 82,100 ha. A co-management programme called the Resource Sharing Project (RSP) was initiated by the Forestry Commission of Zimbabwe (FC), a state agency responsible for forestry conservation, in 1994. In the RSP, local people were invited to participate in the management of the forest and also gained access to non-timber forest products. Products such as timber were however excluded from the RSP, and these continued to be sources of conflict between the FC and local people living around the forest, who continued to access them illegally.

Under the RSP, communities around the forest were divided into 14 Resource Management Committee areas with each community managing access to a certain portion of the forest.[18] Their main roles involved administering permits

---

16 Compilation from interviews with several of John's relatives between July and September, 2011. Interviews and translations done by Simphiwe Tsawu. Part of the narrative of what happened also appears on The Archival Platform 2012: http://www.archivalplatform.org/blog/entry/rights_enshrined/ (accessed 14 February 2014)
17 Cwebe villager, July 2013, interview and translation by Simphiwe Tsawu
18 Mutimukuru-Maravanyika/Matose 2013

for resource users to harvest forest products, monitoring the harvesting process, opening and keeping a community bank account and advising the community on how revenues generated could be spent. Thus, to prevent conflict, a collaborative project was offered to the local people living outside the state forest through which they had access but no enduring rights to forest land. However, the Fast Track Land Reform Programme introduced by the Zimbabwean government in 2000 provided opportunities for local people to reclaim their lost rights to the forest. Some formerly displaced forest residents teamed up with liberation-struggle war veterans and led the resettlement over Zanda Plateau inside the forest, reclaiming their land through illegal settlement. Interviews we conducted with local community members in 2002 revealed that about 75 households had settled in the forest. By 2004 there were over 200 households in Zanda Plateau occupying a forest area that stretched for 16 km.[19] At the last count in 2014, the figures had risen to 880 households.

In the case of Mapfungautsi Forest in Zimbabwe, articulatory resistance took a different form, which is 'squatting' as a means to repossess land from the state. The case below is a compilation from several years' (2006, 2007 and 2013) interviews with different settlers on state forest land.

CASE STUDY 2: RETURNING DISPLACED RESIDENTS

People who were evicted from the forest in 1986 due to a civil war returned to Zanda Plateau in 2000.[20] For example, Sabhuku Dongi, whose father used to be a forest resident prior to 1986, returned with some households to start a new village inside the forest.[21] He took early retirement from Harare to resettle on his ancestral land. His village has 20 households. An FC employee however made a counterclaim that, by the time the forest inhabitants were evicted from the forest in 1986, Dongi's father had already left the forest. Then there was Sabhuku Chikuni who was the first to return to the forest and was also my respondent in 1994.[22] His homestead was the venue for all ruling party rallies in the early 2000s when violence was perpetrated against opposition party supporters outside the forest. Consequently, one of the first makeshift schools was established in his village. Other former residents include Mr Marose and Mr Makosi who did not hold leadership positions. However, when the land reform programme started, they came to settle in the forest and claimed to have had leadership positions before the

---

19 Mutimukuru-Maravanyika/Matose 2013
20 Matose 1994. The civil war was fought in the western part of Zimbabwe over a fall-out between Zapu and Zanu-PF parties between 1983 and 1987.
21 'Sabhuku' refers to a village head, the lowest level of traditional authority and a hereditary position.
22 Matose 1994

evictions. To cement their positions, the two are active ruling party cadres. At the same time, new Sabhuku Marose (he was not a village leader before) showed me the tree under which his late father was buried. Yet another former forest resident was Sabhuku Mandamba who did not previously hold a position of authority. He had been a neighbour to the village head but when the forest invasion started, he came to settle and claimed the authority of Sabhuku Kangazane, who went to settle further away from the forest after the 1986 eviction and never came back. "We belong here, here is home. I will live long now that I am back to my roots. It's good for my spirit," eulogised an elated Mr Marose. Sabhukus were given metal insignias similar to those issued to official village heads and headmen. Chiefs Nemangwe and Njelele facilitated the issue of these insignia of authority.[23] These village heads were not officially recognised by the state yet, as they did not receive monthly allowances accrued to official village heads. Nonetheless, the resettled village heads still enjoyed settlement levies of US$500 for each land-seeking household, which could be paid in kind, in the form of a cow.[24]

Displaced people who were now 'squatting on forest land' took advantage of the land occupations in Zimbabwe to articulate their reclaim and repossession of their ancestral lands lost to the state. They surrounded themselves with households to cushion themselves in the form of villages and collaborated with the ruling party officials to assert their claim on forest lands. At the same time, they also mobilised local chiefs to recognise them through the issue of insignias which will make it difficult to dislodge them. The state, for now, appears to have lost this battle to the articulatory power of local people, formerly displaced forest residents.

The politics of resistance in forestry: a discussion

Both cases, in which the state has retained control of conserved forests through various collaborative management arrangements, demonstrate the hidden politics embedded in the resistance strategies deployed by local people to regain both access and rights to forest resources. In Dwesa-Cwebe the co-management agreement between the state and surrounding seven communities is very slowly unravelling due to the resistance examined here. In Dwesa-Cwebe, the two resistance typologies were deployed against the state as local people strove to regain access to essential natural resources for their day to day survival. Whereas *de jure*, the nature reserve belongs to local people through the 2001 restitution, in practice, however, local people feel the state has retained control of the reserve and thereby continues to

---

23 Chiefs play significant roles in local governance and give recognition to village heads below them in authority terms.
24 Village heads in Zanda, July 2013, interviews and translations by Witness Kozanayi

dispossess them of their rights over the land and access to natural resources.[25] Ultimately this threatened the very existence of local people in different ways through barring them from the nature reserve. The reserve forms people's main access to key resources upon which their lives have depended for many generations. People on the Cwebe side of the reserve have been particularly impaired, as their lives are much more intertwined with resources inside the reserve. If they fail to obtain construction materials then they will be without shelter in the future. This is illustrated by the fact that some of the people have lost their lives in the process of articulating their needs. Overall, the co-management arrangements for managing resources around Dwesa-Cwebe have been rendered ineffectual as the day-to-day hidden battles of the 'weak' demonstrate.

The Mapfungautsi case illustrates 'squatting' or land occupation as an even more overt illustration of 'articulatory resistance' in which local people, particularly those formerly displaced from the forest in the 1980s, fought for their rights to the land. Such displaced people have occupied the forest for more than a decade and continue to grow in confidence as the state slowly begins to concede defeat. The co-management arrangements that were initiated through the resource sharing project have long since been abandoned as local people have taken over parts of the forest that formerly belonged to them. The areas strategically settled are where former forest residents used to farm and had their homes prior to their eviction in 1986. While Mapfungautsi forest might not have as much potential for ecotourism development as Dwesa-Cwebe, the state appears ambivalent about whether to let it revert to community control or to retain it as a state property. Mapfungautsi remains far from the ecotourism routes and is not as endowed with commercial hardwood species as other Kalahari Sand forests in Zimbabwe.[26] The state has been overwhelmed by the land occupation strategies of former displaced people who have gained the upper hand in repossessing their ancestral lands. It may be that the state has lost the battle to the weapons of the weak after all.[27] At the same time settlement of parts of the forest results in forest clearance for cultivation, which can have adverse implications for forest ecology if the clearance is unchecked.[28]

Conclusion

In this chapter I used a typology of forms of resistance deployed by local people around forests in Southern Africa to take up the call by Peluso to disentangle the trajectories of actors, the state and their quotidian effects.[29] The denial of access to

---

25 See also Kepe 2008
26 Matose 2002
27 Scott 1985
28 Forestry Commission 2014
29 Peluso 2012

and rights over forest resources results in complex relations between people, the state and forests. The two cases presented here provide evidence that local people cast away by the state engage in resistance to regain and retain access to their forests for their basic existence, and to articulate their rights. Only two such forms of resistance were used here but the other typologies are developed elsewhere.[30]

By digging into the particularity of place and listening to the voices of the people who live in or near forests, a much more nuanced perspective emerges. These are the 'hidden' struggles that outsiders often do not see. In engaging with resistance debates raised by Scott, Sivaramakrishnan, Holmes and others, I have adapted them to the Southern African context where my particular concern places emphasis on local people's lost rights and access to forest conservation practices.[31] If collaborative projects do not restore rights to forests nor give access to forest resources, then such projects are resisted by local people. The effect of such resistance is mixed. In the Dwesa-Cwebe case a stalemate has been reached and renegotiations are needed. For the Mapfungautsi case, 'squatting' has informally restored lost rights to forest land where access was previously considered adequate by the state.

References

Beinart, W. (1989), Introduction: The Politics of Colonial Conservation. *Journal of Southern African Studies*, 15(2): 143–162.

Borrini-Feyerabend, G., M.T. Farvar, J.C. Nguinguri and A.V. Ndangang (2000) *Co-management of Natural Resources: Organising, Negotiating and Learning by Doing*. Yaoundé: GTZ and IUCN.

Carlsson, L. and F. Berkes (2005), Co-management: Concepts and Methodological Implications. *Journal of Environmental Management*, 75: 65–76.

Fay, D. (2007), Struggles Over Resources and Community Formation at Dwesa-Cwebe, South Africa. *International Journal of Biodiversity Science and Management*, 3(2): 88–101.

Fay, D. (2012), 'The Trust is Over! We Want to Plough!': Social Differentiation and the Reversal of Resettlement in South Africa. *Human Ecology*, 40(1): 59–68.

Forestry Commission (2014), Report on the Visit to Mafungabusi Forest to Assess Land Requested by the Minister of State for Provincial Affairs (Midlands) to Settle More People: September 2014. Harare: Forestry Commission. Unpublished report.

---

30 See Matose forthcoming
31 Scott 1985; 1990, Siviramakrishnan 2005, Holmes 2007

Foucault, M. (1991), Governmentality. In B. Graham, C. Graham. and P. Miller (eds.), *The Foucault Effect: Studies in Governmentality*. London: Harvester Wheatsheaf: 87–104.

Grundy, I.M., B.M. Campbell, R.M. White, R. Prabhu, S. Jensen and T.N. Ngamile (2004), Participatory Forest Management in Conservation Areas: The Case of Cwebe, South Africa. Unpublished report.

Holmes, G. (2007), Protection, Protest and Politics: Understanding Resistance to Conservation. *Conservation and Society*, 5(2): 184–201.

Kepe, T. (2008), Land Claims and Co-management of Protected Areas in South Africa: Exploring the Challenges. *Environmental Management*, 41(3): 311–321.

Kull, C.A. (2002), Madagascar Aflame: Landscape Burning as Peasant Protest, Resistance, or a Resource Management Tool?. *Political Geography*, 21(7): 927–953.

Matose, F. (1994), Local People's Uses and Perceptions of Forest Resources: An Analysis of a State Property Regime in Zimbabwe, (MA Thesis, University of Alberta).

Matose, F. (2002), Local People and Reserved Forests in Zimbabwe: What Prospects for Co-management? (PhD Thesis, University of Sussex).

Matose, F. (forthcoming), *Hidden Politics in Conservation: Forests and the Power of the Weak in Southern Africa*. Tucson, University of Arizona Press.

Mutimukuru-Maravanyika, T. and F. Matose (2013), Applying Adaptive Collaborative Management Approach in Forested Landscapes: Experiences from Zimbabwe. In H.R. Ojha, A. Hall and R.V. Sulaiman (eds.), *Adaptive Collaborative Approaches in Natural Resource Governance*. London: Routledge: 177–215.

Ntshona, Z., M. Kraai, T. Kepe and P. Saliwa (2010), From Land Rights to Environmental Entitlements: Community Discontent in the 'Successful' Dwesa-Cwebe Land Claim in South Africa. *Development Southern Africa*, 27(3): 353–361.

Palmer, R., H. Timmermans and D. Fay (2002), *From Conflict to Negotiation: Nature-based Development on South Africa's Wild Coast*. Pretoria: Human Sciences Research Council.

Paterson, A.R. (2011), Bridging the Gap Between Conservation and Land Reform: Communally-conserved Areas as a Tool for Managing South Africa's Natural Commons, (PhD Thesis, University of Cape Town).

Peluso, N.L. (2012), What's Nature Got to Do with it? A Situated Historical Perspective on Socio-natural Commodities. *Development and Change*, 43(1): 79–104.

Poteete, A. and J.C. Ribot (2011), Repertoires of Domination: Decentralization as Process in Botswana and Senegal. *World Development*, 39(3): 439–449.

Ramutsindela, M. (2004), *Parks and People in Postcolonial Societies: Experiences in Southern Africa*. Dordrecht/Boston/London: Kluwer (Springer).

Ribot, J.C. and N.L. Peluso (2003), A Theory of Access. *Rural Sociology* 68(2): 153–181.

Scott, J.C. (1985), *Weapons of the Weak: Everyday Forms of Villager Resistance*. New Haven: Yale University Press.

Scott J.C. (1990), *Domination and the Art of Resistance: Hidden Transcripts*. New Haven: Yale University Press.

Sitas, A., W. Keim, S. Damodaran, N. Trimikliniotis and F. Garba (2014), *Gauging and Engaging Deviance: 1600–2000*. New Delhi: Tulika Books.

Sivaramakrishnan, K. (2005), Introduction to 'Moral Economies, State Spaces and Categorical Violence'. *American Anthropologist*, 107(3): 321–330.

The Archival Platform (2012), Rights Enshrined Yet Rights Denied. http://www.archivalplatform.org/blog/entry/rights_enshrined. Accessed 14 February 2014.

Timmermans, H.G. (2004), Rural Livelihoods at Dwesa/Cwebe: Poverty, Development and Natural Resource Use on the Wild Coast, South Africa, (MSc Thesis, Rhodes University).

CHAPTER 15

'Before we start': science and power in the constitution of Africa

Elísio Macamo

> Creating new names and assessments and apparent truths is enough to create new 'things'.[1]

Introduction

There is a basic paradox underlying our knowledge of Africa. The assumption that there is any such thing as 'Africa' implies that we know what it is. Yet, much of the search for knowledge on Africa is premised on the assumption that we do not know enough about it to be able to claim that what we do know corresponds to that thing we call Africa. In other words, to know is to be able to judge the validity of what we claim to know. We judge validity by pitting pieces of knowledge against the phenomenon itself and checking whether there is any coherence between what we claim to know, i.e. what we think accurately describes an object, and the object itself. Here, however, we come up against a difficult philosophical problem. To be able to establish the validity of what we claim to know, we must know beforehand the thing about which we are producing knowledge. It feels like a tautological form of reasoning.

Of course, there is a way out of this. It consists in the idea that our knowledge of anything is both cumulative and based on logic. The claim that knowledge is cumulative means that, when we gather knowledge on anything, we are simply adding information to something whose existence we have already established in one form or another. Indeed, gathering knowledge on anything largely depends on the prior existence of objects, however that existence may have been established.

---

1   Nietzsche, quoted by Hacking 2006

The idea that our knowledge is based on logic means that claims to truthfulness are not judged according to whether there is any fit between what we say and the nature of the object itself. Rather, it is based on whether our propositions can withstand a logical test of their soundness.

The basic claim of this chapter is that there is no such thing as 'knowledge of Africa'. What we describe as 'knowledge of Africa' is the process through which we constitute Africa as an object. Everything else that ensues from this process is an elaboration on the conditions under which we can legitimately claim to know. To make this case I will first briefly present some critical injunctions voiced by many scholars in order to sharpen our gaze on what is at stake when claims are made about knowing Africa. Next, I will draw on the work of Ian Hacking to suggest an approach to scientific knowledge and power relations based on the sociology of knowledge.[2] My claim will be that scientific knowledge and power relations conflate into a mandate conferred upon science to speak truthfully about Africa. This yields a construct which I will describe as 'scientific power' that preys on the critical naivety of researchers as evidenced by their apparent reluctance to engage knowledge production where it really takes place, namely in the theoretical frameworks, conceptual categories and methodological procedures that form the basis for the conditions of possibility of any knowledge at all.

The main goal here is to argue against a whole critical tradition in African studies which seems to be premised on the belief that there is a phenomenon out in the world called 'Africa', against the background of which truth claims can be validated. On this account, to speak truth on Africa would be tantamount to checking whether what we claim reflects the true nature of the thing called 'Africa'. This is a scholarly dangerous path, for it leaves scholarly argument at the mercy of ideological preferences. One example may suffice to drive the point home. In a famous debate opposing the late Archie Mafeje, the South African anthropologist, and Sally Falk Moore, an American anthropologist, the former rejected the latter's historical account of the relationship between anthropology and Africa mainly on the grounds that, as a white American scholar, she could not speak truthfully about the relationship.[3] Mafeje's more substantive arguments on the book, namely those concerning the relationship between colonialism and anthropology, as well as those bearing on how anthropologists related to Africans and their cultures, are poignant and relevant. And yet, it is the prerogative claimed by his moral and ideological right as a 'Black African scholar' to question Moore's right to speak truthfully about Africa that lends force to Mafeje's argument. This is a problem and it needs to be addressed. The case I make for identifying a construct by the name 'scientific

---

2 Hacking 2006
3 Mafeje 1996; Moore 1996; Moore 1994

power' is an attempt at suggesting more useful scholarly ways of engaging with the claims that scholars make when they produce knowledge on Africa.

Some critical injunctions

So far, I have been addressing issues of a philosophical nature. They are important caveats to any pursuit of knowledge on Africa, for they draw our attention to very important issues that need to be addressed at the outset of any inquiry into 'Africa'. On a very basic level, one could ask what it is that people are studying when they state that they are studying the geography, history, economy, politics, or even culture of Africa. The question is not whether it is legitimate to use such a broad notion,[4] but rather the assumptions that converged towards producing the very object of that gaze, namely 'Africa' and the processes through which it was naturalised into a legitimate object of inquiry. Since Valentin Mudimbe's path-breaking work on the *Invention of Africa* we have learnt not to take Africa for granted, for much of what stands for Africa is, on Mudimbe's account, simply a (mis)representation of the continent, an artefact, as it were, of a will to power.[5] In this sense, then, the question that we should ask concerns what we need to do before we even start. Are we sure it is Africa that we are addressing? Mudimbe himself would claim, if his argument is taken to its logical end, that true knowledge of Africa is impossible simply because colonial rule and the colonial library that has been mobilised to organise our representations of the continent relied on a discursive power that has effectively rendered it impossible for the real Africa to come to the fore – real Africa is what could have been. What makes the whole situation tragic is the fact, according to Mudimbe, that the conceptual apparatus that we could draw from to recover real Africa is based on epistemological assumptions that erased it through the power of their own discourse.

So, asking whether we are sure that it is Africa we are addressing is a thorny question. This is because the answer is disarmingly simple. Indeed, all that we need to do in order to be able to start talking about Africa is to claim that we are doing just that. What is left unsaid, though, is the possibility that the object whose prior existence is presupposed by our inquiry and curiosity may actually be constituted by that inquiry itself. The assumption that there is an object out there which can be retrieved and rendered intelligible through our inquiry may

---

4 As in 'Africa is not a country'.
5 Mudimbe's argument (Mudimbe 1988) was highly influenced by Edward Said's book on *Orientalism* (Said [1978] 2003), drawing as it did on the more general arguments developed by Michel Foucault (Foucault 2002) in his discussion of the order of knowledge. For the sake of comprehensiveness it is important to mention Walter Mignolo's *The Idea of Latin America* (Mignolo 2005) which does for Latin America the same job that Said's book did for the Middle East and Mudimbe's did for Africa.

belie an insidious intellectual exercise that actually contrives the object through the theoretical, conceptual and methodological tools that are deployed to purportedly produce knowledge on the very same objects. Our theories, concepts and methods are not necessarily resources that we use to render objects visible. Rather, they are resources that we deploy to constitute them in the first place.

This is particularly true of Africa, especially on two accounts. First, in some ways, knowledge about Africa is motivated by interests, for example, the interest of colonial powers, the interest of competing trading partners, the interest of social activists, etc. How Africa is conceptualised under such circumstances will to some extent be a function of the interests underlying the pursuit of knowledge in those particular instances. This is not to say that knowledge is essentially value-laden. Rather, it is a reminder that there is more to knowledge than just curiosity. As far as environmentalism is concerned, for instance, Richard H. Grove argues in his *Green Imperialism* that the colonial state lies at the origin of western environmentalism, particularly in what he calls 'Edenic and Orientalist search'.[6] Agarwal and Narain make the same point about the present by claiming that much global warming discourse is a form "environmental colonialism".[7] Now, this does not undermine whatever good may come from environmentalism. It simply points out a mere truism, namely that knowledge is motivated. This motivation, which can be political, economic or even cultural, can either represent or misrepresent. Secondly, the constitutive role played by theoretical, conceptual and methodological resources is particularly true of Africa to the extent that often these are cognitive resources whose solidity as tools of inquiry came into fruition in alien settings. To be more specific, knowledge of Africa has been produced within what we might define as a Western episteme. The theoretical, conceptual and methodological resources through which Africa is to this day rendered visible and intelligible speak from a place, about that place and in accordance with criteria of plausibility that use that particular place as the normative standard for truth. Kwame Anthony Appiah had already raised this issue in the context of his discussion of the predicament of African scholars' critique of knowledge about Africa. He makes the point in a poignant way: "The Western emperor has ordered the natives to exchange their robes for trousers: their act of defiance is to insist on tailoring them from homespun material. Given their arguments, plainly, the cultural nationalists do not go far enough; they are blind to the fact that their nativist demands inhabit a Western architecture."[8] Again, this paradox does not undermine the legitimate claims to truth that can be made from within a position that resists 'western epistemology'.

---

6   Grove 1995: p. 474; see also Grove 1997
7   Agarwal/Narain 1991
8   Appiah 1992: p. 60

It simply points out the problem and makes clear why 'before we start' is a crucial moment in the production of knowledge about Africa.

Many scholars have drawn our attention to how knowledge production constitutes objects. I have already mentioned Valentin Mudimbe.[9] Paulin Hountondji is another useful reference, especially his injunction against the intellectual division of labour that devalues the work of African scholars to the condition of mere hunters and gatherers of primary data that more intellectually sophisticated scholars and research programmes from the North translate into intelligible accounts of the human condition.[10] Almost a decade ago, Jack Goody added an important dimension to this criticism by describing Western copyright claims over basic human values, institutions and practices (love, democracy, aesthetics, etc.) as tantamount to *The Theft of History*.[11] What makes Goody's accusation particularly powerful is his reminder of how scholars easily fall prey to the normative use of concepts. According to Goody, concepts should be seen as analytical grids, rather than categorical descriptions of the essence of an object. His telling example is the notion of 'feudalism'. Conflating the notion with the particular form which it took in Europe is not advisable. It is better, he argues, to define it as 'bonded labour', for this allows for the identification of various forms that can be taken by 'bonded labour'. This approach is more sensitive to different forms of human experience, practices and values.

To take another example in order to illustrate this point we could draw on the widely-used notion of neo-patrimonialism in the study of African politics. The original notion was introduced into the sociology of domination by Max Weber who used it to describe a form of authority based on the prerogative of one individual to discharge power from his claims to a territory and its possessions.[12] The notion then found its way into the political sociology of Africa, mainly through the work of the French scholar Jean-François Médard, but most forcefully through debates unleashed by Jean-François Bayart's book on the *State in Africa* and the so-called politics of the belly and the highly polemical book by Patrick Chabal and Jean-Pascal Daloz on what they claimed to be the political instrumentalisation of disorder.[13] In all of these publications, albeit less so in the work of Médard, the purveyed view was that African politics constituted a deviation from a norm.[14] The notion of neo-patrimonialism described that deviation.

---

9   Mudimbe 1988
10   Hountondji 1983; see also Connell's critical remarks in Connell 2006
11   Goody 2006
12   Weber 1978; see in particular the chapter on *The types of legitimate domination*, pp. 212–301
13   Médard 1990; Médard 1991; Bayart 1993; Chabal/Daloz 1999
14   The legal-rational norm of the rule of law.

The problem with this is that, by reducing African politics to variations on the theme of neo-patrimonialism, researchers failed to live up to Goody's methodological injunction to identify a general condition that can take different forms across space and time. In this particular case, the general condition could have been something like 'forms of discharging political authority' in which patron-client relations could be one such form. Awarding public sector contracts to party benefactors could be another form. Rewarding loyal party militants with political office or seats on the boards of parastatals could be yet another form. It may be that, at the end of the day, patron/client relations as practised in certain African political settings are so ubiquitous that they define the nature of politics in Africa. However, this would not be the result of a confirmation bias, but rather of applying a conceptual category describing a general condition in non-normative ways. Mahmood Mamdani discusses some of the implications of this in his reflections of what he calls 'history by analogy'.[15] Similar points are made by Jacques Depelchin in his indictment of *Silences in African History*, for what is silenced is that for which there is no room in the conceptual apparatus of hegemonic historical accounts.[16]

To recapitulate, critical injunctions draw our attention to two crucial aspects. First, the claim that we are producing knowledge about Africa is one that cannot be accepted or rejected simply on the merits of the argument according to which the propositions underlying it are consistent with some idea of 'Africa'. In this sense, there does not seem to be any position of authority outside scholarly criteria from which knowledge claims about Africa could be accepted or rejected. Being an 'African' or having the 'right' political frame of mind is not a relevant criterion to assess knowledge claims about Africa. The second aspect follows from this one. There are reasons beyond ethnocentrism, racism and power that could support a rejection or acceptance of knowledge claims about Africa. The most important of these reasons have to do with how the knowledge itself is constructed, i.e. how concepts succeed in establishing a rational link between the theoretical framework and the object that they seek to describe. It is the critical engagement with the challenges posed by this link that not only constitutes scholarly debate, but also provides the basis for assessing the validity of claims made on particular objects. I turn to these issues in the next section by trying to make a case for the existence of a construct which I shall call 'scientific power'. As I will argue, 'scientific power' can be said to mediate our search for knowledge and the limits that we can set to that search.

---

15   Mamdani 1996
16   Depelchin 2005

Knowledge on Africa

"Before I start" is what public debaters in some African settings say in order to preface their intervention. They are aware of the time that has been allotted to them. For this reason, they use this rhetorical trick to make their point and use the rest of the time to embellish it. Something akin to this happens at the interface of scientific knowledge and Africa. What counts as knowledge of Africa is in some very important respects the preface to the real thing, in fact, the thing in itself. There is an excerpt from Nietzsche's *Gay Science* quoted by the Canadian philosopher, Ian Hacking, which is quite instructive in terms of my argument here. It says: "There is something that causes me the greatest difficulty, and continues to do so without relief: unspeakably more depends on *what things are called* than on what they are".[17] Nietzsche ends this thought with the quote that opens this chapter, namely "creating new names and assessments and apparent truths is enough to create new 'things'". My claim is that the relationship of science and Africa is based on naming, not on what Africa is. Of course, one logical difficulty here concerns the paradox of inquiry that I alluded to earlier on in the chapter when I was discussing the difficulty of establishing criteria on the basis of which one could judge the validity of one's knowledge claims. However, there is more to the story.

Nietzsche is drawing our attention to a process described brilliantly by Ian Hacking through the idea of 'engines of discovery'.[18] Engines of discovery are ways of securing knowledge about classes of things but, in the process, they also 'make up' these things. In explaining this notion, Hacking asserts that he is interested in exploring how names interact with the things named.[19] He describes these engines as (a) classifications, (b) people, (c) institutions, (d) knowledge and (e) experts. I would like to suggest that these engines offer a sociology of knowledge of this moment that I call 'before we start'. They encapsulate the assumptions that are constitutive of the object and that belie the assumption of knowledge production underlying much of what we do when we claim to be producing knowledge on Africa. Classifications refer to specific phenomena constituting what we can legitimately describe as the object of our knowledge. Different aspects of 'Africa', i.e. the environment, culture, politics, etc. fall under this term. In fact, the idea of 'classification' suggests a judicious selection of something, a point once again emphasising the importance of the caveat to look at this 'before we speak' moment.

The second engine discussed by Hacking is people. In the context of Hacking's discussion, 'people' refers to the people who are implied by the classification.

---

17 Hacking 2006: p. 23 (italics by Hacking)
18 Hacking 2006: p. 23
19 Hacking himself describes this as a form of nominalism, i.e. dynamic nominalism, which is sensitive to the fact that the things named change to accommodate the ways of knowing that constitute them.

If the phenomenon is child abuse, 'people' would refer to the individuals who have been, or are held to be victims of that particular practice. In the context of scientific knowledge, 'people' refers to the African actors implied by whatever classification establishing a phenomenon. If, for example, the phenomenon is climate change, 'people' might refer to the communities vulnerable to weather vagaries. The third engine, i.e. 'institutions' is connected directly to this. It describes the organised ways in which a phenomenon, i.e. the object of classification and the people thereby implied, is dealt with. To stick to the climate change example, we could say that relevant UN agencies, research bodies, relief organisations and perhaps even government agencies constitute what we can legitimately describe as 'institutions' in Hacking's sense.[20] The fourth and fifth engines are knowledge and experts, respectively. The former describes the collection of facts and causal links (for instance, that climate change is caused by unsound environmental practices) that provide us with coherent accounts of a phenomenon. The latter refers to the purveyors of the knowledge, i.e. to those who draw on acknowledged sources of authority to speak truthfully about the phenomenon.

It is not the purpose of this short chapter to launch into an inquiry as to how these engines of discovery function in the context of the relationship between scientific knowledge and Africa as an object. However, one thing should become immediately obvious. The claim that knowledge is not about something, but rather constitutes things, has far-reaching consequences. Knowledge is an exercise in power. Science is power. Producing knowledge about Africa is an exercise in power. This assertion goes beyond the usual Foucaultian claim of discursive power that lies at the heart of Mudimbe's discussion of the *Invention of Africa*.[21] It addresses a sociological fact that goes beyond the politics of representation to encompass the idea of naturalisation of knowledge as the revelation of the true nature of things. For this reason, the issue is not the relationship between scientific knowledge, on the one hand, and power, on the other. The issue is scientific power, i.e. the power to speak truth. This power, I submit, has operated on the basis of three essential mechanisms. The first mechanism is colonisation. Scientific power, in this sense, is the ability to take charge of the natural and social environment of a continent and set the boundaries of what can be legitimately said about it. This is not to say that what we know about Africa's natural and social world is wrong in any essential way. The point is that the kinds of truth that are purveyed in conversations about Africa's natural and social worlds are those whose legitimacy and plausibility are established on

---

20 'Institutions' function rather like institutions in the sense in which Georg Simmel, the German sociologist, describes 'the poor'". According to him, the poor man is not poor because of any objective criterion pertaining to the conditions of his existence. He is poor because he is the object of institutional intervention (Simmel 1950).
21 Or even Said's critique of "Orientalism" (Said 2003).

the basis of criteria derived from science. In the past, much discussion about local knowledge was in some important respects predicated mainly on the discomfort felt by many who resented the way in which the claims to scientific authority had undermined other ways of knowing.[22] This takes us to the second mechanism. This is the idea which some scholars have described as 'systems of ignorance', i.e. the manner in which the dominance of scientific discourse has undermined local knowledge and forced local specialists on the defensive by placing the onus on them to show the relevance of their knowledge.[23] The third and final mechanism is what I would like to describe as 'paternalistic reason'. Paternalistic reason describes a situation in which problem definitions are foisted upon individuals in the full knowledge that the solutions to these problems are held by those who came up with the problem definitions in the first place.[24] Scientific power is in this sense the power to define what Africa's problems are and to claim the supremacy of the solutions that science suggests while, at the same time, undermining local problem definitions and solutions.

The construct suggested here, namely 'scientific power', operates on two levels. The first level makes the claim that knowledge is reflexive to the extent that it yields the criteria on the basis of which it can be challenged. These criteria entail the exact relationship between concepts and theoretical frameworks on the one hand, and concepts and phenomena or objects on the other. The validity of claims to knowledge at this level can only be usefully made with reference to the internal logic entailed by the links. To put it simply, to claim that a proposition is true or false does not depend on whether it is a truthful representation of reality, but rather whether the linkages are made in sound ways, i.e. in ways that are consistent with the standards shared by the relevant community of scholars. The second level acknowledges the social nature of knowledge production. Here what is assessed is not the claim to truthfulness. Rather, it is the social context within which certain objects become scientifically interesting and the uses to which knowledge so derived can be put to use. Scientific power, in this sense, would refer to the social dynamics that make the production of knowledge possible. While these dynamics can be criticised and deplored, they could not serve as the basis for rejecting the validity of the knowledge produced because this is only possible on the first level.

---

22 Santos 2007; Neubert/Macamo 2003
23 Lachenmann 1994; see also Marglin 1990; Santos 2007; Diagne 2013; Macamo 2011. On the difference between 'experts' and 'specialists' see Neubert/Macamo 2003
24 Stefan Musto, the original inspiration for this, uses the term "manipulative reason" (Musto 1987).

Conclusion

What I have tried to do in this brief comment is to raise issues around our claims to knowledge about Africa by drawing attention to the assumptions underlying the theoretical, conceptual and methodological resources which we deploy to produce knowledge on Africa. The defining moment is a paradox straddling our pursuit of knowledge and the very things about which we make knowledge claims. This paradox refers us to a tautology in the justification of knowledge production, since to know something cannot be justified by the thing itself, but rather by the very claim that we make to the effect that we know something. Owing to this apparent tautology, I drew the conclusion that the claims to knowledge we make about Africa are not accounts of what Africa is. Rather, the claims themselves constitute Africa as an object by rendering visible and intelligible what our theoretical frameworks, conceptual categories and methodological procedures assume. I briefly illustrated this by reference to Hacking's engines of discovery to suggest a sociology of knowledge of the manner in which we constitute Africa as an object of study.

Nowhere is this more insidious than in the scientific study of Africa. To the extent that the scientific study of Africa can be described as a colonial enterprise premised on the production of ignorance justifying itself on the basis of a paternalistic form of reason, it would seem appropriate to be reticent about scientific knowledge and power relations. The crucial moment is not represented by the extent to which claims to knowledge can be validated against any particular standard put forward by science itself. The crucial moment occurs before everything else, i.e. *before we start*. Knowledge of Africa is defined by our ways of knowing, i.e. it is about what we can know and how we can know what we know. This crucial moment establishes the nature of the object in ways which render everything else that follows secondary in the sense that what follows is parasitical on unspoken premises and the credulity that underlies an uncritical attitude to the claims of science.

My case, then, rests on the critical injunction not to take what is regarded as knowledge of Africa as the revelation of truth about this particular object. Contrary to what the direction of the discussion in this chapter may suggest, this suspicion is not founded on a fundamental rejection of the claims of science. In fact, the suspicion is a celebration of science to the extent that it enjoins us to be critical about how we come by our knowledge. This elaborates on the idea that what is distinctive about scientific knowledge is not the quality of the answers given to research questions, but rather the procedures that led to the answers. Questioning scientific power is not an ideological exercise in 'Western bashing'. It is a critical inquiry into how theoretical frameworks, conceptual categories and methodological procedures may fool us into believing that the worlds we are after are to be found outside of the bounds set by these intellectual resources. I hope to have produced reasons that should make us rather circumspect about such claims.

After all, our hold on 'Africa' is a discursive one. The ontological security displayed by this concept is one that is founded on our use of concepts and our agreement over the meanings and definitions that we assign to them. Africa is not Africa because it is. It is Africa because we have agreed to describe it as such. In this sense, then, the very possibility of knowledge on Africa, scientific or otherwise, rests on the verve with which we engage the preliminaries of knowledge production. These preliminaries bear directly on the conditions that must be met for enunciation, the places that make enunciation possible and the kinds of agreements that make it possible for concepts to acquire descriptive and analytical value, not to mention the data collection procedures enabling us to claim that pieces of information can be arrayed to produce intelligible datasets.

References

Agarwal, A. and S. Narain (1991), *Global Warming in an Unequal World: A Case of Environmental Colonialism*. New Delhi: Centre for Science and Environment.

Appiah, K.A. (1992), *In My Father's House: Africa in the Philosophy of Culture*. Oxford: Oxford University Press.

Bayart, J.-F. (1993), *The State in Africa: The Politics of the Belly*. London: Longman.

Chabal, P. and J.-P. Daloz (1999), *Africa Works: Disorder as Political Instrument*. Oxford: James Currey.

Connell, R. (2006), Northern Theory: The Political Geography of General Social Theory. *Theory and Society*, 35(2): 237–264.

Depelchin, J. (2005), *Silences in African History: Between the Syndromes of Discovery and Abolition*. Dar es Salaam: Mbuki na Nyoto Publishers.

Diagne, S.B. (2013), L'encre des savants: Réflections sur la philosophie en Afrique. Paris/Dakar: Présence Africaine/CODESRIA.

Foucault, M. ([1970] 2002), *The Order of Things: An Archaeology of the Human Sciences*. London: Routledge.

Goody, J. (2006), *The Theft of History*. Cambridge: Cambridge University Press.

Grove, R.H. (1995), *Green Imperialism: Colonial Expansion, Tropical Island Edens and the Origins of Environmentalism, 1600–1860*. Cambridge: Cambridge University Press.

Grove, R.H. (1997), *Ecology, Climate and Empire: Colonialism and Global Environmental History, 1400–1940*. Cambridge: The White Horse Press.

Hacking, I. (2006), Making Up People. *London Review of Books*, 17 August, 28(16): 23–26.

Houtondji, P. (1983), *African Philosophy: Myth and Reality*. Bloomington: Indiana University Press.

Lachenmann, G. (1994), Systeme des Nichtwissens: Alltagsverstand und Expertenbewußtsein im Kulturvergleich. In: A. Honer, R. Hitzler and C. Maeder (eds.), *Expertenwissen: Die institutionalisierte Kompetenz zur Konstruktion von Wirklichkeit*. Opladen: Westdeutscher Verlag: 285–305.

Macamo, E. (2011), Afrika stört: Ein Totengespräch über Norm und Wirklichkeit in den Sozialwissenschaften. In J. Fleischhack and K. Rottmann (eds.): *Störungen: Medien/ Prozesse/Körper*. Berlin: Reimer: 23–43.

Mafeje, A. (1996): A Commentary on Anthropology and Africa. *CODESRIA Bulletin*, 2: 6–13.

Mamdani, M. (1996), *Citizen and Subject: Contemporary Africa and the Legacy of Late Colonialism*. Kampala: Fountain Publishers.

Marglin, F.A. (ed.) (1990), *Dominating Knowledge: Development, Culture and Resistance*. Oxford: Clarendon Press.

Médard, J.-F. (1990), L'État patrimonialisé. *Politique africaine*, 39, September: 25–36.

Médard, J.-F. (1991), L'État néo-patrimonial. In J.-F. Médard (ed.), *États d'Afrique*. Paris: Karthala.

Mignolo, W. (2005), *The Idea of Latin America*. Oxford: Wiley-Blackwell.

Moore, S.F. (1994), *Anthropology and Africa*. Charlottes-Ville: University Press at Virginia.

Moore, S.F. (1996), Concerning Archie Mafeje's Reinvention of Anthropology and Africa. *CODESRIA Bulletin*, 3, 20–23.

Mudimbe, V.Y. (1988), *The Invention of Africa: Gnosis, Philosophy and the Order of Knowledge*. London: James Currey.

Musto, S. (1987): Die hilflose Hilfe: Ansätze zu einer Kritik der manipulativen Vernunft. In D. Schwefel (ed.), *Soziale Wirkungen von Projekten in der Dritten Welt*. Baden-Baden: Nomos Verlagsgesellschaft.

Neubert, D. and E. Macamo (2003), Wer weiß hier was: 'Authentisches' lokales Wissen und der Globalitätsanspruch der Wissenschaft. In N. Schareika and T. Bierschenk (eds.): *Lokales Wissen: Sozialwissenschaftliche Perspektiven*. Hamburg/Münster: Lit.: 93–122.

Said, E. ([1978] 2003), *Orientalism*. London: Penguin Books.

Santos, B. de S. (2007), Para além do pensamento abissal: das linhas globais a uma ecologia de saberes. *Revista Crítica de Ciências Sociais*, 78: 3–46.

Simmel, G. (1950), *The Sociology of Georg Simmel*. Glencore: The Free Press.

Weber, M. (1978), *Economy and Society: An Outline of Interpretive Sociology*. Berkeley: University of California Press.

LIST OF CONTRIBUTORS

MELANIE BOEHI is a PhD student in history at the Basel Graduate School of History and Centre for African Studies, University of Basel.

DIANA GIBSON is Professor in the Department of Anthropology and Sociology, University of the Western Cape.

MARNIE GRAHAM is a Formas-funded post-doctoral fellow at the Stockholm Resilience Centre and the Department of Geography and Planning, Macquarie University.

TANJA HAMMEL is a PhD student in history at the Basel Graduate School of History and Centre for African Studies, University of Basel.

GABRIELE KRANZ is a PhD student in history of science in the Department of Biology, University of Hamburg and public relations officer of the Loki Schmidt Haus.

ANNETTE LAROCCO is a PhD student in the Department of Politics and International Studies, University of Cambridge.

LUREGN LENGGENHAGER is a PhD student in the Department of History, University of Zurich.

ELÍSIO MACAMO is Professor of African Studies in the Social Sciences Department, University of Basel.

FRANK MATOSE is a Senior Lecturer in the Department of Sociology, University of Cape Town.

GIORGIO MIESCHER is the Carl Schlettwein Foundation Senior Lecturer and Research Fellow in Namibian and Southern African Studies at the Centre for African Studies, University of Basel.

ROMIE VONKIE NGHITEVELEKWA is a Lecturer in the Department of Sociology, University of Namibia, and a PhD student in Anthropology, University of Freiburg.

MAANO RAMUTSINDELA is Professor in the Department of Environmental and Geographical Science, University of Cape Town.

SANDRO SIMON is a PhD student in Social Anthropology at the a.r.t.e.s. Graduate School for Humanities Cologne and a member of the DELTA project on Volatile Waters and the Hydrosocial Anthropocene in Major River Deltas.

NDIDZULAFHI INNOCENT SINTHUMULE is a Senior Lecturer in the Department of Ecology and Resource Management, University of Venda.

ANNA VOEGELI is a PhD student in the Department of History, University of Basel, and works for the archives of the Basler Afrika Bibliographien.

Index

A
Aawambo societies 209–211
Africa: knowledge of 323–333, 326, 328, 332; object 330, 332; propositions 328
African medicine 129–142; Decade of Traditional Medicine 130, 131, 138; presidential task team 137–138; Thabo Mbeki 129, 146
Amani Institute in German East Africa 75
Anthropocene 9
anti-apartheid movements 149, 170, 171
apartheid 252–276. *See also* post-apartheid; forced removals 254–255; racialised identities 259

B
Bamenda, Cameroon 281–304; city council 298–302; Below-Foncha 291. *See also* wetlands; ecological and demographic change 292–298; Fondoms and Bamenda II/III 289; migration and urbanisation 289; Programme D'Appui Aux Capacites Decentralisees De Developpement Urbain (PACDDU) 290–291, 296, 297
Bamenda Wetlands 17
bantustans 260, 261, 265
Barber, Mary Elizabeth 39–54; butterfly and moth illustrations 42–54; circulation of evolutionary theory 42–43; entomological research 42–54; naturalist 41–54; racism. *See* race, racism; writings 42, 49, 50, 51, 52
Beit Bridge Rural District Council 243–245
biological exchanges: shipment of seeds and seedlings 90
biopiracy and bioprospecting 81–82; herbal medicines/African TMs 132
botanical collections 62–82
botanical diplomacy 149, 151, 158–170; Golden Jubilee 164, 167, 169
botanical gardens. *See* Hamburg, Botanical Garden; *See* National Botanical Gardens (NBG)
Botanical Society of South Africa 150, 152–176; *Journal of the Botanical Society of South Africa* 154, 156, 167
Botswana 179–202, 237, 238, 241, 243, 244, 246; Botswana Tourism Organisation 190; community conservation. *See* Community-Based Natural Resource Management (CBNRM); Department of Wildlife and National Parks 182, 192, 238; laws: 1979 Unified Hunting Regulations 187; Special Game Licences (SGL) 187; Ngamiland 181, 188, 191, 195, 197; politics of conservation policy 181–202; hunting ban 188; policy of sustainable use 181; wildlife tourism. *See* tourism, Botswana
boycott campaigns 150; international 168, 169, 170

C
Cape Flats 252–276. *See also* township; protests and racial tensions 261; residential segregation 255–256; social inequality 256, 274
Cape Floristic Region (CFR) 139–140, 161; fynbos 154, 159, 161
Cape Town 252–276; black rural-urban migration 261; economic and social inequalities 257; urban nature 257
Caprivi Strip 87–90; fauna and flora 97; German colonisers 90; illegal purchase and hunting of animals 90; South African Defence Force (SADF) 91–102
cattle. *See also* Ovambo cattle; exoticisation and musealisation 16; police zone border (the Red Line) 113–121; rinderpest

panzootic 108–113. *See also* rinderpest panzootic; veterinary science 16
circulation of nature 87–89; axis of military control 100; collecting specimens 95–98, 101; colonialism and imperialism 87, 101; exotic trees 99; international trafficking of ivory and rhino horn 93; translocation of animals, SADF 92–97
collectors 62, 63–68, 75–78
colonialism, German 15, 59–82
colonised ecosystems 87, 90, 99
co-management 315–320. *See also* Dwesa-Cwebe, South Africa; *See also* Resource Sharing Project (RSP)
commercial interests (cattle) 15, 113–117, 121
commercial interests (plants) 68–73, 127–142, 130; clinical trials, traditional plant medicines 127, 130, 131; informal market 127; plant medicine markets 128, 133; therapeutic properties 128; traditional healers 132, 133; traditional plant medicines 138; unregulated economy 128
Commission of Inquiry into the Alleged Smugglings and Illegal Trade of Ivory and Rhinoceros Horn in South Africa (Kumleben Report) 93
commonage 16, 210–211, 225–228
Communal Areas Management Programme for Indigenous Resources (CAMPFIRE); Zimbabwe 183, 245
communal land 16, 208–228; administration 212–228; Communal Land Reform Act 223–225
communal land boards (CLBs) 209–228
Community-Based Natural Resource Management (CBNRM) 16, 234; Botswana 180–202; Madagascar 234–235
Community Development Working Group (CDWG) 245
conservation 9–17, 20–33, 152, 281–304; Botswana 179–202. *See also* hunting, Botswana; conservation-adjacent communities 181–202; faunal kingdom 199; participatory conservation 179–202; resistance 193; wildlife: consumptive-to non-consumptive use 179; wildlife tourism. *See* tourism, Botswana; centres of political, economic and academic power 16; collaborative 254–276; control over natural resources 15; ecological experts and armed security units 15; environmental movements 26; forest 311–320. *See* Dwesa-Cwebe, South Africa; *See* Mapfungautsi, Zimbabwe; policy 17, 233; Botswana 185–186, 191, 199; Convention of Biological Diversity (CBD) 29–30; World Conservation Congress 29; World Parks Congress 28–29; political ecology 15; politics and ecology 20–33; politics and scale 26–33; power relations 26–28; colonial Namibia 15; transfrontier conservation areas 15; protection and preservation of fauna and flora 28; South Africa 134–142; community-based 140; land restitution 134; plant diversity 140; traditional healers 134; tourism 28; wildlife corridors 31
conservation, forest 311–320. *See also* Dwesa-Cwebe, South Africa; *See also* Mapfungautsi, Zimbabwe
Conservation International 199
conservation policy 281–285, 298–299, 303–304
conservators 252–276; alien vegetation removal 254

D

Darwin, Charles 42, 43, 48, 49
diamond mines, Botswana 185, 186
disempowerment: criminalisation of border crossing 246; definition 232; lack of consultation 245–247; lack of knowledge about TFCA 241, 245–247; lack of property rights 241–247; limited benefits from nature-based tourism 241
Du Toit's Pan 49
Dwesa-Cwebe, South Africa 311–320; access 311, 314, 316, 318, 320; benefit 311; conflict 311, 314–316; dependence on forest resources 314; dispossession of local people 318–320; land restitution 314; Settlement Agreement 314; shooting incident 315–316

E

Eastern Cape Parks and Tourism Agency (ECPTA) 314–316

ecosystem 282–285, 302
eGazini Memorial Garden 40
eGazini Outreach Project 40
elephants 240, 244; central to Botswana's marketing 199; destruction crops and property 198; hunting 12; poaching 199
empowerment: TFCAs 241–248
environmentalism of the poor 21–33
environmental non-governmental organisations (ENGOs) 31–32
eucalyptus 99–101
exhibitions: Botanical Museum, Hamburg 74–75; colonial plants, Windhoek, Namibia 75; Empire Exhibition: British, 1924–1925 154, 156; Coronation, 1937 156; Johannesburg, 1936 154; exhibition of medicinal and aromatic plants 154; exhibition of medicinal and toxic plants 165; South African government; production of exhibitions 150

F
Farm Industry Commission 119
farming 15, 210, 239–240, 244, 293, 294
festivals: Tercentenary Festival 163
floriography 153
flowers 149, 151–176
flower shows 153–162, 165; Chelsea Flower Show 156–157, 167–170
Fons of Mankon and Nkwen 289–298
forced removals 30, 233; Etosha (Namibia) 30; Gonarezhou (Zimbabwe) 30; Kalahari Gemsbok (South Africa) 30; Kruger (South Africa) 30; Sehlabathebe (Lesotho) 30
Forestry Commission of Zimbabwe (FC) 316

G
game/nature reserves: Dwesa-Cwebe, South Africa 314; Hluhluwe 166; Northern Tuli 237; The Wilds Nature Reserve 159; Venetia Limpopo Nature Reserve 237
gender: agriculture 292–294; bias 291; communal land boards (CLBs); representation of women 212; diamond fields 49; entomology 44; equality 42, 53, 213; feminist entomology 44, 53; politics 13

Global Environment Facility (GEF) 28
Grahamstown. *See* Makhanda
Greater Mapungubwe Transfrontier Conservation Area. *See* national parks; *See also* transfrontier conservation areas (TFCAs)
Griqualand West 50

H
Hamburg 59–82; Botanical Garden 61–64; trading companies 76, 77
Heritage Week: Macassar Dunes 252–276; diverse relationships to nature 252, 254, 262; inter-racial relations 256
HIV/AIDS 131; Treatment Action Campaign 131
horticultural societies 154; Cape Horticultural Society 154; Railway Horticultural Society 154; Royal Horticultural Society 156, 169
human-environment relations 11–13, 20–33; community participation and inequality 16; elite capture 16; policy frameworks impact 16; post-apartheid social reconciliation 17
hunting 12–13, 16, 26–28, 179–202. *See also* conservation, Botswana; 1979 Unified Hunting Regulations 187; access to wildlife resources through community trusts 188; ban: Botswana 16, 179–202; Ngamiland 181; commercial 12–13; wildlife trade 13; elephants. *See also* conservation, Botswana: legalised sale of hunts 198; poaching 186, 191, 196; rights 12–13; Selous Game Reserve, Tanzania 12; Special Game Licences (SGL) 187–188; revoking of licences 192; subsistence hunting 187; transition from/to quota system 188, 192; subsistence hunting 13, 26–28, 186, 187; quota system 188; tourism. *See* tourism, Botswana

I
identity; coloured 255–263, 269; KhoiKhoi 260, 267; language 257–260, 272–273; Rastafari 257–258, 267–270; Xhosa 253–276
ilala palms 240, 244; baskets 240; wine 240, 244

Impalila 94
indigenous Cape flora 150
Indigenous Knowledge Systems (IKS) 127–142; herbal science and medicine research 135
indigenous medicine 127–142; protection 128; traditional healing 128
indigenous people 44, 45, 47, 51, 52, 53, 135, 187, 193
insects 39–54
International Union for Conservation of Nature (IUCN) 28–30, 162, 281, 283
International Wildfowl Research Bureau (IWRB) 283
Istituto Agricolo Coloniale Italiano (Italian Institute for Colonial Agriculture) 77

K
Katima Mulilo 94; Department of Agriculture and Forestry 94
Kenya 235
Kew. *See* Royal Botanical Gardens, Kew
Kirstenbosch. *See* National Botanical Gardens (NBG)

L
land 208–228; access 208–228; administration 213–228; allocation 211–223; claims 208–228; conservation 17; disputes 211–227; land banking 221; landholders and land users 218–223; legitimate and informal land agreements 220–222; Namibian constitution 16; policy 210, 214; Communal Land Reform Act, 2002 209, 215–217, 223–225; Consultative Conference on Communal Land Administration, 1996 213; Traditional Authorities Act, 2000 212, 216; registration 213, 222–226; relations 16; central-north Namibia 208–228; communal land reform 223–224
land reform. *See also* Mapfungautsi, Zimbabwe; Fast Track Land Reform Programme 317; land restitution. *See* Dwesa-Cwebe, South Africa
land tenure 17, 209, 213–215, 218, 223–228, 281–304; commons 281–289, 302; communal land, Botswana, state-owned 241; communal land, Zimbabwe 243–247; customary 213–226, 281–304;
conflict mediation 287, 294–298, 303–304; governmental acquisition and legal pluralism 295–297; hereditary 284, 296–300; women's increased independence 294–295; freehold and communal 209; game farms and commercial agricultural farms 238, 242, 246; nationalisation and privatisation 284–304; regimes 281–291, 303; common (wet-)land use 284; systems 287; tenure arrangements 210, 224
linguistic imperialism 46–48
local communities 231–247, 262–265. *See also* Bamenda, Cameroon; *See* Dwesa-Cwebe, South Africa; *See* Mapfungautsi, Zimbabwe; *See* Resource Sharing Project (RSP); Botswana 239–241; Lentswe Le Moriti; Mathathane; Motlhabaneng; Botswana: Community-Based Natural Resource Management (CBNRM) 180–202; community conservation 234; disempowerment 17; farmworkers, South Africa 242; land claimants 243; Machete and Sematla clans 243; poverty alleviation 236; Zimbabwe 243–247; Machuchuta; Maramani; River Ranch

M
Macassar Dunes Conservation Area 252–276
Madagascar 234–235; Ambovombe-Androy 234
Makhanda (formerly Grahamstown) 39, 54
Makira Natural Park 235
Mankon 289
Mapfungautsi, Zimbabwe 311–320; displaced residents 317–318; land occupation 316–318; Zanda Plateau; civil war 317; resettlement 317–318
medicinal plants 127–142; Cape Nature 140; collections in South Africa and Namibia 135; control of 140; harvesting in the wild 133, 140; intellectual property 133; Khoisan healing practices 135–136; policy developments 134–137; politics, South Africa 129–142; traditional health practitioners 133
methodology; study of Africa 17
museums; Albany Museum, Grahamstown 40–41, 42, 54, 98; Botanical Museum,

Berlin 64; Botanical Museum of Hamburg 15, 59–82. *See also* museums, Loki Schmidt Haus; research for trade 72–73, 79; Herbarium Hamburgense 61–64, 78–81; Kaffrarian Museum (now Amathole Museum) 95; Loki Schmidt Haus, previously the Botanical Museum of Hamburg 61–69, 77–79. *See also* museums, Botanical Museum of Hamburg; link with Colonial Institute, Hamburg 67; Museum of Natural History, Hamburg 62; Onderstepoort 106, 108, 120; Transvaal Museum 120

N
Namibia 88, 108–121, 183, 234; administration: Ministry of Land Reform 211, 213; policy and gender equality 213; African cattle breeding and meat production 109–121; animal husbandry 110–113; central-north region 208–228; colonial war of 1904 111, 113; conservation and tourism 91; emergence of veterinary science and services 108–121; establishment of the police zone border 108; first agricultural exhibition, Windhoek 111; Ohangwena region 209, 211, 217–218; Owambo region 108, 112, 114–120; police zone border 108, 115–118; professionalisation of settler farming 108–121; South African period 88–102
National Botanical Gardens (NBG) 150–171; Kirstenbosch 16
national parks: Kruger National Park 92, 166; Limpopo National Park, Mozambique 27; Mapungubwe 232–247; Memorandum of Understanding (MoU) 237–238, 241; NOTUGRE (private land) 239–241; Tuli Block 239; translocation of game to South Africa 90
natural resource policy, Botswana. *See* conservation
nature 59–82; conservators 252–276. *See* separate entry; culture 128, 134; medicinal plants. *See* separate entry; missionisation 135
Nkwen 289

O
Okavango 99, 100
Okavango Delta 181, 191, 193, 198
Ovambo cattle 106–121. *See also* Namibia; musealisation as an exotic breed 108, 120; scientific standard reference 106; small scale smuggling 119

P
Peace Parks Foundation 245
plants: African 63–64; genera 65, 71; indigenous 68–72, 78–81; industries; cacao, jute, natural rubber, spices, margarine and oil 60; interplay with power and politics 16; medicinal 68, 72, 81; institutionalisation 16; relational objects 16
plant science 127–142, 151; HIV/AIDS controversy 131–133; safety testing 127
poaching 31–32; rhino, Kruger National Park 31; South African National Defence Force 31
political ecology 20–33
politics 9–13, 20–33, 87–92, 128–131, 137–141. *See also* Dwesa-Cwebe, South Africa; *See also* Mapfungautsi, Zimbabwe; environmental 9–17; foreign aid and donor funding 30; hidden struggles 17, 312–320; links with science 13–15; neo-patrimonialism 327–328
politics of gender and race 13
politics of knowledge production 13–15
politics of land 16
politics of nature conservation 20–33, 186, 189, 233–247; bureaucratic centralisation 234; resistance 243
politics of science 9–17, 22, 59–82, 233–247
post-apartheid 151, 254–276; collaborative nature conservation 254–276; historical configurations of racial and ethnic identities 259–265, 273–276; racialised and ethnicised identities 255–276; social reconciliation 254–276
post-colonial 281–287, 302
property rights 16, 208–228, 311–312; individual versus communal 16
protests 149, 170

R

race, racism 43–54; indigenous people 69, 72–73, 78; scientific racism 48; social Darwinism 48

Ramsar Convention 281–285; definition of wetlands 282; global wetland loss 284; The Convention on Wetlands 281–285; wetland management 285

Reconstruction and Development Programme (RDP) 258

resistance: articulatory 17; criminalisation 312; existential 17; strategies 312–320; occupation or squatting 313; typology 17, 312–314, 318–320; power relations 312–320

Resource Sharing Project (RSP) 316

rinderpest panzootic 108–113; commercial impact 111

Royal Botanic Gardens, Kew 156, 157, 162

S

scale 15, 20–33; capital accumulation 25; ecological 20–33; glocalisation 25; political 20–33; power dynamics 25–33. *See also* human-environment relations; power geometries 25

science 9–17; academic exploitation 100; Africa, living laboratory for European science 13; critical history 9–10, 13–15; ecological 89, 90, 92; field laboratories 14; links with politics 13–15; nature 9–17; negotiated racial difference and insects 15; veterinary 14–16

science of ecology 22–33

science projects: BIOdiversity Monitoring Transect Analysis in Africa (BIOTA) 80–81; Southern African Science Service Centre for Climate Change and Adaptive Land Management (SASSCAL) 80; The Future Okavango (TFO) 80

scientific power 324, 328, 330, 331; construction of Africa 17

social relations 20–33

society-nature dualism 12–17

sociology of knowledge 324

Soga, Tiyo 48

South Africa government 128–142; African medicine. *See* separate entry; Department of Science and Technology 132; 2014 Bio-economy Strategy 132; legislation and policies related to plants 128–142; Department of Health's Draft Policy on Traditional Medicine 129–133; Medicines and Related Substances Amendment Act (72 of 2008) 130, 139; National Drug Policy of 1996 130, 139; Policy on African Traditional Medicine 130; Traditional Health Practitioners Act (22 of 2007) 130

South African botany 64–82

South African Defence Force (SADF) 92–102; transfer of fauna/flora to South African mainland 94, 95, 97

South African empire: armed resistance 88–105; Bush War 96; Caprivi Strip. *See* Caprivi Strip; clearing of settlements 96; direct political and military rule over Namibia 88–92; military maps showing natural features 96, 101; overlapping security and academic interests 101; strategy to mask occupation as development 90

South African government 96, 97, 151, 158, 160; advancement of 'indigenous gardening' 150; international relations 151

South African Medical Association (SAMA) 132; KwaZulu-Natal (KZN) Midlands Branch Council 132

South African Medicines Control Council (SAMCC 131

South African Museum 165

South African National Parks (SANParks) 237–238, 242–243

South African Railways and Harbours 154

South Africa's National Science Festival (Scifest Africa) 39

student movement, Rhodes Must Fall 39

T

Tanzania 181

tourism 16, 233; Botswana 182, 185, 191, 194–197, 198, 199, 201; ecotourism 236; ecotourism revenue 315; recreational 233

township: Khayelitsha 252–276; Macassar 252–276; Mitchell's Plain 252–276

traditional authorities (TAs) 209–228; hierarchy 211, 216; *ombadu yekaya* 222

Traditional Medicine (TM) 128–141;

African 137, 141; bossiesdokters (kruiedokters) 135, 141; Cape pharmacopoeia 136; Chinese medicine 130; herbal 130, 135; Indian medicine (Ayurveda) 130; intellectual property 130, 141; Khoisan 135; pseudo-science 139; Rastafarian healers 135, 141
transfrontier conservation areas (TFCAs) 102, 231–247; definition 235; ecotourism 236, 243; empowerment/disempowerment of local communities 232–247; Greater Mapungubwe Transfrontier Conservation Area 27, 237–239; 241–246; livelihoods of local residents 236; Water–Glacier International Peace Park 235
Trilateral Ministerial Committee (TMC) 238
Trilateral Technical Committee (TTC) 238, 245, 246
Trimen, Roland 42, 44, 47, 49
Tulbagh 154
Tuli Circle Safari Area 238

U
UNESCO 281–283
Union of South Africa 90
urban nature 252–276; apolitical spaces of nature 256–276; intersection with poverty and violence 275

V
Van Riebeeck's Hedge 163
veterinary services, colonial Namibia 108, 114, 116–121

W
Western Caprivi 99, 100
wetlands 281–304. *See also* Bamenda, Cameroon; artificial 282, 283; Below-Foncha 288–301; declaration as state land 295; direct-use 283, 302; recreation, transport and research 283; hydrological cycles 285; indirect-use 283, 302; control of water, carbon storage, nutrients 283; loss 282–284; marine, coastal and in-dryland 282; natural 282; natural-anthropogenic ecosystems 282, 302; non-use values 283–284, 290, 302; products 303; fish, timber, wildlife, wild plants 283; water supply for extra-wetland purposes 283; science 281, 282; subsistence and commercial activities 283; threats 281–304; conflicts between users 288; displacement or expropriation 290; ecological damage 294; flooding 290; health risks 294; overstocking, pollution, soil erosion 288; overuse of resources/technology 287; political 287
wildlife management area (WMA) 27–33, 238–239; conflict 31; conservation authority 31; Greater Mapungubwe Transfrontier Conservation Area 27; Machuchuta (Zimbabwe) 238; Maramani (Zimbabwe) 27, 238; River Ranch (Zimbabwe) 238
World Bank 284
World Conservation Union Red List 140
World Health Organization (WHO) 128, 139–140
World Heritage Site 237, 243
World Wide Fund for Nature (WWF) 28

Z
Zambia 91, 183
Zimbabwe 234, 237–238, 243–247; Beit Bridge Rural District Council 238; Communal Areas Management Programme for Indigenous Resources (CAMPFIRE). *See* Communal Areas Management Programme for Indigenous Resources (CAMPFIRE)

www.ingramcontent.com/pod-product-compliance
Lightning Source LLC
Chambersburg PA
CBHW080355030426
42334CB00024B/2881